S0-ADJ-309

THE HOLY REICH

Analyzing the previously unexplored religious views of the Nazi elite, Richard Steigmann-Gall argues against the consensus that Nazism as a whole was either unrelated to Christianity or actively opposed to it. He demonstrates that many participants in the Nazi movement believed that the contours of their ideology were based on a Christian understanding of Germany's ills and their cure. A program usually regarded as secular in inspiration – the creation of a racialist "peoples' community" embracing antisemitism, antiliberalism, and anti-Marxism – was, for these Nazis, conceived in explicitly Christian terms. His examination centers on the concept of "positive Christianity," a religion espoused by many members of the party leadership. He also explores the struggle the "positive Christians" waged with the party's paganists – those who rejected Christianity *in toto* as foreign and corrupting – and demonstrates that this was a conflict not just over religion, but over the very meaning of Nazi ideology itself.

Richard Steigmann-Gall is Assistant Professor of History at Kent State University. He has earned fellowships and awards from institutions in Germany, Israel, and Canada, and he has published articles in *Central European History*, *German History*, *Social History*, and *Kirchliche Zeitgeschichte*.

The Neue Wache during the Third Reich. The Cross was added by the Nazis after the Seizure of Power. Source: *Die Jugend des Führers Adolf Hitler: Bildbuch über die grossdeutsche Judend*, edited by the Reichsjugendführung der NSDAP (Leipzig, 1942).

THE HOLY REICH

Nazi Conceptions of Christianity, 1919–1945

RICHARD STEIGMANN-GALL

CAMBRIDGE
UNIVERSITY PRESS

PUBLISHED BY THE PRESS SYNDICATE OF THE UNIVERSITY OF CAMBRIDGE
The Pitt Building, Trumpington Street, Cambridge, United Kingdom

CAMBRIDGE UNIVERSITY PRESS
The Edinburgh Building, Cambridge CB2 2RU, UK
40 West 20th Street, New York, NY 10011-4211, USA
10 Stamford Road, Oakleigh, Melbourne 3207, Australia
Ruiz de Alarcón 13, 28014 Madrid, Spain
Dock House, The Waterfront, Cape Town 8001, South Africa

http://www.cambridge.org

First published 2003
First paperback edition 2004

Printed in the United States of America

Typeface Sabon 10/12 pt.   System LATEX2e [TB]

A catalog record for this book is available from the British Library

Library of Congress Cataloging in Publication data is available

ISBN 0 521 82371 4 hardback
ISBN 0 521 60352 8 paperback

CONTENTS

LIST OF ILLUSTRATIONS

ACKNOWLEDGMENTS

This book grew out of a Ph.D. dissertation written at the University of Toronto. It gives me great pleasure to name the many people and institutions whose guidance, encouragement, and backing enabled me to write it and then turn it into a book. The Department of History and the School of Graduate Studies at the University of Toronto provided generous support in the form of Simcoe Fellowships, a University of Toronto Open Fellowship, and several travel grants. Doctoral fellowships from the Social Science and Humanities Research Council of Canada allowed me to undertake extensive research in German archives and libraries. An Ontario Graduate Scholarship and a Felix Posen Fellowship from the Sassoon International Center for the Study of Antisemitism helped support me during the last year of the writing phase. A Faculty Research Appointment from the Office of Research and Graduate Studies at Kent State University, and a Summer Fellowship from the Max-Planck Institut für Geschichte in Göttingen, were vital for fine-tuning the manuscript. Without these sources of funding, this book could not have been written.

While in Germany, I benefited from the generous assistance I received at archives and libraries in Berlin and Munich. I want especially to thank Frau Blumberg at the former Bundesarchiv Abteilungen Potsdam and Frau Popp at the Institut für Zeitgeschichte in Munich for their considerable help in locating sources. Without exception, the entire staff of the Bundesarchiv Außenstelle Berlin-Zehlendorf, formerly the Berlin Document Center, was extremely helpful and friendly. They not only helped me navigate the many changes taking place in their holdings at the time, but offered geniality and sociability during the long days I spent there. With the transferal of its holdings to the Berlin-Lichterfelde location, I hope they have all found the new homes they deserve. I particularly wish to thank the staff of the Institut for permission to examine restricted files and of the Bundesarchiv Koblenz for shipping files to the Berlin-Zehlendorf location for my viewing.

My interest in this subject first took tangible form in a graduate seminar paper I wrote at the University of Michigan for Geoff Eley. The theoretical and conceptual rigor he instilled was invaluable, as are the encouragement and support he still provides. My most important debt is to my doctoral supervisor at the University of Toronto, James Retallack. No one could have asked for as much attention and patience as Jim gave me throughout my academic training. His constant guidance and eye for precision steered me away from fallacies and added enormously to the final product. Also at Toronto, Thomas McIntire freely gave his time to discussions of empiricism and theory and greatly assisted me in thinking through larger conceptual approaches to ideology and the intersection of religion and society. Michael Marrus, who privileged me with his personal investment in the topic and Richard Helmstadter both read through the entire dissertation and provided valuable feedback. Eric Jennings and Ian Rutherford also provided encouragement and advice along the way.

Important as well were graduate student friends on both sides of the Atlantic who helped me by providing intellectual exchange, reading my work, providing support, or opening their homes. In Toronto the friendship and support of Hilary Earl and Marline Otte were very valuable to me. They took time to read various drafts of my thesis and considerably enhanced my thinking. Annette Timm generously offered her apartment in Schöneberg as a base of operations on my arriving in Berlin for my major research trip. In Bielefeld and Berlin I benefited very much from the feedback of Stefan-Ludwig Hoffmann and Dirk Bönker at an early stage of research. At all times I have valued the friendship and intellectual exchange that Till van Rahden has freely offered. And in Melle, the Otte family very warmly provided a home away from home.

Since Toronto, I have been honored to accumulate additional debts. Shelley Baranowski has been wonderfully supportive as well as intellectually challenging. Margaret Anderson, Albert Lindemann, and Harry Liebersohn read through parts of the manuscript at an early stage, and I am grateful to them for their suggestions. I have also had the good fortune of incisive critique and advice from Hartmut Lehmann, Helmut Walser Smith, Susannah Heschel, and in particular Bob Ericksen. My thanks to Susannah for allowing me to see the manuscript of *Betrayal: German Churches and the Holocaust* before it was published. Other acquaintances and colleagues in the German history community have offered their advice or assistance at different stages, including Michael Geyer, Doris Bergen, Lucian Hölscher, Peter Steinbach, Larry Eugene Jones, Dagmar Herzog, Bob Gellately, Benita Blessing, Richard Levy, Christopher Browning, Omer Bartov, Celia Applegate, Richard Weikart, and John Conway. I thank them all for their feedback or encouragement, especially where differences of opinion challenged and sharpened my own thinking. It goes without saying that responsibility for any remaining errors is my own. At Cambridge University Press, my editor Frank Smith and his assistant Barbara Chin have been wonderfully supportive from the beginning, getting back readers' reports with amazing speed and in other ways showing their enthusiasm and commitment to the manuscript. In a period that is seeing acute changes in academic publishing, Frank is the kind of editor every author should have. I also thank the

ACKNOWLEDGMENTS

anonymous reviewers at Cambridge for their very helpful comments. Thanks as well to Molly Natt at Audio-Visual Services at Kent State University for assistance with the illustrations.

The two history departments I have been part of since obtaining my Ph.D. have also afforded me many opportunities for professional growth. While at St. Francis Xavier University I prized the intellectual company of Paul Phillips and the friendship of Nancy Forestell. My colleagues at Kent State University have been very supportive, particularly Argyrios Pisiotis, Liz Smith, John Jameson, David Brenner, Shirley Wajda, Nikki Brown, Victor Papacosma, and Felix Ekechi. I have had the particular benefit of Carol Harrison's probing reading of parts of this work, as well as of papers and articles that have originated from it. The students who have taken my classes at Kent State, St. Francis Xavier, and Toronto have in particular been a wonderful part of my professional and personal development, and I thank them for helping me grow as a teacher and scholar.

I would like to acknowledge a few friends and colleagues who have been particularly important to me. Mollie Cavender and Kathy Pence, whom I first met in Ann Arbor, have been close and constant friends since my first year in graduate school. Kathleen Canning at the University of Michigan has been a constant source of guidance and assurance. Her enthusiasm and determination meant a great deal to me when I began considering a graduate career in history, and she has offered her assistance and advice ever since.

Finally, and most importantly, my family has unswervingly been by my side. My parents, Axel and Yolande Steigmann, and my brother, David, have provided a great deal of support, both emotionally through their belief in my abilities and materially through their massive subsidies. As I discovered to my relief some years back, the mix of "hard" and "soft" scientist in one family is not that unusual. I have known my wife Lisa as long as I have worked on this project; once it is put aside I will be able to say I have known her longer. She and our daughter Natalie have been constant sources of inspiration and joy. They have sustained me through the computer failures and other obligatory disasters that befall the typical scholar, but have also shared some very happy moments. I hope this book will begin in some way to thank my family for all they have done.

Göttingen, June 2002

ABBREVIATIONS

AELKZ	*Allgemeine evangelisch-lutherische Kirchenzeitung*
BAP	Bundesarchiv Potsdam (Federal Archive Potsdam)
BAZ	Bundesarchiv Berlin-Zehlendorf (Federal Archive Berlin-Zehlendorf)
BdK	*Bund für deutsche Kirche* (League for a German Church)
BdM	*Bund deutscher Mädel* (League of German Girls)
BK	*Bekennende Kirche* (Confessing Church)
BStA	Bayerisches Hauptstaatsarchiv (Bavarian State Archive, Munich)
CEB	*Christliche Elternbund* (Christian Parents' League)
DAZ	*Deutsche Allgemeine Zeitung*
DC	*Deutsche Christen* (German Christians)
DGB	*Deutsche Glaubensbewegung* (German Faith Movement)
DSP	*Deutschsozialistische Partei* (German Socialist Party)
DVFP	*Deutschvölkischen Freiheitspartei* (German Völkisch Freedom Party)
EZA	Evangelisches Zentralarchiv in Berlin (Protestant Central Archive Berlin)
GStA	Geheimes Staatsarchiv Preußischer Kulturbesitz (Prussian State Archive, Berlin-Dahlem)
HJ	*Hitlerjugend* (Hitler Youth)
IfZ	Institut für Zeitgeschichte (Institute for Contemporary History, Munich)
NSDAP	*Nationalsozialistische Deutsche Arbeiterpartei* (National Socialist German Workers' Party)
NSDStB	*Nationalsozialistischer Deutscher Studentenbund* (National Socialist Student League)
NSEB	*Nationalsozialistische Elternbund* (National Socialist Parents' League)
NSF	*Nationalsozialistische Frauenschaft* (National Socialist Women's Organization)
NSFP	*Nationalsozialistische Freiheitspartei* (National Socialist Freedom Party)

NSLB	*Nationalsozialistischer Lehrerbund* (National Socialist Teachers' League)
NSV	*Nationalsozialistische Volkswohlfahrt* (National Socialist People's Welfare)
PNB	*Pfarrernotbund* (Pastors' Emergency League)
PPK	*Parteiamtliche Prüfungskommission zum Schutze des NS-Schrifttums* (Party Examination Commission for the Protection of National Socialist Literature)
RPL	*Reichspropagandaleitung* (Reich Propaganda Office)
SA	*Sturmabteilung* (Storm Troopers)
SD	*Sicherheitsdienst* (Security Service)
SS	*Schutzstaffeln* (Protection Squads)
StAM	Staatsarchiv München (Munich State Archive)
VB	*Völkischer Beobachter*
WHW	*Winterhilfswerk* (Winter Relief Drive)

NOTE ON TRANSLATION
AND CITATIONS

I have translated *Konfession* as "confession," rather than the more standard "denomination." In Germany, where to this day religion nominally remains an obligatory state affair and not voluntaristic, there are no denominations in the strict sense of the word. Its use in the German context incorrectly suggests an American-style religious "marketplace" and attendant separation of church and state. This is especially relevant when describing certain Nazis like Hitler or Goebbels as "Catholic," even though they expressed antagonism toward their church. Whereas both men ceased to attend Catholic services or take confession long before 1933, up until their deaths neither man actually left his church or refused to pay church taxes. In a nominal sense therefore both men can be classified as Catholic.

I have translated *evangelisch* as "Protestant," except when "Evangelical" is used in cited secondary literature. For North American readers the more conventional translation of "Evangelical" implies a particular type of religious activity not necessarily tied to any one church. By contrast, the German *evangelisch* carries a definite theological–institutional determinacy. To maintain the distinction made between *Volk* and *Nation* in the German language, *Volk* has been translated as "people" or, more commonly, left untranslated. *Heidnisch* is frequently translated as "heathen" or "pagan" in the secondary literature. However, the proponents of a Nordicized religion within the party did not actually practice this religion, let alone devise a coherent religious system that could actually be practiced. Rather, they advocated the establishment of a faith that ultimately never came into being. Therefore, instead of referring to these Nazis as "pagans" or "neopagans," I use the expression "paganist" in all cases.

Documents are cited as follows: "archive, holding/file/page (date: place)." For instance, the citation "BAP R5101/23135/152-153 (21 February 1938: Berlin)," means the document was found in the Bundesarchiv Potsdam (BAP), holding R5101 (Reich Ministry for Church Affairs), file 23135 (correspondence with *Forschungsheim für Weltanschauungskunde*), folios 152–153, date 21 February 1938, and origin Berlin. For files with no pagination, page numbers are omitted.

With the alterations still taking place in the German Federal Archive system, many of the archival citations used here will have changed. During research, plans were being made to phase out the Bundesarchiv Berlin-Zehlendorf (BAZ), formally known as the Berlin Document Center, and transfer its holdings to the new Bundesarchiv Berlin-Lichterfelde location. Similar plans were being made for the Bundesarchiv Potsdam (BAP). As of this writing, both these moves are still ongoing. In addition, several files that were at these locations have now moved back to the Bundesarchiv Koblenz. I have therefore chosen to retain the original citations as the exact location of the holdings currently remains in a state of flux.

INTRODUCTION

Nazism owes nothing to any part of the Western tradition, be it German or not, Catholic or Protestant, Christian....

Hannah Arendt[1]

We will not... be capable of 'thinking the Shoah,' albeit inadequately, if we divorce its genesis and its radical enormity from theological origins.

George Steiner[2]

The 450th anniversary of Luther's birth fell only a few months after the Nazi Seizure of Power in 1933. The celebrations were conducted on a grand scale on behalf of both the Protestant Churches and the Nazi Party. One particular celebration took place in Königsberg, the provincial capital of East Prussia. Present for this event were the region's two highest representatives of the sacred and the secular: Landesbischof Friedrich Kessel and Gauleiter Erich Koch. Koch spoke on the propitious circumstances surrounding Luther's birthday. He implied that the Nazi Seizure of Power was an act of divine will, as it so closely preceded this special anniversary. He explicitly compared Hitler and Luther, claiming that both struggled in the name of belief, that both had the love and support of the German nation, and that the Nazis fought with Luther's spirit.[3] Given the occasion, one might consider such a speech entirely predictable, especially because Nazis were eager to elicit support from what was still a very large churchgoing population in Germany. We might therefore disregard the speech as mere propaganda.

We could pay this occasion no further attention were it not for one important fact: in addition to being *Gauleiter* of East Prussia, Koch was also the elected president of the provincial Protestant Church synod. Such a position confirmed one's credentials as a good Christian as much as Koch's record in the National Socialist German Workers' Party (*Nationalsozialistische*

---

[1] "Approaches to the German Problem," *Partisan Review* 12 (1945), 96.
[2] "Through that Glass Darkly," reprinted in *No Passion Spent: Essays 1978–1996* (London, 1996), 336.
[3] "Luther-Kundgebung im Schloßhof," *Königsberg-Hartungsche Zeitung*, 20 November 1933 (in Bundesarchiv Potsdam [hereafter BAP] R5101/23189/83).

Deutsche Arbeiterpartei) confirmed his Nazism. Yet a question arises: Might an exploration of Koch's church career reveal part of a larger Nazi "fifth column" against the clerical establishment, an infiltration of Christian institutions in order to destroy them from within? After all, on the same occasion, Koch made clear his preference for the German Christians (*Deutsche Christen*), a group long considered an offshoot of the Nazi Party who were intent on suffusing Protestant Christianity with the "anti-Christian" tenets of its parent movement. However, contemporaries regarded Koch as a bona fide Christian who had attained his position through a genuine commitment to Protestantism and its institutions. According to a prominent Königsberg theologian and leader of the East Prussian Confessing Church, Koch spoke "with the deepest understanding of our church," he consistently dealt with the "central themes of Christianity."[4] As Koch himself maintained, "Externally, much has changed. But in our church the Word of Christ according to the doctrine of Luther remains.... Righteousness, truth and love should guide us, not only at the level of charity but also in the joyful and active struggles for our Protestant confession of faith."[5]

By the end of the war, Koch had gained tremendous notoriety as the Reich Commissar of Ukraine, where he established his credentials as a brutal, ruthless Nazi of the first order. Indeed, he personified Nazi barbarity in the East, playing a leading role in the murder of thousands of Jews and partisans, their deportation to camps, the destruction of their villages, and the virtual enslavement of the remaining Slavic population.[6] By then he was no longer president of his provincial church synod: In fact, he had officially resigned his church membership by 1943. Nonetheless, in his postwar testimony, taken by a public prosecutor in Bielefeld in 1949, Koch would insist: "I held the view that the Nazi idea had to develop from a basic Prussian–Protestant attitude [*Grundhaltung*] and from Luther's unfinished Reformation."[7]

In a movement like Nazism, with hundreds of thousands of members and even more supporters, it may not be especially shocking to discover the occasional isolated individual who could embrace two ideological systems long supposed to be polar opposites. Anomalous situations are found in all political movements. It is one thing for such isolated individuals to exist; it is quite another, however, for them to reach a position of power and dominance within their milieu, indeed to achieve elite status in that milieu. Such was the case with Koch, whose well-known identity as a Christian in no way hindered his career as a Nazi. Indeed, Koch grew more powerful as German society became more nazified. And so the questions multiply: Was Koch an exception? Did other Nazis explain their allegiance to the movement or

4 Hans Iwand, *Briefe an Rudolf Hermann*, edited by Karl Steck (Munich, 1964), 251–2.
5 Quoted in ibid.
6 The magnitude of Koch's brutality is detailed in Alexander Dallin, *German Rule in Russia: A Study of Occupation Policies* (New York, 1957); Gerald Fleming, *Hitler and the Final Solution* (Berkeley, 1984), 120–34.
7 Institut für Zeitgeschichte (hereafter IfZ) MC 1 (15 July 1949).

conceive of its goals in specifically Christian terms? And if so, what might this say about the nature of Nazism itself, a movement long believed to be at best unrelated to Christianity, and at worst as anti-Christian as it was antisemitic or anti-Communist?

Nearly all aspects of Nazism have come under revisionist scrutiny in the past twenty years. Debates persist as to whether Nazism was modern or antimodern, progressive or reactionary, capitalist or socialist, middle class or cross class. Even the centrality of antisemitism to the movement has been questioned. However, one important aspect of our understanding of Nazism remains largely uncontested: the belief that, however much Christian clergy welcomed the movement or however much Nazi ideology may have borrowed from Christian traditions, Nazism itself could not be described as a Christian movement. Indeed, it is more often thought to be anti-Christian. Through an examination of the religious views of the Nazi Party elite, including those commonly referred to as "pagans," this work seeks to reexamine this widely held assumption. In what follows, we explore the ways in which many leading Nazis in fact considered themselves Christian (among other things) or understood their movement (among other ways) within a Christian frame of reference. They drew on Christian traditions to articulate their vision of Nazism – not only to the German people, but more importantly to each other and themselves. In the process, these Nazis entered into a struggle with party pagans over religious meanings in their movement, a contest that ultimately became part of a larger debate about Nazi ideology itself.

To assert that leading Nazis conceived their movement to be in some sense a Christian one, or may even have been believing Christians themselves, may seem to some deliberately provocative if not outrageous. This is not to say that the relationship between Nazism and Christianity has not been a topic of scholarly inquiry; quite the opposite. There is a vast and still-growing literature on the churches in the Third Reich, which has explored the ways in which theologians and Christian clergy who were supportive of Nazism often drew connections between their traditions and Nazi ideology; most obviously with regard to the Jews, but also on a wide range of issues such as Marxism, liberalism, women's rights, and homosexuality. But the question of how the Nazis themselves possibly thought about such an ideological coupling has not led to a similar scholarship, largely because it is assumed that the response from the Nazis was overwhelmingly negative. Nazi conceptions of Christianity are understood to run a rather narrow gamut, from at worst a complete rejection of Christianity *in toto* to at best a cynical, opportunistic posturing for the sake of electioneering and political expediency. If we liken public pronouncements by Nazi leaders to the words of actors on a stage, and the German public to their audience, it is almost universally held that these actors completely rejected their Christian script after the curtain came down. According to John Conway, still one of the most prominent scholars on this subject, the Nazi movement and its leadership were little more than wolves in sheep's clothing, placing a "tactical restraint" on their hatred until they had accrued enough power to unfurl their true colors.[8] Others of Conway's generation arrived at very similar conclusions. However, even among a younger generation of scholars, who have argued that there were disturbing connections between Nazi ideology and Christian traditions of antisemitism or anti-Marxism and who have shown just how deeply sympathetic to Nazism certain churchmen and women may have been, it is widely presumed that the Nazis never reciprocated. As one such scholar has recently suggested, Christian support for Nazism was an "unrequited affection."[9]

Between early and more recent scholarship on the churches under Nazism there is considerable difference. Earlier histories of the churches under Nazism were often quite adverse to suggestions that church traditions could in any way have flowed into Nazism; Christianity, so the argument went, offered nothing but spiritual opposition to the "paganism" and "atheism" of the movement. In other words, the antagonism between Christianity and Nazism was not just institutional, but ideological as well.[10] Such a view was in part a result of the war: The histories of the churches during the Third Reich tended to emphasize those clergymen who opposed the Nazi regime. Whereas former German Christians retained an embarrassed silence, the flood of books on the Confessing Church (*Bekennende Kirche*), often written by the historical actors themselves, led to the impression that the position of Christians and their churches toward the Nazi State was one of resistance or opposition.[11] As Karl Barth put it even before the war was over, Christianity was separated "as by an abyss from the inherent godlessness of National Socialism."[12]

A growing number of scholars have, for several years, unearthed growing evidence that points to a rather different conclusion. The debate on the collusion of the German churches under the Third Reich, which began in serious academic terms in the 1960s with Guenther Lewy's *The Catholic Church and Nazi Germany* and Gordon Zahn's *Catholics and Hitler's Wars*, continues today with no apparent abatement. Particularly with regards to antisemitism, church traditions and the ways they fostered support for Nazism are undergoing unprecedented scrutiny. The policies and actions of the Vatican, both

---

[8] John Conway, *The Nazi Persecution of the Churches* (London, 1968), 15–16, 140.

[9] Susannah Heschel, "When Jesus was an Aryan: The Protestant Church and Antisemitic Propaganda," in Robert Ericksen and Susannah Heschel (eds.), *Betrayal: German Churches and the Holocaust* (Minneapolis, 1999), 81.

[10] The literature on the churches under Nazism is vast and still growing. I make no attempt here to provide a comprehensive overview. Some of the more prominent works in the earlier apologetic vein are Hans Buchheim, *Glaubenskrise im Dritten Reich: Drei Kapitel nationalsozialistischer Religionspolitik* (Stuttgart, 1953); John Conway, *The Nazi Persecution of the Churches* (London, 1968); Beate Ruhm von Oppen, *Religion and Resistance to Nazism* (Princeton, 1971).

[11] Besides the works previously cited, there is Hubert Locke (ed.), *The Church Confronts the Nazis: Barmen Then and Now* (New York, 1984) and, more recently, Theodore Thomas, *Women Against Hitler: Christian Resistance in the Third Reich* (Westport, CT, 1995).

[12] Karl Barth, "Protestant Churches in Europe," *Foreign Affairs* 21 (1943), 263–5.

during the Third Reich and long before it, are currently receiving the preponderance of this critical attention.[13] However, the traditions of the Protestant Churches have also been revisited for the ways they sanctified Nazism and have been shown to have been much closer to the Nazi regime.[14] Several scholars have demonstrated the ambivalent and often positive stand that even members of the Confessing Church took toward the regime.[15] We have come to realize with growing empirical certainty that many Christians of the day believed Nazism to be in some sense a Christian movement. Even in the later years of the Third Reich, as anticlerical hostility grew, churchmen of both confessions persisted in their belief that Nazism was essentially in conformity with Christian precepts.

However, this same body of literature has argued with a notable degree of unanimity that Nazi leaders were not themselves believing Christians, however much they may have "borrowed" from Christian traditions in erecting their own policies. Still the only comprehensive work to explore Nazi attitudes toward Christianity in detail is John Conway's *The Nazi Persecution of the Churches*, which argues unequivocally that the Nazis held Christianity in the sharpest contempt. Later generations of church historians do not differ in their basic estimation of a Nazi rejection of Christianity – at least among its ideological elites – even as they have gone much further in implicating Christian churches for their institutional and ideological support of the movement. When church historians ask how there could have been a pro-Nazi element within German Christianity but not a pro-Christian element within Nazism, two types of argument predominate among their explanations: Either such Christians deceived themselves, or they were not truly Christian. The works of Klaus Scholder and Conway illustrate the first approach. Assessing the fact that the Confessing Church made frequent

---

[13] John Cornwell, *Hitler's Pope: The Secret History of Pius XII* (New York, 1999); David Kertzer, *The Popes against the Jews: The Vatican's Role in the Rise of Modern Antisemitism* (New York, 2001); Michael Phayer, *The Catholic Church and the Holocaust, 1930–1965* (Bloomington, IN, 2000).

[14] Again, this is a vast literature, incapable of being summarized. Prominent examples include Robert Ericksen, *Theologians under Hitler: Gerhard Kittel, Paul Althaus and Emmanuel Hirsch* (New Haven, 1985); Manfred Gailus, *Protestantismus und Nationalsozialismus: Studien zur nationalsozialistischen Durchdringung des protestantischen Sozialmilieus in Berlin* (Cologne, 2001); Ernst Klee, *'Die SA Jesu Christi': Die Kirche im Banne Hitlers* (Frankfurt a.M., 1989); Björn Mensing, *Pfarrer und Nationalsozialismus: Geschichte einer Verstrickung am Beispiel der Evangelisch-Lutherischen Kirchen in Bayern* (Göttingen, 1998); J.R.C. Wright, *'Above Parties': The Political Attitudes of the German Protestant Church Leadership 1918–1933* (Oxford, 1974). An excellent overview can be found in Robert Ericksen and Susannah Heschel, "The German Churches Face Hitler." The collection of essays Ericksen and Heschel have edited, *Betrayal: German Churches and the Holocaust*, provides the best compendium of current English-language research on the topic.

[15] Shelley Baranowski, *The Confessing Church, Conservative Elites, and the Nazi State* (Lewiston, NY, 1986); Victoria Barnett, *For the Soul of the People: Protestant Protest Against Hitler* (New York, 1992) (title notwithstanding); Wolfgang Gerlach, *Als die Zeugen schwiegen: Bekennende Kirche und die Juden* (Berlin, 1987).

declarations of loyalty to Hitler, Scholder suggests that "the great majority of the churches persistently refused to see the consequences."[16] Conway similarly argues for "the almost incredible blindness of churchmen to the spread of Nazi totalitarianism."[17] Doris Bergen typifies the second approach. As one of the few to examine seriously the views of the German Christians, Bergen has demonstrated that her subjects were not part of a cynical Nazi strategy, as is often assumed, but were sincere adherents of their church. At the same time, however, she contends that the German Christians were "ultimately non-Christian," based on their racism and antifeminism.[18] These two components of Bergen's argument are problematic, even irreconcilable; only false-consciousness theory allows us to contend that millions of sincere Christians could create a non-Christian movement. Bergen's argument is reinforced through use of analytical categories like "canonicity," which set the bar sufficiently high to prohibit the German Christians from passing the test of true Christianity. Such concepts, however, do not constitute a reliable gauge, as others whose Christian credentials are undisputed would similarly fail to pass. Such an analysis is not peculiar to Bergen, however, but reflects a wider assumption about the German Christians, and by extension about Nazis who may have been active in church life: Even while they adhered to all the requisite criteria for Christian religiosity – church attendance, baptism, communion – they still served to destroy Christianity, whether or not they actually knew it.

Aside from church history, intellectual history is another field in which connections between Christianity and National Socialism have been pondered and the relationship deemed – from the Nazi point of view – at best nonexistent and at worst adversarial. Some forty years ago, Fritz Stern suggested in his classic study *The Politics of Cultural Despair* that Nazism could trace its ideological origins back to apostate German intellectuals, who sought to create a new national religion, one "which hid beneath pious allusions to . . . the Bible a most thoroughgoing secularization. The religious *tone* remained, even after the religious faith and the religious canons had disappeared."[19] Stern, and many scholars after him, sought the roots of Nazi ideology in serious intellectual–historical terms (albeit in a distinctly deterministic fashion), but insisted that those lineages were not only un-Christian, but anti-Christian. Traditional intellectual history of this period posited a Nietzschean "death of God" as the originating moment of Nazism. In this conception, Nazism is understood to have served as a replacement

---

[16] Klaus Scholder, *A Requiem for Hitler and Other New Perspectives on the German Church Struggle* (London, 1989), 109. See also his magisterial *The Churches and the Third Reich*, 2 vols. (London, 1987–8).

[17] Conway, *Persecution*, 14.

[18] Doris Bergen, *Twisted Cross: The German Christian Movement in the Third Reich* (Chapel Hill, 1996), 192.

[19] Fritz Stern, *The Politics of Cultural Despair: A Study in the Rise of the Germanic Ideology* (Berkeley, 1974), xxv (emphasis in the original).

faith (*Religionsersatz*) for a defunct Christianity. Here was no argument about a residual Christian discourse influencing a later generation of National Socialists; whatever discourse remained was, according to this view, used with self-awareness and cynicism as a way of masking the anti-Christian comportment of the new *völkisch* national religion that Nazism was supposed to have embodied. George Mosse, in his *The Nationalization of the Masses*, made a similar argument, stating that the Nazis, like their intellectual "forefathers," poured a new secular wine into the old Christian bottles: "For the National Socialist this basic form could not be abandoned, but should simply be filled with a different content."[20] Within the conceptual framework of "political religion," Michael Burleigh echoes this view when he claims that Christianity's "fundamental tenets were stripped out, but the remaining diffuse religious emotionality had its uses."[21]

We know from recent scholarship that in fact much of the *völkisch* and racialist content of Nazi thought found a receptive home among particular varieties of Christian belief well before the arrival of Nazism and even before the turn of the twentieth century. As Wolfgang Altgeld demonstrates, ideas of a popular "national religion" had found resonance within Protestant circles as early as the Wars of Liberation.[22] As he has recently put it: "In Germany, the idea of the nation and nationalism [is] in the first analysis the fruit of certain intellectual, and not least certain theological, developments in Protestant Germany."[23] Helmut Walser Smith unveils the religious dimensions of German nationalism in the *Kaiserreich*, specifically pointing to the ways in which Protestantism was cast as the natural expression of German nationhood.[24] Whereas the conventional view among ecclesiastical and intellectual historians portrays the relationship between Christian and national identities as innately one of tension, requiring negotiation and contestation to maintain itself, these scholars show how the relationship between being Christian and being national was marked more by synthesis. Beyond nation to race, Rainer Lächele argues that ideas of a specifically *völkisch*–racialist religion had resided within the templates of German Protestantism by the turn

---

[20] George Mosse, *The Nationalization of the Masses* (New York, 1975), 80. See as well Robert Pois, *National Socialism and the Religion of Nature* (London, 1985); James Rhodes, *The Hitler Movement: A Modern Millenarian Revolution* (Stanford, 1980); Klaus Vondung, *Magie und Manipulation: Ideologischer Kult und politische Religion des Nationalsozialismus* (Göttingen, 1971).

[21] Michael Burleigh, *The Third Reich: A New History* (New York, 2000), 256.

[22] Wolfgang Altgeld, *Katholizismus, Protestantismus, Judentum: Über religiös begründeter Gegensätze und nationalreligiöser Ideen in der Geschichte des deutschen Nationalismus* (Mainz, 1992), especially 165–181.

[23] Wolfgang Altgeld, "Religion, Denomination and Nationalism in Nineteenth-Century Germany," in Helmut Walser Smith (ed.), *Protestants, Catholics and Jews in Germany, 1800–1914* (Oxford, 2001), 52.

[24] Helmut Walser Smith, *German Nationalism and Religious Conflict: Culture, Ideology, Politics, 1870–1914* (Princeton, 1995).

of the century.[25] Arguably, *völkisch* thought had emerged within established Protestantism even sooner. As Wolfgang Tilgner and Robert Ericksen have observed, the particular theological construct of *Schöpfungsglaube*, a departure within mainstream German Lutheranism, presaged the same kinds of *völkisch* theories for which the Nazis would later become infamous.[26] Looking to ideology instead of theology, Günther Brakelmann has shown how closely political Protestantism could "overlap" with Nazism on a range of issues.[27] Exploring broader European intellectual trends, historian Maurice Olender has gone so far as to argue that the racialism that would come to its extreme conclusion in Nazism was born of the debates which emerged in biblical criticism in the nineteenth century.[28] Outside of the European context, historians have pointed to very similar connections between religion and racialist politics in the modern world. Work on the ideological roots of the Ku Klux Klan and "Christian Identity" in the United States and the Apartheid system in South Africa says much about two societies whose histories are notable both for their intense Protestant identity and often virulent racism.[29] However, as with the literature on the churches, we have an incomplete coupling. Whereas Nazism's direct or indirect indebtedness to Christianity is debated in terms of intellectual precedents, this literature has not widened its scope further to reconsider the question of whether the Nazis themselves may have recognize these traditions and, if so, how they may have inherited and reproduced them.

This discrepancy is particularly evident in scholarship on antisemitism, the third major locus of inquiry in which we see a discussion of the relationship between Christianity and Nazism. The question of the origins of Nazi antisemitism has of course garnered a vast and still-growing literature.[30]

[25] Rainer Lächele, "Protestantismus und völkische Religion im deutschen Kaiserrreich," in Uwe Puschner, Walter Schmitz, and Justus Ulbricht (eds), *Handbuch zur 'Völkischen Bewegung' 1871–1918* (Munich, 1999), 149–63, here 152.

[26] Wolfgang Tilgner, *Volksnomostheologie und Schöpfungsglaube: Ein Beitrag zur Geschichte des Kirchenkampfes* (Göttingen, 1966); Ericksen, *Theologians under Hitler*. See as well Karl Kupisch, "The Luther Renaissance," *Journal of Contemporary History* 2 (1967), 39–49.

[27] Günter Brakelmann, "Nationalprotestantismus und Nationalsozialismus," in Christian Jansen et al. (eds.), *Von der Aufgabe der Freiheit: Politische Verantwortung und bürgerliche Gesellschaft im 19. und 20. Jahrhundert* (Berlin, 1995), 337–50.

[28] Maurice Olender, *The Languages of Paradise: Race, Religion and Philology in the Nineteenth Century*, trans. Arthur Goldhammer (Cambridge, MA, 1992).

[29] For South Africa, see T. Dunbar Moodie, *The Rise of Afrikanerdom: Power, Apartheid, and the Afrikaner Civil Religion* (Berkeley, 1975), and Leonard Thompson, *The Political Mythology of Apartheid* (New Haven, 1985). For the United States, see Michael Barkun, *Religion and the Racist Right: The Origins of the Christian Identity Movement* (Chapel Hill, 1994); David Chalmers, *Hooded Americanism: The First Century of the Ku Klux Klan, 1865–1965*, 3rd ed. (Durham, 1987); Leo Ribuffo, *The Old Christian Right: The Protestant Far Right from the Great Depression to the Cold War* (Philadelphia, 1983).

[30] Just a few of the many important works include Hermann Greive, *Geschichte des modernen Antisemitismus in Deutschland* (Darmstadt, 1983); Jacob Katz, *From Prejudice to Destruction: Antisemitism, 1700–1933* (Cambridge, MA, 1980); Peter Pulzer, *The Rise of Political*

The long-standing question about the influence of Christian antisemitism on later racial or Nazi antisemitism has recently been the topic of renewed and intense disagreement.[31] Generally those who argue against such an influence contend that the unprecedented brutality of Nazi antisemitism took it outside the parameters of previous Christian forms and was qualitatively different from them (many of these scholars also tie their position to a larger critique of the concept of a German *Sonderweg*).[32] On the other hand, a growing number of historians are beginning to rethink earlier assumptions that religious antisemitism played no part in the formation of its racialist counterpart. For instance, Peter Pulzer writes in the introduction to his revised classic study on the subject: "I am more strongly convinced than I was when I wrote the book that a tradition of religiously-inspired Jew hatred ... was a necessary condition for the success of antisemitic propaganda, even when expressed in non-religious terms and absorbed by those no longer religiously observant."[33] Although this rethinking is gaining currency in recent scholarship, it has suffered from an important drawback: It almost never takes the Nazi ideological elite into account, as their views are usually regarded as proof that the movement was anti-Christian. Rather than presenting direct empirical evidence of a connection, scholars of this school frequently confine themselves to a homology. For instance, Jacob Katz argues that "[M]odern antisemitism turned out to be a continuation of the premodern rejection of Judaism by Christianity, even when it renounced any claim to be legitimized by it or even professed to be antagonistic to Christianity."[34] Even though Saul Friedländer has suggested that Nazi antisemitism contained a religious element (as explicated in his concept of "redemptive antisemitism"), this portion of Katz's argument is in his view "excessive."[35] Convinced of Nazism's ideological indebtedness to Christian antisemitism, other scholars, such as the theologian Richard Rubenstein, concur that the Nazi movement was nonetheless anti-Christian, based again on the statements of Nazis themselves. Unable to overcome this empirical stumbling block, Rubenstein can

Antisemitism in Germany and Austria, 2nd ed. (Cambridge, MA, 1988); Reinhard Rürup, *Emanzipation und Antisemitismus: Studien zur 'Judenfrage' in der bürgerlichen Gesellschaft* (Göttingen, 1975); Uriel Tal, *Christians and Jews in Germany: Religion, Politics and Ideology in the Second Reich 1870–1914* (Ithaca, 1975).

[31] See, among others, Olaf Blaschke, *Katholizismus und Antisemitismus im Deutschen Kaiserreich* (Göttingen, 1997); Gavin Langmuir, *Toward a Definition of Antisemitism* (Berkeley, 1990); Paul Lawrence Rose, *Revolutionary Antisemitism in Germany from Kant to Wagner* (Princeton, 1990); John Weiss, *Ideology of Death: Why the Holocaust Happened in Germany* (Chicago, 1996).

[32] For instance, see Jonathan Frankel (ed.), *The Fate of the European Jews, 1939–1945: Continuity or Contingency?* (Oxford, 1997), in which the majority of the contributors emphatically argue for the latter option.

[33] Peter Pulzer, *Antisemitism*, xxii.

[34] Jacob Katz, *Prejudice*, 319.

[35] Saul Friedländer, *Nazi Germany and the Jews: The Years of Persecution, 1933–1939* (New York, 1997), 85.

argue only that the movement as a whole was paradoxical.[36] Among the questions this work will explore is the meaning of Christian antisemitism for Nazis themselves and whether they may indeed have recognized the intellectual indebtedness that Rubenstein insists on.

In this study, the ideas of a select few within the movement are not regarded as the sole locus of the Nazi *Weltanschauung*. Nor do I subscribe to the view that Hitler himself somehow ranks as a bona fide intellectual, a man of any singular ideological innovation. Hans Mommsen has rightly argued against the intentionalists' "Hitlercentric" interpretation of Nazism, thereby rejecting postwar efforts to off-load as much responsibility on as few people as possible. But the baby of an ideological investigation need not be thrown out with the bath water of resting total blame on Hitler alone. As with the rank-and-file of the Nazi Party, Hitler's own worldview was not created in a void, but rather was the product of a particular sociocultural context, one shared with a great many other party leaders.

This work therefore goes beyond past practices of concentrating solely on the supposed forefathers or designated high priests of the movement to incorporate a wider range of party opinion. At the same time, however, it is essential to concentrate on those Nazis whose ideological credentials were beyond reproach. Whereas zealous Nazis existed in all ranks of the party, only those who displayed ideological commitment by "working towards the Führer" could achieve elite status.[37] For this reason I focus chiefly on the religious views – enunciated in both public *and* in private – of not only Hitler and his immediate circle, but also of the *Reichsleiter* (national leaders), *Gauleiter* (district leaders), and those operating explicitly as ideological or educational leaders, either independently or in party organizations. In this way we can avoid an "*exegetical* focus on Hitler's and other Nazi leaders' immediate ideas,"[38] and at the same time rectify what Jane Caplan has termed the "massive imbalance between the intensive, almost obsessive rereading [of selected Nazi ideologues] on the one hand, and the neglect of their alleged ideological confrères on the other."[39]

In Chapter 1 I investigate those Nazis who insisted that Christianity played a central role in their own lives and in their movement. Many of them articulated this belief through the concept of "positive Christianity." More than just a cynical ploy for winning votes, the proponents of positive Christianity maintained that their antisemitism and socialism were derived from a Christian understanding of Germany's ills and their cure. This development

[36] Richard L. Rubenstein, *After Auschwitz: History, Theology and Contemporary Judaism*, 2nd ed. (Baltimore, 1992), 31. Arguing in a somewhat similar vein is Franklin Littell, *The Crucifixion of the Jews* (New York, 1962).

[37] For more on this concept, see Ian Kershaw, "'Cumulative Radicalisation' and the Uniqueness of National Socialism," in Jansen et al., *Von der Aufgabe der Freiheit*, 323–336.

[38] Geoff Eley, "What is Cultural History?," *New German Critique* 65 (1995), 34.

[39] Jane Caplan, "Postmodernism, Poststructuralism, and Deconstruction: Notes for Historians," *Central European History* 22 (1989), 275–6.

is explored through Nazi conceptions of Jesus, the Bible, and Germany's religious past. Whereas public utterances are explored, private writings and utterances made behind closed doors are given even more weight. In Chapter 2 I explore the hope among the positive Christians to bridge the sectarian divide between Protestants and Catholics in Germany. Although positive Christianity was never an attempt to create a practicable "third confession," discussions about its relevance to sectarianism in German society help reveal basic attitudes about the two established faiths. As is shown, the sectarian divide in German society could also cut through the Nazi Party; more surprisingly, however, several nominally Catholic Nazis actually showed greater preference for the ideological substance of Protestantism over their own original faith. As is shown in Chapters 1 and 2, those aspects of the Nazis' religious views that have conventionally been seen as the hardest to reconcile with Christianity – such as the end of confessional schools or the rejection of the Old Testament – in fact found expression within bona fide varieties of Protestantism. In Chapter 3 I explore the "paganists" of the movement, those who espoused a radically anti-Christian faith and whose religious views have usually been regarded as hegemonic in the party. I demonstrate that their religious agenda in fact brought them into conflict with many people in the party's leadership. Through a close reading of their major works, I also demonstrate that their detachment from Christianity was partial and ambiguous. Their conceptions of Christianity revealed a consistent appreciation for Protestantism in particular.

Having explored Nazi "text" in the first three chapters, in the remaining chapters I explore Nazi "action": in other words, how Nazi rule after 1933 conformed with or departed from Nazi ideology before 1933.[40] In Chapter 4 I examine the first years of the Third Reich and explore how Nazi understandings of their major policies fit within a Christian framework. Christian and anti-Christian themes, as well as ongoing party member activity within religious bodies, are examined to delineate lines of continuity and change, to determine how widespread Christian and paganist identities within the party remained. In Chapter 5 I deal with church–state relations in the Third Reich from the state perspective, focusing on the attempt to establish a Protestant Reich Church that would unite the splintered state churches under the authority of a Reich Bishop. Through an analysis of their involvement in this undertaking, I demonstrate that leading Nazis put great stock in the strengthening of institutional Protestantism, above all as a "bulwark" against the Catholic Church. In the process, they permitted a surprising freedom of expression for members of the Confessing Church. In Chapter 6 I explore the Nazis' claims that a kind of Christian ethic guided them in defining their social policies. I do this by examining the ideological and institutional

---

[40] The conceptual distinctions between fascist "text" and "action," between "essence" and "process," and how this corresponds with the "movement" and "regime" phases of fascism, is brought out very well in Robert Paxton, "The Five Stages of Fascism," *Journal of Modern History* 70 (1998), 1–23.

relationships between the churches' and the Nazis' social networks. Three areas of social policy important to both state and church are explored here: eugenics, women, and youth. Chapter 7 extends the investigation of the Nazis' religious views and policies into the latter years of the Nazi State. In the wake of the failed attempt to create a Reich Church came a wave of measures aimed against church affiliation in the party. In this chapter I also look at the pivotal role played by leading anti-Christians in their attempt to expunge Christian influence from Nazism. The polycratic infighting that took place over the policing of Nazi ideology reveals that Nazism, as a whole, although increasingly hostile to the churches, never became uniformly anti-Christian, displaying instead deep ambivalence and contradiction by the end.

In this study I attempt a critical rethinking of the nature of Nazi ideology and practice and seek to uncover a dimension previously overlooked by scholars of the period. Both the Nazis and their historians have viewed the movement through many frames of reference. I seek to add an additional layer of interpretation rather than replace or reject previous interpretations. To the many ways Nazis identified themselves and their movement – nationalist, socialist, scientific, racialist – many attached the label of Christian as well. While I chart the personal religious feelings of Nazi leaders, I seek foremost to explore the ways in which Nazis claimed their movement and its ideology were related or unrelated to different strands of Christian thought. In a somewhat different context, Geoff Eley has suggested that in fascist ideology "certain beliefs and practices came to reproduce themselves under radically changed circumstances," thereby becoming "subtly transformed in the very process of renewal."[41] In this study I attempt to demonstrate how radical new circumstances present in Germany after 1918 effected the reproduction and transformation of certain Christian traditions within the Nazi movement. I also disclose the contested nature of religious meaning in the movement, one that spanned nearly the entire period of the party's history, and reveal how this shaped larger debates within the party about ideology and its oversight. I do not examine the reception of the German masses to the Nazis' religious claims or how pivotal those claims may have been to the broad social consensus the Nazis attempted. Nor do I seek in a deterministic or monocausal fashion to place the origins of Nazism in a simplified, static concept of Christianity. Rather, I suggest that, for many of its leaders, Nazism was not the result of a "Death of God" in secularized society, but rather a radicalized and singularly horrific attempt to preserve God *against* secularized society.

[41] Geoff Eley, "What Produces Fascism: Preindustrial Traditions or a Crisis of the Capitalist State?," *Politics and Society* 12 (1983), 63.

POSITIVE CHRISTIANITY

The Doctrine of the Time of Struggle

The struggle we are now waging today until victory or the bitter end is, in its deepest sense, a struggle between Christ and Marx.
              Joseph Goebbels[1]

The narrative of the early history of Nazism is well enough known: The trauma of defeat in the First World War, the guilt clause of the Versailles Treaty, and the domestic upheaval of the failed November Revolution all conspired to produce a cacophony of rightist fringe groups determined to overthrow the newly created Weimar Republic. Although distinct in style and organization, all these groups advocated a radical *völkisch* nationalism that embraced antisemitism, anti-Marxism, antiliberalism, and anti-Catholicism to varying degrees. By positing the primacy of race, these groups, and the National Socialists in particular, seemed to represent a radical departure from the norms of the party-political right, which up to that time remained within the parameters of traditional, monarchist conservatism. The turbulence created by events unleashed a movement that, although having ideological roots in the prewar period, had been previously unable to enter the political mainstream. The tumult of Weimar and apparent triumph of the left provided the opportunity to seize the initiative.[2]

There was initially little aspiration for parliamentary success on the extremist right. Up until Hitler's failed *putsch* of November 1923, the Nazis did not take political pragmatism into consideration. Less concerned with garnering an electorate than with forcing through their immediate goals, the party in this period articulated its vision without concern for campaign strategy or electoral posturing. Indeed, postwar Bavaria was particularly noteworthy for its singular disdain of parliamentary principles, being the site of considerable revolutionary activity and numerous attempted coups.

[1] J. Goebbels, *Michael* (New York, 1987 [orig. 1929]), 66.
[2] On the founding of the NSDAP and its early history, see *inter alia* Reginald Phelps, "Hitler and the *Deutsche Arbeiterpartei*," in Henry A. Turner (ed.), *Nazism and the Third Reich* (New York, 1972); Werner Maser, *Die Frühgeschichte der NSDAP: Hitlers Weg bis 1924* (Frankfurt a.M., 1965); Jeremy Noakes and Geoffrey Pridham (eds.), *Nazism 1919–1945: A Documentary Reader*, 4 vols. (Exeter, 1983-98), 1: 7–35.

In such an extremist environment, a tiny party like the National Socialist German Workers' Party (*Nationalsozialistische Deutsche Arbeiterpartei*, or NSDAP) felt little need to tone down its message for the sake of public relations. There was nothing to be lost in a frank expression of the movement's ideology. Hence we can reasonably expect that Nazi speeches, writings, and other public expressions from this period can provide insight into their untempered ideas and provide useful points of comparison with what Nazis said behind closed doors.

Much is already known about the Nazis' public stance toward Christianity. Point 24 of the NSDAP Party Program of 1920, commonly accredited to Gottfried Feder, reads:

We demand freedom for all religious confessions in the state, insofar as they do not endanger its existence or conflict with the customs and moral sentiments of the Germanic race. The party as such represents the standpoint of a positive Christianity, without tying itself to a particular confession. It fights the spirit of Jewish materialism within us and without us, and is convinced that a lasting recovery of our *Volk* can only take place from within, on the basis of the principle: public need comes before private greed [*Gemeinnutz geht vor Eigennutz*].[3]

After it applied the litmus test of compatability with the "Germanic race," the party claimed to uphold a *type* of Christianity. Whereas the Party Program is usually regarded as a true reflection of the Nazis' goals at that time, this passage is commonly regarded as a product of caution, meant to allay fears among religious peoples by posing as essentially favorable to Christianity. The expression "positive Christianity" in particular is commonly regarded as a tactical measure, "cleverly" left undefined in order to accommodate a broad range of meanings.[4] However, on closer examination, the wording of Point 24 readily provides us with three key ideas in which Nazis claimed their movement was Christian: the spiritual struggle against the Jews, the promulgation of a social ethic, and a new syncretism that would bridge Germany's confessional divide. In this chapter we turn our attention to the first two of these components; the third will be treated in the next chapter. Through a survey of some of the leading figures of the Nazi movement, I will demonstrate that positive Christianity was more than a political ploy

[3] As printed in Alfred Rosenberg, *Das Parteiprogramm: Wesen, Grundsätze und Ziele der NSDAP* (Munich, 1922), 15ff, 57f. Jeremy Noakes and Geoffrey Pridham suggest that Hitler and Anton Drexler wrote most of this program, and not Feder: *Reader*, 1: 14. Albrecht Tyrell, in his biographical sketch of Feder, also suggests that he did not directly participate in writing the Party Program: Albrecht Tyrell, "Gottfried Feder: the Failed Policymaker," in Ronald Smelser and Rainer Zitelmann (eds.), *The Nazi Elite*, trans. Mary Fischer (New York, 1993), 33.
[4] Franz Feige, *The Varieties of Protestantism in Nazi Germany: Five Theopolitical Positions* (Lewiston, NY, 1990), 126. See also John Conway, *The Nazi Persecution of the Churches* (London, 1968), 5; George Denzler and Volker Fabricius, *Christen und Nationalsozialisten: Darstellung und Dokumente* (Frankfurt a.M., 1993), 16–20; Kurt Meier, *Kreuz und Hakenkreuz: Die evangelische Kirche im Dritten Reich* (Munich, 1992), 11.

for winning votes and that it was not a loose, unarticulated construct, but instead adhered to an inner logic.

OUR RELIGION IS CHRIST, OUR POLITICS FATHERLAND

If Germany before November 1918 had been a "Christian state," afterward it looked to many people like a godless republic. For most of Germany's Christians, and certainly for German Protestantism, it was a time of deep insecurity. The *Summus Episcopus*, secular guarantor of the Protestant Church's prerogatives, had been overthrown. The churches' constitutional rights, as well as the professional security of the German pastorate, were similarly thrown into question. The brief tenure of Adolf Hoffmann (a member of the future Communist Party and strong advocate of the separation of church and state) as Prussian Minister of Culture further strained relations between the churches and the Weimar "system." However, the strains were not just institutional.[5] Indeed, more important was a larger crisis of Germany's Christian culture. For many Christians, Weimar's very existence signaled a profound assault on God's order. Christians of both confessions had stood at the forefront of nationalist agitation during World War I. The growing inclination among Protestant theologians in particular to view Germany as God's favored nation, a theological trend that began in the latter half of the nineteenth century,[6] culminated in 1914 in "war theology."[7] This theology was fostered by an ethical interpretation of Christianity, by which God worked providentially through history to liberate humanity from materialism in order to realize his moral kingdom on Earth. War theology reduced ethical activity to the nation, conceived as the means through which God revealed his will. The notion that God sanctioned the nation as one of his orders of creation was similarly a theological departure within mainstream Christianity that, although significantly radicalized by the longevity of the Great War, in fact predated it by many years.[8] The result was that most Christian clergy condemned Germany's adversaries in harsh moral terms, elevating the war into a type of crusade in which God had chosen Germany to punish his enemies.

[5] That they largely were is argued by Gerhard Mehnert, *Evangelische Kirche und Politik 1917–1919* (Düsseldorf, 1959). For the general comportment of Protestant churchmen toward the Weimar regime, see as well Karl-Wilhelm Dahm, *Pfarrer und Politik: Soziale Position und Politische Mentalität des deutschen evangelischen Pfarrerstandes zwischen 1918 und 1933* (Cologne, 1965); Jochen Jacke, *Kirche zwischen Monarchie und Republik: Der preussische Protestantismus nach dem Zusammenbruch von 1918* (Hamburg, 1976).

[6] Hartmut Lehmann, "The Germans as a Chosen People: Old Testament Themes in German Nationalism," *German Studies Review* 14 (1991), 261–73.

[7] Wilhelm Pressel, *Die Kriegspredigt 1914–1918 in der evangelischen Kirche Deutschlands* (Göttingen, 1967); Arlie Hoover, *The Gospel of Nationalism: German Patriotic Preaching from Napoleon to Versailles* (Stuttgart, 1986).

[8] See the discussion of the works of Altgeld, Ericksen, Smith, and Tilgner, among others, in the Introduction.

Whereas some quarters of German opinion – beginning with Social Democrats and then Catholics – began to call for a negotiated peace as the war dragged on, many Protestants preached holding out until the very end, endorsing the notion of a "Hindenburg peace," one of total victory and extensive war aims.[9] Many reacted to the peace overtures of socialists and the Vatican by joining the Fatherland Party (*Deutsche Vaterlandspartei*), established in 1917. As an increasing number of Germans – some conservatives now among them – contemplated ending the war, many Protestant pastors continued to assert that victory could be won if only the German people could muster the will to win.[10] When the war was finally lost, such Christians were plunged into a crisis. Instead of interpreting events in military or economic terms, they chose to view defeat in moral terms, believing the cause lay in a domestic betrayal of Germany and God. The first known public articulation of the infamous "stab-in-the-back" legend came, not from a general or politician, but in a sermon preached on 3 February 1918 – nine months before the actual end of the war – by Protestant Court Chaplain Bruno Doehring.[11]

The Versailles Treaty turned nationalist Protestant wrath into rage. An address delivered to the Protestant Upper Church Consistory (*Oberkirchenrat*) by the general superintendents of the Prussian state church read: "The demand that we admit sole guilt for the war places a lie on our lips that shamelessly affronts our conscience. As Evangelical Christians we ceremoniously raise before God and men the holy protest against the attempt to press this scar on our nation."[12] The fervor generated by this moral outrage reached extraordinary heights. Some made clear their preference for "disaster with honor" over a "dishonorable existence." The Association of Protestant Women's Organizations stated with unmistakable zeal: "For German Evangelical women, honor is more important than their own and their children's welfare." Many prominent Christians, most notably the Lutheran thinker Emanuel Hirsch, argued that God had not failed the German people, but rather that the German people had failed God. Others suggested that a materialist spirit had infected the *Volk* and driven God to punishment. The idea that God was an active intervener in human affairs was a long-standing

---

[9] Annexation and reparation demands appeared frequently in church periodicals, including liberal ones. Adolf Stöcker's Christian Social Party specifically called for the "dismemberment and partial annexation of Belgium, adjustment of Germany's borders based on military needs, [and] German control over central Africa": Pressel, *Kriegspredigt*, 270; Daniel Borg, *The Old-Prussian Church and the Weimar Republic: A Study in Political Adjustment, 1917–1927* (Hanover, NH, 1984), 42.

[10] Borg, *Old-Prussian Church*, 37.

[11] Pressel, *Kriegspredigt*, 305–6; Kurt Nowak, *Evangelische Kirche und Weimarer Republik: Zum politischen Weg des deutschen Protestantismus zwischen 1918 und 1932* (Göttingen, 1981), 53–4. This goes against Doris Bergen's suggestion that the church was implicated in the *Dolchstoßlegende*: *Twisted Cross: The German Christian Movement in the Third Reich* (Chapel Hill, 1996), 66.

[12] Borg, *Old-Prussian Church*, 217–18.

tradition within certain Christian theologies, both within and outside Germany. Within Germany, prominent Protestant theologians like Hirsch and Paul Althaus developed this tradition the furthest: According to Althaus, "Since history is full of the will of God, it yields knowledge of God."[13] In light of the crisis that befell Germany after 1918, belief in an active, providential God could lead to only so many conclusions politically. If Germany were to regain God's favor, these Christians suggested, the nation must return to him. The *Volk* had to prepare for the day "when the Lord of history will give [us] the sign for a new fight of liberation."[14]

Liberation from materialism; Germany as God's chosen nation; domestic betrayal of the nation and God; honor and sacrifice; a new fight for liberation – these were not indeterminate tropes readily available to all Germans across the political spectrum in Weimar. Rather, they represented the fixed ideological position of a variety of Christian in postwar Germany. Such views represented an increasingly dualistic thinking among those in Germany who were not just reacting to the material difficulties of postwar inflation and the redrawing of the nation's borders, but who also believed that the country was on the verge of a moral abyss reflected in an inexplicable defeat and the specter of atheistic revolution. This dualism, this understanding of Germany's predicament as a fight of good against evil, precluded a search for answers in the workings of pluralist Weimar democracy, which for many was regarded as illegitimate in the first instance. For them this was instead an all-or-nothing struggle. This same dualistic vision, enunciated within the same Christian parameters, was an ideological centerpiece for many in the new Nazi movement as well.

Dietrich Eckart was perhaps the most important ideologue in the early stages of the movement. It was he who coined the phrase "Jewish materialist spirit within us and without us," used in Point 24, an expression that implied a religious element in the Nazi typology and suggested the Jewish "problem" was not solely racial.[15] Eckart became something of a mentor to Hitler, introducing him to Munich's extremist milieu and strengthening his basic beliefs. Twenty years later, Hitler acknowledged his ideological indebtedness to Eckart, stating that "At the time, I was intellectually a child still on the bottle."[16] Hitler felt so indebted to Eckart he ended *Mein Kampf* with a tribute to him: "And among [our heroes] I want also to count that man, one of the best, who devoted his life to the awakening of his – our – people, in his writings and his thoughts and finally in his deeds: Dietrich Eckart."[17]

One of the earliest works of Nazi ideology was Eckart's *Der Bolschewismus von Moses bis Lenin: Zweigespräche zwischen Adolf Hitler und mir*

---

[13] Quoted in Feige, *Varieties of Protestantism*, 93.

[14] Borg, *Old-Prussian Church*, 219–21.

[15] Dietrich Eckart, "Das Judentum in und außer uns," *Auf gut deutsch* 1 (1919).

[16] Adolf Hitler, *Hitler's Table Talk 1941–1944: His Private Conversations*, trans. Norman Cameron and R. H. Stevens, introduction by Hugh Trevor-Roper (London, 1953), 217.

[17] Adolf Hitler, *Mein Kampf*, trans. Ralph Manheim (Boston, 1962), 687.

Fig. 1 Dietrich Eckart, mentor to Hitler and one of Nazism's most important early ideologues: "In Christ, the embodiment of all manliness, we find all that we need." (Scherl)

("Bolshevism from Moses to Lenin: a conversation between Adolf Hitler and myself"), written shortly before his death in 1923. Although scholars have pointed to the importance of this book as an early instance of Nazi ideology, they generally overlook its strong religious overtones.[18] It is most likely that Hitler in fact held no such conversation with Eckart; these are probably spurious conversations with the Nazi leader. However, because the conversation was manufactured by Eckart, it still remains a reliable indication of his own views.[19] Lamenting the cultural and moral crevasse he believed his country had fallen into, Eckart suggests that Christ provided an important moral compass: "Christ stands never otherwise than erect, never otherwise than upright... eyes flashing in the midst of the creeping Jewish rabble... and the words fall like lashes of the whip: 'Your father is the devil' (John 8:44)."[20] Far from advocating a paganist or anti-Christian religion, Eckart held that, in Germany's postwar tailspin, Christ was a leader to be emulated: "In Christ, the embodiment of all manliness, we find all that we need. And if we occasionally speak of Baldur, our words always contain some joy, some satisfaction, that our pagan ancestors were already so

[18] Ernst Nolte, "Eine frühe Quelle zu Hitlers Antisemitismus," *Historische Zeitschrift* 192 (1961), 585–606; Barbara Miller Lane, "Nazi Ideology: Some Unfinished Business," *Central European History* 7 (1974), 3–30; Barbara Miller Lane and Leila Rupp (eds.), *Nazi Ideology before 1933: A Documentation* (Austin, 1978). Lane and Rupp draw extensively from Eckart's works in their study of early Nazi ideology, but curiously overlook the many references Eckart made to Christianity and how he regarded it as the antithesis of Judaism.
[19] Margarete Plewnia, *Auf dem Weg zu Hitler: Der 'völkische' Publizist Dietrich Eckart* (Bremen, 1970), 94–112.
[20] Dietrich Eckart, *Der Bolschewismus von Moses bis Lenin: Zwiegespräche zwischen Adolf Hitler und mir* (Munich, 1924), 18.

Christian as to have indications of Christ in this ideal figure."[21] The book, published posthumously, ended with an afterword by the publishers: Eckart's death "prevented the completion of this highly significant work showing the Christian approach to the *völkisch* movement."[22]

This dualism, conceived in a specifically Christian language, guided Eckart's thinking on other subjects as well. On the First World War he wrote: "This war was a religious war, finally one sees that clearly. A war between light and darkness, truth and falsehood, Christ and Antichrist."[23] This religious dualism achieved apocalyptic dimensions: "The moment of truth has arrived: humanity once again has the choice between appearance and reality, between Germandom and Jewry, between the all and the nothing, between truth and falsehood."[24] Eckart believed in an ultimate confrontation between these forces: "When light comes to blows with darkness, no pacts are made! There is only struggle for life and death, until the destruction of one or the other. And that is why world war is the only apparent end."[25] In such passages, Eckart makes use of a Christian discourse – an apocalyptic opposition of good and evil – rather than delineating an explicit ideological program with a Christian content. Use of religious metaphors in political movements was certainly nothing new, nor in Weimar Germany was it limited to the Nazi movement. But Eckart goes further than this, demonstrating an underlying assumption that his struggle against the Jews was ontologically bound with the struggle for Christianity. The racial duality between Aryan and Semite overlapped with and was related to a religious duality between Christian and Jew.

Combining a rejection of the Old Testament with esteem for Jesus seems highly idiosyncratic. However, as the case of Artur Dinter reveals, such a seemingly peculiar configuration was in fact common among the positive Christians of the party.[26] Known primarily as an ideologue, Dinter also displayed considerable organizational abilities. As *Gauleiter* of Thuringia he was instrumental to the party's early success in that area: According to one historian, his district was one of the "first and most successful examples of party expansion outside of Bavaria."[27] The selection of Weimar as the site of the 1926 *Reichsparteitag* (National Party Congress), the first to be held after the party's refounding, affirmed the importance of Dinter's *Gau* to the party during this period. Inspired by Houston Stewart Chamberlain's

---

[21] Ibid., 36.

[22] Ibid., 50.

[23] *Auf gut deutsch* 2 (1919), 23.

[24] Alfred Rosenberg, *Dietrich Eckart: Ein Vermächtnis* (Munich, 1935), 86.

[25] Ibid., 84.

[26] On Dinter's political career and his relevance for the NSDAP's early gains, see Donald Tracey, "The Development of the National Socialist Party in Thuringia, 1924–1930," *Central European History* 8 (1975), 26–34; Dietrich Orlow, *The History of the Nazi Party: 1919–1933* (Pittsburgh, 1969), 90–1.

[27] Tracey, "Thuringia," 34, 38. This work also provides a useful overview of the internecine warfare between the competing far-right parties.

Foundations of the Nineteenth Century, which he maintained led to his "total spiritual rebirth," Dinter turned from a career in the theater to writing novels. His most famous, *Die Sünde wider das Blut* ("The sin against the blood"), was published in 1918, and sold 235,000 copies by 1927, making it the most popular novel written by a National Socialist. Two subsequent novels further expounded his world view: *Die Sünde wider den Geist* ("sin against the spirit"), published in 1921, which sold 100,000 copies in its first year; and *Die Sünde wider die Liebe* ("sin against love"), published in 1922, which sold 30,000 copies by 1928. A projected fourth novel on Jesus was never completed.[28] In "Sin against the Spirit," Dinter unveiled an admiration for Jesus that went beyond a mere political appropriation: "Jesus is the only spirit created by God and incarnated on earth who never misused his free will to sin."[29] Dinter also suggested the removal of the Old Testament from the Christian canon: It was too "materialistic" for Christians, a monument to "the religious thinking of the Jews, which is based upon lies and betrayal, business and profit."[30] The expurgation of the Old Testament would bring about a "return" to the unadulterated teachings of Jesus. This leading exponent of the Nazis' race mania was also deeply absorbed with Christ.

Joseph Goebbels' religious views encompassed Jesus as well. Like Eckart and Dinter, Goebbels had literary pretensions. He was one of the most prolific writers of the movement, both in number of published works and in the quantity of unpublished, private material.[31] As the chief architect of the infamous *Kristallnacht* of 1938, he was also an antisemite of the highest order. However, given his role as the Nazis' supreme propagandist, there is a tendency in scholarship to regard him as ideologically lax or even mendacious. Indeed, his role in the *Kristallnacht* is often attributed to his extramarital affairs as much as to a committed antisemitism.[32] However, Goebbels' writings before 1933, both public and private, reveal a committed and consistent ideologue: "Money is the power of evil and the Jew its servant. Aryan, Semite, positive, negative, constructive, destructive. The Jew has his fateful mission to once more dominate the sick Aryan race. Our salvation or our

---

[28] Ibid., 26, no.13; George Kren and Rodler Morris, "Race and Spirituality: Arthur Dinter's Theosophical Antisemitism," *Holocaust and Genocide Studies* 6 (1991), 238.

[29] Arthur Dinter, *Die Sünde wider den Geist* (Leipzig, 1921), 60.

[30] As quoted in Kren and Morris, "Spirituality," 242.

[31] See, *inter alia*, Helmut Heiber, *Joseph Goebbels* (Munich, 1988); Ulrich Höver, *Joseph Goebbels – ein nationaler Sozialist* (Bonn, 1992); Ulrich Nill, *Die 'geniale Vereinfachung': Anti-Intellektualismus in Ideologie und Sprachgebrauch bei Joseph Goebbels* (Frankfurt a.M., 1991); Ralf Georg Reuth, *Goebbels* (Munich, 1990). None of these works address Goebbels' Christian preoccupations: The only one not to overlook this is Claus-Ekkehard Bärsch, *Erlösung und Vernichtung – Joseph Goebbels: Zur Psyche und Ideologie eines jungen Nationalsozialisten* (Munich, 1987). See also the very important collection of Goebbels' diaries: Elke Fröhlich (ed.), *Die Tagebücher von Joseph Goebbels: Sämtliche Fragmente* (Munich, 1987).

[32] For instance, Elke Fröhlich, "Joseph Goebbels: The Propagandist," in Smelser and Zitelmann, *Elite*, 57–8.

ruin is dependent upon us."[33] Such religious imagery ("salvation," "mission") was not simply detached from its originating context. The eternal quality of the struggle was intimately connected with God and with Hitler as "an instrument of divine will shaped by history. . . . Nothing exists outside of God."[34] Here we see reference to the interventionist God of history on which certain Christian theologians in Germany had long ruminated. For Goebbels, the Nazi struggle was innately religious; it was a struggle against the Devil himself: "Whoever cannot hate the Devil cannot love God. Whoever loves his *Volk* must hate the destroyer of his *Volk*, hate him from the depths of his soul."[35]

Goebbels' reference to God was more than a simple deism divorced of Christian content; Christ held a central place in his worldview. Goebbels' fascination with the person of Christ, more than just an appropriation meant to dignify Nazism with pious allusions to the Bible, bordered on a type of evangelism: "I converse with Christ. I believed I had overcome him, but I have only overcome his idolatrous priests and false servants. Christ is harsh and relentless."[36] Through his esteem for Christ, Goebbels also displayed a positive attitude toward the New Testament: "I take the Bible, and all evening long I read the simplest and greatest sermon that has ever been given to mankind: The Sermon on the Mount! 'Blessed are they who suffer persecution for the sake of justice, for theirs is the kingdom of heaven'!"[37] In his novel *Michael*, published in 1923, we also see the unmistakable presence of anticlericalism, but not one rooted in opposition to Christianity itself. Rather, Goebbels suggests that contemporary Christianity is ossified and must be renewed and revitalized by removing it from its institutional shackles: "The various churches have failed. Completely. They are no longer in the front lines, they have long since retreated to the rear guard. From that position, their resentment terrorizes any formation of a new religious will. Millions of people are waiting for this new formation, and their yearnings remain unfulfilled."[38] As a consequence of this anticlerical attack, Goebbels also demonstrates the sincerity of his attitude toward Christianity. Had *Michael* been meant for only public consumption, as an effort to be "all things to all people" typical of the Nazis' alleged opportunism, such an attack on the clergy would have constituted a damaging strategic error. Goebbels' anticlericalism is justified as a preservation of religion, not

---

[33] Fröhlich (ed.), *Tagebücher*, entry for 6 August 1924.

[34] Joseph Goebbels, "Die Revolution als Ding an sich," in idem., *Wege ins Dritte Reich: Briefe und Aufsätze für Zeitgenossen* (Munich, 1927), 48.

[35] Joseph Goebbels, *Michael: Ein deutsches Schicksal in Tagebuchblättern* (Munich, 1929) (English translation hereafter: *Michael: A Novel*, trans. Joachim Neugroschel [New York, 1987], 45). Helmut Heiber, for one, believes that the manuscript was written as early as 1923. It went through seventeen editions by 1945.

[36] Ibid., 38.

[37] Ibid., 120, 44.

[38] Ibid., 120.

an attack on it: "Today's youth is not against God, we are only against his cowardly religious menials, who try to commercialize him as they do everything else. We have to square off against them if we want to square ourselves with God."[39]

Dietrich Klagges, a friend of Goebbels' in the party, almost exactly duplicated these themes. Klagges had the distinction of being one of the first Nazis to attain ministerial office, being appointed State Interior and Education Minister of Braunschweig in 1931. He gained notoriety for providing Hitler with his German citizenship (by making him an official in the Braunschweig government), thereby allowing him to run in the presidential elections of 1932.[40] Klagges published widely and was known for his contribution to Nazi educational philosophy during the Third Reich, having edited and contributed to the enormous four-volume work, "*Volk* and Führer: German History for Schools."[41] He also published many articles on Nazi economic thinking and was considered qualified enough in this area to be appointed head of the Department for the Science of Economics within the party, commissioned "to explore and determine the scientific foundations of National Socialist economic principles."[42] Klagges also turned his attention to Christianity. As a member of the German–Christian Working Group, a precursor to the German Christians, he wrote a work entitled *Das Urevangelium Jesu* ("The Original Gospel of Jesus"), in which he expounded on the meaning of Christ to the Nazi movement. Goebbels took note of his friend's book, writing in his dairy: "Klagges' 'The original gospel of Jesus', perhaps an epoch-making book.... A fabulous book."[43] Klagges closely followed the same ideological pattern laid out by his fellow party members: "Christianity – Judaism, creation – destruction, good – evil, God – Satan, and in the last consequence, redemption – annihilation."[44] However, more than just a model antisemite, Jesus was the son of God.[45] Whereas Nazis tended to emphasize Christ's humanity, Klagges confirmed his divinity.

Even more than Eckart or Dinter, Klagges and Goebbels placed a special emphasis on Christ. Walter Buch also emphasized the inspiration of Jesus as a person. As chairman of the party's Investigation and Conciliation Committee (*Untersuchungs- und Schlichtungsausschuss*) and president of the party's supreme court, he held one of the most powerful positions in Nazism. He had the power to discipline, expel, and punish all party members, and none

---

[39] Ibid., 12–13.

[40] Holger Germann, *Die politische Religion des Nationalsozialisten Dietrich Klagges: Ein Beitrag zur Phänomenologie der NS-Ideologie* (Frankfurt a.M., 1995), 16.

[41] Dietrich Klagges (ed.), *Volk und Führer: Deutsche Geschichte für Schulen*, 4 vols. (Frankfurt a.M., 1937–43). Klagges was also a member of the NSLB.

[42] Avraham Barkai, *Nazi Economics: Ideology, Theory, and Policy* (New Haven, 1990), 33.

[43] Fröhlich (ed.) *Tagebücher*, entry for 29 May 1926.

[44] Dietrich Klagges, *Das Urevangelium Jesu: Der Deutsche Glaube* (Wilster, 1925), 265.

[45] Ibid., 46.

Fig. 2 Walter Buch, head of the Nazi Party court and Martin Bormann's father-in-law: "Christ preached struggle as did no other." (Scherl)

of his judgments could be overturned save for Hitler's direct intervention.[46] Martin Bormann, who would achieve infamy near the end of the party's life, was Buch's son-in-law: According to his biographer, Bormann married Buch's daughter to gain entry to Hitler's inner circle.[47] Otto Wagener, Hitler's confidant in the *Kampfzeit*, named Buch as one of only three men who "were prepared and in a position to tell Hitler their own views when they contradicted his."[48] Like the others surveyed so far, Buch related Nazism as a movement to Christ's own "struggle," sounding a distinct note of triumphalism. Unlike Goebbels or Eckart, Buch was not given to literary flourishes, choosing instead to speak in a more straightforward manner on the relevance of Christ and Christianity for Nazism. To an assembly of the National Socialist Student League (*Nationalsozialistischer Deutscher Studentenbund*, or NSDStB) he declared: "When Point 24 of our program says the party stands for a positive Christianity, here above all is the cornerstone of our thinking. Christ preached struggle as did no other. His life was struggle for his beliefs, for which he went to his death. From everyone he demanded a decision between yes or no.... That is the necessity: that man find the power to decide

[46] See Donald McKale, *The Nazi Party Courts: Hitler's Management of Conflict in His Movement, 1921–1945* (Lawrence, 1974).

[47] Jochen von Lang, *The Secretary – Martin Bormann: The Man Who Manipulated Hitler* (New York, 1979), 47–8. Considering Buch's importance, it is rather surprising that not more has been written on him. Aside from McKale's work, only Lang's book on Bormann contains any substantial biographical information on Buch.

[48] Otto Wagener, *Hitler: Memoirs of a Confidant*, Henry Ashby Turner (ed). (New Haven, 1985), 76. The other two were Gregor Strasser and Franz Pfeffer von Salomon, the supreme commander of the Storm Troopers (*Sturmabteilung*).

between yes and no."[49] This stark black-or-white vision makes clear the dualism of the Nazi worldview. In addition, Buch drew direct comparisons not only between Christ's struggle and the Nazis', but between Christ's followers and members of the NSDAP: "Just as Christianity only prevailed through the fanatical belief of its followers, so too shall it be with the spiritual movement of National Socialism."[50]

Whereas Eckart, Dinter, and Goebbels were all brought up Catholics, Buch was a Lutheran. Unlike his Catholic colleagues, however, Buch held his childhood faith in high esteem. His antisemitism, according to one authority, "he had learned as a young boy from his rigid Lutheran parents."[51] Buch maintained he was guided in his social thought by Martin Luther. This was especially displayed in his concern over the state of German family life; Buch was fond of quoting Luther's adage that the family was "the source of every people's blessings and misfortunes."[52] As we shall see, his reading of Luther would also lead him to a vituperative antisemitism that interwove racial and religious concepts.

A similar reading of Luther as the first antisemite was found in the views of Hans Schemm. Like Buch, Schemm is not usually ranked among the Nazi elite. However, as head of the National Socialist Teachers' League (*Nationalsozialistischer Lehrerbund*, or NSLB) he was in charge of one of the party's most important professional organizations.[53] Typifying the tendency of the Nazi elite to hold many feudalities, he was also *Gauleiter* of Bayreuth – a site of particular symbolism in the Nazi imagination – and after 1933 was Bavarian Minister of Education and Culture. Schemm was also one of the few Nazis who actually adhered to the Aryan ideal of physical beauty and vitality: According to Otto Wagener, he was "tall, blond, blue-eyed, tranquil, athletic. It was characteristic of him that, out of sheer joy for sport, he became a pilot."[54] According to Michael Kater, "he came closer to the *terribles simplificateurs* of Jacob Burckhardt's vision than any of the other Nazi leaders except Adolf Hitler, whom he resembled in charismatic appeal."[55]

Schemm was particularly known throughout the Reich for his slogan "Our religion is Christ, our politics Fatherland!" His speeches, which were

---

[49] Walter Buch, "Geist und Kampf" (speech): Bundesarchiv Berlin-Zehlendorf (hereafter BAZ) NS 26/1375 (n.d., n.p.) (The speech was probably given between 1930 and 1932).

[50] Der Aufmärsch, Blätter der deutschen Jugend 2 (January 1931): in BAZ NS 26/1375.

[51] McKale, Courts, 54.

[52] Ibid., 55–6.

[53] See Willi Feiten, Der Nationalsozialistische Lehrerbund: Entwicklung und Organisation (Weinheim, 1981); Hermann Giesecke, Hitlers Pädagogen: Theorie und Praxis nationalsozialistischer Erziehung (Weinheim, 1993); Franz Kühnel, Hans Schemm, Gauleiter und Kultusminister 1891–1935 (Nuremberg, 1985).

[54] Institut für Zeitgeschichte (hereafter IfZ), ED 60/7 (n.d., n.p.). The book made from Wagener's recollections (Turner [ed.], Memoirs of a Confidant) leaves out this passage.

[55] Kater, Nazi Party, 186.

Fig. 3   Hans Schemm (left), *Gauleiter* of Beyreuth and leader of the National Socialist Teachers' League: "Our religion is Christ, our politics Fatherland!" Source: Theodor Oppermann, *Unter den Sturmstandern des NSKK* (Munich, 1936).

famous in Bavaria, were designed to cast Nazism as a religious revival.[56] As a police report stated, Schemm spoke "like a pastor" and often ended his deliveries with the Lutheran hymn "A Mighty Fortress is our God."[57] Like his fellow Protestant Buch, Schemm held a much more positive view of his confession than did Catholic Nazis like Goebbels. This was not coincidence: As we shall see, a belief that their faith held affinities with their politics – and even helped shape their politics – led Protestants in the Nazi movement to

[56] See, for instance, Geoffrey Pridham, *Hitler's Rise to Power: The Nazi Movement in Bavaria, 1923–1933* (London, 1973), 101–2, who refers to Schemm's unconventional electioneering through the Franconian countryside and the success this had especially among youth. Pridham also points to Schemm's organizational skills in explaining Nazi success in this region. See also Ian Kershaw, *Popular Opinion and Political Dissent in the Third Reich: Bavaria 1933–1945* (Oxford, 1983), 158.

[57] Kühnel, *Schemm*, 134–5.

display far less anticlericalism toward their church than did Catholics, who regarded their confession and its temporal messages as innately antithetical to their politics.

In one of his speeches, Schemm spoke of God in Nazism's conceptual universe: "Our confession to God is a confession of a doctrine of totality.... To give ultimate significance to the totalities of race, resistance and personality there is added the supreme totalitarian slogan of our *Volk*: 'Religion and God.' God is the greatest totality and extends over all else."[58] Here Schemm makes specific reference to the "totalitarian" nature of Nazi discourse. However, he makes it clear that the "totalizing" claims of Nazism as a *Weltanschauung* did not preclude the possibility that that *Weltanschauung* could be based on a variety of Christianity. Far from conflicting loyalties, for Schemm Christianity and Nazism went hand in hand: "We are no theologians, no representatives of the teaching profession in this sense, put forth no theology. But we claim one thing for ourselves: that we place the great fundamental idea of Christianity in the center of our ideology [*Ideenwelt*] – the hero and sufferer Christ himself stands in the center."[59]

These were among the voices of the *Kampfzeit* that displayed an attachment to Christianity and its meaning for the Nazi movement. But what did the top Nazi, Adolf Hitler, have to say? Much is already known through the "Bible" of the Nazi movement, Hitler's *Mein Kampf*. In its pages Hitler gave no indication of being an atheist or agnostic or of believing in only a remote, rationalist divinity.[60] Indeed, he referred continually to a providential, active deity: "What we must fight for is to safeguard the existence and reproduction of our race ... so that our people may mature for the fulfillment of the mission allotted it by the creator of the universe.... Peoples that bastardize themselves, or let themselves be bastardized, sin against the will of eternal Providence."[61] Whereas reference to a vague providential force bears little resemblance to belief in the biblical God, elsewhere in *Mein Kampf* Hitler intones more than a naturalist pantheism devoid of Christian content. Again, it was in the question of race and race purity in which Hitler most frequently intoned such a God: It was, in his view, the duty of Germans "to put an end to the constant and continuous original sin of racial poisoning, and to give the Almighty Creator beings such as He Himself created."[62] Even as Hitler elsewhere made reference to an anthropomorphized "Nature," and the laws of nature that humanity must follow, he also revealed his belief that these were divine laws ordained by God: "The folkish-minded man, in particular, has the sacred duty, each in his own denomination, of making *people stop*

---

[58] Gertrud Kahl-Furthmann (ed.), *Hans Schemm spricht: Seine Reden und sein Werk* (Bayreuth, 1935), 124.

[59] Walter Künneth, Werner Wilm, and Hans Schemm, *Was haben wir als evangelische Christen zum Rufe des Nationalsozialismus zu sagen?* (Dresden, 1931), 19.

[60] As suggested by William Carr, *Hitler: A Study in Personality and Politics* (London, 1978), 135–6.

[61] Hitler, *Mein Kampf*, 214, 327.

[62] Ibid., 405.

just talking superficially of God's will, and actually fulfill God's will, and not let God's word be desecrated. For God's will gave men their form, their essence and their abilities. Anyone who destroys His work is declaring war on the Lord's creation, the divine will."[63] The reference to God as the Lord of Creation, and the necessity of obeying "His" will, reveal a standard Christian conception. As we shall see with regard to his antisemitism, Hitler would return to religious themes in *Mein Kampf* and, in particular, the person of Jesus.

Other sources of Hitler's religious views in this period confirm a Christian element. As early as 1919 Hitler sketched out his basic worldview in an unpublished manuscript. The first section was on the Bible, under which heading Hitler noted: "Monumental History of Mankind – Idealism–Materialism: Nothing without a cause – history makes men . . . the children of God and men."[64] He concluded from these ruminations the first result: "Purification of the Bible – that which is consistent with our spirit. Second result: critical examination of the remainder."[65] This "purification" is almost certainly an allusion to the Old Testament, which both Eckart and Dinter claimed had to be removed from the Christian canon owing to its origins in Judaism. Although such a position brings into question the theological soundness of Hitler's religious views, the idea of expunging the Old Testament from Christianity was not simply a nazification of Christianity. No one less than Adolf von Harnack, one of the leading Protestant theologians of the twentieth century, had conceived such an idea when the Nazi movement was still to be born (see subsequent discussion).

In a speech delivered in front of a Nazi audience in April 1922, Hitler made a more explicit reference to Christianity, referring to Jesus as "the true God." He made it plain that he regarded Christ's struggle as direct inspiration for his own. For Hitler, Jesus was not just one archetype among others, but "our greatest Aryan leader."[66] While emphasizing Jesus' human qualities, Hitler in these instances also alluded to his divinity. At a Christmas celebration given by the Munich branch of the NSDAP in December 1926, Hitler maintained that the movement's goal was to "translate the ideals of Christ into deeds." The movement would complete "the work which Christ had begun but could not finish."[67] On another occasion, this time behind closed doors and to fellow Nazis only, Hitler again proclaimed the centrality of Christ's teachings for his movement: "*We are the first to exhume these teachings! Through us* alone, and not until now, do these teachings celebrate their resurrection! Mary and Magdalene stood at the empty tomb. For they were seeking the dead man. But

[63] Ibid., 562 (emphasis in the original).
[64] Werner Maser, *Hitler's Letters and Notes* (London, 1973), 282–3. Following chapters were to have been on "2. The Aryan; 3. His Works; 4. The Jew; 5. His Work" (ibid.).
[65] Ibid., 282–3.
[66] Eberhard Jäckel (ed.), *Hitler: Sämtliche Aufzeichnungen 1905–1924* (Stuttgart, 1980), 635. Speech of 26 April 1922, originally reported in the *NSDAP-Mitteilungsblatt*, No. 14.
[67] Joachim Fest, *Hitler: Eine Biographie* (Frankfurt a.M., 1973), 354.

we intend to raise the treasures of the living Christ!"[68] In a nearly evangelical tone, Hitler declares that the "true message" of Christianity is to be found only with Nazism. He claims that, where the churches failed in their mission to instill a Christian ethic in secular society, his movement would take up the task. Hitler not only reads the New Testament, but professes – in private – to be inspired by it.

Public sources for Hitler's worldview, such as *Mein Kampf*, enunciate views widely accepted as genuine components of Nazi ideology. If Hitler displays great mendacity about the enemies of Nazism in *Mein Kampf*, he is entirely frank about Nazi beliefs and ambitions. Nonetheless, other historical sources contend that the public stance Hitler took toward Christianity was deceptive, that Hitler was in fact a hater of Christianity who simply posed otherwise for the sake of politics. Historians have long claimed to find Hitler's "real" attitude on religion in the works of Hermann Rauschning. One book in particular, *Hitler Speaks*,[69] is consistently used to argue that Hitler's professions in *Mein Kampf* were nothing more than opportunism; that beneath this cloak of piety stood a duplicitous hater of Christianity and everything it stood for. According to Rauschning, Hitler stated in April 1933:

Neither of the confessions – Catholic or Protestant, they are both the same – has any future left. At least not for the Germans. [Italian] Fascism may perhaps make its peace with the Church in God's name. I will do it too. Why not? But that won't stop me stamping out Christianity in Germany, root and branch. One is either a Christian or a German. You can't be both.... The parsons will be made to dig their own graves. They will betray their God to us. They will betray anything for the sake of their miserable little jobs and incomes.[70]

The conspiratorial tone of this account of the "private" Hitler has convinced many church historians that Hitler was "a wolf in sheep's clothing," anti-Christian to the core and from the outset of his career.[71] The caricature Rauschning presents of Hitler's ranting should alone have raised questions as to its authenticity; but the more troubling fact remains that Rauschning's book stands completely alone in handing down sayings of this nature from this period.[72] It is not for nothing that these factors should raise questions:

[68] Turner (ed.), *Memoirs of a Confidant*, 139–40 (emphasis in the original).

[69] Hermann Rauschning, *Hitler Speaks* (London, 1939). The German edition was published in Switzerland as *Gespräche mit Hitler* (Zürich, 1940).

[70] Rauschning, *Hitler Speaks*, 57–8.

[71] See, *inter alia*, Conway, *Persecution*, 15–16; Denzler and Fabricius, *Christen*, 17–19 ("wolf" quote: 19); Carsten Nicolaisen (ed.), *Dokumente zur Kirchenpolitik des Dritten Reiches*, 3 vols. (Munich, 1971–94), I: 31–4; Hans Buchheim, *Glaubenskrise im Dritten Reich: Drei Kapitel nationalsozialistischer Religionspolitik* (Stuttgart, 1953); Wilhelm Zipfel, *Die Kirchenkampf in Deutschland 1933–1945: Religionsverfolgung und Selbstbehauptung der Kirchen in der national-sozialistischen Zeit* (Berlin, 1965), 9.

[72] Eberhard Jäckel noted long ago that Rauschning was an unreliable source; he painted such a one-dimensional picture of Hitler as an opportunist that, for instance, the Holocaust ended up having nothing to do with antisemitism: *Hitler's Worldview: A Blueprint for Power* (Cambridge MA, 1972), 15–17.

Hitler Speaks is now considered to be fraudulent. As a recent biographer has put it, "Especially the chapter 'Hitler in private'... is untrustworthy through and through – a product of war propaganda.... [Rauschning's] 'conversations with Hitler' are far-off fantasies."[73] Moreover, unlike Otto Wagener, Rauschning was too peripheral to the movement to have been part of Hitler's inner circle of confidants, as he consistently maintained.[74] However, despite the highly questionable nature of Rauschning as a primary source, some historians persist in using him.[75]

ARYAN AND SEMITE, CHRIST AND ANTICHRIST

Attitudes toward the Jews and Judaism are where we see the most frequent reference among Nazis to the relevance of Christian teaching. The ontological priority given in the Nazi worldview to race is undeniable. Among the many targets of Nazi racism, or racialism, the Jews stood squarely in the middle and qualitatively apart. However, the same antisemitism that is usually regarded as a function of racialism was for many Nazis conceived within a Christian frame of reference. Even as they argued that race was the supreme law of life, they did not argue that it overrode religion, since in their view race was God's law. Rather, they commingled racial and religious categories of the Jew and conversely used Aryan and Christian as interchangeable categories as well. In the process, they revealed that their antisemitism was far from a secular or scientific replacement for Christian forms of Jew hatred.

Eckart used a strongly Christian discourse when describing his enmity for the Jews: "Wonders never cease; from the deluge is born a new world, while the Pharisees whine about their miserable pennies! The liberation of

73 Eckhard Jesse, "Hermann Rauschning – Der fragwürdige Kronzeuge," in Ronald Smelser et al (eds.), *Die braune Elite II: 21 weitere biographische Skizzen* (Darmstadt, 1993), 201–2.
74 Theodor Schieder attempted many years ago to defend Rauschning's works: See his *Hermann Rauschnings 'Gespräche mit Hitler' als Geschichtsquelle* (Opladen, 1972). However, a growing amount of literature has proven they are not reliable sources: Besides Jesse, see Wolfgang Hänel, *Hermann Rauschnings 'Gespräche mit Hitler': Eine Geschichtsfälschung* (Ingolstadt, 1984); Fritz Tobias, "Auch Fälschungen haben lange Beine: Des Senatspräsidenten Rauschnings 'Gespräche mit Hitler'," in K. Corino (ed.), *Gefälscht: Betrug in Literatur, Kunst, Musik, Wissenschaft und Politik* (Nördlingen, 1988). In his introduction to Wagener's recollections, Henry Ashby Turner effectively demonstrates why Wagener is more reliable than Rauschning: *Memoirs of a Confidant*, xv–xvii. In his comprehensive biography of Hitler, Ian Kershaw similarly dismisses Rauschning's book, "a work now regarded to have so little authenticity that it is best to disregard it altogether": Ian Kershaw, *Hitler 1889–1936: Hubris* (London, 1998), xiv.
75 This is especially true for church historians: see Denzler and Fabricius, *Christen*, whose revised 1993 edition still relies on Rauschning to support their arguments. However, now nonchurch historians are beginning to use Rauschning through other works, perhaps inadvertently. For instance, Martyn Housden, *Resistance and Conformity in the Third Reich* (London, 1997), 46, cites Zipfel as the source of the famous "betray their God to us" passage; Michael Burleigh, *The Third Reich: A New History* (New York, 2000), 258, cites Conway as the source.

humanity from the curse of gold stands before us! But for that our collapse, but for that our Golgotha!"[76] The antisemitism implicit in the use of such phrases as "Pharisees" and "curse of gold" and the belief that Christianity served as the antipode to the Jew are made more explicit on other occasions: "[The] Jewish conception of God is of no interest to us Germans! We seek God nowhere but in ourselves. For us the soul is divine, of which the Jew, on the other hand, knows nothing: The Kingdom of Heaven is within you (Luke 17:21), thus God also, who belongs to the Kingdom of Heaven. We feel our soul is immortal, eternal from the beginning, and therefore we refuse to be told that we are created from nothingness."[77] Jews, on the other hand, did originate "out of nothingness."[78] We see in Eckart's antisemitism a clear racial element: Christ is cast as the representative of a preexisting Aryan spirit. As important as race belief is in this passage, no less important is Christ's rejection of the Jews. This is further revealed in one of Eckart's poems, called "The Riddle": "The New Testament broke away from the Old/ as you once released yourself from the world/ And as you are freed from your past delusions/ so did Jesus Christ reject his Jewishness."[79] Eckart here suggests that the Old Testament is not only to be superceded by the New Testament, but totally detached from it. The Old Testament's Jewishness, and the call to effectively remove it from the canon of Christianity, would be a theme echoed by others in the Nazi leadership. Eckart's overlapping of racial and religious categories was further revealed when he maintained that "To be an Aryan and to sense transcendence are one and the same thing."[80] Eckart showed here that his religion was not a naturalist pantheism, but a transcendent supernatural faith – one so important that in its absence one could not be considered Aryan. However, Eckart went further than this, demonstrating an underlying assumption that his struggle against the Jews was ontologically bound with the struggle for Christianity. The racial duality between Aryan and Semite was coterminous with a religious duality between Christian and Jew. Eckart made the interchangeability of these categories clear when describing a conversation he had about Freemasonry with Alfred Rosenberg: "In light of the indisputable facts, together with Rosenberg I showed the anti-German or rather anti-Christian, or – what amounts to the same thing – Jewish character of Freemasonry."[81]

The dualism of Christian–Aryan and Jew–Semite was also exhibited in the work of Dinter, one of the Nazi movement's most vituperative anti-semites. His most successful work, the "Sin against the Blood", was a perfect expression of the Nazis' racialist topos, and "stood at the summit of an

---

[76] *Auf gut deutsch* 3 (1919), 297.
[77] Ibid., 38.
[78] *Auf gut deutsch* 1 (1919), 199.
[79] Quoted in Rosenberg, *Eckart*, 112.
[80] Plewnia, *Eckart*, 46.
[81] *Auf gut deutsch* 3 (1919), 36.

enormous production of antisemitic publication."[82] The protagonist of the novel, Hermann Kämpfer, marries a half-Jew who is torn between the "noble and profound" influence of her mother's German blood and the "licentious, pleasure seeking" influence of her father's Jewish blood, and hence personifies the "curse of the sin against the blood to which she owes her existence."[83] They have a child, whose appearance represents the triumph of her father's inheritance. Outraged by this racial contamination, Kämpfer commits himself to the antisemitic cause, founding a society for "race research and hygiene" that is restricted to those who can prove Aryan status up to three generations.[84] Awakened to the malignance of Jewish blood, he remarries, this time to a fully Aryan woman. But amazingly, their child is born with fully Jewish features. As Kämpfer later discovers, his second wife had permanently contaminated herself by having borne a child fathered by a Jew years before. Although fully Aryan herself, this one encounter with Jewish blood was enough to destroy her racial purity. Outraged at this act of defilement, Kämpfer kills the Jewish seducer. He is tried for murder and proclaims before the court that "To lead the spirit to victory over matter, and struggling humanity to its divine destiny: that was the goal God created for himself when he created the Germans! . . . In the Jewish race are found, since time immemorial, those hellish powers which lead man away from God."[85] The jury acquits Kämpfer; racial separation and purity is affirmed as a divine ordinance. Just as with Eckart, for Dinter the question of the German–Jewish duality was as much religious as it was racial. The struggle between Christ and Antichrist was the archetype of the eternal battle between the Aryan and the Semite, between good and evil.[86] According to Dinter, Jesus was the perfect Aryan, who was born among the Jews only to emphasize their polar opposition. Dinter followed Houston Stewart Chamberlain's argument that Galilee was inhabited by Aryans and that Jesus could not have been racially Jewish. Similarly, all the apostles save Judas were Aryan.[87]

In *Michael*, Goebbels revealed the same duality evident in the works of Eckart and Dinter. As in Eckart's writing, in *Michael* we see a use of religious metaphor that, in itself, does not tell us a great deal about a specific commitment to Christianity. However, Goebbels too goes beyond this to a more explicit reliance elsewhere in the book. As Dinter had done, Goebbels created a fictional protagonist, Michael Vormann, through whom he voiced this view: "Christ is the genius of love, as such the most diametrical opposite of Judaism, which is the incarnation of hate. The Jew is a non-race among

[82] Uwe Lohalm, *Völkischer Radikalismus: Die Geschichte des deutschvölkischen Schutz- und Trutz-Bundes, 1919–1923* (Hamburg, 1970), 126.
[83] Arthur Dinter, *Die Sünde wider das Blut* (Leipzig, 1918), 187.
[84] Ibid., 296.
[85] Ibid., 369.
[86] Arthur Dinter, *Die Sünde wider die Liebe* (Leipzig, 1922), 169.
[87] Dinter, *Blut*, 172.

the races of the earth. . . . Christ is the first great enemy of the Jews. . . . That is why Judaism had to get rid of him. For he was shaking the very foundations of its future international power. The Jew is the lie personified. When he crucified Christ, he crucified everlasting truth for the first time in history."[88] In his reference to Jews as a "non-race," Goebbels seemed to question the very scientific or biological nature of the struggle – if only they *were* a race, he suggested. This is also brought out in his reference to Jesus, whom Goebbels insisted was not Jewish: "Christ cannot have been a Jew. I do not need to prove this with *science* or scholarship. It is so!"[89] The evangelical reverence for Jesus that Goebbels revealed pertained especially to antisemitism: "He drives the Jewish money-changers out of the temple. A declaration of war against money. If a man said that today, he would wind up in prison or a madhouse."[90] This reference to John 2:15 was to appear repeatedly in the Nazis' antisemitic ideology. As Julius Streicher insisted in 1924, "[We] relentlessly fight the shady mixing of religion and Jewish party politics, and fight to keep religion pure, as did the Lord when he threw the hagglers and usurers out of the Temple."[91]

In the writing of Goebbels, we see not only a cohabitation of racial and religious tropes for describing the Jew, but an ontological priority given to religion over science. The Jewish threat is primarily spiritual; Jesus' Aryanhood is a matter of *faith*. We see much the same conceptualization in the work of Klagges, who saw the Jews not simply as a harmful race; they were also contaminated by a "satanic spirit" that sought to control the world. And in Christ they found their greatest enemy.[92] Christ was, in Klagges' conception, an Aryan; despite having belonged to the Jewish "faith-community," he was never a Jew inwardly. Christ fought on behalf of his fellow Galileans against the dominant Jews and was to be regarded, not just as one antisemite among many, but as nothing less than the world's "greatest opponent of Judaism."

Buch's antisemitism displayed a more equal reliance on racial and religious tropes. "The Jew," according to Buch, "is not a human being: he is a manifestation of decay." He supposed that the nefarious influence of the Jew was especially notable in the state of German family life. As he said in a speech from 1932, "Never more than in the last ten years has the truth behind Luther's words been more evident: 'The family is the source of everyone's blessing and misfortune'." The Jew caused the breakdown of the German family, since for him marriage was simply a means to an end, a contract concluded for material benefit. The German, on the other hand, entered into marriage to produce children and imbue them with values such as honor, obedience, and national feeling. As with Eckart, Dinter, and Goebbels, for Buch the antithesis of the Jew was the Christian as well as the German: "The

[88] Goebbels, *Michael*, 65.
[89] Ibid., 45 (emphasis added).
[90] Ibid., 38–9.
[91] "Kulturkampf!" (Flugblatt): IfZ MA 740 (10 March 1924: Munich).
[92] Klagges, *Urevangelium Jesu*, 57–8.

idea of eternal life, of which the Jew knows nothing, is just as characteristic of our Germanic forefathers as it was of Christ."[93] Buch's reference to life after death, as with Eckart, revealed belief in a supernatural faith rather than a pantheistic religion of nature. Buch insisted that any mixing of Jews and Germans, whether biological or social, was a violation of the "divine world order."[94] This state of affairs Buch blamed on the liberalism of the previous century: "The heresies and enticements of the French Revolution allowed the pious German to totally forget that the guest in his house comes from the *Volk* who nailed the Savior to the cross. . . . In the nineteenth century the lie of the rabbis' sons, that the Holy Scripture made the Savior into a Jew, finally bore fruit." It was under the auspices of Europe's liberal regimes that Jews were allowed their emancipation, to the detriment of Christian Europe. The nineteenth-century debate over Jesus' Jewishness, exemplified in the debates surrounding biblical criticism, to Buch's mind only facilitated the Jews' hegemony. The truth was that Jesus' "entire character and learning betrayed Germanic blood."[95] In his antisemitic cause Buch was able to appropriate the legacy of Martin Luther: "When Luther turned his attention to the Jews, after he completed his translation of the Bible, he left behind 'On the Jews and their Lies' for posterity."[96] Although his language was unmistakably racialist, he nonetheless maintained Christian references to the Jews as "Christ-killers." Buch regarded both racial and religious antisemitism as equally relevant to Nazism.

Buch's references to race as God's creation, whose purity must be upheld as God's will, was not simply a pious allusion hiding a "most thoroughgoing secularization."[97] Rather, it found expression within certain Christian

---

[93] *Der Aufmarsch* 2. From this evidence we can argue against McKale's assertion that Buch "despised Jews not so much for religious or cultural reasons"(*Courts*, 55).

[94] McKale, *Courts*, 57.

[95] "Niedergang und Aufstieg der deutschen Familie," *Der Schlesische Erzieher*, 18–25 May 1935 (transcript of 1932 speech): in BAZ Personalakt Buch.

[96] "On the Jews and their Lies" is one of the most notorious antisemitic tracts ever written, especially for someone of Luther's esteem. The rising tide of violence in the work finds its climax in the following passages: "If I had power over the Jews, as our princes and cities have, I would deal severely with their lying mouths. . . . For a usurer is an arch-thief and a robber who should rightly be hanged on the gallows seven times higher than other thieves. . . . We are at fault in not avenging all this innocent blood of our Lord and of the Christians which they shed for three hundred years after the destruction of Jerusalem, and the blood of the children they have shed since then (which still shines forth from their eyes and their skin). We are at fault in not slaying them." Martin Luther, "On the Jews and their Lies," in *Luther's Works*, trans. Franklin Sherman (Philadelphia, 1971), 47: 267, 289. At one point, Luther anticipates the medical and the scientific metaphors used by racialist antisemites later: "I wish and I ask that our rulers who have Jewish subjects exercise a sharp mercy towards these wretched people. . . . They must act like a good physician who, when gangrene has set in, proceeds without mercy to cut, saw, and burn flesh, veins, bone and marrow. Such a procedure must also be followed in this instance" (ibid., 292).

[97] Fritz Stern, *The Politics of Cultural Despair: A Study in the Rise of the Germanic Ideology* (Berkeley, 1974), xxv.

circles – specifically Lutheran – as a genuine theological trend. Called the "theology of the orders of creation" (*Schöpfungsglaube*), it valorized the *Volk*, along with the family and state, as God – ordained. With roots in the nineteenth century, *Schöpfungsglaube* promoted the nation as divine because it both transcended the individual and fought the supposedly disintegrating forces of liberal rationalism and materialism. Because God created the order of the nation, it "assumed the form of an involuntary association, a community of fate" invested with values inimical to individualism and class egoism.[98] This theology was advanced by an influential group of Lutheran theologians whose views, significantly, predated Nazism. After the founding of the republic, the theological valorization of the Volk in *Schöpfungsglaube* theology was intensified. As Paul Althaus maintained, "*Volk* and *Volkstum* are God's creation and gift.... We cannot think of volkishness without thanking God."[99] Because God had created the nation as one of his orders, the church had an obligation to serve the *Volk*: "The church has every reason to be happy about the *völkisch* movement."[100] The church also had the duty to recognize the threat Jews, as deniers of Christ, posed to this order. It was essential for the churches to speak out against the Jewish menace in public and even, where necessary, resort to "bold action."[101] In a 1927 speech at the Protestant Church Congress (*Kirchentag*) in Königsberg,[102] Althaus insisted that Christianity in Germany had its own special national character and that any move to promote cosmopolitanism at the expense of *völkisch* interests was unacceptable: "German–Christian and Christian–German coherence stand as a clear, transparent and self-evident fact. The greatest moments and the most splendid figures in our national history bear witness to this."[103] Althaus' theological development was part of a larger "Luther Renaissance" that took place after World War I and involved some of the most prominent Protestant theologians of the day, including Werner Elert and Walter Künneth. Many of them were pupils of Karl Holl, a noted prewar theologian who led the development of a theology of nationalism.[104] In this context Buch's Lutheranism is clearly significant.

An opportunity presented itself in 1931 for Nazis and Protestants to directly debate each other on the theological rectitude of Nazi ideology; representing the Nazi side was Hans Schemm. Held in Berlin in 1931, it concerned

---

[98] Borg, *Old-Prussian Church*, 178.

[99] Paul Althaus, "Gott und Volk," *AELKZ*, as quoted in James Zabel, *Nazism and the Pastors: A Study of the Ideas of Three "Deutsche Christen" Groups* (Missoula, 1976), 66–7.

[100] Paul Althaus, *Evangelium und Leben: Gesammelte Vorträge* (Gütersloh, 1927), 129.

[101] Ibid., 186; idem., *Kirche und Volkstum* (Gütersloh, 1928), 33–4.

[102] The "loudspeaker of German Protestants," the *Kirchentag* was a newly formed body of elected representatives of all the state churches. The theme for that year's congress was *Volk und Vaterland*. In its general statement, the congress declared that the *Volk* was a divine institution. Althaus' speech was the principal one at the congress: Richard Gutteridge, *The German Evangelical Church and the Jews, 1879–1950* (Oxford, 1976), 42.

[103] As printed in Althaus, *Volkstum*, 33.

[104] Karl Kupisch, "The 'Luther Renaissance'," *Journal of Contemporary History* 2 (1967), 44.

the proper comportment of the committed Protestant toward the emergent Nazi movement. The forum served as an explicit point of reference for the ways in which Nazism was received and mediated by certain theologians of the day. Schemm began by directly confronting those who claimed that Nazism replaced Christianity with a new race religion: "Race and religion give rise to each other. I do not believe that the *Volk* are obliged to put aside race for the sake of religion; otherwise all natural and historical development would be invalid." [105] Schemm attempted discursively to reconcile science and religion, instead of simply discarding or demoting science as Goebbels and Eckart did. In Schemm's view, the priority given to the *Volk* in Point 24 of the Party Program did not mean a demotion of Christianity. Suggesting that racialism stemmed from a Christian attitude, Schemm used naturalistic and scientific metaphors to suggest that racial separateness was not only compatible with Christian doctrine, but derived from it:

When one puts steel into fire, the steel will glow and shine in its own distinctive way. . . . When I put the German *Volk* into the fire of Christianity, the German *Volk* will react in its racially distinctive way. It will build German cathedrals and create a German hymn. . . . We want to preserve, not subvert, what God has created, just as the oak tree and the fir tree retain their difference in a forest. . . . We are accused of wanting to deify the idea of race. But since race is willed by God, we want nothing else but to keep the race pure, in order to fulfill God's law. [106]

Here was an explicit evocation of the orders of creation. As did *Schöpfungsglaube* theologians, Schemm postulated the sanctity of racial separation, the theological precondition for positing the Germans as God's chosen people. Such sentiments bear more than a passing resemblance to this passage by Althaus a few years later: "God has given me out of the wellspring of my *Volk*: the inheritance of blood, the corporeality, the soul, the spirit. God has determined my life from its outermost to its innermost elements through my *Volk*, through its blood, through its spiritual style. . . . As a creation of God, the *Volk* is a law of our life." [107] As much as he paid attention to the racial question, however, Schemm did not argue for the *supremacy* of race. Indeed, he explicitly rejected the notion of racial materialism, since he considered materialism of any kind to be Marxist: "The spiritual for us always remains primary, blood and race secondary. The cause of all things is and remains the Creator. . . . Race, *Volk* and nation represent only instruments which lead to God." [108] Schemm even rejected Darwin, whose ideas, along with Marx's, represented the "political formulation of materialism." [109]

[105] Walter Künneth, et al., *Rufe des Nationalsozialismus*, 19.
[106] Ibid., 19–20.
[107] Quoted in Robert Ericksen, *Theologians under Hitler: Gerhard Kittel, Paul Althaus and Emanuel Hirsch* (New Haven, 1985), 103.
[108] Kahl-Furthmann, *Schemm*, 127.
[109] Kühnel, *Schemm*, 123.

As the counterpoint to Schemm, the Protestant side was represented by Walter Künneth, the Berlin University lecturer and *Schöpfungsglaube* theologian. Like other confessional Lutherans of a conservative theology, he criticized the Nazis' violent political practices and doctrinal positions, particularly attacks on the Old Testament. However, he believed that from the point of view of the gospel one could say a "joyful yes" to Nazism specifically on the point of *völkisch* nationalism: "Because we are Christians, we know that God created us as a particular race, as a particular *Volk*.... racial commitment is not coincidence, but divinely ordained destiny."[110] The *Allgemeine evangelisch–lutherische Kirchenzeitung* (*AELKZ*), the most widely circulated Protestant church periodical in Germany, reported on the meeting, stating that Künneth's lecture had been received with "unanimous approval."[111]

In *Mein Kampf*, Hitler undoubtedly spoke of the Jewish "problem" in racial, economic, political, and even eugenic terms, but he frequently concluded on a religious basis: "Hence today I believe that I am acting in accordance with the will of the Almighty Creator: by defending myself against the Jew, I am fighting for the work of the Lord."[112] As did his mentor Eckart, Hitler emphasized the Aryan belief in the afterlife over against Jewish belief, which, according to Hitler, could not even be called religion: "Due to his own original special nature, the Jew cannot possess a religious institution, if for no other reason because he lacks idealism in any form, and hence belief in a hereafter is absolutely foreign to him. And a religion in the Aryan sense cannot be imagined which lacks the conviction of survival after death in some form."[113] While emphasizing again his belief in a supernatural religion instead of a religion of nature, here Hitler speaks of the Aryan rather than the Christian. However, there is an implicit equating of the two, made explicit on other occasions. Consistent with his party comrades, Hitler regarded the antithesis of the Jew to be not only the Aryan, but the Christian – in this case Christ himself:

[The Jew's] life is only of this world, and his spirit is inwardly as alien to true Christianity as his nature two thousand years previous was to the great founder of the new doctrine. Of course, the latter made no secret of his attitude toward the Jewish people, and when necessary he even took to the whip to drive from the temple of the Lord this adversary of all humanity, who then as always saw in religion nothing but an instrument for his business existence.[114]

[110] Ibid., 7.
[111] Klaus Scholder, *The Churches and the Third Reich*, 2 vols. (London, 1987–8), 1: 140.
[112] Hitler, *Mein Kampf*, 65. Saul Friedländer suggests that this passage got to the heart of the Nazis' antisemitism: *Nazi Germany and the Jews: The Years of Persecution, 1933–1939* (New York, 1997), 98. He contends that the Nazis subscribed to a "redemptive" antisemitism, "born from the fear of racial degeneration and the religious belief in redemption" (ibid., 87).
[113] Hitler, *Mein Kampf*, 306.
[114] Ibid., 307.

Here again we see reference to John 2:15. Elsewhere in *Mein Kampf*, the Jew took on the satanic proportions of the Antichrist: "In his vileness he becomes so gigantic that no one need be surprised if among our people the personification of the devil as the symbol of all evil assumes the living shape of the Jew."[115]

Even before his adaptation of a new electoral strategy and the writing of *Mein Kampf*, Hitler had been enunciating these basic themes. At the founding of the NSDAP local office in Rosenheim, in April 1921, Hitler displayed the same dualistic thinking that marked other Nazi leaders surveyed so far, overlapping categories of the Christian and the Aryan on the one hand, the Antichrist and the Semite on the other: "I can imagine Christ as nothing other than blond and with blue eyes, the devil however only with a Jewish grimace."[116] In a party gathering at Munich's Bürgerbräukeller in April 1922, Hitler dealt with the question of whether one could be both antisemitic and Christian: "My Christian feelings point me to my Lord and Savior as a fighter (tumultuous, prolonged applause). They point me toward the man who, once lonely and surrounded by only a few followers, recognized these Jews and called for battle against them, and who, as the true God, was not only the greatest as a sufferer but also the greatest as a warrior."[117]

Hitler's conception of Christianity, consistent with those of other Nazis surveyed so far, contained a good deal that was far from orthodox: namely, the insistence that Jesus had not been a Jew and that the Old Testament was to be expunged from the Christian canon. Were these assertions symptomatic of an allegedly typical Nazi attempt to hammer the round pegs of past traditions into the square holes of their revolutionary politics – or was there a preexisting variety of Christian theology that similarly declared Jesus an Aryan and rejected the Old Testament? How "genuinely" Christian, in other words, were these views? More than a bricolage of idiosyncratic and disparate ideas, might these doctrinal positions have adhered to an inner logic? We have already seen in the case of theologically conservative Christians like Künneth how such positions could be rejected by those who otherwise endorsed Nazi racialism as Christian. However, an interesting clue is provided by a Catholic observer who, in 1930, proclaimed that the Nazis' positive Christianity had nothing to do with Catholic teaching, but was rather a product of "liberal Protestant theology."[118]

Theologically liberal Protestantism, also known as *Kulturprotestantismus*, had no political association with extremist or "proto-Nazi" movements before 1918. Indeed, this variant of Protestantism is more usually associated

[115] Ibid., 324.
[116] *Völkischer Beobachter* (hereafter *VB*), 28 April 1921.
[117] *VB*, 22 April 1922.
[118] "Die Religion in Programm und Praxis der Nationalsozialisten Deutschen Arbeiterpartei," *Fränkischer Kurier*, 31 July 1930, in Bayerisches Hauptstaatsarchiv (hereafter BStA), Presseausschnittssammlung (hereafter PAS), 929.

with Martin Rade and the *Christliche Welt* circle, who were affiliated with political left liberalism before World War I. Nonetheless, this variety of Christianity contained within it doctrinal views strikingly similar to those of the positive Christians. *Kulturprotestanten* of Imperial Germany, like Rade and more importantly Albrecht Ritschl, left no doubt that they considered Protestantism superior to Judaism, which suffered from "national segregation and confining ceremonialism dating from the Pharisees in the time of Jesus."[119] Confessional Lutherans also considered Judaism inferior. Their antisemitism, both before Nazism and during its ascendancy, was often very harsh.[120] But they interpreted the nature of the "Jewish problem" differently. Such theologically conservative Protestants claimed to respect the historical importance of biblical Judaism and professed no animosity toward the Jew who maintained his divinely ordained separation from the Christian: "I do not attack the Jews," Adolf Stöcker insisted, "but only that light-minded Judaism that is without fear of Heaven, that pursues material gain and practices deceit."[121] In other words, Stöcker's antisemitism was a reaction to emancipation, which undermined the precepts of the Christian state. He wished to keep Jews politically, socially, and economically ghettoized. The liberal Protestant answer to the "Jewish problem" was just the opposite. They shared the desire to see Jews convert to Christianity in order to effect the second coming and complete the eschatological process of salvation, but believed the way to achieve this was by granting the Jews total freedom through emancipation and engaging with them theologically. However, this should not lead us to the belief that emancipationism per se was the opposite of antisemitism[122]; liberal Protestants were in general motivated to give Jews their freedom in order to end Judaism, not to promote a new pluralistic society.[123] The *Christliche Welt* repeatedly called for the Jews to relinquish their religion and become an integral part of Christian culture. Given the choice to do so, liberal Protestants claimed, Jews would recognize their religion as a "petrified pharisaism" and see in Christianity the legitimate heir of Israel.[124] According to theologically liberal scholars such as Julius Wellhausen and Adolf von Harnack, Judaism was only the "withered branch of the religion of the Old Testament whose sap and vitality, by virtue

---

[119] Quoted in Uriel Tal, *Christians and Jews in Germany: Religion, Politics and Ideology in the Second Reich, 1870–1914* (Ithaca, 1975), 169.

[120] See, inter alia, Wolfgang Gerlach, *Als die Zeugen schwiegen: Bekennende Kirche und die Juden* (Berlin, 1987), and the articles by Doris Bergen, Shelley Baranowski, Susannah Heschel, and Kenneth Barnes, in Robert Ericksen and Susannah Heschel (eds.), *Betrayal: German Churches and the Holocaust* (Minneapolis, 1999).

[121] Quoted in Tal, *Christians*, 250.

[122] As Shulamit Volkov argues in her article "Antisemitismus als kulureller Code," in idem., *Jüdisches Leben und Antisemitismus im 19. und 20. Jahrhundert* (Munich, 1990), 12–36.

[123] Gangolf Hübinger, *Kulturprotestantismus und Politik: Zum Verhältnis von Liberalismus und Protestantismus im wilhelminischen Deutschland* (Tübingen, 1994), 275.

[124] Tal, *Christians*, 192.

of the New Dispensation, have passed to the side of Christianity. . . . the time of Judaism is now over."[125]

When mass conversion did not occur, *Kulturprotestanten* were thrown into a crisis. As Uriel Tal puts it, "The main hope and purpose of Liberal Protestantism, namely the national and cultural unity of the Second Reich based on historical and Christian principles, had broken against the stiff neck of Judaism."[126] If liberal Protestant relations with Jews had been marked by dialogue at the time of emancipation, by the turn of the century this dialogue had largely broken down. Seeking an explanation for Jewish "stubbornness" without undermining their own theological system, some liberal Protestants called for a complete doctrinal separation of Christianity from Judaism. They also increasingly suggested that Jewish deafness to their religious plea was attributable to a racial disposition.

This development is illustrated in the liberal Protestant reception of Houston Stewart Chamberlain, and in particular Chamberlain's relationship with the theologian von Harnack. According to his biographer, Chamberlain both influenced and was influenced by liberal Protestantism.[127] Harnack's polemics against Judaism were used by Chamberlain in his own *Foundations of the Nineteenth Century* (1899), a Christian–racialist tract widely regarded as one of the most important antecedents of Nazi ideology. According to a review in *Christliche Welt*, "this book . . . carries in it an apologetic strength for which our 'Christian world' will have much to thank." The highly charged attacks on Catholicism and scientific materialism in *Foundations* also ensured a warm reception among liberal Protestants. While confessional Lutherans firmly rejected Chamberlain's critique of organized religion,[128] liberal Protestants found their own views echoed in Chamberlain's call for a nationalist *Kulturreligion*.

The antisemitism of Chamberlain's book, which argued that Jesus was not a Jew, was directly linked with the racialist and by extension racist implications of liberal Protestantism. Another review in *Christliche Welt*, reflecting exasperation with the Jews' refusal to convert, explicitly agreed with the racist thrust of the book: "We theologians have even now failed to take up a real position but for the present continue to operate calmly with the notion of equality for all men before God, as if this also includes equality with each other. However, the emphasis on race expresses a new important knowledge for our time. Today even the Jews . . . no longer hide [this fact] as more and more they give vent in public to the racial consciousness which

---

[125] As quoted in Hübinger, *Kulturprotestantismus*, 273; Tal, *Christians*, 192. Tal provides ample evidence that such views were widely held among theologically liberal Protestants (ibid., 192–6).

[126] Tal, *Christians*, 164.

[127] Geoffrey Field, *Evangelist of Race: The Germanic Vision of Houston Stewart Chamberlain* (New York, 1981), 238–9.

[128] Ibid., 236.

they have always had."[129] The emphasis on race made its way into wider liberal Protestant circles. By the turn of the century it had entered the ranks of the Protestant League, where the arguments in *Foundations* were enthusiastically greeted.[130] Some liberal Protestants took issue with the hostility of Chamberlain's antisemitism. Harnack, a friend of Chamberlain's, flatly told him he was "possessed by an anti-Jewish demon." However, this did not prevent Harnack from admiring Chamberlain's work in general. In a letter to Chamberlain, Harnack disquietingly assured him: "Still enough – the Jew shall not have the last word. Rather, may he disappear completely and may there remain between us only the conviction of a broad and deep unity and agreement."[131] Harnack's wish for Judaism's "complete disappearance," although not a call for genocide, nonetheless demonstrates how the conceptual boundaries of Christian antisemitism became alarmingly ill defined in this period. Liberal Protestantism's derision of Judaism, its call for national unity based on Christian principles and culture, and its bias against a separate Jewish existence were all easily adapted by a "thoroughgoing antisemite like Chamberlain."[132] Liberal Protestants' dialogue with their Jewish counterparts led to the problem of determining the uniqueness of Jesus' message and the boundary between liberal Protestantism and liberal Judaism. The theological self-doubt that ensued motivated certain Protestant theologians to propound a new race theory: According to Susannah Heschel, "while the content of Jesus' message may have been identical to Judaism, his difference could be assured on racial grounds."[133] This development both paralleled and informed the wider sentiment among antisemites in Germany that emancipation had only allowed the Jew to become more insidious. Because the conversion of Jews was increasingly viewed to be opportunistic and therefore fraudulent, among antisemitic nationalists, and liberal Protestant Christians in particular, racialist discourse was increasingly used to argue that a "Jew remains a Jew."

Harnack went further down this path in his later theological development. As World War I was coming to an end, he attempted to resuscitate the second-century Christian Marcion, who had taught that the God of love in the New Testament bore no relation to the imperfect God of the Old Testament and that Christianity and Judaism had to be totally separated. Although he professed to take a critical view of Marcion's thought, Harnack nonetheless came to a conclusion that the present age was ripe for Marcion's thinking: "The rejection of the Old Testament in the second century was a

---

[129] Quoted in ibid., 240.

[130] Helmut Walser Smith, *German Nationalism and Religious Conflict: Culture, Ideology, Politics, 1870–1914* (Princeton, 1995), 225; Field, *Evangelist*, 237.

[131] Quoted in Field, *Evangelist*, 242.

[132] Ibid., 311.

[133] Susannah Heschel, "When Jesus Was an Aryan: The Protestant Church and Antisemitic Propaganda," in Ericksen and Heschel (eds.), *Betrayal*, 69. My thanks to Professor Heschel for making the prepublication manuscript available to me.

mistake which the great church rightly avoided; to maintain it in the sixteenth century was a fate from which the Reformation was not yet able to escape; but still to preserve it in Protestantism as a canonical document since the nineteenth century is the consequence of a religious and ecclesiastical crippling."[134] As "Jewish carnal law," the Old Testament as a unity "lies below the level of Christianity."[135] Harnack sadly acknowledged that Luther did not expunge the Old Testament from Protestantism – "What an unburdening of Christianity and its doctrine it would have been if Luther had taken this step!" – but nonetheless, his emphasis on gospel over law meant that "Luther's concept of faith actually is the one that stands nearest to the Marcionite concept."[136] Nowhere in his book *Marcion* did Harnack engage in a political antisemitism aimed directly against contemporary Jewry. In fact, like many other liberal theologians, he would later take exception to the "rabble-rousing" of the Nazis. However, the work influenced the growing pro-Nazi thrust of *Kulturprotestantismus* after 1918; more importantly, it predated and overlapped completely with Nazi attitudes toward the Old Testament.[137] So long as departures such as Harnack's existed within the parameters of legitimate Protestant theology, the Nazi rejection of the Old Testament cannot be used to demonstrate an antithesis to Christianity.

According to Wilhelm Pressel, it was a combination of Ritschlian *Kulturprotestantismus* and confessional Lutheran *Schöpfungsglaube* that lead to the "war theology" of 1914–18.[138] Confronted with a secular, antinational Weimar, liberal Protestantism would continue in this political direction during the 1920s and in many ways flow directly into the theology of the German–Christians, the group of pro-Nazi Protestants who, like the Nazis themselves, rejected the Old Testament and contended that Jesus was Aryan.

CHRIST SOCIALISTS

Aside from a spiritual struggle against the Jews, the party's positive Christianity pointed as well to a social ethic in the expression "public need before private greed." The Nazis' opposition to the socioeconomic system of communism is well known. However, the Nazis also insisted they were against "mammonism." Nazi economic theorists Gottfried Feder and Gregor Strasser advanced the idea of a socially oriented, ethical productive

---

[134] Adolf von Harnack, *Marcion: The Gospel of the Alien God*, trans. John Steely and Lyle Bierma (Durham, 1990 [orig. 1920]), 134.

[135] Ibid., 135.

[136] Ibid., 135, 139.

[137] This point is also made by Rita Thalmann, "Die Schwäche des Kulturprotestantimus bei der Bekämpfung des Antisemitismus," in Kurt Nowak and Gérard Raulet (eds.), *Protestantismus und Antisemitismus in der Weimarer Republik* (Frankfurt a.M., 1994).

[138] Pressel, *Kriegspredigt*, 179–82, 191–3. Pressel bases this estimation on a close reading of Protestant war sermons, in which a loving, benevolent God – one in keeping with the liberal Protestant view of the New Testament "God of love" – was constantly emphasized (ibid., 180ff).

capitalism (*schaffendes Kapital*), contrasting it with a selfish "rapacious capitalism" (*raffendes Kapital*).[139] Party members designated as economic experts cast their views in similar language. Dietrich Klagges, charged with the task of helping to define Nazi economic theory, made a fairly typical call for the ethical–moral supervision of the economy in a 1929 article: "Comprehensive social justice can be brought to bear only by withdrawing the decision making on interest rates, prices, and wages from the sphere of economic power and transferring it to the sphere of justice and legal authority."[140] As a professed follower of Christ, Klagges doubtlessly would have found inspiration for his ethical imperative in Christ's whipping of the usurers and the money changers. We cannot rehearse the many controversies that surround the persistence or curtailment of capitalism in the Nazi system[141]; but it is clear that Nazi ideology sought a "third way" between Marxist and liberal socioeconomic modes.[142] The Nazi movement espoused a national, anti-Marxist ethic that would finally end class strife in Germany, forging the People's Community (*Volksgemeinschaft*) as an organic, harmonious whole. More important than the programmatic details of the Nazis' social policy, which changed frequently, was the underlying logic of cross-class solidarity. In this sense, the factory communities of the Third Reich associated with "Beauty of Labor" campaigns – meant to impart a sense of honor to manual labor and largely successful in integrating the German worker into the *Volksgemeinschaft* – were just as, if not more, significant as any long-term restructuring of property relations.[143]

A similar brand of "ethical socialism," one that sought a third way between the anomie of capitalism and the atheism of Communism, had been available within political Christianity in Germany well before the Nazis. Particularly notable in this regard was the Christian Social movement of Protestant Court Chaplain Adolf Stöcker. The Stöckerite brand of Lutheranism professed a sympathy with the lower classes, arguing they were equal and valued members of the *Volk*, but that they also had a responsibility to the *Volk*. It tried to turn workers away from Marxism and class

---

[139] Barkai, *Economics*, 23.

[140] Quoted in ibid, 195.

[141] See Peter Hayes, *Industry and Ideology: IG Farben in the Nazi Era* (Cambridge, 1987); Richard Overy, *War and Economy in the Third Reich* (Oxford, 1994); Henry Ashby Turner, *German Big Business and the Rise of Hitler* (Oxford, 1985).

[142] Barkai, *Economics*; Jeffrey Herf, *Reactionary Modernism: Technology, Culture and Politics in Weimar and the Third Reich* (Cambridge, 1984). As Peter Hayes puts it, "to German industry, the emergent economic system was still capitalism, but only in the same sense that for a professional gambler poker remains poker, even when the house shuffles, deals, determines the ante and the wild cards, and can change them at will, even when there is a ceiling on winnings, which may be spent only as the casino permits and for the most part only on the premises": Hayes, *IG Farben*, 79.

[143] See, for instance, Alf Lüdtke, "The 'Honor of Labor': Industrial Workers and the Power of Symbols under National Socialism," in David Crew (ed.), *Nazism and German Society 1933–1945* (London, 1994), 67–109.

conflict through a return to *Gemeinschaft* and curtailment of capitalism, suggesting that management also had a responsibility to maintain social harmony. This was directly connected to the confessional Lutheran emphasis on *Schöpfungsglaube*, which would gain a new currency in the republic. As Daniel Borg points out, Protestant social ethics in Weimar and *völkisch* nationalism demonstrated another affinity by "orienting the individual's attention toward the national commonweal as the touchstone of what constituted 'social' behavior and what not."[144] Even before Weimar, this "social Protestantism" carried strong *völkisch* undertones. The Christian Trade Union movement was founded during the *Kaiserreich* to keep German Catholics away from the temptations of social democracy. By contrast, the few Protestant workers who sought an explicitly religious organization could look to the *Evangelische Arbeitervereine* (Protestant Workers' Associations). Their name notwithstanding, their ranks were filled more with shopkeepers, craftsmen, teachers, and civil servants than with workers.[145] As a Wilhelmine "outpost of Protestantism" they had no interest in propagating working-class consciousness, but aimed rather to "combat the red and the black and the gold internationals as diabolical powers of selfishness and hold high our banner: the Evangelical faith."[146] Here we see a conception of social Protestantism defined by what it opposed: the red of Marxism, black of Catholicism, and gold of liberal capitalism.

This social ideology was evident in wider Protestant circles as well. During the *Kaiserreich* the *AELKZ* consistently attacked the "gold" of capitalism, often in explicitly antisemitic terms. Defending the "little man," the newspaper viewed the speculation of the liberal 1870s as a "dance with the golden calf."[147] "Liberal terrorism" was held accountable for class warfare and ultimately the rise of social democracy. These forces were directly associated with the "liberal, capitalistic, antireligious Jewish press, the partisan of the stock exchange.... Thus the greatest discontent is produced; through this machinery the *Volk*, the *Mittelstand* is expropriated for the favor of the money potentates, which means first and foremost the Jews.... That is the reason why the social question is also called the 'Jewish Question'."[148] The connection between the two made here also points to why Stöckerite social ethics were innately tied to antisemitism. By limiting the influence of the "mammonistic" Jew, Stöckerites believed they would simultaneously curtail the power of "mammonistic" capitalism. As Stöcker wrote, "It would

---

[144] Borg, *Old-Prussian Church*, 206.

[145] W. R. Ward, *Theology, Sociology and Politics: The German Protestant Social Conscience 1890–1933* (Berne, 1979), 73.

[146] Quoted in Vernon Lidtke, "Social Class and Secularisation in Imperial Germany: The Working Classes," *Leo Baeck Institute Yearbook* 25 (1980), 33.

[147] Quoted in Thomas Kremers-Sper, "Antijüdische und antisemitische Momente in protestantischer Kapitalismuskritik," *Zeitschrift für Religions- und Geistesgeschichte* 44 (1992), 233.

[148] Quoted in ibid., 233–4.

never have occurred to me to take up my stand against purely economic errors, if this frivolous chase against all Christian elements in our life were not connected with them."[149] His use of antisemitism, although intensely vituperative, was not only cynical demagogy: It was tied to his concern for the little man. Like the Nazis, Stöcker was not a single-issue politician.

In the Nazis' conceptual universe, the struggle against Marxism and liberalism was similarly bound up with antisemitism. Those who revered Jesus as the first antisemite often cast him as the first socialist as well. Joseph Goebbels, for whom the "socialism" in National Socialism was of particular importance, was a notable example in this regard. In *Michael*, the evil of Communism finds its greatest enemy in Christ, who is elevated as the ideal expression of "German" socialism: "The idea of sacrifice first gained visible shape in Christ. Sacrifice is intrinsic to socialism.... The Jew, however, does not understand this at all. His socialism consists of sacrificing others for himself. This is what Marxism is like in practice.... The struggle we are now waging today until victory or the bitter end is, in its deepest sense, a struggle between Christ and Marx. Christ: the principle of love. Marx: the principle of hate."[150] Goebbels' reference to "Christ Socialists" (*Christussozialisten*) as opposed to "Christian Socialists" (*Christliche Sozialisten*) emphasizes the nearly evangelical nature of the struggle: An unadulterated return to Christ's teachings, free of the temporal church, is the only way to German salvation. "The modern man is intrinsically a seeker of God, perhaps a Christ–man.... We modern Germans are something like Christ Socialists."[151] Even in private, without the requirements of political expediency that otherwise might have compelled him to cynical posturing, Goebbels similarly wrote: "Speaking does not help. Action! Be socialists of action. There is too little of that. Be true Christians!"[152] This emphasis on an active morality, a "practical" Christianity, would be a continuous theme for Goebbels well into the Third Reich.

Walter Buch also touched on the social dimension of positive Christianity. Addressing himself to Nazi youth, he wrote on the party's social philosophy: "Public need before private greed.... So important and meaningful is this phrase that Jesus Christ placed it in the center of his religious teaching. However, since Christ was not a politician, since his *Reich* was not of this world, he put the calling into other words. He taught: love your neighbors as yourself! National Socialism is therefore nothing new, nothing that a person after much consideration would not come upon as the solution to the economic plight of the Germans."[153] Buch plainly states that the socialism of National Socialism is "nothing new," but rather the simple fruit born of Christian love

---

[149] Quoted in Peter Pulzer, *The Rise of Political Antisemitism in Germany and Austria*, 2nd ed. (Cambridge, MA, 1988), 95.

[150] Goebbels, *Michael*, 66.

[151] Ibid., 65.

[152] Fröhlich (ed.), *Tagebücher*, entry for 27 June 1924.

[153] *Der Aufmarsch, Blätter der deutschen Jugend* 2 (January 1931): in BAZ NS 26/1375.

of neighbor, in which the neighbor, or *Volksgenossen*, is defined by his racial belonging. Even in a system in which priority was given to race, Nazis like Buch believed that Christianity was basic to *völkisch* socialism.

A leading proponent of Nazi economic theory, Joseph Wagner, similarly suggested a link between Nazi and Christian conceptions of socialism. *Gauleiter* of Westphalia, Wagner made numerous speeches in the *Kampfzeit* on the Nazis' economic agenda.[154] Like Klagges, he was considered an expert in economic questions, which ultimately led in 1936 to his appointment as Reich Commissioner for Price Setting (*Preisbildung*), an occasion lauded in the Nazi press as the final realization of Hitler's will to command the economy.[155] In a typical speech from the *Kampfzeit*, Wagner outlined the contours of the party's economic platform, stating that three main tendencies stood opposed to it: Marxism, "the enemy of private property, the national state and Christianity"; political Catholicism; and "Jewish liberalism, the antithesis of Christianity and, as the champion of economic permissiveness and piracy by the stock exchange and banks, the mortal enemy of socialism."[156] Private property was sanctified as such, but not the excesses of an egoistic capitalism. Here we see the same reference to the "red–gold–black" internationals that a prior generation of social Protestants had defined themselves as being against in precisely the same manner.

Some Nazis suggested that a Christian ethic was also vital in bridging the confessional divide that separated the *Volk* into Protestant and Catholic. Bernhard Rust, *Gauleiter* of South Hanover-Braunschweig and Reich Education Minister after 1933, felt this was a particularly important element of positive Christianity. Making specific reference to "practical Christianity," Rust spoke of both confessions in a tone of equity: "Neither the Reformation nor the Counter-Reformation fully conquered all of Germany, nor did either create a Christian state religion. The National Socialist program commits itself to positive Christianity. However, the German *Volk*, split into two religions, cannot express one confession to Christian dogma, but only to practical Christianity. The two confessions can find each other in Christian ethics, whereas in dogma the *Volk* breaks in two."[157] Rust lamented the inconclusive outcome of the Reformation, but rather than advancing the radical solution of completing it, he sought to sublimate it by emphasizing ideological commonalities. In this context Rust also suggested that the moral

---

[154] See, *inter alia*, "Weltwirtschaft und Sozialismus," *VB*, 27 November 1926; "Das Verbrechen der sog. Wirtschaftspartei," *VB*, 28 June 1929; "Wirtschaft und Sozialpolitik," *Rote Erde*, 24 April 1935: all found in BStA, Sammlung Rehse (hereafter Rehse)/P5049.

[155] *VB*, 14 June 1936; *Westfälische Landeszeitung*, 30 October 1936: in IfZ Fa 223/95. Barkai suggests that translating *Preisbildung* as "price controls" overlooks the fact that the Nazis wanted "not merely price control but *the setting of prices* by the government": Barkai, *Economics*, 188 (emphasis in the original).

[156] "Gauleiter Wagner vor dem nationalen Köln," *Westdeutscher Beobachter*, 9 April 1932: in BStA Rehse/P5049.

[157] *Deutsche Allgemeine Zeitung* (hereafter *DAZ*), 23 March 1935.

teachings available in Christianity, rather than theological doctrines, were what counted: "What Christianity achieves is not dogma, it does not seek the outward ecclesiastical form, but rather ethical principles. . . . There is no religion and no philosophy that equals it in its moral content; no philosophical ethics is better able to diffuse the tension between this life and the hereafter, from which Christianity and its ethic were born."[158] As we shall see in the next chapter, the sublimation of confessional differences was another ideological touchstone of positive Christianity; here Rust linked it directly with the erection of a National Socialist Peoples' Community.

If Hitler saw his movement's antisemitism in Christian terms, what of its socialism? In *Mein Kampf*, he made explicit reference to the threat of mammon and insisted that "industry, technology, and commerce can thrive only as long as an idealistic national community offers the necessary preconditions. And these do not lie in material egoism, but in a spirit of sacrifice and joyful renunciation."[159] This was the standard rendering of Nazi socialism as the *gemeinschaftlich* antithesis of *gesellschaftlich* capitalism and communism; but aside from the use of Christian metaphors such as mammon and renunciation, there is no explicit reference to a Christian content in this socialism. However, in a private meeting on Nazi economics with his inner circle, held in 1930, Hitler elaborated his ideas on "real" socialism once again, but now with explicit reference to Christ: "It is such a far-reaching and complete conversion that the adult is no longer capable of it. Only youth can be converted, newly aligned and adjusted to the socialist sense of obligation toward the community. For almost two thousand years the Gospel of Christ has been preached, for two thousand years the sense of community has been taught. . . . But today, at the end of these two thousand years, economic liberalism flourishes as never before!"[160] This view resonated Goebbels' notion of the German as a "Christ Socialist." For Hitler, the answer to the current state of affairs lay in a resurrection of Christ's ideas: "As Christ proclaimed 'love one another', so our call – 'peoples' community', 'public need before private greed', 'communally-minded social consciousness' – rings out through the German fatherland! This call will echo throughout the world!"[161]

Without reference to a particular variety, "positive" or otherwise, Hitler insists that Christianity is at the center of Nazi social thought. As with Buch and Goebbels, Hitler regards the teachings of Christ as direct inspiration for the "German" socialism advanced by the party. At another private meeting of his confidants, Hitler explained why economics must be subordinate to politics: "Socialism is a political problem. And politics is of no concern to the economy. . . . Socialism is a question of attitude to life, of the ethical

---

[158] *Reichsbote*, 31 March 1935: in Bundesarchiv Potsdam (hereafter BAP), 62 Di 1/106/266.

[159] *Mein Kampf*, 423.

[160] Turner (ed.), *Memoirs of a Confidant*, 56.

[161] IfZ ED 60/7 (n.d., n.p.). This passage in Wagener's memoirs is left out of the volume edited by Turner, including the lengthier German edition, *Hitler aus nächster Nähe: Aufzeichnungen eines Vertrauen 1929–1932* (Frankfurt a.M., 1978).

outlook on life of all who live together in a common ethnic or national space. Socialism is a *Weltanschauung*!" He then went on to maintain that the ideological content of this socialism was derived from the original message of Christianity:

But in actual fact there is nothing new about this *Weltanschauung*. Whenever I read the New Testament Gospels and the revelations of various of the prophets...I am astonished at all that has been made of the teachings of these divinely inspired men, especially Jesus Christ, which are so clear and unique, heightened to religiosity. *They were the ones who created this new worldview which we now call socialism, they established it, they taught it and they lived it!* But the communities that called themselves Christian churches did not understand it! Or if they did, they denied Christ and betrayed him![162]

The tendency for the positive Christians of Nazism to reduce the economic problems of the day to a conflict over mammonism, making the question of the economic order a moral–ethical issue, closely resonated with the prior "social Christian" belief that socialism was a matter of ethics and morality over the free play of unrestrained capitalism.[163] This was evident among Nazism's Christian contemporaries as much as with Christians of the *Kaiserreich*. One of Weimar's most notable Lutheran social theorists was Friedrich Brunstäd. As a friend of Chancellor Brüning, he never aligned himself with the Nazis; but, like Althaus, he subscribed to *Schöpfungsglaube*.[164] Brunstäd believed the causes of economic injustice ultimately lay in the atomistic ideology of the Enlightenment. He did not condemn capitalism as such, because the acquisition of property was a God-given instinct. What Brunstäd objected to was its "perversion" by mammonism. Brunstäd also criticized Marxian socialism for trying to extinguish "natural" differences through artificial means.[165] According to Brunstäd, both Marxian socialism and mammonistic capitalism, as materialist forces, found their roots in democracy, which degenerated the state by turning it into a marketplace of interest groups. For the fight against Marxism and capitalism to be won, Weimar's parliamentary democracy had to be defeated.

Other Protestant churchmen went further, explicitly sanctioning Nazi socialism as Christian. In the same debate with Hans Schemm on the nature of Nazi racialism, Walter Künneth stated that "The basic principle of 'public need before private greed' is a belief and demand which meets Protestant desires and resembles the demands of Luther's Reformation."[166] In the Bethel newspaper *Aufwärts*, the Wolfsberg pastor Herbert Plesch wrote on the Christian socialism that he believed Hitler had inherited: "Hitler has set the great goal of creating a national block, embracing all German *Stände*

[162] Turner (ed.), *Memoirs of a Confidant*, 139–40 (emphasis in the original).
[163] Pulzer, *Antisemitism*, 43; Barkai, *Economics*, 23.
[164] Ward, *Theology*, 229; Borg, *Old-Prussian Church*, 206.
[165] Friedrich Brunstäd, *Deutschland und der Sozialismus* (Berlin, 1927), 303–11.
[166] Künneth et al., *Rufe des Nationalsozialismus*, 7.

[estates], including the *Stand* of the industrial worker. He affirms the workers' movement as such and therefore also its interest in coalitions and tariffs. Adolf Stöcker also advanced these interests." He then went on to claim that Hitler's social struggle was reflective of a larger Christian imperative:

Hitler has taken up the mighty struggle against gold. "Gold determines economic worth," says Americanism. "Man and his labor determine economic worth," declares National Socialism. According to the will of the Creator, gold has no value in itself.... Through the sins of the world economy, gold has received intrinsic value. Man and his work have been made worthless. The Hitler Movement is a large-scale protest against this world injustice. It wants to throw gold off its throne and give back man and his work their value.[167]

Another article in *Aufwärts* similarly praised Strasser's economic views, agreeing that the German economy could be built neither with Communist–Marxist nor liberal–capitalist methods and praising Strasser's commitment to private property and its "ethical power."[168]

Many Lutheran state bishops saw in Nazism the fulfillment of a Protestant social vision. In 1931 the Lutheran *Landesbischof* of Mecklenburg, Heinrich Rendtorff, proclaimed that "Many members of the Protestant Church live with their complete thought and feeling in the National Socialist movement.... The National Socialist movement passionately affirms social thought and brotherhood. Therefore it stands for a concern which is also one for the Protestant Church.... The Protestant Church must, for the sake of its calling, hear and thankfully greet the great intent coming out of the National Socialist movement."[169] After Hitler's appointment, Rendtorff was no less enthusiastic: "The Protestant communities of Mecklenburg should know in this hour that their state church in its faith says a joyful and strong yes to German *Volkstum*...to the German nation...to the German Reich."[170] Althaus alluded to the commonalities between the Nazis' social philosophy and his own as he detailed his reasons for rejecting the republic: "[T]heology has waged a determined struggle against the individualistic and collectivistic attack on single marriage, against irresponsibility, contraception and abortion, against the liberal–capitalist and marxist spirit in economy and society, against deflation of the state, against pacifist effeminacy of political ethos, against the destruction of penal law and the surrender of the death penalty – in general, for the order of God as the standard for the human shaping of common life."[171] After the seizure of power he proclaimed: "Our Protestant

[167] "Um Hitler," *Aufwärts: Christliches Tageblatt,* 5 November 1932: in BAZ NS 12/819.
[168] "Gregor Strassers Wege zu Arbeit und Brot," *Aufwärts: Christliches Tageblatt,* 5 November 1932: in BAZ NS 12/819.
[169] *Mecklenburgische Zeitung,* 24 April 1931.
[170] As quoted in Scholder, *Churches,* 1: 235.
[171] Paul Althaus, *Theologie der Ordnungen,* 2nd ed. (Gütersloh, 1935), 39 (1st ed. 1934, based on lectures and addresses given in Fall 1932).

churches have greeted the turning point of 1933 as a gift and miracle of God."[172]

CONCLUSION

More than just a useful slogan, positive Christianity was a religious system that not only tied racial antisemitism and the Nazi social ethic to Christianity, but suggested that both these aspects of the movement's ideology flowed from a particular understanding of Christianity. The language of Point 24 of the Party Program gave ontological priority to the "customs and moral sentiments" of the *Volk*. This was not meant as a way to exclude a particular variety of Christianity: No variety was explicitly privileged or maligned. Rather, it was a way of double casting the Jew as both Nazism's and Christianity's "other." Leading Nazis appropriated Christ, not just as *a* socialist or antisemite, but as the *original* socialist and antisemite. In various ways, the Nazis examined here staked a discursive claim to represent the "true" political manifestation of Christianity. They all held that Christianity was a central aspect of their movement, shaped its direction, or in some cases even helped explain Nazism. The themes common among them – a binary opposition of good against evil, God against the Devil; of struggle for national salvation against the Jews, Marxism, and liberalism – were inscribed in a strongly Christian language. However, positive Christians did not simply rummage through the discourse of Christianity, picking out metaphors like "salvation" or "redemption" and voiding them of their content. Whereas public professions of upholding Christianity certainly had their political usefulness, at other times they were more than that. Indeed, none of the Nazis who proclaimed a positive attitude toward Christianity in public revealed themselves as anti-Christian in private. Therefore the insistence that the Nazis practiced "sheer opportunism" or placed a "tactical restraint" on their supposed hatred for Christianity "which had been imposed during the years of struggle to achieve power"[173] cannot be sustained. Not only is there no proof of such a fine-tuned misinformation campaign, but the internal structure of the Nazi movement was far too polycratic, individual leaders too autonomous, for the kind of central coordination and planning such a broad conspiracy of deception would have required.

Positive Christians may have said little or nothing about the Augsburg Confession or other signifiers of theological orthodoxy, but they nonetheless regarded Christian social theories – "practical Christianity" as it was also known – as a linchpin of their worldview. Although generally unconcerned with dogma, many of these Nazis nonetheless adhered to basic precepts of

---

[172] Quoted in Ericksen, *Theologians*, 85.
[173] Stanley Payne, *A History of Fascism, 1914–1945* (Madison, 1995), 200; Conway, *Persecution*, 140.

Christian doctrine, most importantly the divinity of Christ as the son of God. Although they clearly departed from conventional theology in their rejection of the Old Testament and insistence on Christ's Aryanhood, they were not simply distorting Christianity for their own ends or engaging in idiosyncratic religious meandering. Only by ignoring the intellectual precedents for these ideas can we argue that positive Christianity was an "infection" of an otherwise pristine faith. Rather, these ideas found expression among bona fide voices of *Kulturprotestantismus* before the Nazi Party ever existed. Some Nazis, like Eckart and Goebbels, may never have acknowledged this religious connection; but others, like Schemm and Buch, did. That the former were Catholics and the latter Protestants is itself significant. Buch and Schemm, raised within a Protestant way of seeing, would have been more aware of the original sources.

This brings us to the third component of positive Christianity: the attempt to create a new syncretism, a new national religion that would bind Catholic and Protestant in Germany in elective affinity. Like German nationalists before them, the Nazis saw the confessional divide in Germany as the strongest impediment to true national unity. Like previous generations of nationalists, their attempt was based not on doctrine but on a value system. In the next chapter we shall explore the positive Christians' conceptions of confessionalism and how to overcome it. Would this new national religion put both faiths on an equal footing? Did the emphasis on a syncretic form imply an equally syncretic content? What kinds of preferences did positive Christians reveal, and what kinds of solutions did they suggest, as they discussed bridging the religious divide?

2

ABOVE THE CONFESSIONS
Bridging the Religious Divide

We all say a Lord's Prayer, we all have a Savior, we all have a Christmas celebration. The banner above both confessions is: Christianity.
Hans Schemm[1]

The Protestant League stands very close to the NSDAP. It is consciously German and, through moral and religious power, wants to contribute to the building up of the German people.
Hans Schemm[2]

When incorporating different strands of Christian antisemitism or socialism, Nazis spoke in undifferentiated, nonconfessional terms. In large part this was one of the very purposes of positive Christianity: to bridge the religious divide by making no specific references to a particular confessional bias. Any direct allusion to a particular theological lineage would have worked against the priority of the nation. Insofar as this allowed the NSDAP to appeal to all of Germany's Christians, it had potential as an effective political strategy. However, it was also central to the inner logic of their worldview: By appealing to what the Nazis regarded as the commonalities that joined Protestants and Catholics, they hoped to unify the nation and end a long, often bloody history of sectarianism in Germany. In this sense, the Nazis undoubtedly put the nation above confession, but in ways strikingly similar to those attempted by prior generations of German nationalists. This goal notwithstanding, the sectarian fault line that ran through German society – illustrated in conceptions of Luther and the Reformation – could be found within the Nazi movement as well. In this too, the Nazis duplicated the patterns of previous generations of German nationalists who advocated a "national religion." Even though they upheld the need to place Germans under the common banner of "Christianity," many positive Christians in the party displayed clear allegiances and often lent ideological favor to one confession over the other – even ones that were not nominally their own.

[1] Künneth et al., *Rufe des Nationalsozialismus*, 22–3.
[2] Bundesarchiv Berlin-Zehlendorf (hereafter BAZ), NS 12/638 (6 March 1931: Berlin).

BETWEEN SECTARIANISM AND SYNCRETISM

Many of the leading German nationalists of the nineteenth century saw the confessional divide between Protestants and Catholics as the greatest stumbling block to national unity. In their view, a politically unified nation was untenable without a common culture – which for many of them meant as well a singular religion. For some nationalists, the necessity of a common religion was so great that confession became the measure of national belonging: According to one writing in 1806, the "noble German fatherland ... the splendid Germanic tribe in its unity and power" could be found only in the Protestant North, in "purely German Prussia and among the 'peoples' between Westphalia, Mecklenburg, Franconia and Saxony ... This is where culture thrives [and] religious culture in particular."[3] Although this particular sentiment was expressed by a theologian, "secular" nationalists similarly found themselves eliding German nationhood and Protestantism: As the Napoleonic Wars were coming to a close, Ernst Moritz Arndt proclaimed that "Protestantism seems to be purely Germanic ... it effortlessly attracts all things Germanic to it."[4] For this kind of nationalist, the emergent German state had to perforce exclude the Catholic portion of German-speaking Central Europe. However, other kinds of nationalists, just as intent on a unitary German culture, nonetheless wanted all German speakers, regardless of confession, to be politically united. Because Protestantism for them could not serve as the barometer of Germanhood, a different kind of national religion would need to be found. For some, an answer was a generalized and rather diffuse notion of simple Christianity. For others, it meant dabbling in a paganistic faith that predated Christianity entirely. Whatever the incarnation, the very idea of a national religion was at one level innately Protestant, which Catholic Germans never subscribed to: For them, a rather more universalistic notion of religion prevailed, as did a definition of the nation that did not rely on religion as a constituent category. Those who advanced the idea of a *syncretic* national religion could not but betray the essentially Protestant character of their vision.

Advocates of a national religion were particularly unsuccessful in laying out any idea of what the new faith would actually look like; what its dogmas, creeds or institutions might be, aside from a de facto appropriation of aspects of Protestantism. On the other hand, there is no evidence that – aside from the paganists of the *Kaiserreich* – they made any particular effort to do so. One way in which diffusely Christian nationalists attempted concretely to bridge the confessional divide was through antisemitism. Antisemitism as part of the proposed national religion was often used as a "vehicle to disguise the reality of confessional, and thus cultural, rifts in a nation imagined as

---

[3] Quoted in Wolfgang Altgeld, "Religion, Denomination and Nationalism in Nineteenth-Century Germany," in Helmut Walser Smith (ed.), *Protestants, Catholics and Jews in Germany, 1800–1914* (Oxford, 2001), 54–5.

[4] Quoted in ibid., 52.

united in a trans-confessional German Christianity." More than simply a political calculation, such use of antisemitism illustrated the heartfelt anti-Jewish enmity of nationalists themselves. In spite of the hopes they held for an integrative, interconfessional antisemitism, such nationalists could not disguise the fact that behind the syncretic window dressing they were essentially disguising a sectarian content. According to one Jewish observer, such nationalists sought simultaneously to unite "all Germany in one faith" and establish "Protestantism as the only source of Germany's salvation." As Wolfgang Altgeld puts it, "The Jews constituted a negative point of reference for an ideology of national–religious integration."[5] Up until the First World War, attempts to create a national religion were all unsuccessful; in many ways, the Nazis' positive Christianity continued the attempt almost precisely. As we survey positive Christian attitudes toward the two confessions in Germany, we can see that many of them similarly conceived of a national religion as a unifier, bringing Catholics and Protestants together in opposition to the shared "other," the Jew. As well, many of these Nazis revealed a clear preference for the ideological content of Protestantism, even if they simultaneously insisted they were rising "above confessions."

In his observations on Germany's religious past, Dietrich Eckart betrayed a Catholic sensibility. Whereas Luther was to be applauded for revealing the Jewish danger as none of his contemporaries could, by attacking Catholicism he inadvertently did the Jews' bidding: "There would never have been a schism, never the war which for thirty years shed torrents of Aryan blood, as the Jews wanted."[6] Even though he criticized Luther, Eckart approved of Luther as a great antisemite and nationalist, an appreciation of the Reformer very rare among even nominal Catholics. This is not purely coincidental; Eckart's mother was Lutheran.[7] His mixed confessional heritage may account for Eckart's simultaneous approval of Luther and criticism of the religious wars he helped unleash, as well as his known predilection for the "conciliatory," interconfessional nature of positive Christianity.[8]

The nominally Catholic Goebbels also had mixed views on Luther and his religion. True to the positive Christian premise to be "above confessions," he praised Protestantism, even while defending Catholicism from party members' sectarian attacks: "Catholicism and Protestantism.... Catholicism is music (feeling), Protestantism poetry (reason and personal responsibility). It is no coincidence that Beethoven and Mozart are Catholics, Goethe and Schiller Protestants.... Every great German is Catholic in his feelings, Protestant in his actions. Protestantism is defined: Luther! Here I stand, I can do

---

[5] Ibid., 59.

[6] Dietrich Eckart, *Der Bolschewismus von Moses bis Lenin: Zweigespräche zwischen Adolf Hitler und mir* (Munich, 1924), 31.

[7] Barbara Miller Lane and Leila Rupp (eds.), *Nazi Ideology before 1933: A Documentation* (Austin, 1978), 147.

[8] Margarete Plewnia, *Auf dem Weg zu Hitler: Der 'völkische' Publizist Dietrich Eckart* (Bremen, 1970), 53.

no other, God help me, amen!"[9] In his own literary fashion Goebbels attempted here to synthesize the best attributes of each confession. Without explicitly using the term, he nonetheless argued that an *Überkonfessionalismus* is innate to the character of German greatness. Regardless of one's confession, elements of both exist in the truly great. Goebbels' claim that Germans are "Protestant" in their actions suggests that he believed that the Nazis themselves, as "men of action," were similarly Protestant in sensibility. A few years later, however, Goebbels' assessment of Luther was much more negative: "Luther does not give us much more today. He did not measure up to the highest standards. Either he could not come at all, or he had to be a revolutionary and bring everything to his knees. But here stands before us a fellow who left behind nothing else but a religiously divided people.... Catholicism and Protestantism are both rotten. Luther was the first religious liberal."[10] Unlike other Nazis, who recognized the tragic consequences of Luther's Reformation but blamed Catholicism for not giving way, Goebbels blamed Luther. The very attributes other Nazis found so inspiring – the totalizing revolutionary recasting everything before him – were not appreciated by Goebbels. Instead of admiration of each confession for it own strengths, we see here a rejection of both confessions similar to the attacks on the churches in *Michael*. Taken as a whole, Goebbels' attitude toward the confessions was ambivalent. He could defend Catholicism while praising Protestantism or attack both. Goebbels nonetheless retained a distinction between the confessions and Christianity. Shortly after attacking both churches as "rotten," he triumphantly wrote in his diary: "We have brought back the image of Christ."[11]

A supraconfessionalism found resonance within larger circles as well. As early as 1920, the German Socialist Party (*Deutschsozialistische Partei*, or DSP), an early rival of the NSDAP that counted Julius Streicher among its leaders, addressed the issue of religion in their first party congress in Hanover. The leadership agreed to take the "Protestant and Catholic religion into account" equally, and a nonconfessional platform was readily agreed to: "We are friends and supporters of religion and Christianity, and welcome all efforts that work toward a deeper religious understanding and a reminder of our Christian nature."[12] Years after he left the DSP, Streicher maintained this theme of confessional supercession, tying it in with the common denominator of Jew hatred: "Every National Socialist has the freedom to think what

9 Elke Fröhlich (ed.), *Die Tagebücher von Joseph Goebbels: Sämtliche Fragmente* (Munich, 1987), entry for 26 March 1925.

10 Ibid., entry for 16 September 1928 (emphasis in the original).

11 Ibid., entry for 9 December 1928. *Michael* having first been published in 1929 – all of its Christian references intact – is also a fair indication that his anticonfessional feelings of this period in no way conflicted with an attachment to Christianity itself.

12 "Verhandlungsschrift des 1. Parteitages der Deutschsozialistischen Partei in Hannover": Insitut für Zeitgeschichte (hereafter IfZ), MA 734 (24–26 April 1920: Hanover) (emphasis in the original).

he wants about Catholicism or Protestantism.... Instead of the Bavarian Peoples' Party asking the question, 'where is Christian unity in the struggle against the Christ-killers?' it is proclaiming 'Hand in hand with the Christ-killers'."[13]

If Eckart and Goebbels took an ambivalent stance toward Luther, or at least showed no preference for Protestantism, there were others who freely placed Luther in the Nazi pantheon along with Christ. As the product of a pious Protestant upbringing, Walter Buch was particularly fond of the Reformer: "Many people confess their amazement that Hitler preaches ideas which they have always held.... From the Middle Ages we can look to the same example in Martin Luther. What stirred in the soul and spirit of the German people of that time, finally found expression in his person, in his words and deeds."[14] Buch was fond of quoting Luther even privately. As he wrote to a friend in 1929, "Luther's eloquent words, 'the intellect is the Devil's whore,' confirm my belief that the human spirit of the greatest magnitude is too small to alter the laws of life. And the highest law of life is *struggle*.... Nothing comes from 'yes, but' [*Zwar-Aber*]."[15]

Hans Schemm presented a particularly interesting case. He made strong references to the syncretic nature of positive Christianity: "Each confession in honor, but the common holy bond, which is tied together through both confessions, must always be emphasized on account of the German and Christian community. We all say a Lord's Prayer, we all have a Savior, we all have a Christmas celebration. The banner above both confessions is: Christianity."[16] Yet Schemm was an ardent admirer of Luther and attempted to connect him with racial thought: "What went for Luther goes for us as well: only through the mirror of our blood and our race are we able to see God as he must be seen."[17] Schemm also attacked the signifiers of German Catholicism, most notably the Center Party. He castigated them as the ruling party for placing a speaking ban (*Redeverbot*) on a prominent Nazi speaker, retired Protestant Pastor Ludwig Münchmeyer, while allowing "free room for maneuver" for the Social Democrats.[18] (Schemm failed to mention that

---

[13] *Stenographischer Bericht über die Verhandlungen des Bayerischen Landtags*, Siebenundfünfzigste öffentliche Sitzung (29 January 1930): in Bayerisches Hauptstaatsarchiv (hereafter BStA), MInn/81630/75–76.

[14] "Geist und Kampf" (speech): BAZ NS 26/1375 (n.d., n.p.). The same reverence for Luther was found in Buch's family. According to Lang, Buch's wife was delighted with the prospect of having Bormann as a son-in-law because "Soon we'll have a Martin in our family too!": Jochen von Lang, *The Secretary – Martin Bormann: The Man who Manipulated Hitler* (New York, 1979), 47. He also refers to "the stern Protestant morality of the Buch family" (ibid.).

[15] BAZ NS 26/1375 (1 December 1929: Berlin) (emphasis in the original).

[16] Walter Künneth, Werner Wilm, and Hans Schemm, *Was haben wir als evangelische Christen zum Rufe des Nationalsozialismus zu sagen?* (Dresden, 1931), 22–3.

[17] Gertrud Kahl-Furthmann (ed.), *Hans Schemm spricht: Seine Reden und sein Werk* (Bayreuth, 1935), 126.

[18] *Stenographischer Bericht über die Verhandlungen des Bayerischen Landtags*, Siebenundfünfzigste öffentliche Sitzung (29 January 1930): in BStA MInn/81630/71–72.

Münchmeyer commonly referred to the Center Party as "the biggest Jew in the Reich.")[19] In 1931 Schemm contributed to a dialogue with Lutheran theologians meant specifically for the Protestant German giving consideration to the Nazi movement. Here he attacked "political" Catholicism once more: "The political organizations that in Germany today have betrayed Christianity are the Center and Bavarian Peoples' Parties. One cannot join hands in league with the mortal enemy [e.g., social democrats] and then still say: 'Vote Center! God wills it!'."[20] The Nazis regularly attacked "political Catholicism" as a political rival. Usually, however, they refrained from attacking the religion the Center Party claimed to uphold, instead casting the Center Party as a betrayer of Christianity, since it worked closely with the Social Democratic Party during much of Weimar. Schemm went beyond this. In party correspondence regarding the intensely sectarian Protestant League (*Evangelischer Bund*), which was seeking active political cooperation with the Nazis, Schemm stated that "The Protestant League stands very close to the NSDAP. It is consciously German and, through moral and religious power, wants to contribute to the building up of the German people.... [It has] the same line as the NSDAP against the Center as [representatives of] political, ultramontane Catholicism."[21]

Protestant sectarianism was notable in wider circles, especially the German Völkisch Freedom Party (*Deutschvölkische Freiheitspartei*, or DVFP). An antisemitic offshoot of the German Nationals, the DVFP actively cooperated with the Nazis, especially in the north, where its organization was much stronger than Hitler's party. After the failed Beer Hall *putsch* and Hitler's imprisonment, it joined forces with NSDAP elements to create the National Socialist Freedom Party (*Nationalsozialistische Freiheitspartei*, or NSFP). A rivalrous relationship with the NSDAP resumed after Hitler's release, but the two parties had "no real programmatic differences."[22] Indeed, some of the most notable DVFP members, such as Wilhelm Kube and Graf Zu Reventlow, were to achieve positions of status in the NSDAP. Despite these affinities, on confessional issues there was an explicit Protestant sectarianism within DVFP that was largely lacking in the NSDAP. In a revealing comparison, Goebbels claimed: "the two certainly do not belong together. The one wants Prussian Protestantism (they call it the 'German Church'), the other a Greater German compromise – perhaps something with a Catholic touch. Munich and Berlin

---

[19] Geheimes Staatsarchiv Preußischer Kulturbesitz (hereafter GStA) I Rep 77/Tit 4043/Nr 188/2–18 (23 March 1931: Oberhausen).

[20] Künneth et al., *Rufe des Nationalsozialismus*, 20.

[21] BAZ NS 12/638 (6 March 1931: Berlin). In his original letter to Schemm, Wilhelm Fahrenhorst, head of the Protestant League, indicated that he had spoken with Göring on the NSDAP's connection to Protestantism: BAZ NS 12/638 (20 December 1930: Berlin).

[22] Thomas Childers, *The Nazi Voter: The Social Foundations of Fascism in Germany, 1919–1933* (Chapel Hill, 1983), 53–6; Dietrich Orlow, *The History of the Nazi Party: 1919–1933* (Pittsburgh, 1969), 49–50, 62.

remain opposed."[23] In 1924, the DVFP proclaimed: "The *völkisch* freedom movement is a religious movement to the core. It wants a deepening of the German people and knows that the German without religion is unthinkable. In its ranks are positive Protestants; prominent ministers of this tendency fight for our movement... [theological] Liberals as well as German Christians are in our ranks." They claimed "hundreds of thousands of Catholics" were followers, but in the same breath urged: "Protestant Christians, defend your Christianity against party politics."[24] Elsewhere they were more plain in their antagonism to Catholicism. *The Völkisch*-Social Block, an immediate predecessor to the NSFP, went beyond attacking political Catholicism to aim its propaganda against the Vatican itself: "We *völkisch* understand Ultramontanism to be the international political activity of the Pope, and hence reject it, since it was harmful to the history of Germany's development and inner freedom and is still harmful today."[25]

The close association of some in the *völkisch* movement with Protestantism was noted with alarm in the Catholic press. According to a writer in the *Bayrischer Kurier*, "Not only in Bavaria do the *Völkisch* stir up their Kulturkampf: what they demonstrate here is neither new nor created by them.... It is the *furor protestanticus* they want to do business with, the hatred against everything Catholic, to help realize their dream of a Protestant Reich."[26] As further proof of the Protestant leaning of the *völkisch* movement, the paper reported on a meeting held by the Protestant League in Nuremberg in February 1924, in which a speech was delivered by a Nazi Party member: "Two ideologies stand opposed in Germany today: the *völkisch*–Christian and the Jewish–social–democratic with its variations, among them the Jesuit–ultramontane.... The pillar Ludendorff threw himself against the sea of the Counterreformation. On the 9th of November Ludendorff behaved like a true German and a convinced Protestant.... For us Protestants it is most painful that on 9 November 1923 the Protestant [Bavarian state commissioner] Kahr worked against the realization of the Protestant, Greater German State."[27] Other speeches on the failed *putsch* similarly suggested that it was primarily an act against Rome in defense of Wittenberg. The Luther League (*Lutherbund*) sponsored a speech in Hof, Bavaria, by one Pastor Hoch, an ex-monk. Devoted mostly to questions

---

[23] Fröhlich (ed.) *Tagebücher*, entry for 30 June 1924.

[24] "Evangelische Christen, schützt Euer Christentum vor Parteipolitik" (Flugblatt): IfZ MA 740 (1924: Berlin). The reference to "hundreds of thousands of Catholics" is a vast exaggeration.

[25] "Kirche und Politik" (Flugblatt): IfZ MA 740 (1924: Amberg).

[26] *Bayrischer Kurier*, 9 April 1924: in Staatsarchiv München (hereafter StAM), PolDir/6687/23.

[27] *Bayrischer Kurier*, 27 February 1924: in StAM PolDir/6687/8. Kahr, an extreme reactionary in the Bavarian government, was at best a hesitant participant in the failed *putsch* and later served as a witness for the prosecution at Hitler's trial: Jeremy Noakes and Geoffrey Pridham (eds.), *Nazism 1919–1945: A Documentary Reader*, 4 vols. (Exeter, 1983–98), 1: 26–35. The orator is identified only as "the engineer Herr Born."

of religion and politics, the speech ended with reference to the *putsch*: "Through some miracle Hitler and Ludendorff were saved. The driving force [behind their suppression] was the Jesuits, who in reality govern Munich. Their aim is the creation of a purely Catholic state (Bavaria–Austria) under a 'Catholic' dynasty. The Protestant north cannot assent to this."[28]

As to the Nazi Party itself, the evidence so far suggests that confessional preferences followed personal affiliation; Eckart and Goebbels, critical of Luther, were themselves nominally Catholic, whereas the strongly Protestant Buch and Schemm were unsurprisingly laudatory. Others however, did not follow this basic pattern. Arthur Dinter was a nominal Catholic like Eckart. And, like Eckart, he expressed regret with the sectarian divide in Germany; it was, as he put it, "our whole sorrow and misery," as it accounted for the nation's political and spiritual disunity.[29] He advocated an undogmatic or, as he called it, "spiritualistic" Christianity, bringing together Protestants and Catholics in the face of their common enemy, the Jew. Unlike Eckart, however, he cast Luther as a religious and national hero who freed the Germans from the stranglehold of the Pope.[30] Dinter took his admiration for Luther further than any other party member: He formulated a platform for "completing" the Reformation in Germany. Luther had failed to unite all Germans under the banner of "true" Christianity: it would now be the responsibility of the Nazi Party to complete the process. Dinter enunciated this vision in 1926 through his *197 Thesen zur Vollendung der Reformation* ("197 Theses for Completion of the Reformation"), in which he declared that the only path to German political renewal was through a religious revolution. The following year in Nuremberg he established his own organization, the Christian-Spiritual Religious Association (*Geistchristliche Religionsgemeinschaft*) and a periodical, *Das Geistchristentum*. In this departure Dinter felt he had an ally in the nominally Catholic Julius Streicher, whom he endorsed as being "one of the very few in the party who have a natural feeling for religion and a general understanding of the religious question."[31]

Dinter's personal religious agenda – attempting to turn the Nazi movement from a political party into a sectarian religious revival – led to his expulsion from the party. As an episode that helped shape the religious and confessional policy of the NSDAP, it is worth discussing in some detail.

---

[28] Eisenbahnüberwachungsstelle Hof, "Versammlungsbericht": StAM PolDir/6687/7 (26 February 1924: Hof i. Bayern). The report adds that "Heil Hitler!" and "Heil Ludendorff!" could be heard from the audience during the speech.

[29] Artur Dinter, *Die Sünde wider die Liebe* (Leipzig, 1922), 206–7.

[30] Ibid. George Kren and Rodler Morris suggest that "The adolescent Dinter experienced a spiritual crisis, the immediate occasion of which may have been a failed love affair with a Protestant girl, that led him to reject Catholicism as irreconcilable with the truths of evolution": George Kren and Rodler Morris, "Race and Spirituality: Arthur Dinter's Theosophical Antisemitism," *Holocaust and Genocide Studies* 6 (1991), 234. Whether something more substantial may have been behind such a profound turning point is not considered.

[31] BAZ Personalakt Dinter (28 June 1928: Weimar).

According to Roger Griffin, "at the level of ideology mainstream Nazism was intensely anti-Christian, except for individual followers, such as Dinter, who was eventually ousted from the party."[32] Griffin fundamentally misinterprets the events surrounding Dinter's expulsion. Far from being too Christian, Dinter was expelled from the party for not being Christian enough, in the sense of positive Christians' claim to be "above confessions." After the party's refounding, Hitler regarded Dinter's religious agenda a threat to his reworked political strategy: As Hitler is supposed to have said, "I need Bavarian Catholics as well as Prussian Protestants to build up a great political movement."[33] In the same year Dinter created his association, Hitler expressly forbade sectarian dissension: "Arguments on these matters may not be carried into the ranks of the NSDAP."[34] Dinter's assault on the "Judeo–Roman" church drew the ire of Catholics – even those within the party.[35] Despite party requests that he moderate his line, he continued his polemics unabated. The party leadership regarded this as a threat to their prospects. Whereas attacks on "political Catholicism" were a cornerstone of the movement's politics, the party's positive Christians generally refrained from openly attacking the Catholic religion itself.

Another factor was of far greater consequence for Hitler; his political philosophy. By the time he wrote *Mein Kampf*, Hitler was firmly opposed to any suggestion that Nazism should take the form of a *völkisch*–religious movement. Explicitly rejecting the role of a *völkisch* prophet, he unequivocally stated that "Not for nothing did the young movement establish a definite program in which it did not use the word 'völkisch.' The concept, in view of its conceptual boundlessness, is no possible basis for a movement and offers no standard for membership in one."[36] He disdained "those German-*völkisch* wandering scholars whose positive accomplishment is always practically nil, but whose conceit can scarcely be excelled."[37] The attempt at making Nazism a religious movement, or a "political religion" as some have described it, came in for total reproach: "Especially with the so-called religious reformers.... I always have the feeling that they were sent by those powers which do not want the resurrection of our people." Hitler stated that the common enemy of the Christian, the Jew, could only profit from such efforts: "For their whole activity leads the people away from the common struggle against the common enemy, the Jew, and instead lets them waste their strength on inner religious squabbles as senseless as they are disastrous.... I shall not even speak of the unworldliness of these völkisch Saint

---

[32] Roger Griffin, *The Nature of Fascism* (London, 1991), 32.
[33] As quoted in J.R.C. Wright, *'Above Parties': The Political Attitudes of the German Protestant Church Leadership 1918–1933* (Oxford, 1974), 78.
[34] Quoted in Klaus Scholder, *The Churches and the Third Reich*, 2 vols. (London, 1987–8), 1: 95.
[35] BAZ Personalakt Dinter (12 June and 19 June 1928: Essen).
[36] Adolf Hitler, *Mein Kampf*, trans. Ralph Manheim (Boston, 1962), 362.
[37] Ibid., 360.

Johns of the twentieth century or their ignorance of the popular soul."[38] As
we shall see in the next chapter, this was actually more of an attack on the
paganism so *de rigueur* among some of the Nazi Party's elite. However, elsewhere in *Mein Kampf* Hitler made positive references to being *völkisch* and
used the term uncritically. He rejected the phrase primarily where he saw
it being used as a means to turn Nazism from a political movement with a
religious deportment into a religious movement with a political deportment.

Two years after Hitler expressed this view in Landsberg prison, it was
exactly the latter course that Dinter was proposing: "If the *völkisch* movement gets stuck in the lowlands of merely political struggle, it will certainly
become bogged down again ... it will only reach its goal when it raises itself to the pure moral and spiritual heights which shine upon us from the
teaching of the greatest antisemite and antimaterialist of all time, the hero
of Nazareth."[39] As a "second Luther" increasingly obsessed with a sectarian revolution, Dinter might possibly have left the NSDAP on his own, had
he realized the futility of influencing the party in this direction. He slowly
turned against Hitler, to whom he was previously so loyal. While still in the
party, Dinter accused him of blindness to the fact that "the Roman Pope's
church is just as terrible an enemy of a *völkisch* Germany, to say nothing
of a *völkisch* Greater Germany, as the Jew."[40] Before expelling him from
the party, Hitler instructed Gregor Strasser to solicit the party leadership
to gauge how widespread Dinter's views may have been. The form they received read: "We, the undersigned leaders of the National Socialist German
Workers' Party, Protestants and Catholics, decisively reject [Dinter's] attempt. Without prejudice to our respective personal views on religion, we
will not allow the political movement to be drawn into the whirlpool of religious struggle."[41] Among those responding were Goebbels, Göring, Wilhelm
Kube, Rudolf Buttmann, and Hanns Kerrl: All affirmed this position.
Streicher and Rosenberg were among those who did not respond.[42] Hitler
won: Nazism remained "not a religious reformation, but a political reorga-
nization of our people."[43] A few weeks after Dinter's expulsion, Hitler gave
a speech in Passau: "We are a people of different faiths, but we are one.
Which faith conquers the other is not the question; rather, the question is
whether Christianity stands or falls.... We tolerate no one in our ranks who
attacks the ideas of Christianity ... in fact our movement is Christian. We
are filled with a desire for Catholics and Protestants to discover one another

[38] Ibid., 361, 363.
[39] *Das Geistchristentum* 1 (1928), 4.
[40] Ibid., 274.
[41] BAZ NS 26/487 (8 October 1928: Munich).
[42] BAZ Personalakt Dinter.
[43] Dinter lashed out at this decision. According to a police report, "Dinter called Strasser's
Aryanness (*Ariertum*) into question. In his *Das Geistchristentum* he writes: 'The name Strasser
is a good Jewish name ... a look at his characteristic business methods ... is enough to confirm
his racial composition' ": BAZ NS 26/1370.

in the deep distress of our own people."[44] Hitler unequivocally wished to cast Nazism as religious politics rather than a political religion.

Hitler's dictum was not enforced against Dinter alone. In fact, his attack was leveled more against Erich Ludendorff, early on the greatest luminary of the Nazi Party, who, like Dinter, attempted to create a new religious movement and was expelled from the party (see Chapter 3). But if Hitler rejected the idea of Nazism as a political religion, what did he have to say about politics *and* religion? Put differently: If he rejected Dinter's suggestion that Nazism should take on a religious form, did this also entail a rejection of the religious content?

To help answer this question, we need to examine Hitler's description of his political "evolution" in prewar Vienna and his evaluation of the two antisemitic movements there: the Christian Socials under Karl Lueger and the Pan-Germans under Georg von Schönerer. Hitler makes it plain in *Mein Kampf* that his "sympathies were fully and wholly on the side of the Pan-German tendency...compared as to abilities, Schönerer seemed to me even then the better and more profound thinker in questions of principle. He foresaw the inevitable end of the Austrian state more clearly and correctly than anyone else." In Pan-Germanism Hitler was primarily attracted to the ideological substance; in Christian Socialism, on the other hand, he was attracted to the political *style*: "if Schönerer recognized the problems in their innermost essence, he erred when it came to men. Here, on the other hand, lay Dr. Lueger's strength."[45] Lueger was the supreme tactician, "inclined to make use of all existing implements of power, to incline mighty existing institutions in his favor, drawing from these old sources of power the greatest possible profit for his own movement."[46]

For Hitler, the most important issue in all this was the Catholic Church: "[Lueger's] policy toward the Catholic Church, fashioned with infinite shrewdness, in a short time won over the younger clergy to such an extent that the old Clerical Party was forced either to abandon the field, or, more wisely, to join the new party, in order slowly to recover position after position."[47] On the other hand, the most important reason for Schönerer's failure was his attack on this institution: "The hard struggle which the Pan-Germans fought with the Catholic Church can be accounted for only by their insufficient understanding of the spiritual nature of the people," who in German-speaking Austria were overwhelmingly Catholic: "The struggle against the Catholic Church made it impossible in numerous small and middle circles, and thus robbed it of countless of the best elements that the nation can call its own." The result was that "The Pan-German deputies could talk their throats hoarse: the effect was practically nil."[48] However, if Lueger was

[44] BAZ NS 26/55 (27 October 1928: Passau).
[45] Hitler, *Mein Kampf*, 88–9.
[46] Ibid., 100.
[47] Ibid.
[48] Ibid., 108, 117, 104.

the better politician, his lack of ideological insight meant that his ultimate goal, the maintenance of the Habsburg Empire, was doomed: "What he had done as mayor of Vienna is immortal in the best sense of the word; but he could no longer save the monarchy, it was too late. His opponent, Schönerer, had seen this more clearly." Hence there were problems with both: "All Dr. Lueger's practical efforts were amazingly successful; the hopes he based them on were not realized. Schönerer's efforts were not successful, but his most terrible fears came true."[49]

What was needed was a synthesis of both – the ideological substance of a Schönerer and the political style of a Lueger. Therefore Hitler the *politician* came to the conclusion that "For the political leader the religious doctrines and institutions of his people must always remain inviolable; or else he has no right to be in politics, but should become a reformer, if he has what it takes! Especially in Germany any other attitude would lead to a catastrophe."[50] His decision to remove a sectarian reformer like Dinter is entirely congruent with this strategic policy. However, just like a prior generation of nationalists searching for an interconfessional religion, Hitler the *ideologue* revealed an unmistakable preference for the content of Protestantism. With the "anti-German" efforts of the Habsburgs, "The general impression could only be that the Catholic clergy as such was grossly infringing on German rights. ... The attitude of the Pan-German movement toward the Catholic Church was determined far less by its position on science, etc., than by its inadequacy in the championing of German rights and, conversely, its continued aid and comfort to Slavic arrogance and greed." In other words, even though Schönerer's attack on the Catholic Church was political suicide, it was ideologically sound. In spite of Schönerer's incapacity for *Realpolitik*, Hitler left no doubt that he sympathized with Schönerer on this score: "The 'Away-from-Rome' [*Los von Rom*] movement seemed the most powerful, though to be sure the most difficult, mode of attack, which would inevitably shatter the hostile citadel. If it was successful, the tragic church schism in Germany would be healed, and it was possible that the inner strength of the Empire and the German nation would gain enormously by such a victory."[51]

For Schönerer, as for Dinter, the schism was to be healed under the banner of Protestantism, "completing the Reformation" among irredentist Germans. The *Los von Rom* slogan, "one God, one emperor, one people," symbolized an understanding of Protestantism as the natural religion of the German.[52] According to Helmut Walser Smith, the leaders of this movement

---

[49] Ibid., 101.
[50] Ibid., 116.
[51] Ibid., 109–110.
[52] Lothar Albertin, "Nationalismus und Protestantismus in der österreichischen Los-von-Rom Bewegung um 1900," Ph.D. dissertation (Cologne, 1953); Wolfgang Altgeld, *Katholizismus, Protestantismus, Judentum: Über religiös begründete Gegensätze und nationalreligiöse Ideen in der Geschichte des deutschen Nationalismus* (Mainz, 1992), 5; Helmut Walser Smith, *German Nationalism and Religious Conflict: Culture, Ideology, Politics, 1870–1914* (Princeton, 1995), 206–34.

viewed Protestantism as "the religion of master nations," whereas Catholicism was regarded as "the religion of peoples in decline.... Germany could only survive [in their view] if it became completely Protestant."[53] Whereas Hitler did not attack Catholicism in the same way, he took an equally favorable view of Protestantism: "Protestantism as such is a better defender of the interests of Germanism, in so far as this is grounded in its genesis and later tradition.... Protestantism will always stand up for the advancement of all Germanism as such, as long as matters of inner purity or national deepening as well as German freedom are involved, since all these things have a firm foundation in its own being." Schönerer's Pan-Germanism failed because it took place in "a province absent from the general line of [Protestantism's] ideological world and traditional development."[54] Positive Christianity is usually considered an "infected" Christianity because it insisted that the Germanic race took ontological precedence over the sacrament of baptism. Here, however, Hitler plainly stated his belief that a preexisting variety of Christianity already held up to his racialist scrutiny. His understanding of Protestantism, much like that of nineteenth-century nationalists, supposed that it already corresponded with Germanic values. Looking back fifteen years after *Mein Kampf* was published, Hitler recalled in private conversation how he "had certain impressions which he had brought from his Austrian background, where the Protestants had been a national church."[55] Although Hitler was not ready to elevate Luther to the heights Dinter placed him, he nonetheless regarded Luther as a *völkisch* hero, equaled only by Richard Wagner and Frederick the Great.[56]

In contrast, Hitler's attitude toward Catholicism revealed ambiguity. On the one hand, the Catholic confessionalist would indeed be incorporated into the nation: "it will be seen that in Germany, as in Ireland, Poland, or France, the Catholic will always be a German."[57] On the other hand, his church was inimical to the national cause. Regardless of his ideological preferences, Hitler insisted that there would be no sectarian warfare. The fight against the Jew was too important for that: "Catholics and Protestants wage a merry war with one another, and the mortal enemy of Aryan humanity and all Christendom laughs up his sleeve.... [I]t is the Jewish interest today to make the *völkisch* movement bleed to death in a religious struggle at the moment when it is beginning to become a danger for the Jew."[58] More than a coy political strategy, positive Christianity was a genuine effort to unite Germans under the banner of a shared religion aimed against the Jew, who would thereby face a united front he had hitherto, according to the

---

[53] Smith, *Nationalism*, 208–9.
[54] Hitler, *Mein Kampf*, 112–13.
[55] Hans-Günther Seraphim (ed.), *Das politische Tagebuch Alfred Rosenbergs 1934/35 und 1939/40* (Göttingen, 1956), entry for 19 January 1940.
[56] Hitler, *Mein Kampf*, 213.
[57] Ibid., 114.
[58] Ibid., 564.

Nazi imagination, managed to keep disunited. Here we see how the basic elements of the movement's positive Christianity were interrelated.

Hitler's basic policy to welcome Catholics and preserve them from *völkisch* attack cost him the support of elements previously loyal to him. The DVFP asked "Is Hitler still *völkisch*?" and answered by accusing Hitler of selling out: "*Völkisch* means fighting against all three supranational powers; Freemasons, Jesuits and Jews. Hitler fights for Rome and the Jesuits. ... Does Mussolini, Hitler's model, fight against the Vatican? No. Against Freemasons? Only by half. Who are the mainstays [*Hauptstützen*] of Fascism? The almighty financier, the Jew Olivetti; the Jewish editor of the Fascist newspaper, Margareta [sic] Sarfatti."[59] On the occasion of the Vatican's attempt to conclude concordats with the individual German *Länder*, the DVFP played the sectarian Protestant card it had previously used in a more subdued manner: "You Protestants among the Germans, protect your people! Stay true to Dr. Martin Luther and his Reformation! You know the danger that comes from Rome! No Protestant German can enter into a Reich or state concordat with Rome, as the German Nationals want!" To counter the danger of Nazism's supraconfessionalism, they announced the creation of a German Reformation Party, which would "have no connection with high finance and Jewish banks! For that very reason it can find its political home with Protestant working people." The party was founded by the Protestant pastor Bruno Doehring, the same man who originated the stab-in-the-back legend in 1918 and who had since become head of the Protestant League. Hand in hand with the religious commitment of this new party was a nationalist one: "The occupation of the Rhineland must cease! The brutal nonsense of the Polish corridor must be done away with! In order to reach this goal, all those Germans must unite for whom Luther's holy defiance and Bismarck's national will still live. The domination of international Marxism, which has thoroughly ruined our *Volk*, must be broken."[60] In attacking the Concordat the party also attacked what would become the Nazis' own political and foreign relations policies. Indeed, they professed to "have nothing in common with the National Socialists." In fact, the ideology was largely the same. However, by failing to differentiate Hitler's acceptance of Catholics from an

---

59 "Ist Hitler noch völkisch?" (Flugblatt): IfZ MA 740 (n.d.: Leipzig). They also could have pointed out that Margherita Sarfatti was one of Mussolini's most famous mistresses: Victoria de Grazia, *How Fascism Ruled Women: Italy, 1922–1945* (Berkeley, 1992), 229. The DVFP ignored the fact that Sarfatti was in fact a baptized Catholic, thereby underscoring the racialist antisemitism of this explicitly Protestant party.

60 "Deutsche Reformationspartei im Völkisch-nationalen Block" (Flugblatt): IfZ MA 740 (9 May 1928: n.p.). This party was short lived, joining the DVFP in a "Völkisch-national block" and garnering little more than 250,000 votes throughout Germany in 1928. See Herbert Gottwald, "Detsche Reformationspartei," in Dieter Frick (ed.), *Lexikon zur Parteiengeschichte: Die bürgerlichen und kleinbürgerlichen Parteien und Verbände in Deutschland (1789–1945)*, 4 vols. (Leipzig, 1984), 2: 60–2; Kurt Nowak, *Evangelische Kirche und Weimarer Republik: Zum politischen Weg des deutschen Protestantismus zwischen 1918 und 1932* (Göttingen, 1981), 153–7.

ideological or institutional allegiance with Ultramontanism, they assumed – as Ludendorff put it – that Hitler had become "the servile tool of the romish priests."[61] Dinter reached a similar conclusion. In his *Geistchristentum* he accused Hitler of betrayal: "His personal power and money interests – I emphasize again: money interests – will not let him go the way of his earlier honest convictions, but rather ties him to the Jesuit fraud, which he commits against his followers with the Concordat and Rome questions."[62] In 1930, the remnant of the DVFP not incorporated into the NSDAP similarly attacked Hitler for his ongoing rapprochement with the Catholic Church, based on a defense of Protestantism: "Never can the German freedom movement be led by followers of the Jewish–Roman race-killing religion! For this reason Germany's liberation could never come from Jewish–Roman Bavaria, but only from Protestant Prussia!"[63]

Even though Hitler consistently rejected sectarianism and never attacked the faith of Catholicism, he resonated Streicher's contention that the Catholic establishment was allying itself with the Jews. The following attack on the Catholic Church, made privately behind closed doors, would have pleasantly surprised his *völkisch* opponents:

[The Jews] have even succeeded within the Church of Rome in falsifying this high Christian teaching of the community ordained by God. . . . And the struggle which the world and those churches that falsely designate themselves Christian wage against National Socialism – against us, who want only the fulfillment of Christ's lifework – is nothing more than the continuation of the crime of the Inquisition and the burning of witches, by which the Jewish–Roman world exterminated whatever offered resistance to that shameful parasitism.[64]

This is not an anticlericalism leveled at both churches; as we shall see, whereas the Catholic Church and the Nazi Party kept a distance from each other, relations between the Protestant churches and the party were much more amiable. In a subsequent meeting, in which he compared the German National and Center parties, Hitler even more sharply revealed his ideological affinity for Protestantism over Catholicism, claiming that the Center Party represented "those people who have kept the servile slave mentality inculcated during the period that lasted from Roman military despotism to Ultramontane papal dominance. Precisely as the German Nationals allow us to recognize the Germanic will to rule and the spirit of Protestantism

---

[61] Quoted in William Carr, *Hitler: A Study in Personality and Politics* (London, 1978), 134.

[62] *Das Geistchristentum* 2 (1929), as reprinted in "Mitteilungen zur weltanschaulichen Lage," 23 October 1936: in Bundesarchiv Potsdam (hereafter BAP), 62 Di 1/71/43–54.

[63] "Hitler und Rom" (Flugblatt): IfZ MA 740 (15 October 1930: Berlin). In defense of this position the party quoted extensively from the Catholic Dinter.

[64] Otto Wagener, *Hitler: Memoirs of a Confidant*, Henry Ashby Turner, ed. (New Haven, 1985), 65.

against dogmatization of faith and the stifling of conscience, so we see here those people and tribes that were gradually trained in passive obedience to authority."[65] The emphasis on the spiritual freedom of the Protestant and independence from Roman domination was part of a continuous nationalist narrative in German history, which had long esteemed the "freedom from hierarchy...the true, free spirit of Protestantism."[66] Ironically, passive obedience to authority would be a quality greatly appreciated in the Third Reich.

Indeed, the Catholic "slave mentality" that Hitler derided would be cast in a more positive light on another occasion. Otto Wagener and Franz Pfeffer von Salomon, top-ranking leaders of the Storm Troopers (*Sturmabteilung*, or SA), asked Hitler to help them interpret a map showing uneven distribution of SA and SS (*Schutzstaffeln*) recruitment. After looking at the map for "three or four minutes," Hitler claimed the distribution correlated with Germany's confessional divide: "Do you see the Roman frontier wall, the *limes*? . . . To the south and west of this line the SA is thin; to the north and northeast of it, it is strong. To the south and southwest of this line Germany is predominantly Catholic; to the north and northeast it's Protestant." Having claimed to discover the key to SS recruitment in Catholic areas over against SA recruitment in Protestant areas, he elaborated on what he saw as the pivotal difference explaining the discrepancy: "Where the Germanic breed predominates, the people are Protestants; where Romanism has left its mark, the people are Catholic. . . . The SA attracts the militant natures among the Germanic breed, the men who think democratically, unified only by a common allegiance. Those who throng to the SS are men inclined to the authoritarian state, who wish to serve and obey, who respond less to an idea than to a man."[67] According to Hitler, the SA's greater strength in Protestant Germany is based on an attraction to Nazism's ideological *substance*, whereas the SS's greater strength in Catholic Germany is based on an attraction to Nazism's authoritarian *style*. However much this helps to explain actual differences in SS and SA recruitment, what is just as revealing is that Hitler believed it to be so. His comparison bears striking similarities to Goebbels' characterization of Protestantism as "action" and Catholicism as "feeling."

PRACTICING CHURCH LIFE

So far we have explored the ways in which leading Nazis believed their movement was in some sense Christian. How did the practices of the movement conform to this belief? Did the totalitarianism of Nazism prohibit involvement with Christian institutions and organizations? Or were Nazis able to take part in Christian life?

---

[65] Ibid., 210.
[66] Altgeld, "Religion, Denomination and Nationalism," 53.
[67] Wagener, *Memoirs of a Confidant*, 19–21.

Party leaders often expressed antagonism for the "Roman" Church, even as they insisted their movement was a Christian one. For its part, the Catholic Church opposed the Nazi Party for these attacks, but also for the Nazis' racialist dogma and extreme nationalism. In several parts of Germany, Catholics were explicitly forbidden to become members of the Nazi Party, and Nazi members were forbidden to take part in church ceremonies and funerals. The bishop of Mainz even refused to admit NSDAP members to the sacraments.[68] This stance was initially met with concern from other bishops, who were hesitant about turning their backs on a movement that fought Marxism, liberalism, and the "Jewish danger." Nevertheless, in 1931 the bishops of Bavaria, the upper Rhine, Köln, and Paderborn all issued statements proclaiming the incompatibility of National Socialism and Catholicism. By the end of the year, the entire German episcopacy had declared itself against the movement.[69] Those isolated Catholic churchmen who publicly supported Nazism – like Benedictine Abbot Alban Schachleiter or Badenese Priest Wilhelm Senn – were exceptions that proved the rule. The lower ranks of the Nazi Party were known to include church-going Catholics; but, whether they were anticlerical like Goebbels or relatively philoclerical like Governor Franz Ritter von Epp of Bavaria, almost none in the ideological or political leadership of the party were active participants in Catholic Church life. Concomitantly, the Catholic Church hierarchy refused all formal contact with the party before 1933.

By contrast, the first official contact between the party leadership and the Protestant authorities took place in March 1931, when Franz Stöhr, a member of the executive committee of the NSDAP, met with Gustav Scholz, an official with the Federal Organization of Protestant State Churches (*Kirchenbundesamt*). The meeting was requested by the church authorities to determine the exact position of the party toward religion. Rosenberg's paganist work, "The Myth of the Twentieth Century," had been published the year before, and the churches feared that it represented an influential segment of party opinion, if not the official party line. Stöhr began by assuring Scholz that the NSDAP entered the Reichstag only as a means to an end, to effect "the creation of the real German Reich of German men." He maintained the anti-Dinter position that the "character of a Christian party was fundamentally rejected," that the party was secular and political, but that nevertheless it was "supported and led by Christian people who seriously intend to implement the ethical principles of Christianity in legislation, and to bring them to bear upon the life of the people." The existence of at least nominal Catholics in the party was defended by virtue of the need to create a united *Volkstum*. Nevertheless, the party leadership was "shaped by Protestantism." Those

---

[68] John Conway, *The Nazi Persecution of the Churches* (London, 1968), 6–7; Scholder, *Churches*, 1: 132–3.

[69] Scholder, *Churches*, 1: 133–5. This picture of Weimar Catholicism as anti-Nazi is affirmed in the classic by Guenther Lewy, *The Catholic Church and Nazi Germany* (London, 1964), especially pp. 3–25, which is nonetheless critical of the church's stance after 1933.

leaders who belonged to the Catholic Church were, in spite of their nominal affiliation, also inclined toward Protestantism. There was no danger that "the movement will be pulled into the Catholic stream or be caught up in the Catholic church": It was a national movement that rejected the claims of the Catholic hierarchy. These principles were reflected in Nazi education policy, which Stöhr acknowledged was a single school for both Catholics and Protestants with common religious instruction. Until such a school was practicable, however, the party would support denominational schools, while at the same time carefully resisting Catholic prerogatives: "The German state should be master of the German school." Stöhr asserted that Nazism was opposed to the individual man of liberalism, the collective man of Marxism, and the hierarchical man of Catholicism; that its ideal was the independent German who lived not for himself but for the community; and assured Scholz that what he said could be regarded as "official party statements."[70]

The party would maintain a stance of formal neutrality over against the churches, but Stöhr firmly maintained that the substance of Nazism was in accord with Protestant Christian precepts, that party members were free to participate in church-related activities, and that, indeed, the party as a whole was "shaped" by Protestantism. For its part, broad sections of the Protestant establishment warmly supported the Nazi Party. After Hitler's appointment, Lutheran State Bishop Rendtorff proclaimed that "The Protestant communities of Mecklenburg should know in this hour that their state church in its faith says a joyful and strong yes to German *Volkstum* . . . to the German nation . . . to the German Reich."[71] Other Lutheran bishops expressed identical views. The bishop of Schleswig-Holstein proclaimed that "a German freedom movement with a national consciousness has emerged from the distress in Germany. . . . The leaders have acknowledged openly that only on a Christian basis can a healthy state develop. This is a change for which we thank God with all our hearts."[72] Initially reserved about the Nazi movement, Theophile Wurm of Württemberg praised it a few days after the Seizure of Power: "One must recognize that the National Socialist movement has with great sacrifice broken a terror. Where would the millions of young people be if this movement had not existed? It has welded together classes which had been estranged from one another. I believe that especially our consciously Protestant people who stand in the National Socialist camp will particularly welcome this welding. The church can also welcome the struggle against undermining influences in our cultural life."[73]

[70] Nowak, *Evangelische Kirche*, 317–18; Wright, '*Above Parties*', 81–2.

[71] As quoted in Scholder, *Churches*, 1: 235.

[72] *Das evangelische Deutschland* 10 (1933), 105. This was the semiofficial periodical of the Church Federation (*Kirchenbund*).

[73] "Frage einer kirchlichen Stellungnahme zu den gegenwärtigen politischen Verhältnissen und Bestrebungen": BAP R5101/28/22–24 (2–3 March 1933: Berlin).

Even many confessional Lutherans who would later join the Confessing Church received the Nazi movement warmly. Otto Dibelius, General Superintendent of the Kurmark, was one of the most conservative in the Confessing Church. Like other confessional Lutherans, he drew his inspiration from Stöcker, calling for an activist, anti-erastian church that would take part in the showdown between the Christian west and the atheistic east and fight the "antireligious crusade" of world communism.[74] After the NSDAP's electoral breakthrough in September 1930, he certified the Nazi movement as Christian: "The National Socialists, as the strongest party of the right, have shown both by their program and their practical deportment in Thuringia that they have a firm, positive relationship to Christianity.... We may expect that they will remain true to their principles in the new Reichstag."[75] After the Seizure of Power, Dibelius continued to view Nazism this way, even to the point of excusing Nazi brutality. At a 1933 service in Berlin's Nikolaikirche for the new Reichstag, Dibelius announced: "We have learned from Martin Luther that the church cannot get in the way of state power when it does what it is called to do. Not even when [the state] becomes hard and ruthless.... When the state carries out its office against those who destroy the foundations of state order, above all against those who destroy honor with vituperative and cruel words that scorn faith and vilify death for the Fatherland, then [the state] is ruling in God's name!"[76]

Aside from individual Protestant church members, the main pillar of Protestant associational life also displayed an essentially favorable attitude toward the Nazis. The Protestant League became the first of any Christian organization formally to support the party. More than lending outside support, many of the league's leaders took part in the movement: Heinrich Bornkamm, president of the league after Doehring, was a member of the SA, the National Socialist Teachers' League (*Nationalsozialistischer Lehrerbund*, or NSLB), and the National Socialist University Teachers' League (*NS-Dozentenbund*); league director Fritz von der Heydt belonged to the Working Group of National Socialist Pastors (*Arbeitsgemeinschaft NS-Pfarrer*).[77] In its 1924 Munich assembly, presided over by Doehring, the league endorsed the essential components of Nazi ideology. Doehring proclaimed that "Neither the cries of the ultramontanist press nor the harsh protests of its Jewish confederates will get in our way."[78] Whereas such statements conceived the Jewish enemy as a tributary of the Catholic one, they nonetheless indicate the strong presence

[74] Otto Dibelius, *Nachspiel* (Berlin, 1928), 21–6.

[75] Quoted in Nowak, *Kirche*, 297.

[76] Günther van Norden, *Der deutsche Protestantismus im Jahr der nationalsozialistische Machtergreifung* (Gütersloh, 1979), 54.

[77] Nazi Party membership in the Protestant League was not limited to these two men. League notables Hermann Beyer and Wilhelm Wehner were respectively in the SA and NS-Volkswohlfahrt, and NS-Volkswohlfahrt, SS and DAF: BAP R5101/23126/85a (n.d., n.p.).

[78] Scholder, *Churches*, 1: 109.

Fig. 4 Wilhelm Kube, *Gauleiter* of Brandenburg and cofounder of the Protestant church party "German Christians": "Christianity and Germanhood have come together in so infinitely many respects that they cannot be separated." (SV-Bilderdienst)

of antisemitism within the league when compared with that at its inception. This, combined with the strident nationalism the league had always espoused, made the Nazi appeal almost immediate. This enthusiasm was felt right through to the end of Weimar. At the league's 1931 general assembly in Magdeburg, the Rhineland pastor Hermann Kremers spoke on "National Socialism and Protestantism." He was careful to suggest that, like the churches, the Protestant League was not making a political endorsement. He made the entirely academic, but nonetheless significant, point that his views related to Nazism as a movement, not a party.[79] Despite this caveat, Kremers was emphatic about the nationalist and antisemitic goals of Nazism, critical only of Hitler's supposed blindness to the Ultramontane threat: "Our Christian duty towards this movement is to protect and preserve it, so that it not be silted up by naturalism, nor, caught by the age old enemy of Germanhood, wither to the roots under the alien sun of Rome."[80]

As a counterpoint to Nazi Christians within the ecclesiastical sphere, there existed many Christian Nazis among the party leadership who were active in the church. One of the most important Nazis to engage in Protestant life was Wilhelm Kube. Beginning his postwar political life as General Secretary of the German National People's Party (*Deutschnationale Volkspartei*, or DNVP), Kube migrated by way of the DVFP to the NSDAP in 1928, where he was quickly awarded the job of *Gauleiter* of Brandenburg (later "Kurmark"). He was also the caucus leader of the Nazi Party in the Prussian Landtag. Although Kube was stripped of his power in 1936 after accusing Buch's wife of being half-Jewish, he was nonetheless able to retain Hitler's

---

[79] Hermann Kremers, *Nationalsozialismus und Protestantismus* (Berlin, 1931), Foreword.
[80] Ibid., 52.

favor.[81] Kube also played a very central role in establishing the German Christians (*Deutsche Christen*, or DC), a party within the Protestant Church that originally went by the name Protestant National Socialists. This group has traditionally been cast as an opportunist organization, an arm of the Nazi Party more interested in the "coordination" of yet another social institution than in honestly taking part in church life.[82] In party correspondence, Kube himself referred more than once to the need to "gain control of the churches," to "bring the churches in hand."[83] However, this was not motivated solely by tactical considerations: Kube had more lasting links with Protestantism. He had been active in a parish community council in Berlin after the First World War, and was additionally a member of the synod of the Diocese of Berlin.[84] His role in founding the DC was propelled more by his conviction that Nazism represented the true interests of German Protestantism than by cynical posturing for the sake of winning votes.

An early opportunity for expressing his views arose with the issue of *Protestant* Church concordats in 1929. Sounding a potentially anticlerical note, Kube declared the Nazi view in a session of the Prussian Landtag: "The question of Christian education or the organization of church life is in the final analysis a question of legislation by the state. In accordance with these views, we are unable in any circumstances to accept an equation of the two parties, state and church." For Kube, however, this was in no way antithetical to Christianity, "precisely because we affirm it, because we are convinced that Christianity and Germanhood have come together in so infinitely many respects that they cannot be separated.... We have confidence in the German state, that its politics are not opposed to Christian interests and Christian sensibilities, but rather that it will look after these interests in all circumstances." His attack on the notion of Protestant concordats was not simply a disguised hostility to Protestantism: As Klaus Scholder points out, "a section of the Prussian Synod had actually rejected categorically any concordat resolution because it was incompatible with the idea of the sovereignty of the state."[85] Kube regarded any deal making between the Protestant Church and the socialist-controlled Prussian government as treason. In party correspondence to Gregor Strasser he wrote: "The current leadership of the church want to conclude an unheard-of treaty with the marxist Prussian state." According to Kube, "the position, dignity and self-respect of the Protestant

---

[81] Kube was actually allowed to keep the title of *Gauleiter:* Peter Hüttenberger, *Die Gauleiter: Studie zum Wandel des Machtgefüges in der NSDAP* (Stuttgart, 1969), 216. Kube was rehabilitated into the active ranks of the Nazi elite when he was appointed General Commissioner for White Russia in the Occupied East.

[82] For a convincing counterargument, see Doris Bergen, *Twisted Cross: The German Christian Movement in the Third Reich* (Chapel Hill, 1996). See in general Kurt Meier, *Die Deutsche Christen: Das Bild einer Bewegung im Kirchenkampf des Dritten Reiches* (Göttingen, 1964); Hans-Joachim Sonne, *Die politische Theologie der Deutschen Christen* (Göttingen, 1975).

[83] See, *inter alia*, BAZ NS 22/1064 (7 January 1931: Berlin).

[84] Scholder, *Churches*, 1: 197.

[85] Ibid., 198.

Fig. 5   Erich Koch, *Gauleiter* of
East Prussia and later Reich
Commissioner for Ukraine. He
served as President of the East
Prussian Protestant Church
Synod when the Third Reich
began. (Scherl)

churches" should have prevented them from "placing themselves under the
influence of marxist-infiltrated governments."[86] As "an old fraternity student," he informed the general superintendent in Lübben that "with the
next church vote we will create a representation in the Protestant Church,
which is essential in the interest of the revival of church life on German and
Christian foundations."[87]

Toward this end Kube suggested the creation of a church party known
as the "Protestant National Socialists," to be separate from the NSDAP itself. Such a plan, however, would do well to have Strasser's approval as the
party's chief administrator. Strasser responded by saying that "in every case
we must attempt to take part in the Protestant Church vote in accord with the
size and strength of the party."[88] In addition, Strasser told Kube to inform
the rest of the Prussian *Gauleiter* of his plans, adding that *Kirchenfachberater*
(consultants for church affairs) should be set up in each *Gau*. Hitler, although
more worried on account of the Dinter episode, nonetheless also endorsed
Kube's plan, based on the assurance that this group would not be an institutional branch of the NSDAP. Furthermore, true to the *Überkonfessionalismus*
of positive Christianity, Hitler suggested "German Christians" as a more appropriate name.[89]

None of the Prussian *Gauleiter* voiced disapproval with Strasser's and
Kube's religious plans for the party. Their own religious involvement confirmed that many of them were actively interested in church life. Erich Koch,
as we have already seen, was actually president of his provincial church

[86] BAZ NS 22/1064 (27 October 1931: Berlin).
[87] BAZ NS 26/1240 (1 December 1931: Berlin).
[88] BAZ NS 26/1240 (17 December 1931: Munich).
[89] Wright, *'Above Parties'*, 92.

synod. Even before, however, he was closely involved with the church: The future *Reichsbischof*, Ludwig Müller, was his pastor, and he was involved in furthering Müller's career.[90] Renowned as one of the most autonomous of *Gauleiter*, Koch fashioned his own regional variation of the DC and sounded a less belligerent note than Kube: "We commit ourselves, and we demand this commitment not only from the elected representatives of the church, but above all from all Protestant men and women, to service in our communities! We want to serve: through tireless recruitment to our worship; through chivalrous intervention for the poor and needy, through defence of our faith; ... through true Evangelical witness in public."[91] Others, like Otto Telschow and Bernhard Rust, actively sought and welcomed the participation of pastors in the movement.[92] The *Gauleiter* of Silesia, Helmut Brückner, sent Strasser an internal "Special Circular" he had issued to his *Gau* officials on the party's official church–political stance. Its contents became common knowledge once a copy came into the hands of the *Kirchenrat* and the newspapers *Tägliche Rundschau* and *Christliche Welt*. As a confidential document, however, it provides a glimpse into the Nazis' feelings about the institution of the Protestant Church[93]: "We struggle for a union of the small Protestant state churches into a strong Protestant Reich Church.... We are acting not as a party, but as Protestant Christians who only follow a call to faith from God, which we hear in our *Volk* movement. As true members of our church we have a legitimate claim to have appropriate consideration given to the greatness and inner strength of National Socialism in church life and the church administration."[94]

Protests to the contrary notwithstanding, this was indeed a politicization of the church. Such a practice was not, however, limited to the Nazis: Most other existing church parties had connections with political parties as

[90] In a monthly report to Strasser, Koch noted that "Röhm was here and has had several discussions regarding the Reichswehr with my pastor." Although Koch does not mention his pastor's name, it was very likely Müller, as Müller came from Königsberg, counted Koch among his friends, and was intimately knowledgeable in military affairs as the *Wehrkreispfarrer* (military chaplain) for East Prussia: BAZ NS 22/1065 (22 July 1931: Königsberg).

[91] As quoted in Scholder, *Churches*, 1: 212. On Koch's independence, see Hüttenberger, *Gauleiter*, 52–3, 72–3; von Lang, *Secretary*, 122, 151.

[92] Telschow, *Gauleiter* of East Hanover, was a good friend of Protestant Pastor Ludwig Münchmeyer; BAZ NS 22/1063. On Rust, see the correspondence between him and Strasser, in which he endorses the establishment of a National Socialist Pastors' Working Group to facilitate the completion of the Nazis' "final struggle" (*Endkampf*): BAZ NS 22/1071 (1 June 1932: Hannover). In Rust's *Gau* alone, seventeen pastors belonged to the Nazi Party: Nowak, *Kirche*, 305.

[93] This was confirmed by Strasser, who noted in a letter to Brückner that he could find nothing objectionable in the circular: BAZ NS 22/1068 (17 November 1932: Munich).

[94] "Richtlinien für Kirchenfragen," BAZ NS 22/1068 (10 November 1932: Breslau). Note that the more menacing translation in Scholder (*Churches*, 1: 203), "Purging of the small Protestant Landeskirchen...," bears no resemblance to the original German ("Vereinigung der kleinen evangelischen Landeskirchen...").

well. As Jonathan Wright has suggested, "It is easy to find fault with the anti-German Christian argument that the church must be kept free of politics . . . as the German Christians pointed out, politics were already in the church: the church leadership was simply conservative or national liberal not national socialist."[95] However, whereas German Christians were very often party members, they remained a separate organization, with their own leadership and policy-making apparatus. It is all the more significant therefore that section III-3 of Brückner's circular stated that "Participation in the church vote is mandatory for every party member."[96]

Nazis could be found in other Protestant Church organizations as well. One of the most important was the League for a German Church (*Bund für deutsche Kirche*, or BdK), which counted Walter Buch among its leaders. The League was founded in 1921, much earlier than the DC, by Joachim Niedlich, who came from a pastor's home described by one scholar as "politically conservative as it was religiously orthodox."[97] Included among its members was no one less than Houston Stewart Chamberlain. The BdK remained separate from the DC, but much of its program was the same, not least the aspiration for a Protestant Reich Church. Like the DC, the BdK was also opposed to paganism.[98] Their agenda was to build "a church that will fight – not, as up to now, unconsciously pave the way for – both the Jesuit spirit and semitic degeneration through education and instruction, which through the German soul and German Christianity will again provide us a mighty fortress."[99] Another BdK leader, the Flensburg pastor Friedrich Andersen, elaborated on this theology in his book *Der deutsche Heiland* ("The German Savior"), published one year after von Harnack's *Marcion*. In it, Andersen identified Christianity as the religion of progress, emphasizing Christ's loneliness, individuality, and ascent to spiritual mastery.[100] Andersen also reduced Christianity to the person of Christ alone, insisting that "foreign underpinnings" like the Old Testament were unnecessary. In his argumentation, Andersen made explicit reference to both Chamberlain and Harnack.[101] Andersen's rejection of the Old Testament was based on an insistence that the Christian God of the New Testament was a God of love, not the vengeful, unjust God of the Old Testament. He also posited Christian spirituality and belief

95 Jonathan Wright, "The German Protestant Church and the Nazi Party in the Period of the Seizure of Power 1932–3," in Derek Baker (ed.), *Renaissance and Renewal in Christian History* (Oxford, 1977), 413.

96 Kube had his *Gau* church expert come up with a similar *Rundschreiben*, which also made voting in the church elections mandatory: BAZ, Sammlung Schumacher (hereafter Schu), 205/2/149–50 (1 September 1931: Berlin).

97 Daniel Borg, *The Old-Prussian Church and the Weimar Republic: A Study in Political Adjustment, 1917–1927* (Hanover, NH, 1984), 183.

98 Ibid., 188.

99 *Allgemeine Rundschau*, 25 October 1923: in StAM PolDir/6686.

100 Friedrich Andersen, *Der deutsche Heiland* (Munich, 1921), 10, 15.

101 Ibid., 19–20.

in the eternal over against Jewish carnality and crass materialism.[102] These views were established widely in the BdK. Reinhold Krause, whose call for the removal of the Old Testament caused such a controversy at the German Christian *Sportspalast* assembly of November 1933, had been a member of the BdK. Significantly, several moderate leaders of the later German Christian movement, while acknowledging their overall indebtedness to the ideas of the BdK, rejected the anti–Old Testament thrust of its doctrine, explicitly blaming this on theological liberalism.[103]

In the *Kampfzeit*, rivalry soon arose between the two groups, especially regarding the DC's status as the only church party to be endorsed by the NSDAP leadership. BdK officials wrote to the party leadership, suggesting that this endorsement violated the party's official neutrality in church affairs and pointing out that numerous Nazis had been actively involved with their own organization, both as spokesmen and members. They also insinuated that the DC membership was "Jewish," owing to its ties with a slightly more moderate predecessor, the Christian–German Movement, which did not call for the removal of the Old Testament.[104] They asked Rudolf Hess' cousin, Gret Georg, presumably a BdK member, to intervene with Hess on their behalf, in the hope that they might salvage their position by forming an alliance with the DC for the upcoming church elections.[105] Kube violently rejected the BdK's suggestions and brought himself into potential conflict with Buch, who claimed he had Hitler's ear in Protestant Church matters.[106] Kube assured Buch that he was giving his endorsement of the DC to other *Gauleiter*, not as party functionaries, but as "private people interested in the church."[107] Buch, in turn, recommended to other BdK leaders that they try to avoid any factionalism among Nazi members of the Protestant Church, as this would only serve to weaken the Nazi cause.[108]

Links between the Protestant Church and the Nazi Party could be found lower down the party hierarchy as well. In the Reichstag elections of

---

[102] Ibid., 59–62. Compare with *Mein Kampf*, 306. Andersen joined the NSDAP in 1928 and immediately became active as a party speaker (Nowak, *Kirche*, 249).

[103] See, for instance, Arnold Dannemann, *Die Geschichte der Glaubensbewegung 'Deutsche Christen'* (Dresden, 1933), 11–12; Constantin Grossmann, *Deutsche Christen – Ein Volksbuch* (Dresen, 1934), 24–5.

[104] BAZ NS 22/1064 (23 October 1931: Berlin). Although the DC were to get into hot water after one of its leaders, Reinhard Krause, similarly suggested the removal of the Old Testament at the famous *Sportspalast* meeting of November 1933, many DC members themselves regarded this as excessive. Another DC leader, Friedrich Wieneke, tried to explain this position as a carryover from Krause's days in the BdK: *Das Evangelium im Dritten Reich* 2 (3 December 1933), 514.

[105] BAZ Schu 245/1/40 (26 October 1931: Berlin). The letter pointed out that Buch and another prominent Nazi by the name of Löpelmann could be counted as members of the BdK.

[106] BAZ NS 22/1064 (27 October 1931: Berlin), for Kube's attack on the BdK; BAZ Schu 245/1/39 (23 October 1931: Munich), for Buch's position.

[107] BAZ Schu 245/1/42 (2 November 1931: Berlin).

[108] BAZ Schu 245/1/44 (14 November 1931: Munich).

May 1924, five Protestant theologians ran as NSDAP candidates; six in the December 1924 elections.[109] In the Prussian *Landtag* elections of December 1924, eight Protestant pastors stood as party candidates.[110] By contrast, no Catholic priests or theologians ran for the party. One of the most famed heroes of the Nazi rank-and-file, Horst Wessel, who died in a street brawl with the Communists in 1930 and gained immediate martyr status thereafter, was the son of a Protestant pastor. By one estimate, 120 pastors counted themselves members of the party in 1930 – a very small portion of the approximately 18,000 Protestant pastors then practicing in Germany, but rather more significant when it is remembered that the Protestant Churches discouraged their clergy from formally joining any political party.[111] Relations at the local level could be quite close as well. The local NSDAP branch in Gladbeck was established in the town's Protestant parish hall, which also served as the permanent meeting place for the party.[112] In East Prussia, especially the Catholic enclave of Ermland, Protestant congregation centers were often the primary meeting places for the Nazi Party.[113] Protestant clergymen could be found in the ranks of the district and local party leadership (*Kreis-* and *Ortsgruppenleitung*), as in the case of Pastor Michalik of Altmark, Pastor Melhorn of Lauenberg, and Pastors Leffler and Leutheuser of the Wiera valley in Thuringia, who actually founded the local NSDAP in Altenburg.[114]

A CHRISTIAN, NATIONAL EDUCATION

Aside from relations with the churches themselves, Nazi designs for the schools are often taken as a barometer of the party's religious views. The most obvious starting point is the NSLB. Although nominally a professional association, the NSLB was in fact one of the most important ideological ancillaries of the Nazi movement.[115] We have seen Schemm's personal view on Christianity and Nazism; but was this also the official program of the

---

[109] Herbert Christ, "Der Politische Protestantismus in der Weimarer Republik: Eine Studie über die politische Meinungsbildung dürch die Evangelischen Kirchen im Spiegel der Literatur und der Presse," Ph.D. dissertation (Bonn, 1967), 278.

[110] Ibid., 278–9.

[111] Albrecht Tyrell, *Hitler befiehl... Selbstzeugnisse aus der 'Kampfzeit' der NSDAP: Dokumentation und Analyse* (Düsseldorf, 1969), 379–80. Wright's reference to the "majority" of this number being Protestant (*'Über den Parteien'* [Göttingen, 1977], 140) is not quite correct, as Catholic clergy were prohibited from joining the party altogether, under pain of expulsion.

[112] Frank Bajohr, *Verdrängte Jahre: Gladbeck unterm Hakenkreuz* (Essen, 1983), 190–1.

[113] Gerhard Reifferscheid, "Die NSDAP in Ostpreussen: Besonderheiten ihrer Ausbreitung und Tätigkeit," *Zeitschrift für die Geschichte und Altertumskunde Ermlands* 39 (1978), 72.

[114] On Michalik: GStA I Rep 77/Tit 4043/Nr 423/79 (20 August 1931: Berlin); on Melhorn: Nowak, *Kirche*, 305; on Leffler and Leutheuser: Scholder, *Churches*, 1: 194.

[115] As the party administration (*Organisations-Abteilung VII*) explained when rejecting the idea of a Nazi Dentist League, "Special organizations based primarily on economics would fritter away the fighting strength of the movement.... The special organizations which the party has allowed, lawyers', doctors' and teachers' leagues, are of a decidedly ideological and not economic nature": BAZ NS 22/1065 (23 March 1931: Munich).

organization he headed? Ian Kershaw argues that the NSLB was "prepared to take the initiative and lead the way in expressions of support for Nazi policy," thereby pointing to its commitment to Nazi goals, but suggests that for this very reason the organization was anti-Christian.[116] An examination of the NSLB's own position lends evidence to the contrary. The organization's newspaper published a "School policy statement of the NSDAP" in 1931, which mapped out the fundamentals of their platform. Along with emphasizing the "coordination" of all education under the German state, the statement also insisted that "The German school shall be the Christian community school.... Education should not offer dead knowledge, but should impart those things that mold the soul and character of young people. The living sources are the German *Volkstum*, the German *Heimat* and the eternally living antecedents of the German people. The basic premise of education is active Christianity."[117] The article made no attempt to disguise the party's essential opposition to confessional schools, but at the same time affirmed the importance of Christianity: The Nazi ideal of the *Gemeinschaftschule* was not just German, but also Christian. Such a policy, aimed at sublimating the confessional divide in German society, was totally consistent with the syncretism of positive Christianity.

The same principle was affirmed throughout the ranks of the NSLB. The Saxon branch enunciated its views on religious education in a letter to Schemm: "1) We declare ourselves for Christianity as the singular, towering and irreplaceable spiritual power and reality of life.... 3) Through religious education, youth [will] be prepared for the future growing German *Volk*, to become part of the eternal, living force, as it appeared in Jesus as the power of deliverance, creation and redemption."[118] In the same statement the transformation of the Protestant State Church, erastian and statist by tradition, into an activist "people's church" was affirmed, as was the desire to actively cooperate with it in educational issues. With regard to the religious curriculum, the Old Testament, "in no way comparable to the New Testament, is to be treated as the origin of the Jewish religion and view of history." Its "Jewish–Oriental" spirit was rejected in favor of the gospel of Jesus: "Jewish legalism and materialism [*Lohnsucht*], late-classical intellectualism, and Roman striving for power are not compatible with a German understanding of Christianity."[119] Cooperation would be sought with the church, but the state would not delegate any power to it. This view was shared by the regional leadership for Berlin-Brandenburg, which was opposed to church prerogatives to oversee religious instruction in nonconfessional schools. No suggestion was made that this would be too expensive

---

[116] Ian Kershaw, *Popular Opinion and Political Dissent in the Third Reich: Bavaria 1933–1945* (Oxford, 1983), 147, 216.
[117] *Nationalsozialistische Lehrer-Zeitung* (n.d.[1931]): clipping in BAZ NS 22/446.
[118] "Grundlinien zur Gestaltung der religiösen Erziehung im nat.-soz. Staate": BAZ NS 12/808 (13 December 1933: Dresden).
[119] Ibid.

or too time consuming; rather, the objection was made solely on the grounds that this would "contradict the National Socialist conception of the state school."[120] The existence of religious education in state schools per se was not at issue for the NSLB. Rather, the following question was raised: "Who is master over the school, the church or the state?" However, this led to potential conflict only with regard to the Catholic Church. As the press office of the NSLB wrote to Strasser, "our revolutionary convictions, for which we are always reproached . . . always find resistance in the reactionary leaning of the Roman church."[121] The Baden leadership opposed confessional schools on the grounds that they undermined unity in the Volk, but also because they would allow the Catholic church to become a "state within a state." It was additionally noted that in Baden confessional schools were not an issue, as the existing Badenese system of Christian Simultanschule (undenominational schools) was satisfactory to everyone, "save for a few Center party agitators."[122] In a similar vein, the Ruhr leadership wrote: "National Socialism wants to built a common cultural consciousness and edifice for the entire Volk. . . . The best type for this purpose is the Christian-national community school, which is not separated by confession."[123]

Such a frontal attack on confessional schools was certainly received negatively by confessional Lutherans, not to mention Catholics, and would seem – like their attitude toward the Old Testament – to confirm the anti-Christian comportment of the Nazi movement as a whole. However, as with the question of the Old Testament, here again we see an aspect of Nazi belief that bears striking resemblance to the position of theologically liberal Protestantism dating back from the nineteenth century. In large measure, liberal Protestantism was directed against the Lutheran defense of the confessional school and the "Christian state" that defended it. Although liberal Protestants believed in the church as a community of believers within the state, they maintained that it would ultimately be absorbed by the state. According to Richard Rothe, a leading exponent of liberal Protestantism, the state itself would then be imbued with ethical and religious principles derived from the gospels: The ecclesiastical stage in the historical development of Christianity

---

[120] BAZ NS 12/638 (n.d. [1932]: Berlin).

[121] BAZ NS 22/446 (6 May 1931: Nürnberg).

[122] BAZ NS 22/446 (17 June 1931: Heidelberg). No mention was made of Protestant Church machinations similar to those apparently undertaken by the Catholic Church. The letter was in fact passed on to the Reichsleitung by Heinrich Scharrelmann, a member of the Protestant National Socialist Pastor's Working Group.

[123] BAZ NS 22/446 (19 June 1931: Dortmund). The NSLB files contain many essays written by league Mitarbeiter confirming the positive position that the organization took to Christianity, most of which maintain that Christianity in fact played a central role in the Nazi Weltanschauung: see, inter alia, G. Förster, "Nationalsozialismus und die christlichen Kirchen": BAZ NS 12/808 (10 December 1932: Münster); Johannes Schwager, "Religiöse Erziehung im neuen Deutschland": BAZ NS 12/808 (n.d., n.p.); Oskar Winter, "Die Innere Erneuung Deutschen Lebens: Deutsche Erkenntnis, Deutsche Bildung, Deutsche Liebe, Deutscher Glaube": BAZ NS 12/1499 (28 February 1934: Straubing).

would pass, and the Christian spirit would enter its ethical and political stage.[124] In other words, Christianity would culminate in a secular society on the one hand, with the political state being thoroughly imbued with the spirit of Christianity on the other. Certainly liberal Protestants did not seek the disappearance of the Protestant Church as an institution. However, many of them did support Rothe's central thesis that infusing society in general with Christianity was to be done, not through political or ecclesiastical institutions, conformity to external standards, or participation in established rites, but through the power of the human personality: "The Kingdom of Heaven is within you (Luke 17:21)."[125]

The implications of *Kulturprotestantismus* for the confessional school were entirely congruent with this ecclesiological position. For liberal Protestants, education was meant to be not a study of humanity, which was the goal of rational liberalism and "atheism," but a tool for character building. Truth was not gained through rational thought alone, but also through piety. The entire educational system therefore had to be infused with a Christian ethos. As a consequence, liberal Protestants did not want religion treated as a special subject or confined to confessional schools, which they thought furthered "religious particularism."[126] They believed that confessional Lutherans, because of their defense of confessional schools, were actually causing the exclusion of believing Christians from the *Volksgemeinschaft*. For liberal Protestants, the Christian spirit had to imbue all studies.[127] The answer for them lay in nonconfessional *Simultanschule*. This understanding of religion as a cultural ethos also carried implications for anti-Catholic sectarianism. Concerned with the cultural unity of the nation, liberal Protestants saw the *Simultanschule* as a means to decatholicize Germany, as Catholic youth would now be taught "to be patriotic Germans and loyal subjects of a Protestant monarch."[128] Only in those areas where Catholics predominated did some liberal Protestants express reservations about introducing *Simultanschule*, because such schools would be de facto Catholic schools and act against national and Protestant consciousness.[129] For the nation as a whole, however,

---

[124] Thomas Nipperdey, *Deutsche Geschichte 1800–1866: Bürgerwelt und starker Staat* (Munich, 1983), 429.

[125] Uriel Tal, *Christians and Jews in Germany: Religion, Politics and Ideology in the Second Reich, 1870–1914* (Ithaca, 1975), 168, 172.

[126] Gangolf Hübinger, *Kulturprotestantismus und Politik: Zum Verhältnis von Liberalismus und Protestantismus im wilhelminischen Deutschland* (Tübingen, 1994), 183.

[127] Tal, *Christians*, 171.

[128] Marjorie Lamberti, *State, Society, and the Elementary School in Imperial Germany* (New York, 1989), 208.

[129] Ibid., 65–7, 78–9. Some right-liberal Protestants gave up on *Simultanschule* entirely once the *Kulturkampf* proved to strengthen, not weaken, Catholic consciousness in Germany (ibid., 184–6). Others, however, continued to be opposed, fearful that a return of confessionalism would mean "in Prussian primary schools ... it should be possible to teach that Luther was a scoundrel and a suicide tortured by qualms of conscience." Cited in J. Alden Nichols, *Germany after Bismarck: The Caprivi Era, 1890–1894* (New York, 1958), 172.

this was never an explicit attempt to stamp out Catholicism; rather, it was a way to foster the cultural hegemony of liberal Protestantism in Germany by simply removing reference to confessionalism of any kind, be it Lutheran or Catholic.

In a similar process, some within the NSLB revealed a preference for the substance of Protestant Christianity even while they upheld the nonconfessional style of positive Christianity. One *Mitarbeiter* of the league stated in a report: "Far and wide in nationalist circles in northern Germany, the prevailing opinion is that nationalist ideas and education are best served by the Protestant clergy. This belief happens to be well founded. About Catholic clergy with ultramontane inclinations – and which are not? – we cannot make the same claim."[130] He went on to warn that "a great danger lies in the conclusion of a concordat," and pointed to the Badenese system as an appropriate model for the Nazi Party to follow: "The Christian *Simultanschule* in no way lags behind the confessional school in its results. . . . If we compare the administering of sacraments and church attendance in Baden with that of areas with confessional schools, we find a picture favorable to Baden."[131]

For many, the hostility to confessional schools was in reality aimed against Catholic confessionalism. This became especially evident in the case of Bavaria. Rudolf Buttmann, caucus leader of the Nazi Party in the Bavarian *Landtag* (whose other members included Schemm and Streicher), and later head of the Cultural Division of the Reich Interior Ministry under Frick, attempted to placate the concerns of Catholic Bavarians about his movement: "Our worldview is not directed against Catholicism or Protestantism, not against Christianity, but rather is based on Christianity and against cultural bolshevism, against the false liberalism of the Enlightenment, and against materialism."[132] During another speech in the *Landtag*, he restated the argument with specific reference to the school issue: "One has opportunity enough to see how our party governs in Thuringia, where party member Dr. Frick has reintroduced Christian morning prayer in school. . . . Not through us is religion in danger, but rather through the conditions we know of in Russia, and which they now boast of in Berlin. First we shall sweep clean the recesses of filth of the city – the cinemas and theaters – with an iron broom."[133] In these instances Buttmann reinforced well-known party views. However, Buttmann went one step further when he suggested that the confessional school could find a place in the future Nazi State. Members of the NSLB were especially incensed, and complained to Strasser: "Now that Dr. Buttmann has committed the party to the confessional school, we might as well cease our work, for now we are exactly the same as the others. . . . What Dr. Buttmann said was not just a harmless remark: no, it

---

[130] G. Förster, "Staat – Kirche – Schule: Unter Berücksichtigung besonders der badischen christlichen Simultanschule": BAZ NS 12/808 (n.d.[1932], n.p.).
[131] Ibid.
[132] *Völkischer Beobachter* (hereafter *VB*), 5 January 1931.
[133] *VB*, 13 December 1930: in BStA Sammlung Rehse (hereafter Rehse)/P3432.

was the declaration of the caucus leader in the most important school policy debate of the legislative year." [134]

Confusion on the issue ensued. In private correspondence, league member Baarß in Mecklenburg tried to clarify the party's position for Johannes Stark, the Nobel prizewinner and author of "National Socialism and the Catholic Church," a work that argued that, in attacking Marxism, the Nazis were more Christian than the Center Party. To this convinced Catholic, Baarß made no pretense that the party was in favor of confessional schools: "Indeed all German children should receive a Christian education. With confessional schools, however, children are compelled by their parents to choose one dogma or the other.... One can be a positive Christian without receiving the teachings of Christ through one particular dogma. A non-dogmatic school would undoubtedly be an important step forward in the religious development of our *Volk*." [135] No secret was made of the league's opposition to confessional schools, even for a rare pro-Nazi Catholic whose endorsement would be needed to further the Nazi cause among cautious Bavarians or Rhinelanders. Baarß added that matters were not made easier when party leaders like Buttmann and Strasser publicly committed the party to preserving confessional schools.

Buttmann, having received a copy of this letter from Strasser's Reich Leadership Office, wrote Baarß to clarify his position. Reminding Baarß that the whole issue was tied to the unfortunate history of sectarian conflict in Germany, Buttmann assured him that "with the emergence of a National Socialist state, this historical state of affairs will be altered: not abruptly, but with historically consistent necessity." He admitted that, given the prevailing circumstances in Bavaria, he preferred the confessional over the nonconfessional school. He noted that this was for tactical reasons, however, and specifically requested that Baarß not let his views reach the public: The Bavarian Peoples' Party, Buttmann contended, was attempting a "systematic recatholicization" of the Protestant segment of Bavaria, which comprised roughly 30% of the population. Should the nonconfessional school be instated in Bavaria, he warned, Catholic teachers would infiltrate this population, "grievously affecting the Protestant consciousness of growing school children.... The recatholicization of Germany from the south up is the program of the BVP power brokers [*Drahtzieher*], and for the present we unconditionally need the Protestant confessional school in Bavaria as a bulwark." [136]

Buttmann solicited Baarß's appreciation of the regional differences between Bavaria and Mecklenburg: "When you lay down the demand that dogma disappear from the school, it is conceivable for a purely Protestant region: but for the entire Reich it is impossible." In other words, where the

---

[134] BAZ NS 22/446 (6 May 1931: Nürnberg).
[135] BAZ NS 12/638 (16 June 1931: Lübz).
[136] BAZ NS 12/638 (23 June 1931: Munich).

population was solely Protestant, the formal removal of "dogma" would not engender a weakening of Protestant consciousness, which, according to Buttmann, would be beneficial to the future Nazi State. Such confessional consciousness constituted a threat, however, where Catholics were concerned. Here Buttmann closely followed the anticonfessional logic of *Kulturprotestanten* who had argued in almost exactly the same terms against the *Simultanschule* for majority Catholic areas. Buttmann concluded his letter to Baarß on a defensive note: "Believe me, we south German National Socialists know the enormous danger of political Catholicism at least as well as you in the purely Protestant north!"[137]

This position was all the more remarkable for the fact that Buttmann was nominally Catholic. Like many other Nazis, including Hitler himself, Buttmann seems to have preferred Protestantism over Catholicism on ideological grounds. The Catholic Church and Ultramontanism was similarly criticized by Gregor Strasser, the party's chief administrator and one of the most powerful Nazis of the *Kampfzeit*.[138] He publicly supported confessional schools and refused to grant party membership to members of Ludendorff's Tannenberg League because of their anti-Christian attacks on the Nazi leadership.[139] However, in private he himself attacked institutional Catholicism: "History teaches that the Vatican has never had an interest in a strong and independent Germany. Therefore it wants a strong Germany just as little today or in the future. Indeed we all know from Bismarck's time how much Ultramontanism – one can also say the Center was and is mindful of this – will not let Germany back on her feet."[140]

Further evidence of a much warmer attitude to institutional Protestantism was provided by the NSLB when it decided to sponsor the creation of the National Socialist Pastors' Working Group (*Arbeitsgemeinschaft national-sozialistischer Pfarrer*). Although it counted few members – largely because of the formal "above parties" stance of the Protestant churches – its relevance lay in the fact that a major Nazi organization should have advocated it in the first place. Bernhard Rust endorsed the idea of such a group, as did Strasser.[141] Whereas some thought was given to creating an actual pastors' league on par with the NSLB, this would have abrogated the party's formal "above churches" stance; hence it remained a looser "working group" affiliated with Schemm's organization. The first meeting of the group took place in February 1931, at the Berlin home of the mother of the ambassador to

---

[137] Ibid.

[138] Peter Stachura, *Gregor Strasser and the Rise of Nazism* (London, 1983), 58.

[139] For instance, see the case of Captain August Fleck: BAZ NS 22/1069 (28 November 1930: Munich).

[140] BAZ NS 22/1068 (31 October 1932: Munich). The late date of this letter, barely a month before his sudden resignation, indicates that Strasser did not let any pro-Catholic feelings give way by this time, as Stachura suggests (*Strasser*, 59). In his private correspondence, Strasser pointed out that any alliance with the Center Party was to be made in spite of his ideological convictions, not because of them.

[141] BAZ NS 22/446 (12 January 1931: Munich).

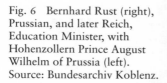

Fig. 6 Bernhard Rust (right), Prussian, and later Reich, Education Minister, with Hohenzollern Prince August Wilhelm of Prussia (left). Source: Bundesarchiv Koblenz.

Moscow. Among the notables present were Hohenzollern Prince August Wilhelm and his brother Eitel Friedrich (Wilhelm II's sons and party members since 1930) and Goebbels, who gave a talk on church and state.[142] In May 1931, the first regional branch of the group was founded in Bremen, with Gauleiter Telschow of East Hanover in attendance.[143] The Reich Leadership took an active interest in the group, overseeing appointments of other regional branches in Pomerania and Brandenburg.[144] Others were established throughout the Reich, including Baden, where, according to the *Kölnische Volkszeitung*, half the Protestant pastors belonged to the Nazi Party.[145] This small group had an impact out of proportion to its size. Their meetings served as forums for some of Schemm's many speeches, and Prussian government officials reported that their speakers were frequent guests at Nazi women's assemblies, where religion was usually strongly emphasized.[146] (Aside from serving as speakers to Nazi women, pastors were also involved in the running

[142] GStA I Rep 77/Tit 4043/Nr 392/1 (23 February 1931: Berlin). The report on this meeting, from the Prussian Interior Ministry, provides no detail as to the substance of Goebbels' speech.

[143] *VB*, 1 June 1931: in GStA I Rep 77/Tit 4043/Nr 423/75.

[144] GStA I Rep 77/Tit 4043/Nr 423/78 (19 July 1931: Köln).

[145] *Kölnische Volkszeitung*, 28 March 1931: in GStA I Rep 77/Tit 4043/Nr 423/74. In light of the probable figure of 120 pastors for the entire Reich, the article most likely meant the political preferences of the pastors, as opposed to their actual party membership.

[146] GStA I Rep 77/Tit 4043/Nr 423/76 (n.d.[1931], n.p.). The Nazis themselves acknowledged the important role played by Working Group speakers at women's rallies: *Westfälische Allgemeine Volks-Zeitung*, 8 September 1931: in BStA Presseausschnittssammlung (hereafter PAS), 929.

of their organizations; one Pastor Lossin was the administrative leader of the German Women's Order, the main Nazi women's organization up until the formation of the NSF in 1931.[147])

CONCLUSION

The Nazi approach to confessionalism displayed a general disregard for doctrine. Positive Christianity was not an attempt to make a complete religious system with dogma or ritual of its own: It was never formalized into a faith to which anyone could convert. Rather, this was primarily a social and political worldview meant to emphasize those qualities in Christianity that could end sectarianism. Even while the inner logic of positive Christianity demanded that neither confession be officially privileged over the other, there was a clear ideological preference for Protestantism over Catholicism. Catholicism was always viewed with hostility by the Nazi leadership, but this did not make the Nazis anti-Christian, as is so often assumed.[148] Rather, many of them regarded Protestant Christianity as innately suited to the needs of the movement. This was not limited to beliefs: Other Nazis went further, taking an active part in religious activities and church organizations. Far from simply professing adherence to Christianity, they were often active in church life and had been even before political expedience alone would have dictated such practice.

Despite attempts to bridge religious differences, there was considerable disagreement on Germany's religious past. Protestant and Catholic Nazis alike acknowledged the schism created by the Reformation. However, whereas certain Catholics like Eckart and Goebbels blamed Luther, Protestants uniformly upheld Luther as a nationalist and antisemitic hero. For them, it was not the Reformation itself but the reaction from Rome that had destroyed German unity. In many ways, the Nazi movement reflected the larger sectarian fault lines that ran through Germany. Just as significant, however, was the existence of nominal Catholics in the party – including Hitler – who demonstrated an admiration, and even preference, for Protestantism over Catholicism. For some, this was a function of anti-Ultramontanism; for others, Protestantism meant a greater theological accommodation with nationalism. In a larger sense these Nazis were entering into a nationalist narrative in Germany that, for the previous half century, had been written in a distinctly Protestant language. This is not to suggest that a deterministic

---

[147] BAZ NS 22/1064 (28 May 1931: Berlin). See also Jill Stephenson, *The Nazi Organisation of Women* (London, 1981), 45.

[148] See, for instance, Gilmer Blackburn, "The Portrayal of Christianity in the History Textbooks of Nazi Germany," *Church History* 49 (1980), 433–45, who uses Nazi vituperation against the "papist will to power" and "Roman spiritual proscription," as well as their dismay with the partial results of the Reformation, to argue that the Nazi movement sought nothing less than the "utter annihilation of the Christian faith," without giving any consideration to the Nazis' esteem for Protestantism and how this might qualify his arguments.

"Luther-to-Hitler" teleology is being proposed, anymore than scholars of the French Revolution would propose an "Athens-to-Paris" teleology due to the Jacobins' understanding of their republic as a revival of ancient Greece. What is revealing, rather, are the ways in which the Nazis – as the Jacobins before them – attempted to claim a certain past for themselves, to position themselves as the inheritors of a venerable but nonetheless vital cultural patrimony.

However instrumentalist the Nazi attraction to Protestantism was, it was often predicated on the same things that Protestants themselves heavily emphasized. This is seen not only in the reaction of Protestants of the day, the most enthusiastic of whom were of a theologically liberal bent; it was also visible in the Nazi conception of the nonconfessional school, a means to bridging Germany's confessional divide that had first been devised by *Kulturprotestanten* for remarkably similar reasons. This affinity for Protestantism was also evident in the anticlerical attacks made during this time, expressed both privately and publicly. Catholic Nazis in particular articulated a negative attitude toward their own church, whereas Protestants, such as Buch, Kube, and Schemm, displayed little if any enmity toward theirs. In the majority of cases, "confessionalism" meant Catholic confessionalism, "the church" meant the Catholic Church – even when the precepts of positive Christianity stipulated that Catholics too had a place in the "Peoples' Community."

However, there were others in the party, a vocal minority, who claimed to make no distinction between church and Christianity. Represented by such prominent Nazis as Ludendorff and Rosenberg, these men rejected both the institution of the church and the ideology of positive Christianity, espousing in their place a different national religion, a "paganist" faith of blood and soil. This faith sought to replace an "alien" religion with something exclusively Germanic in character, whose myths and rituals would seek to reestablish a pre-Christian past. In the next chapter, we will examine the religious views of the party's paganists. How influential was this segment of party opinion? What was their relationship to the positive Christians of the party? Did paganists distinguish between Christianity as doctrine and Christianity as ethic? Did they distinguish between the confessions, or were they equally opposed to both? Was the paganist battle against Christianity unequivocal, or could it display signs of tension and ambiguity?

3

BLOOD AND SOIL

The Paganist Ambivalence

The men of the coming age will transform the heroes' memorials and glades of remembrance into the places of pilgrimage of a new religion; there the hearts of Germans will be constantly shaped afresh in pursuit of a new myth.
  Alfred Rosenberg[1]

Jesus is a linchpin of our history . . . the God of the Europeans.
  Alfred Rosenberg[2]

So far we have surveyed those in the Nazi movement who described themselves as Christian or their movement as based on a Christian social philosophy. Rarely did they elaborate on doctrinal questions. Seldom did these party members disclose their thinking on original sin, the resurrection of Christ, or the communion of the saints. Even though Hitler indicated his belief in an afterlife, he, like all Nazis who expressed an opinion, rejected the Old Testament and believed Jesus was an Aryan. If a strict theologian would have found this far from orthodox, theologically liberal Protestants would have recognized these positions as residing, if not originating, within their own religious system. Their frequent references to biblical passages and reliance on them in constructing their image of Jesus and his social message indicate that a large number of Nazis believed that they were following, if not Christian metaphysics, at least Christian ethics. Because most positive Christians of the movement believed their kingdom was of this world, their attraction to Christianity rested primarily with its temporal message, its political and social meanings. Many of these Nazis were capable of accepting certain Christian dogmas, gaining inspiration from the gospels and their conception of Christ. In general, however, most of them were less concerned with the doctrine of Christianity than with its political ideologies.

However, other voices in the movement argued a quite different position. Not only did they suggest that Christian dogma was unrelated to Nazism; they went one step further, suggesting that Nazism actually opposed such dogma. In its place, they argued for a "pagan" faith based on a return to the

[1] *Mythus des 20. Jahrhunderts* (Munich, 1930), 365.
[2] Ibid., 391.

Nordic mysticism of the past. According to some scholars, this ersatz religion was also predicated on a Nietzschean rejection of Christian ethics. We now survey those party leaders commonly regarded as the Nazi "pagans," here referred to as "paganists." What did these paganists have to say about the ideologies and doctrines of Christianity? What were their attitudes to the different confessions? How complete was their rejection of Christ? And how powerful were they in shaping the overall direction of Nazism?

A GERMAN CONCEPTION OF GOD

Erich Ludendorff was arguably the first paganist of the Nazi movement and easily the most recognizable of all early Nazis. He was one of the most notable military leaders of the First World War, who, in partnership with Hindenburg, won some of Germany's greatest victories, most famously the Battle of Tannenberg on the Russian Front. During the last two years of the war, he and Hindenburg assumed near-dictatorial powers as the civilian authorities began to lose credibility. Having advocated a negotiated peace after the collapse of the Western Front in 1918, Ludendorff soon became involved in the *völkisch* movement. It is perhaps no coincidence that one of the men most responsible for Germany's surrender that year would become a leading propagandist of the stab-in-the-back legend (*Dolchstoßlegende*). Ludendorff took part in the failed Kapp Putsch of 1920, shortly afterward becoming a figurehead of the Nazi movement and taking part in the failed Hitler Putsch of 1923. At the *putsch* trial, his enormous prestige ensured that he, unlike Hitler, would be acquitted of all charges. During Hitler's brief imprisonment, Ludendorff attempted a takeover of the NSDAP with a new National Socialist Freedom Party (*Nationalsozialistischer Freiheitspartei*, or NSFP), which fought with Streicher's Greater German People's Community (*Grossdeutsche Volksgemeinschaft*, or GDVG) for the mantle of Nazism.

It was during this time that Ludendorff, like Dinter, attempted to turn Nazism into an explicitly religious movement. While Dinter attempted a "reform" of Christianity, however, Ludendorff's religious agenda was anti-Christian and pagan. Indeed, Ludendorff proclaimed a divorce from Christianity – a position that Dinter would have rejected utterly. According to Ludendorff's adjutant Wilhelm Breucker, in 1924 "Ludendorff charged Hitler with having expressly based the party on positive Christianity in his program and sought to demonstrate to him with biblical quotations that Christianity was and by nature had to be the sharpest opponent of every *völkisch* movement."[3] Ludendorff's anti-Christian ideology was strongly influenced by his second wife, Mathilde von Kemnitz. The daughter of a theologian, von Kemnitz came to hate everything associated with Christianity, creating in its place a philosophy she called *Deutsche Gotterkenntnis* ("German

---

[3] Wilhelm Breucker, *Die Tragik Ludendorffs: Eine kritische Studie auf Grund persönlicher Erinnerungen an der General und seine Zeit* (Oldenburg, 1953), 107.

conception of God"). As early as 1920, von Kemnitz had attempted to infuse the Nazi movement with her paganistic religious views, but had received a "brusque rejection" from Hitler, "to whom her ideas and teachings seemed like confused delusions."[4] In Ludendorff, however, she found a more receptive audience. He used his power in the NSFP to bring Kemnitz into prominence. At a party conference held in August 1924, the Ludendorffs attempted to impose their religious views. The main speech of the conference was read by von Kemnitz, who insisted on the centrality of a new religion for the Nazi movement that was anti-Christian in tone.[5] Like her husband, she believed that, behind the international powers of Marxism, Catholicism, capitalism, and Freemasonry, the Jews were at work. But even the Jews were tools of another force – namely the Dalai Lama, who sought to destroy Germany from faraway Tibet.[6] This fantasy was too much even for Alfred Rosenberg, who later wrote that Kemnitz "made world history into an affair of mere secret conspiracies."[7]

With Hitler's release from prison, Ludendorff was increasingly marginalized, especially after the latter's disastrous showing in the 1925 presidential elections. In the same year Ludendorff founded the Tannenberg League (*Tannenbergbund*) as an exclusively mystical–religious sect. As we have seen in relation to Dinter's ultrasectarian Christianity, Hitler rejected any attempt to turn Nazism into a political religion. However, whereas Hitler adhered to many of Dinter's and Eckart's religious views, he was totally opposed to Ludendorff's. As Hitler wrote in *Mein Kampf,*

The characteristic thing about these people is that they rave about old Germanic heroism, about dim prehistory, stone axes, spear and shield, but in reality are the greatest cowards that can be imagined. For the same people who brandish scholarly imitations of old German tin swords, and wear a dressed bearskin with bull's horns over their bearded heads, preach for the present nothing but struggle with spiritual weapons, and run away as fast as they can from every Communist blackjack.[8]

Two years later Hitler expelled Ludendorff from the NSDAP. He additionally forbade members of the Nazi Party to enter the Tannenberg League.[9] Undeterred, the Ludendorffs continued along their religious path. In 1931,

---

[4] Ibid., 108.
[5] Erich Ludendorff, *Vom Feldherrn zum Weltrevolutionär und Wegbereiter Deutscher Volksschöpfung: Meine Lebenserinnerungen von 1919 bis 1925* (Munich, 1941), 350–1. Ludendorff makes no mention of the reception her speech received.
[6] Peter Viereck, *Metapolitics: From the Romantics to Hitler* (New York, 1941). Viereck erred when he asserted that Ludendorff's personal influence on Hitler was "enormous" (297).
[7] Quoted in Robert Cecil, *The Myth of the Master Race: Alfred Rosenberg and Nazi Ideology* (London, 1972), 36. Rosenberg's own historical theories hardly revealed a level-headed scholar. While he rejected Kemnitz's mythology, he propagated his own, firmly arguing that European civilization began with the lost continent of Atlantis: *Mythus*, 24–8.
[8] Adolf Hitler, *Mein Kampf*, trans. Ralph Manheim (Boston, 1962), 361.
[9] Albrecht Tyrell, *Führer befiehl…Selbstzeugnisse der 'Kampfzeit' der NSDAP* (Düsseldorf, 1969), 165–6.

Mathilde wrote a book titled *Erlösung von Jesu Christo* ("Redemption from Jesus Christ"), which sought to replace Jesus with a pantheistic adoration of nature. In it, and in her other writings of the period, Jesus was not the heroic Aryan leader, but an alcoholic Jew who did not even die on the cross. In this account, the Bible was a Jewish fraud that destroyed every *völkisch* impulse. Christians, often innocently unaware of the consequences, were propagating a faith that would lead to the destruction of Germany.[10] The search for God was not to lead to Christ, but rather to the German countryside, to a divine "blood and soil": "Because the entire world is permeated with God's soul, the German plants and animals are not soulless, like the servants of Yahweh."[11] Here was a literal deification of Germany, the search for a replacement for Christianity.

If the Ludendorffs represented a clear break with, and attack on, Christianity, for Erich Ludendorff at least the transformation was not without its ambiguity. Although Christian doctrine and metaphysics were rejected, Ludendorff's sectarian obsessions were still tied to a Protestant way of seeing. In 1923 Ludendorff suggested there could be no compromise "in the struggle of the Christian–Germanic worldview against the three Internationals."[12] At his *putsch* trial in February 1924, Ludendorff attributed Germany's malaise not only to Marxism and Judaism, which corrupted the German people "physically, racially and morally," but also to "political Catholicism" and Ultramontanism, which he blamed for the destruction of the *Kaiserreich* as well.[13] As of yet, however, Ludendorff offered no comparable attack on Protestantism. Instead, he made more than one reference to Germany's "Protestant Dynasty," for which he fought loyally in the Great War and which he accused political Catholicism and Bavarian particularism of trying to destroy.[14]

That same year Ludendorff laid out his feelings on the Protestant faith in an extended interview. He was, for the moment, turning away from his struggle against Bolshevism to fight the Roman Church, which was attempting to conquer northern Germany: "The black threat in Germany has become greater than the red." Ludendorff asserted that he had done his best to rouse the Protestant Church of northern Germany to this danger, but with little effect. He emphasized that Prussia was the bulwark of Protestantism in Germany; "indeed, the world has received Protestantism from Prussia." However, since the return of the Jesuits to Germany after the Revolution,

---

[10] Ekkehard Hieronimus, "Zur Religiosität der völkischen Bewegung," in Hubert Cancik (ed.), *Religions- und Geistesgeschichte der Weimarer Republik* (Düsseldorf, 1982), 172–3.

[11] Mathilde Ludendorff, *Deutscher Gottglaube* (Munich, 1932), 20.

[12] As quoted in *Bayrischer Kurier*, 27 March 1924: in Staatsarchiv München (hereafter StAM) PolDir/6687/20. The *Bayrischer Kurier* consistently published anti-Ludendorff opinions, and so questions can be raised as to the veracity of the quotation. However, the paper names its source: the extreme nationalist periodical *Fridericus* (1923, no. 50).

[13] Ludendorff, *Feldherrn*, 271.

[14] Ibid., 272.

the Catholic Church was making "terrible inroads" into the Protestant Church.[15] Here Ludendorff was being both critical and sympathetic. While he lamented that the Protestant Church in his view was not sufficiently anti-Catholic, he nonetheless betrayed his belief that, by nature, it *should* be. Instead of blaming the state of affairs on a weakness of Protestantism, he looked instead to the organizational strength of international Catholicism: "In contrast to the situation of the Protestant Church in northern Germany, the Catholic Church of southern Germany is extremely organized and well financed, and under the leadership of Rome has opened a determined but secret conversion campaign." The danger for Ludendorff was clear: If nothing were done to reverse the process, then Protestants would flock to the Catholic fold, making the entire nation once again Catholic.[16] However, Ludendorff overstated the degree of Protestant indifference toward the Catholic threat. Many Protestants, especially those in the Protestant League, saw the Catholic danger in much the same way as he. As we have seen, they even depicted Ludendorff as a Protestant warrior fighting Catholicism's supposedly ongoing counterreformation.

Catholics also tended to see Ludendorff in these terms. To a writer in the *Augsburger Postzeitung*, it was no coincidence that Ludendorff was descended from Lutheran pastors. As a Prussian Protestant, he was considered "predestined" to join the Protestant League in opposition to Catholic Bavaria.[17] A contributor to the *Bayrischer Kurier* picked up on this relationship as well, suggesting that the Protestant League wanted "to wage its religious–political struggle against Rome with the help of the *völkisch* party movement, because it is quite firmly convinced of the intrinsic similarity of its own worldview to the worldview of [this] movement." The paper suggested that both came together in the name of Ludendorff.[18] In the *Allgemeine Rundschau* it was pointed out that Ludendorff was born in the frontier territory of Posen: "There, to be German is to be Protestant, and to be Polish is to be Catholic.... A sensitive national feeling [is] intimately tied with confessional tradition. Catholicism, the faith of the subjugated foreign people, is despised." Then came a revealing parallel: "Ludendorff is thus a type of Ulsterman, something of a German Carson."[19]

[15] *Bayrischer Kurier*, 31 January 1924: in StAM PolDir/6687/65.
[16] Ibid.
[17] "Die wahren Ziele der deutsch-völkischen Bewegung," *Augsburger Postzeitung*, 10 May 1924: in StAM PolDir/6687/41. The article also referred to Heinrich Hermelink, who after the war wrote *Kirche im Kampf: Dokumente des Widerstandes und des Aufbaus der Evangelischen Kirche in Deutschland von 1933–1945* (Tübingen, 1950), a work suggesting that the Protestant churches were unambiguously anti-Nazi. In the *Postzeitung* article, reference is made to Hermelink's claim that Protestants in Germany then, unlike twenty years before, were no longer anti-Catholic.
[18] Quoted in Klaus Scholder, *The Churches and the Third Reich*, 2 vols. (London, 1987–8), 1: 109.
[19] "Mitten im Kulturkampf," *Allgemeine Rundschau*, 6 April 1924: in StAM PolDir/ 6687/89. Sir Edward Carson was the leader of the Ulstermen in the first decades of the twentieth century.

The same year that he was expelled from the NSDAP, Ludendorff formally left the Protestant Church. In a letter to church authorities, he declared that he no longer believed in the Protestant religion. However, perhaps more important was his resentment that the anti-Ultramontanist and anti-Masonic campaign was insufficiently championed by his church.[20] Given his attack on Hitler for supposedly going to Canossa, we can safely discount his polemic against the Protestant establishment as equally inflated. In return for feeling snubbed by the church, Ludendorff would later profess his disgust that Protestant pastors, "who were supposed to be especially 'national'," could read from psalms full of reference to Zion, Yahweh, and Jerusalem.[21]

THE MYTH OF ROSENBERG

Perhaps the most prominent paganist in the Nazi Party was Alfred Rosenberg. More than any other National Socialist, Rosenberg had pretensions to becoming the movement's great intellect and official ideologue. He failed in both efforts. Early scholars of Nazism, taking Rosenberg's self-promotion at face value, greatly overestimated the importance of his ideas for the movement as a whole.[22] The sheer volume of published works and administrative paperwork produced by Rosenberg and his offices lent weight to this impression. Karl Bracher came somewhat closer to gauging Rosenberg's true influence when he described him as "the administrative clerk of National Socialist ideology."[23] However, even in his role as "protector" of the Nazi worldview, scholars have shown that Rosenberg encountered resistance and ultimate defeat at the hands of rival offices within the Nazi Party and state.[24] In spite of these findings, however, other scholars – especially those who espouse "political religion" theories of Nazism – still maintain that Rosenberg's ideas were hegemonic in the party.[25]

For a discussion of Protestant sectarianism in the frontier areas of the German East, see Helmut Walser Smith, *German Nationalism and Religious Conflict: Culture, Ideology, Politics, 1870–1914* (Princeton, 1995), especially 167–205: "Religious and Nationality Conflict in the Borderlands of the Imagined Community."

[20] J.R.C. Wright, *'Above Parties': The Political Attitudes of the German Protestant Church Leadership 1918–1933* (Oxford, 1974), 75.

[21] Ludendorff, *Feldherrn*, 362.

[22] Church historians in particular have argued that Rosenberg's ideas represented the party's ideology as such. See, *inter alia*, the various contributions in Franklin Littell and Hubert Locke (eds.), *The German Church Struggle and the Holocaust* (Detroit, 1974).

[23] Karl Dietrich Bracher, *The German Dictatorship: The Origins, Structure and Effects of National Socialism* (New York, 1970), 281.

[24] The best account of Rosenberg's many failures in the Nazi Party polycracy is Reinhard Bollmus, *Das Amt Rosenberg und seine Gegner: Studien zum Machtkampf im nationalsozialistischen Herrschaftssystem* (Stuttgart, 1970). On Rosenberg's contests for ideological oversight of the party, see Chapter 7 below.

[25] Aside from the older works mentioned in the Introduction, see Philippe Burrin, "Political Religion: the Relevance of a Concept," *History and Memory* 9 (1997), 321–49; Michael Ley and Julius Schoeps (eds.), *Der Nationalsozialismus als politische Religion* (Bodenheim, 1997), esp.

Fig. 7   Alfred Rosenberg, the
leading theorist of Nazism's
paganist faction: "In *spite* of all
the Christian churches, Jesus is a
linchpin of our history. He
became the God of the
Europeans." (Scherl)

Born in Estonia of *volksdeutsch* parents, Rosenberg fled to Germany after
the start of the Russian Revolution. Like Hitler, Rosenberg received his entrée
into the rightist fringe through Dietrich Eckart. It was through Eckart that
Rosenberg first met Hitler and in Eckart's *Auf gut deutsch* where Rosenberg
published his first article. After Eckart's death in 1923, Rosenberg took over
as editor of the Nazis' official newspaper, the *Völkischer Beobachter* (*VB*). His
only other organizational accomplishment before 1933 was to have founded
the relatively minor Fighting League for German Culture (*Kampfbund für
deutsche Kultur*) in 1928.[26] Other than this, Rosenberg's *Kampfzeit* activity
was limited to writing a slew of books detailing his version of Nazism and the
threat Judaism, Bolshevism, Romanism, and Freemasonry posed to German
nationhood.

By far the most important of these books was *The Myth of the Twentieth
Century*, published in 1930.[27] Significantly, it was published as a private
work, never becoming an official guide to Nazi thinking, as *Mein Kampf*
was. It never received the official stamp of the NSDAP, nor did the party's
official publisher publish it. Given the fate that awaited Dinter and Ludendorff when they tried to make their religious views official party doctrine,
Hitler would not have countenanced its publication any other way. Indeed,
in the same book that put forth a new religious doctrine, Rosenberg felt compelled to assure his reader that he was not trying to resurrect a dead religion

the contributions of Klaus Vondung and Ernst Piper; Robert Pois, *National Socialism and the
Religion of Nature* (London, 1986).

[26] Alan Steinweis contends that the *Kampfbund* was a preexisting nationalist organization
that Rosenberg later took over: "Weimar Culture and the Rise of National Socialism: The
Kampfbund für deutsche Kultur," *Central European History* 24 (1991), 406.

[27] Alfred Rosenberg, *Der Mythus des 20. Jahrhunderts: Eine Wertung der seelisch-geistigen Gestaltenkämpfe unserer Zeit* (Munich, 1930).

and that it should not be Nazi policy to engage in religious matters.[28] Most of Rosenberg's opponents in the churches assumed that it was nonetheless the *true* guide to Nazi thinking – some people even supposed it was more influential in the NSDAP than Hitler's own book.[29] The party in fact largely ignored it, as Rosenberg himself would later discover.[30] Over 700 pages long, it was easily the most abstruse book ever written by a Nazi. In keeping with their own religious views, party leaders like Hitler and Goebbels heaped enormous scorn on it. According to one biographer, "Hitler completely rejected...the mysticism with which Rosenberg, in his main work...attempted to give a religious intensity to a racist interpretation of history."[31] Goebbels was characteristically succinct, describing the book as an "ideological belch."[32]

Although Hitler was known for tailoring his remarks to please his audience, even in Rosenberg's presence he was less than enthusiastic. Before publishing it, Rosenberg asked Hitler for his opinion of the book (six months after receiving the manuscript, Hitler still had not read it). Hitler coolly replied: "It is a very clever book; only I ask myself who today is likely to read and understand such a book."[33] It was a reflection of the insecurity of Rosenberg's position that he replied by asking whether he should suppress it or even resign party office. Hitler supposedly said "no" to both, maintaining that Rosenberg had a right to publish his book as it was his "intellectual property."[34] However, on later occasions Hitler would express regret that Rosenberg had written the book in the first place. According to Albert Speer, Hitler referred to it as "stuff nobody can understand," written by a "narrow-minded Baltic German who thinks in horribly complicated terms....A relapse into medieval notions!"[35] On another occasion, Hitler made reference to its "heretical outpourings."[36] In rare moments Rosenberg even admitted to himself that Hitler ultimately rejected his religion: "[Hitler] set his face from the beginning against racial cultism."[37] Although it is true that Rosenberg's *Mythus* sold hundreds of thousands of copies, this figure is not a real reflection of its popularity. As another

---

[28] Ibid., 5–7.

[29] Jonathan Wright points to some in the clerical establishment who believed "that Rosenberg's views were more widely held in the party than Hitler's": 'Above Parties', 89.

[30] Reinhard Bollmus, "Alfred Rosenberg: National Socialism's 'Chief Ideologue?'," in Ronald Smelser and Rainer Zitelmann (eds.), *The Nazi Elite* (New York, 1993), 187.

[31] Ibid., 185.

[32] Quoted in Joachim Fest, *The Face of the Third Reich: Portraits of the Nazi Leadership* (New York, 1970), 168.

[33] Quoted in Cecil, *Master Race*, 100.

[34] Ibid., 101.

[35] Albert Speer, *Inside the Third Reich* (New York, 1970), 96. For Goebbels' views on and relationship with Rosenberg, see ibid., 122–5; Ralf Reuth, *Goebbels* (New York, 1993), 201–5.

[36] Adolf Hitler, *Hitler's Table Talk 1941–1944: His Private Conversations*, trans. Norman Cameron and R. H. Stevens, Introduction by Hugh Trevor-Roper (London, 1953), 555.

[37] Cecil, *Master Race*, 100.

of Rosenberg's biographers points out, "Secondary schools and institutions of higher education were required to have copies in their libraries; but to what extent these were read cannot now be estimated."[38] We can therefore safely discount Robert Pois' assertion that "Rosenberg's view of religion ... was *widely held* by most committed National Socialists."[39]

This being said, *Mythus* represented the views of at least one Nazi when it was written: Rosenberg himself. And because Rosenberg remained a "Reich leader" throughout the course of the party's history (even if one of the least successful), the views found in the book are worth our consideration. Speaking of the need to create a new religion, Rosenberg proclaimed that "Today a new faith is awakening: the myth of blood, the faith that the divine essence of mankind is to be defended through blood; the faith embodied by the fullest realization that Nordic blood represents the mystery which has supplanted and surmounted the old sacraments."[40] This new religion would place the highest value in the idea of racial honor: "The idea of honor – national honor – is for us the beginning and end of all our thoughts and deeds. It can endure no equivalent center of power of any type, neither Christian love nor freemasonic humanism nor Roman dogmatism."[41] This Christian "brotherhood of man" was nothing more than an attempt to allow Jew and "Turk" to take precedence over the European. In the name of Christian love, Europe was besieged by unrest and chaos: "Thanks to preachings on humanity and the equality of all peoples, every Jew, Negro and Mulatto can be a full citizen of a European state."[42] When the Nordic states of Europe were overwhelmed by the Roman south, the concept of honor was overtaken by that of Christian love: "Christianity ... did not know the idea of race and nationality, because it represented a violent fusion of different elements; it also knew nothing of the idea of honor, because in pursuance of the late Roman quest for power it subdued not only the body, but also the soul."[43] This emphasis on love brought Christianity in alliance with Marxism. If the concept of national honor was once again to be dominant, it could happen only when the "true workers" of the German *Volk* formed a united front against all forces associated with economy, profit, and money, "regardless of whether these forces were hidden under the cloak of democracy, Christianity, internationalism [or] humanism."[44]

Rosenberg also rejected the Christian doctrine of original sin: "The sense of sin always goes together with physical and racial cross-breeding. The abominable mixing of races creates ... inner uncertainty and the feeling that

---

[38] Ibid., 103.
[39] Robert Pois, *National Socialism and the Religion of Nature* (London, 1986), 41 (emphasis in the original).
[40] Rosenberg, *Mythus*, 114 (Rosenberg's *opus magnum* remains untranslated to this day).
[41] Ibid., 514.
[42] Ibid., 203.
[43] Ibid., 155–6.
[44] Ibid., 204–5.

our whole existence is sinful."[45] The Romans had been racially aware, according to Rosenberg, and so could only reject this Christian crossbreeding: "Everything still imbued with the Roman character sought to defend itself against the rise of Christianity, all the more because it represented, next to its religious teaching, a completely proletarian–nihilistic political trend."[46] Rosenberg was also opposed to the Trinity, which he believed overlooked the spirituality of racial nationalism and lead to the "nihilism" implicit in the biblical expression of Paul: "Here is neither Jew nor Greek, neither bond nor free, neither man nor woman." This nihilism led to the purposeful destruction of Greek and Roman civilizations as culturally worthless. Another Christian doctrine rejected by Rosenberg, this time explicitly Catholic, was the "dogmatization" of the birth of the Virgin Mary, which was regarded as a negation of nature. In addition, he also attacked the biblical emphasis on the resurrection.[47]

Hence we have a near-total denunciation of Christian doctrines. Unlike other Nazis, who for the most part left doctrinal questions unexamined, Rosenberg actively rejected them. Whereas other Nazis referred to positive Christianity as a fundament of party ideology, in *Mythus* Rosenberg made no mention of it. As Robert Cecil puts it, "If we accept that the basic Christian beliefs are that Jesus Christ was God, that through His death and resurrection man is redeemed from original sin and that the soul survives the death of the physical body, it is clear that Rosenberg was no Christian."[48] But if Rosenberg was not himself a Christian, how opposed to Christianity was his new religion? Here we are confronted with even more ambiguity than in the case of Ludendorff. For in spite of Rosenberg's denunciation of Christianity's history and his desire to build a new racialist faith, time and again he excluded the most important figures of the Christian faith – Jesus most importantly – from his attacks, and upheld another Christian – the medieval mystic Meister Eckhart – as the inspiration of his new belief system. Indeed, as we shall see, in the *Mythus* Rosenberg ultimately argued that Christianity itself could be reformed and saved from the "Judeo–Roman" infections of its clerical representatives.

Unlike the Ludendorffs, Rosenberg believed that Jesus had been an Aryan. Here he followed his greatest mentor, Houston Stewart Chamberlain, who had maintained that "in all probability" Jesus had not been a Jew.[49] Rosenberg affirmed his belief that, whereas Jesus was born into a Jewish culture, "there was not the slightest reason" to assume that Jesus was Jewish. Christ's teaching that the Kingdom of Heaven is within us was a "thoroughly

---

[45] Ibid., 71.
[46] Ibid.
[47] Ibid., 77–8.
[48] Cecil, *Master Race*, 84.
[49] The very title *Myth of the Twentieth Century* was a tribute to Chamberlain's *Foundations of the Nineteenth Century* of 1899, a work that Rosenberg adored and for which *Myth* was designed as a type of sequel.

un-Jewish, mystical teaching."[50] The traditional, ecclesiastical picture of Jesus had been a distortion of the Roman Church to present a picture of submission and meekness in order to create an ideal that would foster servility. In its place Rosenberg called for a new, manly image of Christ: "Today Jesus appears to us as the self-confident Lord [Herr] in the best and highest sense of the word. It is his *life* which holds meaning for the Germanic people, not his agonizing death, which is the image of him among the Alpine and Mediterranean peoples. The mighty preacher and wrathful one [Zürnende] in the temple, the man who swept along his followers, is the ideal which today shines forth from the Gospels, not the sacrificial lamb of the Jewish prophets, not the crucified."[51] Instead of the conventional image of Jesus as the sufferer, an old–new (alt–neues) picture had to emerge: Jesus the hero.[52] Jesus was not the "hook-nosed, flat-footed savior" of Southern European depiction, but the "slim, tall, blond" savior of northern European portrayals.[53] His entire being was a fiery resistance: For *that* reason he had to die.[54]

Although Rosenberg emphasized Jesus' human, temporal acts over his divine transcendence, this did not necessarily mean that Jesus had lost his divinity altogether. "In *spite* of all the Christian churches, Jesus is a linchpin of our history. He became the God of the Europeans."[55] Rosenberg made many other references of Christ's divinity. In the context of the "Nordic" Meister Eckhart, whom he regarded as both the ultimate Germanic religious hero and the "poet of the Savior," Rosenberg suggested that humanity should be independent of the clergy, made aware of their own spiritual uniqueness, and follow the example of Christ's own "holy union of divine and human natures."[56] Rosenberg even adhered to conventional Christology when discussing Chamberlain's religious views: "A totally free man, who inwardly disposed with the total culture of our time, demonstrated the finest feeling for the great superhuman simplicity of Christ...as the mediator between man and God."[57]

Rosenberg's frequent references to Christ (mentioned far more than Wotan or Nietzsche in *Mythus*) and his positive engagement with Jesus' historical and contemporary significance revealed an ambivalence hardly marking an unequivocal enemy of Christianity. These attachments signified an ambiguous revolution against the cultural heritage of Christianity. However, did Rosenberg admit to this lingering affection? The existing confessions were regarded as inadequate, especially the Roman Church, which was considered beyond redemption. Institutional arrogance and a greed for power massively

---

50 Rosenberg, *Mythus*, 76.
51 Ibid., 604 (emphasis in the original).
52 Ibid., 414.
53 Ibid., 616.
54 Ibid., 607.
55 Ibid., 391 (emphasis in the original).
56 Ibid., 230.
57 Ibid., 623–34.

corrupted the papacy. The Catholic priesthood was, in Rosenberg's view, a racially defiled mixture of "Etrusco–Syro–Near Easterners and Jews" who had infiltrated and infected ancient Rome. Rosenberg accused Catholicism of superstition, pointing to the "millions" of Europeans killed in the medieval frenzy of witch-hunts and belief in magic.[58] In his view, the papacy and its racial contamination had destroyed the Germanic Middle Ages, marked by racial consciousness and productivity; it achieved this by creating a raceless theology of hereditary sinfulness that could be redeemed only through grace.[59] The institution of the papacy was interested in nothing more than the eternal submissiveness of the servile masses.[60] As such, "eternal Rome" represented a "Jewish–clerical 'Christianity',", which propagated the theological "separation of personality from God" against which Jesus had worked.[61] Rome had blocked out Christ, indeed put itself above Christ, separating him from the people and neglecting his teachings.[62]

In contrast to Catholicism, Protestantism was viewed by Rosenberg with more ambivalence. Protestantism in the beginning meant "the blooming of the Germanic will to freedom, national self-determination, personal spirituality. Without question it paved the way for what we now call the highest works of our culture and science."[63] Like Ludendorff early on, Rosenberg essentially asserted that the present-day representatives of Lutheranism, through their approximation of the Roman system, had become un-Lutheran. For Rosenberg, Luther's great deed had been the destruction of the priesthood and the Germanification of Christianity. Rosenberg also regarded Luther as nothing less than the greatest forerunner of German nationalism, racial purity, and spiritual independence.[64] Luther's attack on Rome was especially praiseworthy: "However much Luther was still rooted in the Middle Ages, his action brought about the greatest revolution in Europe after the invasion of Roman Christianity."[65] Through his fight against Rome's clerical power, he saved the west from "Tibetan–Etruscan Asian" influences. Here again Rosenberg got his cue from Chamberlain, who had declared Luther "the greatest man in world history."[66] Rosenberg could not be quite this effusive, however: Luther's shortcoming had been his adherence to the "Hebraic" Old Testament. Although this was compensated for by his later tract, "On the Jews and their Lies" and his declaration that Christianity would have nothing more to do with Moses, the Old Testament nonetheless remained part of Luther's canon.[67]

[58] Ibid., 67.
[59] Ibid., 70–1.
[60] Ibid., 397.
[61] Ibid., 396.
[62] Ibid., 161.
[63] Ibid., 129.
[64] Ibid., 84–5, 397.
[65] Ibid., 183.
[66] Houston Stewart Chamberlain, *Die Grundlagen des 19. Jahrhunderts* (Munich, 1899), 26.
[67] Rosenberg, *Mythus*, 129.

As with other Nazi leaders, Rosenberg believed the Old Testament had to be removed from Christianity's corpus: "As a religious book the so-called Old Testament must be abolished for all time. With it will end the failed attempt of the last fifteen hundred years to spiritually make us Jews.... "[68] However, whereas other Nazis were largely content to stop at the Old Testament, Rosenberg went a step further, calling as well for the removal of "obviously distorted" portions of the New Testament. In addition, a new "Fifth Gospel" should be introduced.[69] Rejecting so much of Christianity and suggesting alternatives clearly prohibits Rosenberg from being considered Christian. However, his agenda did not amount to a total negation of preexisting gospel. Rosenberg approved of two in particular, those of John and Mark. John held out the "first ingenious interpretation, the experience of the eternal polarity between good and evil," and stood "against the Old Testament delusion that God created good and evil out of nothing."[70] The Gospel of Mark signified "the real heart of the message of kinship with God, against the semitic teaching of God's tyranny."[71] Even the Christian notion of love, although it had wrought racial contamination in Nordic Europe, could in some instances be salvaged: "Love, humility, charity, prayer, good works, mercy and repentance are all good and useful, but only under one condition: if they strengthen the power of the soul, elevate it and make it more God-like."[72]

Rosenberg would overcome Christianity's drawbacks through the appropriation of Meister Eckhart. Rosenberg regarded Eckhart as "the greatest apostle of the Nordic west [who] gave us our religion...who awoke God in our hearts, that the 'Kingdom of Heaven is within us'."[73] This reference to Luke 17: 21 – "The Kingdom of Heaven is within you" – was found as well in the works of Dietrich Eckart, who, like Rosenberg, considered it a centerpiece of his theology.[74] For Rosenberg, it was Meister Eckhart's era of the thirteenth and fourteenth centuries, not the Renaissance or even the Reformation, that signaled the birth of the new Germanic man and his culture.[75] Rosenberg was attracted by Eckhart's credentials as a medieval mystic twice tried for heresy by Pope John XXII and the Curia at Avignon. By displaying his defiance of the Pope and rejection of Roman scholasticism and ecclesialism, Eckhart was a particularly appropriate candidate for the new faith. Eckhart proclaimed that the "noble soul," not the church, the bishop, or the pope, was God's representative on Earth.[76] This emphasis on the individual soul and its self-determination was paramount for Rosenberg. God is not

---

[68] Ibid., 603.
[69] Ibid. Rosenberg made no mention of what this new Gospel would look like.
[70] Ibid., 604.
[71] Ibid.
[72] Ibid., 238.
[73] Ibid., 218–19.
[74] Dietrich Eckart, *Auf gut deutsch* 3 (1919), 38.
[75] Rosenberg, *Mythus*, 220.
[76] Ibid., 219.

above man, Rosenberg believed, but lives in the individual soul. Rather than "surrender" to or fear God, the inner soul must be totally free, must communicate with God.[77] In this way, the individual could follow the example of Christ, who strove for a sacred union of divine and human natures.[78] Rosenberg's view of God revealed itself in a direct quote from Meister Eckhart: "God is not an annihilator of works, but an accomplisher. God is not a destroyer of nature, but its perfecter."[79] This view of God as the Creator, as the God of Love rather than the Destroyer, could be found among other Nazis, notably Goebbels, who viewed Christ as the "incarnation of love."[80] This emphasis on an unmediated relationship between man and God meant that the clergyman, be he Catholic or Protestant, would cease to exist.[81] However, unlike the priesthood, which would be annihilated, the church was to be sublimated. Rosenberg left open the possibility that it could find a place in his new religious order, provided it "did not prevent the Nordic soul from unfolding itself."[82] Hence his call for a "German Peoples' Church" (*Deutsche Volkskirche*), which would embrace the faith propagated by (Rosenberg's interpretation of) Eckhart: "In place of a Jewish–Roman worldview steps the Nordic–western soul-faith."[83]

Although it may appear plain that Rosenberg's ideology constituted a rejection of Christianity, Rosenberg himself saw it instead as a radical revision. Although he made reference to Nordic gods in *Mythus*, this was not a typically paganist appropriation: "Wotan was and is dead."[84] Nor was Rosenberg tolerant of all religiomystical sects: He frequently attacked the growth of astrology and other superstitions in Nazi Germany; he also opposed Rudolf Steiner's Anthroposophists, whose organization reminded the Nazis of Freemasonry.[85] Whereas Ludendorff left the Protestant Church in 1927, Rosenberg did not leave it until 1933. Waiting until his party was safely in power does not quite explain Rosenberg's timing. Rather, it was brought on by the dismissal of the leader of the German Christians, Joachim Hossenfelder, by the Reich Bishop of the Protestant Church, who considered Hossenfelder too radical and a threat to his own position within the growing storm of the "Church Struggle."[86] Until this time, Rosenberg held out the

[77] Ibid., 223.
[78] Ibid., 230.
[79] Ibid., 231.
[80] Joseph Goebbels, *Michael: a Novel*, trans. Joachim Neugroschel (New York, 1987), 65–6.
[81] Rosenberg, *Mythus*, 227.
[82] Ibid., 219.
[83] Ibid., 252. This call for a German Peoples' Church was unrelated to the League for a German Church, which was a church–political party within the established Protestant Church. Although there were common ideological denominators between Rosenberg and the BdK, most importantly the lionization of Houston Stewart Chamberlain, there was no formal contact between them.
[84] Rosenberg, *Mythus*, 219.
[85] Cecil, *Master Race*, 83–4.
[86] Bundesarchiv Berlin-Zehlendorf (hereafter BAZ), NS 8/256/173 (15 November 1933: Berlin).

hope that a space could be created in institutional Protestantism for his own views.

Even in Rosenberg's other writings, an element favorable to Christianity (albeit radically reformist) is found. In his 1920 book *Unmoral im Talmud* ("Immorality in the Talmud"), Rosenberg attempted to show that the Jews' "rise to power" had come by way of lies and treachery motivated by a hatred of Christianity, which "has reached its summit in the systematic persecution of Christians by the Jewish Bolshevik rulers in Russia."[87] In the second book he wrote that year, *Die Spur des Juden im Wandel der Zeiten* ("The Tracks of the Jew in the Change of Time"), Rosenberg called for an attack on Jewish materialism. A sharp distinction was to be made between it and Christian spirituality. The antimaterialist, Nordic religious renascence was to take place by the purging of the Old Testament from Christianity, which would raise Christian belief above the "Jewish slag."[88] A preference for Protestantism over Catholicism was also evident outside the confines on the "Myth." Just a few years before the Nazis took power, Rosenberg gave vent to his sectarian preferences when he expressed his belief that Catholic Chancellor Heinrich Brüning was "an emissary of the Vatican, [who] had only one task: by his policy of emergency regulations and the consequent inevitable impoverishment of ever-widening circles of the population to deliver up Protestant North Germany to Communism, in order by the purgatory of this affliction to leave it ripe for a second counterrevolution with the restoration of the Catholic princely houses."[89] Rosenberg's overall estimation of Protestantism, varying between highly conditional and highly laudatory, was presaged in Chamberlain's own estimation of a nonconfessional, nonecclesiastical Protestantism as the "natural" religion of the Germans.

Chamberlain appears time and again as Rosenberg's primary – and acknowledged – intellectual inspiration. As Chamberlain's biographer puts it, "When as a youth in Riga he first encountered the *Foundations*, it struck him with the force of a revelation."[90] As Richard Wagner's son-in-law, Chamberlain served as a living link between the Wagner legacy and the Nazis, living just long enough to see the movement become a political force and endorsing it as Germany's only hope. That Chamberlain was also associated

[87] Alfred Rosenberg, *Unmoral im Talmud*, as quoted in Cecil, *Master Race*, 74. This was not simply a feigned sympathy for Slavs. As would become evident during his failed career as Reich Minister for the Occupied Eastern Territories, Rosenberg was perhaps the most sympathetic of any Nazi to the conditions of the Slavic population, and often fought with his nominal underlings to lessen the brutality of their rule (Cecil, *Master Race*, 189–216, esp. 200). Whereas Rosenberg had envisioned a system of Slavic satellite states under German suzerainty, most other Nazis preferred a simpler system of direct German administration and exploitation. The man who most undermined Rosenberg's ministerial authority in the East was none other than the Christian Erich Koch.

[88] Alfred Rosenberg, *Die Spur des Juden im Wandel der Zeiten* (Munich, 1920), 321–2.

[89] Quoted in Fest, *Face*, 169.

[90] Geoffrey Field, *Evangelist of Race: The Germanic Vision of Houston Stewart Chamberlain* (New York, 1981), 453.

with liberal Protestant theologians like Harnack is more than coincidence. Perhaps most revealing, however, is that in the Third Reich it was not only Nazis who revered Chamberlain. Members of the Confessing Church, a group often cast as the "true" anti-Nazi wing of Protestantism, believed he was their intellectual property as much as Rosenberg's or the DC's. In a 1936 article in the Confessing Church journal *Junge Kirche*, Chamberlain was described as "outstanding among the confessors of Jesus Christ at the turn of the century."[91]

Like Chamberlain, Richard Wagner himself is often cast as a forerunner of paganist religion.[92] He was perhaps more responsible than anyone else in the *Kaiserreich* for introducing the parlor mysticism in which Nazi paganists would later dabble. Wagner's operas openly celebrated the pagan, tribal gods of a mythical pre-Christian Germany. For Wagner, however, this was not a turn against Christianity. Commenting on the Nordic legends that he popularized through his *Ring* operas, Wagner believed paganism's highest God, Wotan, became "completely identified" with "Christ himself, the son of God." He contended that, in German antiquity, "fidelity and attachment were transferred to Christus all the easier, as one recognized in him the stem-god once again."[93] This is especially evident in Wagner's epic *Parsifal*. Whereas Rauschning interpreted *Parsifal* as a story of "pure blood" versus "corrupted blood," and Thomas Mann believed that it was "a dramatization of proto-Nazi racialist thinking," Friedrich Nietzsche denounced the work, claiming Wagner "sank down before the cross." Like all Nazis save Ludendorff, Wagner was convinced that Jesus was Aryan: "That the God of our Saviour should have been identified with the tribal god of Israel, is one of the most terrible confusions in all world-history." Rejecting Jesus' Jewishness, however, did not mean rejecting his divinity. In exchanges with his wife Cosima, this hero of Nazism often stated his belief that "Jesus was the source of all morality ... that Christ brought salvation and joy ... that Jesus was the true redeemer."[94]

FUROR PROTESTANTICUS

Rosenberg and Ludendorff were the most prominent paganists in the party. However, they were not alone: A circle of like-minded party members could be found in the ranks of the NSDAP. One of them was Richard Walther Darré, the party's leading agrarian specialist. After the Seizure of Power, he would become Reich Peasant Leader (*Reichsbauernführer*) and Reich Minister

[91] Quoted in Richard Gutteridge, *The German Evangelical Church and the Jews, 1889–1950* (New York, 1976), 35.

[92] The most recent scholarly treatment of this subject is Joachim Köhler, *Wagner's Hitler: The Prophet and His Disciple* (Cambridge, 2000). See as well Jacob Katz, *The Darker Side of Genius: Richard Wagner's Antisemitism* (Hanover, NH, 1986).

[93] Quoted in Robert Michael, "Wagner, Christian Anti-Jewishness and the Jews: A Re-examination," *Patterns of Prejudice* 26 (1992), 87.

[94] Ibid., 87–8.

for Agriculture. In tune with Rosenberg's mysticism, he envisioned an agrarian return to the soil in Nazi Germany, whereby the peasant and the small landowner would be privileged at the expense of the "nomadic" city dweller. He joined the Nazi movement as a known figure, playing an immediate and central role in shaping the NSDAP's agrarian election strategy. Like fellow Nordicist Rosenberg, Darré had pretensions to being an ideologue, having written *The Peasantry as Life Source of the Nordic Race* three years before joining the party.[95] The other main work of his career, *A New Aristocracy from Blood and Soil*, was published three years later.[96] Darré also influenced Himmler in his attempt to transform the SS from a guard unit into a new racial aristocracy. This took shape in practical measures: Darré drew up the strict marriage regulations for SS men, which included a "rigorous" racial inspection of the individual and his genealogy.[97] Like Rosenberg, however, Darré fell from grace, and was formally replaced as Reich Agriculture Minister in 1942 by Göring's subordinate Herbert Backe. Even before this date, Darré's adherence to a recrudescent, paganist–agrarian ethos was losing him influence.[98] It is perhaps no coincidence that Rosenberg's greatest adversary in the party, Erich Koch, would quickly emerge as one of Darré's staunchest opponents as well.[99]

Whereas Darré's works were primarily concerned with the secular past and future of the Nordic *Landvolk*, they did touch on religious elements as

---

[95] R. Walther Darré, *Das Bauerntum als Lebensquelle der Nordischen Rasse* (Munich, 1927). Like Kube and Reventlow, Darré defected from the DVFP, although with no discernible fanfare.

[96] R. Walther Darré, *Neuadel aus Blut und Boden* (Munich, 1930). Both books were published through the radical right-wing publisher Lehmanns Verlag, not through the NSDAP's own Eher Verlag.

[97] Anna Bramwell, *Blood and Soil: Richard Walther Darré and Hitler's 'Green Party'* (London, 1985), 90; Paul Weindling, *Health, Race and German Politics between National Unification and Nazism, 1870–1945* (Cambridge, 1989), 476. The attempt to turn the SS into a new aristocracy is a theme taken up in Herbert Ziegler, *Nazi Germany's New Aristocracy: The SS Leadership, 1925–1939* (Princeton, 1989).

[98] See Paul Weindling, "Understanding Nazi Racism: Precursors and Perpetrators," in Michael Burleigh (ed.), *Confronting the Nazi Past: New Debates on Modern German History* (New York, 1996), 76, who points to "the disillusion of Richard Walther Darré and Hans F. K. Günther as agrarian ideologists with the power of industrial lobbies in the Nazi State."

[99] Darré's conflict with Koch occurred almost immediately after the Seizure of Power, when Koch announced plans to industrialize his *Gau*, East Prussia. This horrified Darré, who tried to enforce his own vision of an agrarian East Prussia through his *Land* representatives. When they challenged Koch's authority, Koch had them arrested. The case was brought before Buch's party court, with the final decision going to Koch. Henceforth, regional peasant leaders were responsible to the *Gauleiter*, not to the Reich Peasant Leader (Darré): BAZ Personalakt Koch (1 August 1933: Keppurren); Institut für Zeitgeschichte (hereafter IfZ) Fa 199/15/9 (16 April 1934: Königsberg); BAZ Personalakt Koch (8 November 1934: Königsberg). This episode provided a paradoxical demonstration that industrialization and modernization could be supported by a strong Christian in the Nazi movement, whereas ideas of agrarianism and rural communalism were advanced by a professed anti-Christian.

well. In *Neuadel*, Darré stated his case rather plainly: "The conversion of the Teutons to Christianity, which means to the teaching of the anointed, deprived the Teutonic nobility of its moral foundations."[100] Darré believed that the doctrinal teaching of the equality of men before God robbed the settler race of the north of its innate sense of superiority over the nomadic tribes of the Near East. Their conversion was not the product of popular feeling, but was imported by the Franks and enforced by ruling kings for political reasons.[101] Darré attributed this same teaching to the destruction of the aristocratic structure of ancient civilization (even while he admitted that a new, Christian aristocracy emerged under the Franks).[102] Under Charlemagne, this new ruling class mercilessly destroyed the "old Germanic paganism" of the Saxons: Therefore Charlemagne could in no sense be considered "purely Germanic."[103] In *Bauerntum*, Darré reiterated the same essential arguments.[104]

In both works Darré referred to Christianity only in the larger context of peasant history: He did not address religious issues as such. No mention was made of Christ the Hero or Luther the German. In neither work did he make reference to Protestants or Catholics or positive Christianity: Nor did he recommend a reform of the Christian ethos. However, this should not lead us to presume that he was ready to dispose of Christianity altogether. Like Ludendorff and Rosenberg, Darré tempered his apparently unambiguous opposition to Christianity with an admiration for Protestantism. In a letter to his wife Alma, he declared the individual relationship to God found in Protestantism far more to his liking than the Catholic emphasis on clerical mediation, describing this theological breakthrough as the great achievement of the Reformation. He also pointed out that this preference for Protestantism was rooted in family history: His father's ancestors were French Huguenots who had migrated to Brandenburg some 250 years before; his mother came from Sweden, which Darré described as the land of the great Gustav Adolf, leader of the Protestants in the Wars of Religion.[105] According to Anna Bramwell, Darré belonged to that group of Nazis who "offered Northernness as the *best*, the most important part of the German heritage. In doing so, they excluded the Catholic parts of Germany, including the blonde, blue-eyed German Catholics....The Nordics preferred Protestantism to Catholicism, because Protestantism was seen as the Northern reaction

[100] Darré, *Neuadel*, 19.
[101] Ibid., 20.
[102] Ibid., 25, 27.
[103] Ibid., 30–1. Portrayals of Charlemagne as a foe of the German past, not a hero, were common among paganist Nazis. They rejected the historical title "Karl the Great" for the partisan "Karl the Saxon Slaughterer." Himmler, on adopting paganism in the 1930s, was a classic example of this: See Josef Ackermann, *Heinrich Himmler als Ideologe* (Göttingen, 1970), 56. Significantly, Hitler repudiated this trend and regarded Charlemagne as a great man of German history (see Chapter 4).
[104] Darré, *Bauerntum*, 345–7.
[105] IfZ Nachlaß Darré: ED 110/6/98–99 (27 October 1919: Witzenhausen).

to an alien Christianity, a move back to the purer, more individualistic spirit of the north."[106] Bramwell also mirrors the conceptual fallacies of the paganists she studies: By conflating anti-Catholicism with hostility to Christianity per se, she inexplicably leaves Protestantism outside the boundaries of Christianity.

A clear admiration for Protestantism was also discernible in the writings of two of the most reputed paganist "scholars": the racial anthropologist Hans F. K. Günther and the philosopher Alfred Bäumler. More than any other personality in German science, Günther lent a spurious sheen of empirical rigor to Nazi racialism, having written *Rassenkunde des deutschen Volkes* ("Racial Study of the German People") in 1922.[107] In this work, Günther perfected the classic Nazi cliché of racial superiority embodied in blond-haired, blue-eyed Nordicism. He attempted to define the Nordic race on the basis of Gobineau's theories of the previous century and wrote a flood of similar books in the 1920s detailing various aspects of his racial typology. He was a confrere of Darré and became so renowned in Nazi circles that in 1931 he was given a chair in social anthropology at the University of Jena in Thuringia, at the time the only state with a Nazi Minister of Education (Wilhelm Frick). By 1932, over 30,000 copies of *Rassenkunde* were sold.[108]

In a second work, *Rassenkunde Europas* ("Racial Study of Europe"), Günther mapped out the same racial typology for the entire continent. Here we see a seemingly undifferentiated attack on Christianity, which "in its origin and in the blood of its early followers . . . stood nearer to the Oriental standpoint than to the Nordic standpoint." He pointed out that, under Constantine, the first Christian emperor of Rome, foundling homes were built for the racially unfit: "In bringing up the blind, the deaf, the dumb, and the deformed, [such homes] also made their propagation possible."[109] By contrast, he held the Nordic myths of the Edda and the Niebelungen in high regard.[110] When he specified his critique, however, Catholicism became the actual target: "When the Roman Church through its political skill in the seventh century destroyed the Arian [heresy], a strong check on race mixture had gone."[111] When he turned his attention to Protestantism, the tone changed completely. Referring to the Huguenots, he claimed that "the Nordic man is Protestant by his disposition."[112] In a remarkable conflation of race and religion, he argued that "It is noteworthy that the temporary refuge of the Huguenots, the town of La Rochelle and its neighbourhood,

---

[106] Anna Bramwell, *Blood*, 42 (emphasis in the original).
[107] H. F. K. Günther, *Rassenkunde des deutschen Volkes* (Munich, 1922), published by the *völkisch* Lehmann Verlag.
[108] Weindling, *Health*, 312.
[109] H. F. K. Günther, *Rassenkunde Europas* (Munich, 1927), translated as *The Racial Elements of European History* (London, 1927), 191.
[110] Ibid., 193.
[111] Ibid., 205–6.
[112] Ibid., 219.

still strikes one today by the blondness of its people." More than making Protestantism the product of a racial condition, Günther indicated that adherence to Protestantism was itself a marker of Nordic superiority.

Like Günther, Alfred Bäumler bestowed academic legitimacy on the Nazis, in his case through philosophy. Along with Heidegger, Bäumler was the most notable philosopher to back the Nazi regime with his intellectual prestige. Unlike Heidegger, however, Bäumler maintained and indeed strengthened his links with the Nazis well into the Third Reich. Shortly after the Seizure of Power, he was appointed to a newly created chair in philosophy and political pedagogy at the University of Berlin. Present at the infamous book burning in Berlin's Opera Square in May 1933, he went so far as to deliver his inaugural lecture as a prelude to this event.[113] Bäumler served as a liaison man between Rosenberg and the German universities and shortly after war broke out became head of the Academic Division in Rosenberg's office. As Hans Sluga puts it, "Bäumler was... more than any other German philosopher, the typical fascist intellectual."[114]

Bäumler's greatest claim to fame was the nazification of Friedrich Nietzsche. Two years before the Seizure of Power, he wrote *Nietzsche the Philosopher and Politician*, which sought to cast him as the greatest intellectual forefather of Nazism. He emphasized the political style of Nietzsche's thought, the heroic "will to power" of the Nietzsche who had written: "The time for petty politics is over: the very next century will bring the fight for the dominion of the earth – the *compulsion* to large-scale politics."[115] In the process, Bäumler also undertook enormous distortions of Nietzsche's ideological substance, overlooking or negating the Nietzsche who emphasized the individual over the communal.[116] Regarding Nietzsche's contempt for antisemitism, Bäumler had a great deal of explaining away to do. As Steven Aschheim puts it, Bäumler insisted that Nietzsche's "philo-Semitic comments were an attention-getting device – playing the Jews against the Germans was part of his strategy to get the Germans to listen to him!"[117] His work in Rosenberg's office and general stature as a leading philosophical "radical" gained Bäumler considerable influence over Rosenberg. Whereas Rosenberg had made almost no mention of Nietzsche in his early works, his interest in Nietzsche would flourish in the Third Reich "under Baeumler's skillful tutelage."[118] Rosenberg in turn increasingly brought Bäumler into his confidence.

---

[113] Hans Sluga, *Heidegger's Crisis: Philosophy and Politics in Nazi Germany* (Cambridge, MA, 1993), 125.

[114] Ibid., 127.

[115] Quoted in Steven Aschheim, *The Nietzsche Legacy in Germany 1890–1990* (Berkeley, 1992), 234.

[116] Alfred Bäumler, *Nietzsche der Philosoph und Politiker* (Leipzig, 1931), 171–2.

[117] Ibid., 157, as cited in Aschheim, *Legacy*, 250–1.

[118] Sluga, *Heidegger's Crisis*, 224. See as well Rosenberg's assessment of Bäumler in a letter to Hess: IfZ MA 595 (6 November 1937: Berlin).

Bäumler not only overlooked Nietzsche's philo-Semitism, but his hostility to Christianity as well. Like all the paganists surveyed so far, Bäumler was an ardent admirer of Luther and the Reformation. Looking back to history as Himmler had done, in 1936 Bäumler published two articles in the Nazi periodical *Schulungsbrief* on the historical significance of the Reformation.[119] In them, he praised Luther as nothing less than the original German and the Reformation as the liberation of the German soul from Roman theocracy. Bäumler explicitly stated that Nietzsche had erred in condemning Luther: "His thesis on the role of the Reformation in German history is false."[120] Relating Luther to contemporary Protestantism, Bäumler wrote: "Protestantism is strong when it finds itself engaged in struggle, when it does what its name implies. It is strong when the heroic key of Luther, who mercilessly fought for God's Kingdom against the Devil's Kingdom, prevails in it. Outside the context of struggle Protestantism degenerates very quickly into brittle orthodoxy or effeminate pietism."[121] This criticism notwithstanding, Protestantism was more praised than pilloried: Protestant spirituality was about the inner soul, the personal. Protestantism returned a sense of honor to the worldly calling: "Work in the world is service to God." Unlike most paganists, however, Bäumler did not detach Protestantism from Christianity: In his view it was simply "the northern form of Christianity."[122] Luther was also praised as the pioneer of German racial self-awareness: "It is in this setting that his work 'On the Jews and their Lies' belongs."[123] As one Catholic party member would write in response to the article, "The Catholic Church is portrayed as alien, purely Roman and un-German. . . . If this really represents the official position of the party, then logically party members will have to leave the Catholic Church, or else whomever chooses to remain true to the church will be requested to leave the NSDAP."[124] As the case of Gauleiter Josef Wagner would later demonstrate, this was a very prescient observation (see Chapter 7).

Among the party leadership or ideological elite of the movement, there were no other paganists at this time. Whereas Heinrich Himmler would emerge as a committed paganist after the party came to power, he had yet to discover the mysticism and occultism for which he later became famous. Far from being anti-Christian, in Nazism's early years Himmler maintained a strong Catholic piety. In 1919, before he joined the party, Himmler wrote in his diary: "Come what may, I shall always love God, shall pray to Him, and shall remain faithful to the Catholic Church and shall defend it even

[119] Alfred Bäumler, "Der weltgeschichtliche Wendepunkt des Mittelalters," *Der Schulungsbrief* 3 (October–November 1936).
[120] Ibid., 391.
[121] Ibid., 395.
[122] Ibid., 429.
[123] Ibid., 397.
[124] IfZ MA 256 (n.d.[1936], n.p.)

if I should be expelled from it."[125] At this time he took great pleasure in attending church: Confession and communion were important for him.[126] According to Himmler's biographer, he had not seen the war that had just ended "as contradictory to the refining and spiritualization of cultured life and of Christian humanity."[127] He was particularly interested in the writings of Conrad von Bolanden, a Catholic apologist of the prior century whose real name was Joseph Bischoff, which he regarded as an "edifying hymn to Christianity." His only complaint about Bolanden's work was its negative attitude toward – Protestantism: "I doubt that the Protestant religion is so lacking in content.... On the contrary, it must have good ingredients, but Bolanden won't credit Protestantism with anything good. We should be happy when this grave division is healed."[128]

While Ludendorff was waging his war against Christianity, Himmler, who had by now joined the NSDAP and participated in Hitler's failed *putsch*, was still attending church. However, although he enjoyed church life, his attitude toward Catholicism began to change. His diary entries of 1923–4 criticized books on Catholicism that he read as "too doctrinaire" or "fanatical." Of the Jesuits he wrote: "It is now clearer to me than ever that it was a beneficial act of Bismarck's when he expelled the Jesuits."[129] He sympathetically related the experience of a fellow Catholic who, like himself, was involved in the *völkisch* movement: "He would like to confess but cannot believe in certain dogmas, thus [making confession] impossible. Yet he would like to, because he considers it cowardly to call the priest [only] at the moment of dying." Himmler added: "This is an exceedingly decent point of view."[130] Himmler had not yet abandoned Christianity. He attacked the anti-Christian tone of a book on scientific theory by Ernst Haeckel: "The section that...concerns his suppositions and attack on, and denial of, a personal God, is just terrible." Himmler also read Renan's *Life of Jesus* and enjoyed it, save for one major flaw: "Renan believed that Jesus was a Jew, and he is from all appearances a friend of the Jews." For Himmler, this was unacceptable: "However, he proves to me by his whole book that Jesus was no Jew, and that Christianity was and is the most important protest of the Aryans against the Jews, of good against evil."[131] These lines bear a striking similarity to Eckart's, Goebbels', and even Hitler's religious views. Although Himmler would later profess hatred for Christianity, his basic characterization of Jesus as the great antisemite would remain unaltered. Following the

---

[125] Quoted in Werner Angress and Bradley Smith, "Diaries of Heinrich Himmler's Early Years," *Journal of Modern History* 31 (1959), 271.

[126] Bradley Smith, *Heinrich Himmler: A Nazi in the Making, 1900–1926* (Stanford, 1971), 98.

[127] Josef Ackermann, "Heinrich Himmler: Reichsführer-SS," in Smelser and Zitelmann (eds.), *Elite*, 101.

[128] Smith, *Himmler*, 99.

[129] Ibid., 145.

[130] Angress and Smith, "Diaries," 218.

[131] Smith, *Himmler*, 145.

pattern of other Nazis who would end up pagan, Himmler the Catholic began to have high regard for Protestantism and accepted "without comment *völkisch* arguments identifying Protestantism with Germandom and reserved his wrath for Catholics."[132]

Perhaps puzzling in Himmler's diary is the reference to Ernest Renan, who – far outside the circle of German *völkisch* philosophy, a Frenchman rather than a German – is usually left out of the pantheon of proto-Nazis or intellectuals whom Nazis read. However, as Susannah Heschel has recently pointed out, particular racialist concepts that the Nazis would later extend, especially the notion of the "Aryan Christ," could first be found in Renan's writings.[133] It was the discipline of philology developed in Renan's time that had originally devised the very concept of Aryan. Notions of Aryan and Semitic, long associated with the Nazis' own racial categories, began as linguistic concepts invented by philologists in the middle of the nineteenth century. The discourse of Aryan and Semite first arose as an intellectual debate within Christianity, specifically from that school centered around Renan that "exchanged the particular for the general" in order to "restore the historical centrality of Christ."[134] What began in the nineteenth century as an academic attempt to assign essential characteristics to the ancient languages of the biblical era – meant as a way of discovering the place of Indo-European languages in Christianity's originating moment – became a way of assigning essential characteristics to the peoples who spoke them. Chamberlain's own conception of Christ's un-Jewishness, which he described by using racialist discourse, found its origin in this new discipline, of which Renan was a leading exponent.

Unlike Himmler, Rosenberg never credited Renan. However, the similarities between Rosenberg's and Renan's concepts are striking. In a manner to be directly copied by Rosenberg, Renan insisted that "real" Christianity had nothing to do with Judaism: "The special task of Jesus was to break with the Jewish spirit ... [Christianity's] completion will consist in returning to Jesus – certainly not in returning to Judaism."[135] Elsewhere Renan wrote with greater racialist overtones: "Originally Jewish to the core, Christianity over time rid itself of nearly everything it took from the race, so that those who consider Christianity to be the Aryan religion are in many respects correct." Renan stipulated furthermore that the genius of Christianity was expressed in only the European race. If Rosenberg insisted that Jesus became the "God of the Europeans," Renan had done so some sixty years before: "Christianity improved itself by moving farther and farther away from Judaism and seeing to it that the genius of the Indo-European race triumphed within its blossom." As he said in another context, in ways that paganists would mimic

[132] Ibid., 146.
[133] Susannah Heschel, *Abraham Geiger and the Jewish Jesus* (Chicago, 1998), 154–8.
[134] Maurice Olender, *Race, Religion and Philology in the Nineteenth Century*, trans. Arthur Goldhammer (Cambridge, MA, 1992), 15.
[135] Ernest Renan, *The Life of Jesus* (Boston, 1907), 418.

almost to the word: "The North alone created Christianity." Even Rosenberg's call for a "fifth Gospel" was strikingly close to Renan's conception: "I beheld before my eyes a fifth Gospel, torn but still legible."[136] Rosenberg's redemption of Christian charity and love, provided it upheld racial honor and rejected the Jewish God of destruction, was also to be found in the works of Renan, who insisted that these ideas "come more from our ancestors, pagans perhaps, than from the selfish David or the exterminator Jehu."[137] Nowhere did Rosenberg credit Renan for having originally authored these concepts: Undoubtedly his own philosophical pretensions would have prohibited him from acknowledging the unoriginality of his ideas, especially if they were found to originate in a Frenchman. At the very least, however, the proximity of Rosenberg's ideas with Renan's means that proof of paganist hostility to Christianity cannot be found in their Nordic mania, racialist Judeophobia, or call for a "fifth Gospel."

Lower down the ranks of the party could be found a cadre of paganists. One of the most prominent in the *Kampfzeit* NSDAP was Ernst Graf zu Reventlow. He had made a name for himself before the war as a radical nationalist journalist, whose attacks on the government earned him an entry into the inner circle of the Pan-German League.[138] A member of the DVFP after the war, he and Wilhelm Kube defected to the NSDAP in 1927. Although he was a notable in his own right, having come from an established family, he held no important office or position of power within the party. He was, however, the editor of the paganist newspaper *Reichswart*, which later served as a mouthpiece of the German Faith Movement (*Deutsche Glaubensbewegung*, or DGB), of which he also shared the leadership. This was not a Nazi newspaper, but it reflected the views of a small number in the party who, like Rosenberg, advocated a new religion. Reventlow called for equal status among Christian and non-Christian faiths, but he did not count himself as an active opponent of the churches. The year he switched over to Hitler, he wrote an article in his paper on "Politics and Confession," in which he pledged himself to Hitler's position of confessional neutrality. Along with Hitler, he formally rejected any notion that the *völkisch* movement should be engaging in a new *Kulturkampf*: "The Protestant and the Catholic hit each other over the head to the Jews' musical accompaniment."[139] According to a report in the *Augsburger Postzeitung*, Reventlow's article caused great indignation among the ranks of the DVFP, which, as Goebbels had pointed out, were guided by a Protestant sectarian ethos.[140]

---

[136] Quoted in Olender, *Languages*, 70–2.
[137] Quoted in ibid., 78.
[138] Geoff Eley, *Reshaping the German Right: Radical Nationalism and Political Change after Bismarck*, 2nd ed. (Ann Arbor, 1991), 112.
[139] *Reichswart*, 5 February 1927.
[140] *Augsburger Postzeitung*, 15 March 1927: in StAM PolDir/6687/63; Elke Fröhlich (ed.), *Die Tagebücher von Joseph Goebbels: Sämtliche Fragmente* (Munich, 1987), entry for 30 June 1924.

The other leader of the DGB – which was not actually founded until 1933 – was Jakob Hauer. Like Reventlow, he never came close to the leadership circles of the NSDAP; but this did not stop him from portraying his movement as the true religious expression of Nazism. He tried to gain such recognition in a letter he sent to Hitler, in which he requested public, legal recognition of his organization. He claimed that all segments of German society – workers and youth in particular – wanted "in the main not Christianity but rather a German faith." However, like Reventlow, he foresaw coexistence between his paganist faith and the preexisting confessions. He rejected a *Kulturkampf* and saw the German people organizing itself "into the three great religious domains:...Catholic Church...Protestant Church...and German Faith Community." All three were to work together in a "Religious Working Group of the German Nation."[141]

Consistent with the lingering attachment of Ludendorff, Rosenberg, and Darré, Hauer's movement – even while proclaiming itself non-Christian – exhibited an ambiguous attitude toward the Protestant faith. This was demonstrated in July 1933 in the formation of a collective *germanisch–deutsch* faith movement at the Wartburg, a site sacred to the memory of Martin Luther. Present for the ceremony were not only Reventlow and Hauer, but also Fritz von der Heydt, one of the directors of the Protestant League and a member of the National Socialist Pastor's Working Group.[142] In a memorandum sent to Hitler in August 1933, Hauer commented on the "Church Struggle" taking place in Protestantism between the DC and the progenitors of the Confessing Church. He had held out his hand to Protestantism, he wrote, stating that "either the Protestant church must widen itself into a religious *Volksgemeinschaft* of all non-Catholic Germans, or the creation of an independent German Faith community will be necessary." In Hauer's view, the DC had rejected his offer, and hence it was now essential to go forward with the DGB.[143]

Lines of social intersection between Protestants and paganists could be seen elsewhere in the ranks of the DGB. Hanno Konopath, a member of the Race and Culture Division in the Reich Leadership Office, was also the leader of the paganist "Nordic Ring," an association that predated the DGB and would later merge with it. He was slated to take over the administration of the German Christians from its cofounder, Wilhelm Kube, who, as leader of the NSDAP in the Prussian parliament, was too burdened with other responsibilities. However, it was soon discovered that he belonged to a "school of thought that even the most radical of Kube's group could no longer consider Christian." Soon afterward, leading figures in the DC, including Kube and Joachim Hossenfelder, had him ejected from his DC responsibilities. It was

---

[141] Quoted in Scholder, *Churches*, 1: 452.
[142] Bundesarchiv Potsdam (hereafter BAP), R5101/23139/52 (29–30 July 1933: Wartburg).
[143] BAZ NS 8/256/73 (24 August 1933: Tübingen). There is no evidence that Hitler responded to the letter.

reflective of the marginalized status of paganists in the NSDAP at this time that he was additionally deprived of all his party offices by the Buch's party court on "grounds of immorality."[144]

In Rosenberg's employ in the party could be found several expastors. One was Matthes Ziegler, one of Rosenberg's most important lieutenants after the Seizure of Power. Rosenberg engaged him as head of the Office of Ideological Information and editor of the internal party report, "Information on the State of Ideology." Before 1933 he, like Hauer, had been a Protestant theologian.[145] Another ex–pastor, Hubert Grabert, worked in the "Religious Studies" section of the Office.[146] These lines of intersection were more than coincidental. As Steven Aschheim observes, "A quite disproportionate percentage of those who articulated the various versions of [paganist] religion were Protestants or ex-Protestant pastors and theologians."[147] He accounts for this in a *fin de siècle* crisis within Protestantism, brought about by a Nietzschean "Death of God" in which these theologians attempted to overcome this crisis through the protean redemptive philosophy of Nietzsche, which ran its course in an "anti-Christian" Germanic faith.[148] However, although this may have accounted for Hauer's philosophy, it does not necessarily account for Nazi philosophy. Hitler had almost as little fondness for Nietzsche as he had for Ludendorff's and Rosenberg's ersatz religions. As became evident at a strained visit to Nietzsche's sister Elisabeth, Hitler was not at all an admirer of the philosopher.[149] In a conversation he held with Hans Schemm and Otto Wagener during the *Kampfzeit*, Hitler derided paganists and "the rubbish they dredge up from German prehistory! Then they read Nietzsche with fifteen-year-old boys."[150] Hitler's mentor Dietrich Eckart had rejected Nietzsche as early as 1917: "We Germans, who profess through and through our faith in the Christian worldview, reject this despiser of our religious foundations."[151] Even Rosenberg, in his *Mythus*, barely mentioned Nietzsche, and he showed little engagement with Nietzsche's

---

[144] Scholder, *Churches*, 1: 205–7.

[145] "Niederschrift der Unterredung des Herrn Professor Dr. habil. Wilhelm Brachmann," IfZ ZS 210 (29 October 1952: Munich). According to Brachmann, who also worked in the *Amt Rosenberg* after 1933, Ziegler returned to his pastoral occupation after 1945.

[146] BAP R5101/23141/137 (11 October 1937: Berlin).

[147] Steven Aschheim, *The Nietzsche Legacy in Germany, 1890–1990* (Berkeley, 1992), 230.

[148] Ibid. Aschheim avoids the common fallacy of ascribing this crisis to all Protestants. He shows how several Protestant theologians engaged with Nietzsche's thought without falling into apostasy (*Nietzsche*, 203–8).

[149] See Hans Sluga, *Heidegger's Crisis: Philosophy and Politics in Nazi Germany* (Cambridge, MA, 1993), 180. Sluga contends that a picture of Hitler looking at Nietzsche's bust on this visit shows "how little the Führer and the philosopher had to say to each other. The encounter is formal and silent, each of them remains quite evidently enclosed in his own world" (ibid., 186). According to Sluga, Hitler's real philosophical heroes were Schopenhauer and especially Richard Wagner, with whose politics Nietzsche violently disagreed.

[150] Henry Ashby Turner (ed.), *Hitler: Memoirs of a Confidant* (New Haven, 1985), 277.

[151] Margarete Plewnia, *Auf dem Weg zu Hitler: Der 'völkische' Publizist Dietrich Eckart* (Bremen, 1970), 45.

philosophy when he did. In comparison, Christian figures like Jesus, Luther, and Meister Eckhart received far greater attention.

CONCLUSION

Many of the paganists examined in this chapter were deeply concerned with discovering new forms of faith, new objects of veneration that they believed were more suitable to their times. In their search for a new dogma they adulated heroism over humility, racial distinctiveness over universalism. Other paganists, less concerned with mapping out a new *völkisch* doctrine, nonetheless articulated a racialist, mystical interpretation of the German past. Regardless of their different emphases, they refuted much that was central to Christian belief. However, theirs was only a partial rejection of Christianity. If their new religious system was meant as a replacement faith, a way of pouring new anti-Christian wine into old Christian bottles, the paganists demonstrated just how much old wine they were willing to retain in the process. By their own admission, that part of Christianity they most opposed was specifically "Roman." The institutional arrogance they decried was specifically "papal." Lutheranism, in its intent if not in its implementation, was often cast as the antidote; in contrast to Catholicism, it was national, personal, spiritual. Protestantism after Luther had taken a wrong turn down the road to freedom; but it was because "Rome" and "Judah" made it veer off course. Therefore the established Protestant clergy, because "Romanized," also had to be rejected. Protestantism's renewal would be contingent on a rejection of the Old Testament and much Christian dogma, but not on a rejection of Christ himself. These paganists upheld an image of Christ the fighter, Christ the antisemite. The only paganist to reject Christ – and the only paganist to be expelled from the Nazi Party – was Ludendorff.

On some occasions paganists seemed to deny simultaneously the validity of any kind of Christian teaching and then to demonstrate just how much of that teaching they still retained. On other occasions, paganists chose between what they revered and what they condemned. In other words, they seemed to oscillate between ambiguity and ambivalence. Such equivocation clearly precludes them from being considered Christian. However, it also precludes them from being anti-Christian. No single aspect of paganist doctrine – most obviously, but not exclusively, with regard to the Old Testament – constituted an attack on Christianity as such. The elements that made up this doctrine could all, in one form or another, be found within Christian theological departures that *preceded* the paganists themselves. Hotly anticlerical they were certainly known to be; but anticlericalism cannot be conflated with hatred of the religion clerical institutions claim to represent.[152] At a more immediate level, paganists themselves could temper their anticlericalism in

---

[152] See, for instance, the special issue of *European Studies Review* on the subject: René Rémond (ed.), "Special Issue: Anticlericalism," *European Studies Review* 13 (1983).

surprising and revealing ways. The only solid empirical evidence we have that the paganists hated Christianity *in toto* is their professions to this effect, fraught with such ambiguity and even contradiction as to make them far from conclusive.

It could be argued that any attempt to create a new religion in Germany would have had to appropriate Luther in some way. However, if the paganist agenda was to create a new national religion that would replace Christianity in Germany, Luther and the sectarian divide his name evoked for the country's Catholics (who comprised approximately half the German population after 1938) would have been precisely the wrong symbol for their purposes. Rather, such an appropriation revealed just how reliant on Protestantism paganist thought was. Regardless of the considerable accommodation that paganists provided for Protestantism, the positive Christians of the party did not welcome their attack on established Christianity. Before the Seizure of Power, most other Nazis regarded paganist mysticism as laughable. Paganists certainly constituted a bona fide segment of Nazi opinion, and indeed a few acquired real power after 1933. However, if they comfortably resided in the party, it was because they contributed to it in other ways, not because their religious beliefs were hegemonic. Although the conflict between Christianity and paganism in the movement would give rise to considerable factionalism between Nazis, the highest paganist hopes for recognition were never achieved.

4

NATIONAL RENEWAL

Religion and the New Germany

When I hear that a 'Germanic wedding' is to be celebrated, I have to ask: my God, what do you understand to be a Germanic wedding? What do you understand to be National Socialism?

Hermann Göring[1]

1933 was an important year in both secular and sacred terms. Ten years after the failed Beer Hall Putsch, the Nazis' legal path to power finally bore fruit. Without breaking a law, Hitler and his movement achieved their Third Reich. For some members in the movement, this was a time to "unite" the country; for others, the revolution was just beginning. 1933 was also a momentous year for Christian Germany. The years of Weimar had been marked by a growing loss of church membership, especially for the Protestant churches. In a movement known as *Kirchenaustritt*, approximately 200,000 people a year had formally rescinded their membership in their Protestant Church since the mid-1920s, whereas approximately 50,000 a year had joined. In 1933, however, the rate of church leaving plummeted to a little over 50,000 whereas the number joining the churches skyrocketed to almost 325,000.[2] There could have been no clearer sign that national renewal and religious renewal were believed to be deeply connected. As Margaret Anderson has pointed out, for nineteenth-century German Catholics, religious revival could stimulate and facilitate political mobilization. In a similar process, millions of German Protestants, who were so overrepresented in the Nazi electorate, saw in the Seizure of Power a return to Christianity; for many of them, the Nazi Party served as a Protestant Center Party, achieving a longed-for rallying together of Protestants in a unitary *Volkspartei*.[3]

[1] *Positives Christentum*, 3 November 1935.

[2] Rita Thalmann, *Protestantisme et nationalisme en Allemagne de 1900 à 1945* (Paris, 1976), 37.

[3] See Margaret Lavinia Anderson, "Voter, *Landrat*, Junker, Priest: The Old Authorities and the New Franchise in Imperial Germany," *American Historical Review* 98 (1993), 1448–74. On the role of Protestantism in the rise of the Nazi movement, see Wolfram Pyta, *Dorfgemeinschaft und Parteipolitik, 1918–1933: Die Verschränkung von Milieu und Parteien in den protestantischen Landgebieten Deutschlands in der Weimarer Republik* (Düsseldorf, 1996); Richard

The Nazis raised certain expectations about their commitment to Christianity while a movement: How did this compare with their policies as a state? Did the paganists of the movement rise to hegemonic dominance in the party? Did the "regime" phase of Nazism betray an anti-Christian agenda hidden from view during the "movement" phase?

Lines of continuity between the *Kampfzeit* and the first years of the Third Reich were considerable. The basic contours of religious affiliation remained unchanged, even as new voices were added on either side: most important, Hermann Göring's and Wilhelm Frick's among the positive Christians, Heinrich Himmler's and Reinhard Heydrich's among the anti-Christians. The intersections of religious and secular identities remained as complex as before. Even on public occasions, the positive Christians did not pretend that the churches would be equal partners with the new state. They left no doubt that the state and the *Volk* held absolute priority over any one church or confession. At the same time, these party leaders maintained that the new state's practical policies were the fruit born of Point 24 of the Party Program. On the other side, some paganists rose to prominence. These Nazis were strikingly honest about their dislike of the Christian religion. Even though the public ideology of the Nazis after 1933 is usually regarded as nothing if not opportunistic, "paganist" Nazis refused to pose as Christians for propaganda purposes. They rejected making pious allusions to the Bible for the sake of public consumption and were quite open about their own religious agendas. However, in spite of the personal power that individual paganists accrued, their ambitions to project their religious platform on the party were rebuffed. Within the party, positive Christians showed no sign of losing power to the paganists on the issue of religious affiliation. Both retained their adherents and relative strengths, even as the paganists made persistent efforts to gain hegemony.

PRACTICING AN "ACTIVE" FAITH

On 1 February 1933, two days after the Seizure of Power, Hitler addressed the German nation as Reich Chancellor for the first time. His first words were: "We are determined, as leaders of the nation, to fulfill as a national government the task which has been given to us, swearing fidelity only to God, our conscience, and our *Volk*." Later in the speech, Hitler proclaimed: "Thus the national government will regard its first and foremost duty to restore the unity of spirit and purpose of our *Volk*. It will preserve and defend the foundations upon which the power of our nation rests. It will take Christianity, as the basis of our collective morality, and the family as the nucleus of our *Volk* and state, under its firm protection." After outlining the agenda of the new government – the defeat of Communism, compulsory

Steigmann-Gall, "Apostasy or Religiosity? The Cultural Meanings of the Protestant Vote for Hitler," *Social History* 25 (2001), 267–84.

labor service, return to the land, and an aggressive new foreign policy – the speech ended once more on a pious note: "May God Almighty take our work into his grace, give true form to our will, bless our insight, and endow us with the trust of our *Volk*."[4]

Always insistent that actions meant more than words, the Nazi State began to implement an ideological agenda it had outlined in the *Kampfzeit*. This was positive Christianity turned into "active" Christianity. As Goebbels put it in speech from 1935, "A verbal confession cannot suffice; we require an active confession. Christianity to us is no empty form, but rather a continual action."[5] On 23 March 1933, the day the Enabling Law was passed, Hitler addressed the new Reichstag for the first time, touching on two themes simultaneously – the Christian comportment of the new state and the need for the churches to conform to that state:

The national government sees in the two Christian confessions the most important factors for the preservation of our nationality. It will respect the treaties concluded between them and the states; their rights shall not be violated. But the government expects and hopes that the work on the national and moral renewal of our *Volk* which it has made its task will, on the other hand, be equally respected.... The struggle against a materialistic conception of the world and for the production of a true Peoples' Community serves both the interests of the German nation and our Christian faith.[6]

This speech had its political uses, for instance, helping to secure the Center Party's endorsement of the Enabling Law.[7] Indeed, most church historians have noted the frequency of Hitler's religious intonations in the year of the Seizure of Power with great skepticism.[8] The "Potsdam Day" of 21 March 1933, when the new Reichstag was opened with a state ceremony in the Protestant Garrison Church, replete with numerous religious services, is regarded by Klaus Scholder as a "masterpiece of propaganda."[9] Another

[4] Max Domarus (ed.), *Hitler: Reden und Proklamationen 1932–1945*, 2 vols. (Würzburg, 1962–64), 1: 191–4.
[5] *Völkischer Beobachter* (hereafter VB), 5 August 1935.
[6] Carsten Nicolaisen (ed.), *Dokumente zur Kirchenpolitik des Dritten Reiches*, 3 vols. (Munich, 1971–94), 1: 23–4.
[7] See, for example, Rudolf Morsey, *Die Protokolle der Reichstagsfraktion und des Fraktionsvorstandes der deutschen Zentrumspartei 1926–1933* (Mainz, 1970), 627 ff. Klaus Scholder contends that the Center voted for the Enabling Law, and its own extinction, in return for Nazi assurances of a Concordat with the Vatican: *The Churches and the Third Reich*, 2 vols. (London, 1987–8), 1: 244–8.
[8] See, inter alia, Conway, *The Nazi Persecution of the Churches* (London, 1968), 20; Georg Denzler and Volker Fabricius, *Christen und Nationalsozialisten: Darstellung und Dokumente* (Frankfurt a.M, 1993), 59–60. Günter Brakelmann notes that Hitler made more references to Christianity in his public speeches than did any other chancellor since 1918: See his "Nationalprotestantismus und Nationalsozialismus," in Christian Jansen et al. (eds.), *Von der Aufgabe der Freiheit: Politische Verantwortung und bürgerliche Gesellschaft im 19. und 20. Jahrhundert* (Berlin, 1995), 338.
[9] Scholder, *Churches*, 1: 225. Scholder also refers to the occasion as the "Fraud of Potsdam."

authority contends that Hitler's affirmation of Christianity in his public speeches marked a "policy of studied duplicity which characterized his government's attitude toward religion from the start.... behind the scenes [he was] craftily planning the utter annihilation of the Christian faith."[10] Such an argument entirely overlooks the private views Hitler had enunciated during the *Kampfzeit*. Although the famous image of Hitler obsequiously shaking Hindenburg's hand at the end of the ceremony was an obvious deceit, there is no evidence that Hitler's religious expressions were likewise deceptive. Even though Scholder takes a cynical view of Potsdam Day, he concedes that "It is too simple to see all this as no more than a National Socialist propaganda show."[11]

In a speech celebrating Germany's exit from the League of Nations, Hitler again maintained that the Third Reich was actively implementing a Christian agenda: "Along with the fight for a purer morality we have taken upon ourselves the struggle against the decomposition of our religion.... We have therefore taken up the struggle against the Godless movement, and not just with a few theoretical declarations; we have stamped it out. And above all we have dragged the priests out of the lowlands of the political party struggle and have brought them back into the church."[12] This declaration was quite consistent with Hitler's speeches earlier in the year and also with the basic attitude he laid out – privately as well as publicly – in the "time of struggle." Insisting that Nazism as a *state* would not distinguish between Protestant and Catholic, he recognized only a common supra-Christian faith. True to his promise, Hitler defended Christianity against the "Godless" movement, outlawing the Socialist and the Communist parties very early after the Seizure of Power. In exchange for remaining "above churches," Hitler expected the churches to remain "above politics" and quite openly attacked the "meddling" of priests in parliamentary politics. However, this attack was not aimed at both confessions equally: the political engagement of Catholic priests by means of the Center Party was being attacked here,[13] not the political engagement of Protestant pastors, who, after the Seizure of Power as before it, frequently could be counted among the members of the NSDAP.

In the *Kampfzeit*, Hitler had insisted that the Nazi fight against the Jew accorded with Christian values. In the Third Reich, he maintained that these values were now being put into practice. In a reception for Catholic Bishop Berning on 26 April 1933, Hitler freely conceded: "I have been attacked because of my handling of the Jewish question." However, he immediately tied his attitude toward the Jews with the church's historical position: "The Catholic Church considered the Jews pestilent for fifteen hundred years, put

---

[10] Gilmer Blackburn, "The Portrayal of Christianity in the History Textbooks of Nazi Germany," *Church History* 49 (1980), 433.

[11] Scholder, *Churches*, 1: 226–7.

[12] *Dokumente zur Kirchenpolitik*, 1: 166.

[13] The reference was to article 32 of the Concordat with the Vatican, which specifically prohibited Catholic clergymen from engaging in political activity (ibid., 166, 198).

them in ghettos, etc, because it recognized the Jews for what they were." Hitler suggested that the antisemitic legislation being taken was in line with Christian principle: "I recognize the representatives of this race as pestilent for the state and for the church and perhaps I am thereby doing Christianity a great service by pushing them out of schools and public functions."[14] The strategic usefulness of such a statement – to disarm possible criticism of Nazi antisemitism from Catholic quarters – is self-evident. However, there is again no direct evidence that Hitler did not believe what he said on this occasion.

In a speech at the Ehrenbreitstein fortress in Koblenz on 26 August 1934, Hitler directly addressed the tensions that were already beginning to emerge between the party and certain sections of the clerical establishment:

There has been no interference, nor will there be any, with the teachings or religious freedom of the confessions. To the contrary, the state protects religion, though always under the condition that that it will not be used as a disguise for political purposes. . . . I know that there are thousands of priests who are not merely reconciled with the present state, but who gladly cooperate with it. . . . Where can our interests be more convergent than in our struggle against the symptoms of degeneracy in the contemporary world, in our struggle against cultural bolshevism, against the Godless movement, against criminality, and for a social conception of community, for the conquest of class war and class hatred, or civil war and unrest, strife and discord. These are not anti-Christian, but rather Christian principles![15]

Here Hitler affirmed the view he put forward before the Seizure of Power that "we intend to raise the treasures of the living Christ!"[16] Throughout the first years of the Third Reich, Hitler continued to maintain that the Nazi State was limiting the power of the clergy on the one hand and bringing Christianity into effect on the other. He enunciated such views *privately* as well. As late as February 1937, at a closed meeting of his immediate circle, Hitler spoke of the rift that by then had widened significantly with the churches. "Not party versus Christianity," Goebbels noted him as saying, "rather, we must declare ourselves as the only true Christians. . . . Christianity is the watchword for the destruction of the [Confessing Church] pastors, as once was socialism for the destruction of the marxist bigwigs." This is not merely a conspiratorial Hitler adapting a Christian mantle to better undercut and attack clerical enemies, although such considerations played a role. Rather, this was the same attempt to claim ownership of a "true" Christianity – one that had been corrupted by later interlopers – as was evident in the *Kampfzeit*. Hitler's comparison of Christianity and socialism is particularly revealing on this point: "The Führer on Christianity and Christ. [Christ] was also against Jewish world

[14] Quoted in Saul Friedländer, *Nazi Germany and the Jews: The Years of Persecution, 1933–1939* (New York, 1997), 47.
[15] *VB*, 28 August 1934.
[16] Henry Ashby Turner (ed.), *Hitler: Memoirs of a Confidant* (New Haven, 1985), 139–40 (emphasis in the original).

domination. Jewry had him crucified. But Paul falsified his doctrine and undermined ancient Rome. The Jew in Christianity. Marx did the same with the German sense of community, with socialism. That must not prevent us from being socialists."[17] Nor, Goebbels implies, must Paul prevent them from being Christian. Just as a "pure" socialism could be redeemed from a "Jewish" or Marxist corruption, so could a pure Christianity be redeemed from a Jewish or Pauline corruption. For Hitler, Nazism represented not only the antithesis of these later defilements, but the defense of the original forms.

Many of these themes were echoed by others in the Nazi leadership, notably Hermann Göring. Göring played a very minor role in expounding Nazi ideology before 1933, but there were significant, if fleeting, indicators from the *Kampfzeit* that he considered himself to be a religious Protestant. When defending the Nazi Party's refusal to commit to paganism in a letter to the Tannenberg League, Gregor Strasser pointed out that many members of the party's leadership were known Protestants; along with the outspokenly Protestant Walter Buch and Wilhelm Frick, Strasser named Göring.[18] In 1930, when the Protestant League was considering political cooperation with the Nazis, Wilhelm Fahrenhorst, the head of the League, wrote to Göring to determine the NSDAP's ideological relationship to Protestantism.[19]

In a speech he gave on 12 November 1933, Göring picked up on the themes Hitler had sounded earlier that year, but with greater stridency: "In our ten year struggle we have changed the people, that they would no longer be republicans or monarchists, Catholics or Protestants, but Germans.... He who would violate this unity of the *Volk* betrays the entire nation! Neither the red rats nor the black moles shall ever rule over Germany."[20] The reference to the Catholic clergy as "black moles" corresponds (albeit with greater vituperation) with Hitler's reference to "political priests," but the Protestant clergy are left unmaligned. Nor does Göring's reference to "German" replacing "Catholic" and "Protestant" suggest a fundamental antagonism to Christianity. In a 1935 speech, Göring upheld positive Christianity: "We have told the churches that we stand for positive Christianity. Through the zeal of our faith, the strength of our faith, we have once again shown what faith means, we have once again taken the *Volk*, which believed in nothing, back to faith." In the same speech, he attacked the party's paganists with unmistakable derision:

Naturally there are always people at work who represent a type of provocateur, who have come to us because they imagine National Socialism to be something other than it is, who have all kinds of fantastic and confused plans, who misunderstand

[17] Elke Fröhlich (ed.), *Die Tagebücher von Joseph Goebbels: Sämtliche Fragmente* (Munich, 1987), entry for 23 February 1937.

[18] Bundesarchiv Berlin-Zehlendorf (hereafter BAZ), NS 22/1069 (28 November 1930: Munich).

[19] BAZ NS 12/638 (20 December 1930: Berlin). Göring was at this point not yet the "number two man" in the Nazi movement. Göring suggested that Fahrenhorst get in touch with Schemm, describing him as the party's spokesman on religious questions.

[20] *Kreuzzeitung*, 12 November 1933: in Bundesarchiv Potsdam (hereafter BAP), 62 Di 1/106/105.

National Socialist racial thought and overstate their declaration to blood and soil [*Blut und Boden*], and who in their romantic dreams are surrounded by Wotan and Thor and the like. Such exaggerations can harm our movement, since they make the movement look ridiculous, and ridiculousness [*Lächerlichkeit*] is always something most harmful. When I hear that a 'Germanic wedding' is to be celebrated, I have to ask: my God, what do you understand to be a Germanic wedding? What do you understand to be National Socialism?[21]

That year Göring demonstrated his disdain for paganist weddings by marrying his second wife, Emmy, in a Lutheran service officiated by Reich Bishop Müller. He would also give his daughter Edda a Lutheran baptism, much to the chagrin of paganists and those who had left the church.[22] Göring had delivered almost the same speech in Breslau a week before, at a party leadership meeting, but on this occasion combined his attack on paganism with an attack on Rosenberg: "When it is maintained today that we spread an anti-Christian ideology, with reference made to certain writings, then I must reply: No! We National Socialists know only one fundamental work and it is called: Adolf Hitler's *Mein Kampf*! Nothing else is official."[23] Some years later, Göring complained in private that if Rosenberg had had his way, there would be "only cult, *Thing*, myth, and that sort of swindle."[24]

On another occasion, in which he explained the expulsion of Catholic civil servants from the government, Göring affirmed the Christian connection, signaling an adherence to the theology of the orders of creation (*Schöpfungsglaube*): "When the churches assert that first come they, and then the *Volk*, then we must say that God did not create the German person as Catholic or Protestant: He gave him his soul in a German body with German blood. . . . The National Socialist state does not ask whether the civil servant is Catholic. No one has had their post taken away because they confessed the Catholic faith – but there was a time when Catholic officials were members of the Center Party."[25] In other words, only "political Catholics" were expelled. There was no comparable concern expressed for Protestant officials. This was due in part to the fact that the Nazis could not yet dispense with "at least partial agreement with traditional conservative values and their spokesmen" entrenched in the civil service, army, and other sections of the established ruling classes.[26] However, it was also due to an adherence

---

[21] *Positives Christentum*, 3 November 1935: in BAP 62 Di 1/106/113.

[22] Many letters of complaint were written by low-ranking paganistic Nazis, expressing varied levels of dismay, all of them addressed to Rosenberg. See Leon Poliakov and Josef Wulf (eds.), *Das Dritte Reich und seine Denker* (Munich, 1978), 211–17.

[23] *VB*, 28 October 1935: in BAP 62 Di 1/106/125. See also "Aus der Breslauer Rede des Ministerpräsidenten Göring am 26. Oktober 1935": BAP R5101/20.

[24] Fröhlich (ed.), *Tagebücher*, entry for 13 April 1937. *Thing* refers to the "Thing" places, sites set up by Nordic paganists for their religious ceremonies.

[25] *Kölnische Volkszeitung*, 29 June 1934: in Bayerisches Hauptstaatsarchiv (hereafter BStA), Presseausschnittssammlung 929.

[26] Martin Broszat, *The Hitler State: The Foundation and Development of the Internal Structure of the Third Reich* (London, 1981), 233.

Fig. 8 Joseph Wagner (left), the
only *Gauleiter* to have two
separate *Gaue*, with Wilhelm
Frick (right), Reich Interior
Minister and most important
"state" Nazi in the first years of
the Third Reich.
(SV-Bilderdienst)

to Protestantism. In a meeting of the Prussian state council the same month, Göring addressed the conflict taking place in Protestantism between the German Christians (DC) and the Confessing Church (*Bekennende Kirche*, or BK). He hoped that they could overcome their disagreements, otherwise "the leading role of the Protestant Church would be denied to Germany – which up until now has counted as the leading Protestant country, from which the ideas and beliefs of Luther flowed over the world."[27]

Like Göring, Wilhelm Frick was not a notable spokesman of Nazi ideology in the *Kampfzeit*, although he served as the NSDAP caucus leader in the Reichstag. More importantly, he was the first party member to hold governmental power before the Third Reich, serving as state interior minister and culture minister for Thuringia. His governmental experience led Hitler to appoint him as Reich Interior Minister, making him the most important "state Nazi" immediately after the Seizure of Power (*Machtergreifung*). At a party convention in Thuringia in 1935 Frick affirmed that "the party stands for positive Christianity. The National Socialist state is absolutely ready to work with the Christian churches, but the solidarity of the churches to the *Volk* must be a matter of course; that means that the churches must feel bound to the *Volk* and may never come into opposition to the National Socialist leadership of the state."[28] This was again a call for the churches to remain "above politics." In accord with the "above churches" aspect of positive Christianity, Frick, like Göring, lamented the existence of "confessional"

[27] *Dokumente zur Kirchenpolitik*, 2: 140.
[28] *Deutsche Allgemeine Zeitung* (hereafter *DAZ*), 2 June 1935.

public servants. In a speech to the *Gau* leadership of Münster in 1935 he proclaimed: "We National Socialists demand a full deconfessionalization of all public life." But as Frick immediately demonstrated, confessional principally meant Catholic: "Does it still make sense to have a Catholic civil servant association? We want only German civil servants. Or does it make any sense to have a Catholic press?"[29] However, whereas "confessionalism" could not be tolerated when it was Catholic, it was quite a different matter when the confession was Protestant. In his Thuringia speech, Frick stated: "I can State with pleasure that exactly in the state of Thuringia the Protestant State Church has acknowledged this *Volk* solidarity."[30] Frick was himself a member of the Protestant Church, and as Reich Interior Minister had jurisdiction over the affairs of the Protestant Church until the creation of the Reich Church Ministry in 1935.

Particularly in the field of education, positive Christians demonstrated a commitment to turning the ideological pronouncements of the *Kampfzeit* into tangible policy. The *Völkischer Beobachter* (*VB*) announced Bernhard Rust's appointment as Prussian Minister of Education and Culture (*Kultus*) under the headline "Our Confession of Christianity: Education Minister Rust on his Task." Taking up the nonconfessional theme of positive Christianity, Rust declared: "In the 150-year Wars of Religion we were, as a Reich and *Volk*, almost destroyed. Today we stand in a bitter struggle for existence against Bolshevism. I appeal to the Christian churches of both confessions to join with us against this enemy in defense of their living values of belief and morality."[31] Rust reiterated these themes in another speech on 23 February 1933, inviting the churches of both confessions "to cooperation against the Godless movement."[32] Rust backed up his claim two days later, actually ordering teachers who had left their church to return to religious schools of their original confession.[33] He ordered as well that religious instruction be introduced to trade schools and that the number of secular schools be reduced, "in order to prevent the return of paganism."[34] On the subject of paganism Rust's tone became distinctly negative. In a speech of July 1934, he stated: "We have not fought to build a paganistic temple, but to unite the German *Volk* for all eternity. We do not build temples against the Christian church, we do not want Valhalla as a substitute for a Christian heaven."[35] Through his later fights with Rosenberg, Rust would prove that he indeed had little sympathy for paganism. He even found the variety of Christianity propagated by Arthur Dinter, Nazism's erstwhile "second Luther," unacceptable.

[29] *VB*, 8 July 1935.
[30] *Dokumente zur Kirchenpolitik*, 2: 310.
[31] *VB*, 9 February 1933. *DAZ* published an article on Rust's appointment with the title "Christlichnationaler Wahlblock," 7 February 1933: in BAP R5101/23138/6.
[32] *VB*, 24 February 1933.
[33] *Dokumente zur Kirchenpolitik*, 1: 5.
[34] *Nationalsozialistische Erziehung*, 15 April 1933: in BAZ NS 12/8.
[35] *Das Evangelische Deutschland*, 1 July 1934: in BAP 62 Di 1/106/263.

In December 1935 Rust ordered that no members of Dinter's *Deutsche Volk-skirche* sect would be allowed to sit on school boards. He additionally prohibited them and others of the "same line" from engaging in Protestant religious instruction.[36]

On 28 March 1933, twelve days after taking office as Bavarian *Kultus-minister*, Hans Schemm laid out the official policy of his ministry: "It is henceforth the goal of the Education Ministry that every child in Bavarian schools shall be made familiar with the principles of the Christian and national state. . . . Religious instruction is nothing other than service to the soul of children. Faith in God and the personality of the teacher must be expressed in a realistic instruction filled with religious sincerity."[37] When Hitler created a Reich Education Ministry in 1934, Schemm lost to Rust in his bid to lead it.[38] Nonetheless, Schemm was just as committed as Rust to putting Christian words into action. On 26 April, he formally restored obligatory religious instruction and student participation in church festivities.[39] In June, Schemm again acted according to these convictions, ordering that sporting activities were not to be held on Sunday mornings in order to accommodate church services. Leaders of all youth groups were to make necessary arrangements for students under their supervision.[40] The Nazi *Kultusminister* of Baden, in a confidential June 1933 letter to Frick, fully endorsed Schemm's enforcement of compulsory religious instruction.[41]

After the *Machtergreifung*, as before it, Schemm never publicly declared that Protestantism was to be favored by the Nazis. However, a telling episode revealed that behind the stated confessional neutrality of Schemm's positive Christianity still stood an agenda designed to protect Protestant interests. In February 1935 the Reich Governor of Bavaria, Franz Ritter von Epp, received an anonymous letter of complaint about anti-Christian actions being taken in the schools. That year, Schemm ordered that the new school year would begin on 24 April, which was also Ash Wednesday. The first Sunday of the

---

[36] *Germania*, 8 December 1935: in BAP 62 Di 1/71/91.

[37] *Dokumente zur Kirchenpolitik*, 1: 28–9. Schemm reiterated these points in a document written in late June 1933, when the NSDAP no longer needed to court the political favor of the Reichstag's Christian parties: "Die wichtigeren Massnahmen des Bayer. Staatsministeriums für Unterricht und Kultus seit der nationalen Erhebung. Gegenwärtige Aufgaben und Probleme," BAZ NS 12/8 (27 June 1933: Bayreuth).

[38] Hitler's confidant Otto Wagener believed Schemm was easily the more qualified candidate. According to him, the Reich education portfolio was originally intended for Schemm: "But instead of Schemm came Rust, who was indeed a man of education, but *only* that: he had no geniality, no instinct, no creative talent." Wagener suggested that Rust was appointed to appease the "reactionary" members of Hitler's coalition, but in fact Rust was a long-standing Nazi who never left his office, as conservative ministers did, with the progress of *Gleichschaltung*. Institut für Zeitgeschichte (hereafter IfZ), ED 60/7 (n.d., n.p.) (emphasis in the original). The book made from Wagener's recollections, *Memoirs of a Confidant*, leaves out this passage.

[39] Evangelisches Zentralarchiv in Berlin (hereafter EZA), 50/420/8 (7 June 1933: Karlsruhe).

[40] *Dokumente zur Kirchenpolitik*, 1: 54.

[41] EZA 50/420/8 (7 June 1933: Karlsruhe).

school year would therefore fall on the Pentecost (Whitsun). The author asked the following question: "How are the final preparations for the first communicants possible, when the children are kept in school the entire day?... Such an order... arouses deep indignation in the entire Catholic population." The author suggested that this made a mockery of the party's positive Christian platform: "[Schemm states] 'We stand on the foundation of Christianity', but it does not occur to him to respect Catholic celebrations, as he simply eliminates our beautiful holidays without consulting pope or bishops, while Catholics, on the other hand, have to keep the *Buß- und Bettag*. Which Catholic celebrations must the Protestants keep?"[42] Citing disturbing trends in government practice, the complainant did not look to atheism or paganism to explain this anti-Catholic behavior: "It is not enough that only Protestants obtain leading posts in the *Kultus* department, apparently on principle – now Protestants have been appointed as principals in the old and new grammar schools [*Gymnasien*] in Würzburg, even though at both institutions there are almost no Protestant students, so that in Würzburg all the higher institutions of learning are headed by Protestants."[43] This complainant could have pointed to Schemm himself, who had the distinction of being Bavaria's first ever Protestant *Kultusminister*.

Catholic positive Christians, whose new state authority would allow them to turn their anticlericalism into policy, insisted that they and their movement were nonetheless Christian. Joseph Goebbels showed no diminution of his religious convictions. Speaking as Reich Propaganda Minister in March 1934, Goebbels alluded to the "practical" Christianity that the Nazi State was now putting into effect: "When today a clique accuses us of having anti-Christian opinions, I believe that the first Christian, Christ himself, would discover more of his teaching in our actions than in this theological hair-splitting."[44] The following month, Goebbels contended that churches should be thankful that "National Socialism preserved them from the assault of atheists and Bolsheviks.... A government which last winter spent 320 Million Marks for the poorest of the *Volk* need provide no further evidence of its Christian convictions."[45]

In a speech on December 1935, Goebbels argued that practical measures to build the *Volksgemeinschaft* demonstrated that the Nazi State was Christian rather than paganist: "Is it paganist to mount a winter relief drive, thereby feeding millions of people? Is it paganist to give back the *Volk* its inner freedom? Is it paganist to help poor brothers and neighbors? Is it paganist to restore the ethos of the family? And to give the worker a sense of purpose to his life? Is it paganist to erect a state upon moral principles, to expel

---

[42] The "Buß- und Bettag" is a Protestant day of repentance and prayer held in November, and is considered the functional equivalent of the Catholic All-Saints Day. As a religious holiday unique to Germany, it has no English translation.

[43] BStA Epp/644/5 (12 February 1935: Würzburg).

[44] EZA 50/428/47 (2 March 1934: Hamburg).

[45] EZA 50/428/47 (25 April 1934: Düsseldorf).

Godlessness, to purify theater and film from the contamination of Jewish–
liberal Marxism – is that *paganist*?"[46] The theme of practical Christianity implicit in Goebbels' expression "Christ Socialists" was still apparent
eight years later: the return to morality; the sanctity of the family; brotherly
love toward fellow *Volksgenossen*; the conquest of godlessness and Judeo–
Bolshevism. This is especially evident in his reference to the Winter Relief Drive (*Winterhilfswerk*, or WHW), an example of "active Christianity"
in which both the Nazi State and the Christian churches were involved.[47]
"If *that* is paganist," Goebbels concluded, "then to be sure we are grateful to a Christianity that has done the contrary!"[48] The private Goebbels
demonstrated the sincerity of these sentiments, summarizing his disdain for
Nazism's leading paganist in his reference to him as "Almost Rosenberg":
"Rosenberg almost managed to become a scholar, a journalist, a politician –
but only almost."[49]

Like Goebbels, the nominally Catholic Julius Streicher acquired a reputation in the Third Reich as a vituperative anticlerical; and, like Goebbels,
he insisted that this did not make him an enemy of Christianity. In a 1937
edition of the *Stürmer*, the antisemitic newspaper he edited, Streicher praised
Christianity to the extent of attacking his own anti-Christian colleagues in
the party. Far from an alien faith that Nazism had to combat, Christianity
was "one of the greatest anti-Jewish movements." Neither Jesus nor the dis-
ciples were Jewish, save the betrayer Judas: "The crucifixion of Christ is the
greatest ritual murder of all time." Streicher also faulted the churches with attempting to convert the Jews to Christianity, who would thereby contaminate
it.[50] If the appearance of such sentiments in a highly disreputable newspaper
like the *Stürmer* leaves room for skepticism, then views expressed in private
party functions should be more convincing. One such function was a special
course given by members of the party elite at the National Socialist Student League's (*Nationalsozialistischer Deutscher Studentenbund*, or NSDStB)
Reichsschule in Bernau, in July 1935. Remarks made at this confidential meeting give a frank picture of the religious views of those Nazis in attendance,
who, beside Streicher, included Robert Ley, the head of the German Labor
Front. The first day a lecture was given by Hannes Schneider, the head of the
school, who rejected both the Old and New Testaments: "If we accept either
of these writings, then we accept the Jews as the Chosen People, to whom

---

[46] Helmut Heiber (ed.), *Goebbels-Reden*, 2 vols. (Düsseldorf, 1971–2), 1: 274–5 (emphasis in
the original).

[47] Jochen-Christoph Kaiser, "NS-Volkswohlfahrt und freie Wohlfahrtspflege im Dritten Reich,"
in Hans-Uwe Otto and Heinz Sünker (eds.), *Politische Formierung und soziale Erziehung im
Nationalsozialismus* (Frankfurt a.M., 1991), 84. See Chapter 6.

[48] Heiber, *Goebbels-Reden*, 1: 274 (emphasis in the original).

[49] Albert Krebs, *Tendenzen und Gestalten der NSDAP: Erinnerungen an die Frühzeit der Partei*
(Stuttgart, 1959), 166.

[50] Quoted in Nathaniel Micklem, *National Socialism and the Roman Catholic Church* (Oxford,
1939), 174–5.

revelation was given."[51] Here was an open door for other Nazis to reveal confidentially their hatred for Christianity. But Streicher, who gave a lecture some days later, did not share his fellow party member's feelings: "The clergyman cannot teach religion – at most a confession.... There is a difference between a churchly and a true Christian." This was the anticlericalism to be expected of Streicher. However, although the Catholic Church was attacked, Christianity was not at all rejected: "Hitler speaks simply, as did Christ. Christ could not speak as openly as he wished. He spoke in parables, for instance he spoke of the flower and the weed (weed = Jew)." Directly contradicting the views of Schneider, Streicher then proclaimed: "The Bible is a great work when viewed from the perspective of race. Schopenhauer: 'The Jew is the master of lies.' Luther: 'Who ever buys from a Jew is a criminal.' Jesus had been a Nordic, Aryan man.... Christ was the greatest antisemite of all time."[52]

WE MUST FINISH WITH CHRISTIANITY

On the anti-Christian side no attempt was made to erect a rival "practical" religion on par with positive Christianity. None of them sought to paganize Winter Relief or imbue the larger German society with a particular social ethic. Rather, they spent the first years of the Third Reich propounding their new faith and trying to claim new adherents. New voices were heard after 1933 that added to their numbers. Some had not been prominent enough in the party to have a platform for their views, while others underwent a transformation. Among the former was Robert Ley. Although he had been a *Gauleiter* in the *Kampfzeit*, he came into prominence only when he became the new Reich Organization Leader (ROL) just before the Seizure of Power. Hitler saw to it that this office lost much of its power after Gregor Strasser unexpectedly left the post in December 1932. But Ley would soon acquire a much more powerful position as head of the German Labor Front (*Deutsche Arbeitsfront*, or DAF), a mass organization of workers that replaced the labor unions promptly banned by the Nazi State. At the same *Reichsschule* course in July 1935, Ley revealed a clear rejection of Christianity. He went further than Streicher, attacking not only the priest but Christianity itself: "Struggle has given us more religion and faith than Christianity.... In our struggle against Christianity we do not need the hammer, but only the arrow tip of our worldview. Every good SA man stands head and shoulders above the priest. Hitler has and will demand great sacrifice from the *Volk*. Neither Frederick the Great, nor Bismarck, nor Luther had this divine quality."[53] Ley was one of the very few to repudiate not only Christianity, but even its historical figures.

[51] "Einleitungsvortrag," IfZ MA 130 (10 July 1935: Bernau).
[52] "Vortrag vom Pg. Streicher," IfZ MA 130 (23 July 1935: Bernau). "Weed = Jew" reference in the original.
[53] "Vortrag von Pg. Dr. Ley," IfZ MA 130 (16 July 1935: Bernau).

On another occasion, Ley revealed more of his own theological view-point: "At last through Adolf Hitler I have found my Lord again. Before that, I no longer had a God. Today I believe in a personal God who is near to me.... There is nobody more religious and God-fearing than Adolf Hitler. We believe that the Lord sent us our Führer so that he might free Germany from hypocrites and Pharisees."[54] No mention is made of Christ here. But Ley's tone indicates belief in an active, interventionist God. Although there is no evidence that Ley was anything more than a nominal Protestant, he was close to several German Christian leaders, especially fellow Rhinelander Gottfried Krummacher.[55] And he had no hesitance in throwing the weight of the party organization behind the DC in their electoral campaign of 1933. Nonetheless, unlike the DC, Ley never referred to Christ. Neither did he intone a heroic Jesus or express an interest in a mystical medieval past. Although he shared the antipathy to Christianity of the paganists, he did not take any apparent interest in their ersatz faith. Ley was, however, instrumental in getting Rosenberg his only real job after 1934: The Führer's Delegate for the Supervision of the Entire Intellectual and Ideological Education and Training of the NSDAP. Needless to say, this appointment was very alarming to the representatives of the churches, who supposed that this would make *Mythus* the official basis of the party's ideology.[56] However, Rosenberg's appointment was not the opening of a generalized attack by the Nazi Party on Christianity or even, at this point, the churches. Rather, as Reinhard Bollmus convincingly demonstrates, it simply arose out of "a chance constellation of interests within the party which existed for only a short time."[57]

Rosenberg's ideological stance changed little after 1933. Evidence for this is provided in two works he wrote in response to the critical reactions of Catholics and Protestants to his *Mythus*. (Of the many clerical attacks on

---

[54] *Westdeutscher Beobachter*, 14 July 1936.

[55] See, for instance, the correspondence between Krummacher and Ley, in which the former refers to Ley as "Du" and "Lieber Robert": BAZ NS 22/415 (31 January 1933: Berlin); BAZ Personalakt Hossenfelder (6 February 1933: Berlin).

[56] Conway, *Persecution*, 72; Scholder, *Churches*, 2: 102–3. Rosenberg did have a second job: head of the Foreign Policy Office of the NSDAP (*Aussenpolitisches Amt der NSDAP*, or APA), founded in 1933. Rosenberg imagined this would lead to his appointment as foreign minister, but instead it remained a dead-end office with no influence, intended by Hitler to be "harmless compensation [for Neurath's hold on the Foreign Ministry], in order to be rid of Rosenberg": John Heineman, *Hitler's First Foreign Minister: Constantin Freiherr von Neurath, Diplomat and Statesman* (Berkeley, 1979), 122.

[57] Bollmus, *Amt Rosenberg*, 55. Ley and Rosenberg formulated the wording of the commission that Hitler then signed. As in his relations with others in the Nazi elite, here Rosenberg would find his ambition stymied: "Ley did not allow Rosenberg to play any practical part in training. He stressed... that 'supervision' meant only the preparation of written material": Bollmus, "Rosenberg," 190. This was in part a function of Ley's own ideological pretensions: He had a hand in setting up the Adolf Hitler Schools, and edited his own educational periodical, *Der Schulungsbrief*: Robert Cecil, *The Myth of the Master Race: Alfred Rosenberg and Nazi Ideology* (London, 1972), 124.

Rosenberg published after 1933, none were censored or banned by Nazi authorities.[58]) A comparison of the two demonstrates that Rosenberg continued to show a preference for Protestantism over Catholicism as a worldview, even while he eagerly attacked the clergy of both. His attack against the Catholic Church, called *On the Dark Men of Our Times: A Reply to the Attacks against the Myth of the Twentieth Century*, was published in 1935. He dismissively suggested that religious Catholics should stay away from his *Mythus*, as it had not been written for them. He even suggested that it was their opposition to his book that had boosted its sales.[59] He claimed that behind Catholic attacks against him stood a greater Catholic conspiracy to separate the Catholic parts of Germany from the Protestant and merge them with France or Austria. During Weimar, the Center Party was the political arm of this conspiracy and rightly feared that the assent of Nazism would put an end to these plans.[60] The Roman Church, Rosenberg claimed, had always used all means at its disposal to accrue power to itself. In this drive for domination, deceit and falsifications became standard practice. For instance, Rosenberg denied St. Matthew's claim that Jesus had assigned Peter to establish a church. Peter's episcopate in Rome was a falsehood, as the position of bishop was incompatible with the professions of an apostle.[61] Roman Christianity was accused not only of hypocrisy, but also of actively seeking to destroy German national character.[62]

Rosenberg's counterattack on Protestantism, published two years later, was given quite a different title: *Protestant Pilgrims to Rome: The Treason against Luther and the Myth of the Twentieth Century*.[63] Rosenberg fundamentally detached the contemporary Lutheran Church from its founder by suggesting that, whereas the Reformation began as a rebellion against Rome, the current leadership of the Protestant Church was slowly moving back in the direction of St. Peter.[64] Ignatius Loyola, not Martin Luther, was now being made head of German Protestantism, thanks largely to the work of the BK.[65] Sterile dogmatism and clerical infantilism were replacing Luther's fiery spirit of protest "against Rome and Jerusalem." The BK in particular was accused of treachery, of becoming "Jewish prophets" through their maintenance of the Old Testament.[66] Calvinists came in for sharp condemnation, as they frightened people with notions of Hell and self-disdain, and inculcated a

---

[58] As pointed out by Reinhard Heydrich: BAP R5101/23139/239 (20 July 1935: Berlin).

[59] Alfred Rosenberg, *An die Dunkelmänner unserer Zeit: Eine Antwort auf die Angriffe gegen den Mythus des 20. Jahrhunderts* (Munich, 1935), 5–6. This was Hitler's opinion as well: Scholder, *Churches*, 2: 112.

[60] Rosenberg, *Dunkelmänner*, 9.

[61] Ibid., 13–14.

[62] Ibid., 18.

[63] Alfred Rosenberg, *Protestantische Rompilger: Der Verrat an Luther und der Mythus des 20. Jahrhunderts* (Munich, 1937).

[64] Ibid., 10.

[65] Ibid., 16.

[66] Ibid., 24.

"Syrian inferiority complex." Rosenberg regarded Karl Barth as a "Calvinist pseudo-pope" who worked for nothing less than the "Calvinization" – and therefore the destruction – of German Protestantism.[67] Rosenberg also attacked Anglicanism for trying to propagate an "ecumenical League of Nations." Its attempt to create a world Protestantism was similarly regarded by Rosenberg as an attempt at recatholicization.[68] But after this litany of condemnation, Rosenberg ended on a positive note: Not all was lost for Protestantism. It could restore its credibility if it returned to Luther's original intent, recognized the "genuine original forces of Protestantism," abandoned the Old Testament, and divested itself of doctrines like original sin.[69]

Beside Rosenberg, Himmler would now emerge after the *Machtergreifung* as a leading paganist in the party. As the Reich Leader of the SS and Chief of German Police, he was immeasurably more powerful than Rosenberg. Whereas Rosenberg's star would fall in the course of the Third Reich, Himmler's would rise: The height of his power came in 1943, when he replaced Frick as Reich Interior Minister. If Himmler still held an affection for his church in the *Kampfzeit*, by the time of the Seizure of Power this had been extinguished. After 1933 Rosenberg said of Himmler: "Our thoughts ran along similar lines; he always stressed that his attitude was close to mine."[70] They and Darré had a romantic attitude concerning the peasantry and a fascination with German prehistory, which Himmler interpreted as an Aryan struggle against malevolent Jewish–Roman forces. In 1934, Rosenberg noted with approval how Himmler's SS, "together with the Peasant Leadership, openly educates its men ... in an anti-Christian fashion."[71] Himmler viewed the SS as something of a new priesthood or a knight's order. In fact, he drew comparisons between it and the Teutonic Knights, the (Christian) order of crusaders that had led the "civilizing mission" to the East.[72] However, although Himmler had nothing more to do with his original faith, he still retained a deep religiosity. In 1935 he professed belief in "a Lord God who stands over us, who made us and our Fatherland, our *Volk* and the earth, and sent us our Führer."[73] He made no hesitation that his new religion would serve as a replacement for Christianity: "Our business is to spread the knowledge of the race in the life of our *Volk* and to impress it upon the hearts and heads of all, down to the very youngest, as our German gospel."[74] To an assembly of the SS he stated that Christianity would play no part in the organization: "The guideline for us in our struggle is neither

[67] Ibid., 47.
[68] Ibid., 62–74.
[69] Ibid., 77.
[70] Hans-Günther Seraphim (ed.), *Das politische Tagebuch Alfred Rosenbergs 1934/35 und 1939/40* (Göttingen, 1956), 119.
[71] Ibid., 56 (entry for 19 August 1934).
[72] Josef Ackermann, *Heinrich Himmler als Ideologe* (Göttingen, 1970), 103; Felix Kersten, *The Kersten Memoirs, 1940–1945* (New York, 1957), 32.
[73] VB, 17 November 1935.
[74] VB, 1 July 1935.

the Old nor the New Testament, but the political testament of Adolf Hitler."[75] He never spoke of positive Christianity, and at a private speech in Berlin stated flatly: "We must finish with Christianity."[76] He reserved special wrath for the Catholic priesthood, which he denounced as a "homosexual erotic men's league."[77]

In place of Christianity, Himmler advocated ancestor worship and a myth of "Blood and Soil," both of which stood opposed to Christian dogma,[78] and belief in immortality and an omnipotent God, whose anti-Christian credentials was considerably more uncertain. The exact form his replacement faith would take led Himmler down several roads. One was an adoration of the ancient King Heinrich I. Himmler celebrated the 1,000th anniversary of his death at Quedlinburg Cathedral in 1936 and was so enthralled with this medieval figure that he believed himself to be Heinrich's reincarnation.[79] Another road was the obscure occultism of Hanns Hörbiger, who had propagated a theory of "Glacial Cosmogony," in which world history was a record of the eternal struggle between fire and ice, "linking the flood of Genesis and the destruction of the Teutonic kingdom of Atlantis to 'gravitational catastrophes' supposedly unleashed when the Earth 'captured' a moon in its orbit."[80] Even among the party's other paganists, Himmler's religious views were regarded as bizarre. Himmler unwittingly acknowledged this, warning his underlings that no polemics against Hörbiger's theories would be tolerated.[81] This particular obsession was too much even for Rosenberg, who sent a circular to all NSDAP offices, assuring them that "adherence to these theories was no part of being a National Socialist."[82]

Just as Hitler had no time for Rosenberg's plans to create a new, mystical religion to replace clerical Christianity, so he found Himmler's dilettantish religious explorations absurd. As he told a circle of confidants, "What nonsense! Here we have at last reached an age that has left all mysticism behind, and now he wants to start that all over again.... To think that I may some day be turned into an SS saint!" Whereas Himmler attacked

---

[75] Ackermann, *Himmler*, 40–1.

[76] Bradley Smith and A.F. Peterson (eds.), *Heinrich Himmler: Geheimreden 1933 bis 1945* (Frankfurt a.M., 1974), 159.

[77] IfZ MA 311 (18 February 1937: Tölz).

[78] In a 1937 speech, Himmler declared "The worst blow which Christianity ever took against us has been the blow against ancestors and ancestor worship": IfZ MA 311 (18 February 1937: Tölz).

[79] Ackermann, *Himmler*, 60–2; Kersten, *Memoirs*, 153.

[80] Jost Hermand, *Old Dreams of a New Reich: Volkish Utopias and National Socialism* (Bloomington, 1992), 193; Ackermann, *Himmler*, 45.

[81] Hermand, *Dreams*, 64.

[82] Cecil, *Myth*, 119. Given Hitler's utter contempt for Himmler's endless mysticism and pseudoreligious babble, not to mention Rosenberg's own rejection of it, it is extremely unlikely that Hitler "respected" Hörbiger's work, as Jost Hermand and Philippe Burrin both suggest: Hermand, *Dreams*, 193; Philippe Burrin, "Political Religion: The Relevance of a Concept," *History and Memory* 9 (1997), 338.

Charlemagne as an agent of Christianity against pagan-Germanic tribes, Hitler declared: "Killing all those Saxons was not a historical crime, as Himmler thinks. Charlemagne did a good thing in subjugating Widukind and killing the Saxons out of hand. He thereby made possible the empire of the Franks and the entry of Western culture into what is now Germany."[83] Hitler was equally dismissive of Himmler's forays into German prehistory: "Isn't it enough that the Romans were erecting great buildings when our forefathers were still living in mud huts; now Himmler is starting to dig up these villages of mud huts and enthusing over every potsherd and stone axe he finds."[84] According to Albert Speer, "The whole thing was beginning to assume far-fetched pseudo-religious forms. Goebbels, with Hitler, took the lead in ridiculing these dreams of Himmler's, with Himmler himself adding to the comedy by his vanity and obsessiveness."[85] Hitler even approached Himmler himself in 1935, fully rejecting the foundation of a new religion, calling it a "chimera." Rather than attack Himmler frontally, however, he took the indirect route of attacking Himmler's paganist ally Rosenberg, stating that he intended to take action against Rosenberg's *Mythus*.[86]

As outlandish as many of his ideas were, and his own insistence to be thoroughly anti-Christian notwithstanding, Himmler's views on Christianity were fraught with ambiguity. For instance, he still believed that Jesus was not a Jew. Himmler feared that the average SS man would be unable to distinguish between attacks on the churches and a preservation of Christ. Therefore, in a 1937 memorandum marked "to all SS leaders from Standartenführer up," Himmler instructed: "In ideological training I forbid every attack against Christ as a person, since such attacks or insults that Christ was a Jew are unworthy of us and certainly untrue historically."[87] He then added significantly, "I desire that SS men be convinced of the worth of our own blood and our past, through knowledge of the actual history of our *Volk*, the prehistory of our *Volk*, the greatness and culture of our ancestors, so that they will totally root themselves in the value of the past, present and future." Not only Christ, but belief in Christ as a part of German history, was to be respected in the SS. Such proclamations were not simply for public consumption. When a member of the Hitler Youth (*Hitlerjugend*, or HJ) wrote to Himmler asking if he was to believe a Nazi lecturer who claimed that Jesus was a Jew, Himmler's secretary Rudolf Brandt replied, indicating

[83] Albert Speer, *Inside the Third Reich* (New York, 1970), 94.

[84] Ibid., 94–5.

[85] Ibid., 122.

[86] "Aktennotiz Himmlers über eine Besprechung mit Hitler, 23. Oktober 1935," as quoted in Ackermann, *Himmler*, 90. There is no indication whether Hitler followed up on this particular threat. Judging from the continued publication of *Mythus*, he made no serious effort to do so. However, Rosenberg's book was occasionally banned lower down the ranks of the party, for instance, by the Breslau branch of the NSLB: BAZ NS 22/410 (8 September 1935: Breslau).

[87] BAZ Sammlung Schumacher (hereafter Schu) 245/2/150 (28 June 1937: Berlin).

that "The Reichsführer-SS is of the conviction that Jesus was not a Jew. You must have misunderstood the speaker."[88]

Further indications of Himmler's positive feelings about Christianity arose in discussion of SS policies regarding the religious feelings of its members. In a speech to SS leaders in 1936, Himmler spoke of his own family's Christian attachment and maintained that, even as he departed from his parents' religion, he still maintained respect for their feelings: "Not once did I touch his convictions, nor he mine." He then indicated that religious tolerance would be embraced by the SS as well: "I believe that we must maintain such a position towards those elderly who cannot bring themselves to our path. For this reason I have also demonstrated understanding, and will continue to do so in the future, when someone tells me: out of respect for my parents I must have my child baptized. Please! Certainly!...There is no use in disturbing the peace of mind of those with 60 or 70 years behind them."[89] This meant that even the burial of SS men's parents could be conducted in the Christian fashion. For a supposedly fanatical anti-Christian this was an exceedingly mild approach to take.

Himmler consistently maintained that even *within* the SS, Christian viewpoints, although not endorsed by the organization, were nonetheless to be respected. Two years earlier, in reaction to a particular incident, he announced: "I forbid SS members to pester, annoy or mock another due to his religious views. Just as the German has never tolerated religious constraint on himself, so are the religious convictions of his neighbors holy and inviolable to him." This pertained not only to the religious views of individual SS men, but also to their conduct regarding religious institutions: "I most strictly forbid any disturbance as well as any tactlessness regarding religious events of all confessions (i.e. processions of the Catholic Church). Likewise, a tactful deportment when churches are visited out of historical or artistic interest goes without saying." Himmler added that this order was to be enforced on pain of expulsion.[90] A year later he renewed this order, explicitly basing it on the "National Socialist version of the age-old German right of freedom of conscience." This freedom of conscience did have its institutional limits. In the same memorandum, Himmler forbade members of the SS from "any leadership activity in any kind of religious or faith community (for instance, German Faith Movement etc)."[91] Holding a position of responsibility in the Christian churches was thus forbidden: But it was also forbidden for the churches' paganist rivals. (Simple membership in a religious community, Christian or otherwise, was still allowed.) Hence, although Himmler rejected Christianity both as doctrine and as institution, he allowed considerable latitude of Christian expression not only for SS men, but in some senses even

---

[88] BAZ NS 19/3134/2 (16 June 1937: Berlin).
[89] "Rede des Reichsführer-SS anlässlich der Gruppenführer-Besprechung am 8. November 1936 in Dachau," IfZ F 37/3 (8 November 1936: Dachau).
[90] BAZ Schu 245/2/133 (15 September 1934: Berlin).
[91] BAZ Schu 245/2/134-135 (20 September 1935: Munich).

for himself. Christ could not be saddled with the curse of Jewishness. Even to his SS associates he professed a respect and esteem for his family's Christian piety. Himmler would later take this to a degree that made even his close associates question the sincerity of his anti-Christian commitment.

The most important anti-Christian at this time beside Himmler was his subordinate Reinhard Heydrich, whose career in the NSDAP was meteoric. Having joined the party only in 1930, by the next year he became head of the Security Service (*Sicherheitsdienst*, or SD) under Himmler. In 1933 he joined Himmler in the Bavarian Political Police and again accompanied Himmler when the latter transferred to Berlin. He soon took over as head of the office of the Gestapo and by the beginning of the war became head of the immensely powerful Reich Security Main Office (*Reichssicherheitshauptamt*, or RSHA), which essentially made him the leading policeman of Germany. In this office he was perfectly positioned to cause the Catholic Church maximum difficulty, which he lost no time in doing. He was at the forefront of most anticlerical actions taken by the Nazi State, most notably the Morality Trials of 1936, in which over 250 Catholic priests were accused of crimes against the nation. That year Heydrich stated in an internal report: "Of all the supranational powers, political Catholicism has shown itself time and again as our major opponent."[92] His deportment toward the Catholic Church was summarized in the testimony of a fellow Nazi, who pointed out that when Heydrich was assassinated in Prague in 1942, "the Christian churches were rid of their toughest opponent."[93] John Conway similarly points out that Heydrich, along with Himmler, far outstripped other Nazis in his anticlerical extremism.[94]

Like Himmler, Heydrich had been raised in a strongly Catholic environment, "in his case verging on the fanatical."[95] Like Ley, Heydrich did not pursue the esoteric mysticism of paganists like Himmler; but he would far outstrip Ley in turning against his nominal faith. According to his biographer, "even had he never belonged to the SS, his reaction to his intensely Catholic upbringing would have resulted in an increasing indifference to the Catholic faith."[96] Usually regarded as much more of a technocrat of power than an ideologue, his views on Catholicism nonetheless led him to write a book, *The Fortunes of Our Struggle*, in 1936.[97] In it, he declared that all opposition to Nazism ultimately originated in two forces: "Jews and politicized clergy." Heydrich did not concern himself with Christianity in the book, but rather with the secular power of the churches, which, "not content with attempting for centuries to destroy the racial and spiritual values of our *Volk*, . . . now

[92] Quoted in Günther Deschner, *Reinhard Heydrich: A Biography* (New York, 1981), 105.
[93] Quoted in ibid., 109.
[94] Conway, *Persecution*, 169. Conway also argues that "the murder of Heydrich in 1942 led to a certain improvement in the situation of the Churches" (ibid., 301).
[95] Deschner, *Heydrich*, 102.
[96] Ibid., 106.
[97] Reinhard Heydrich, *Die Wandlungen unseres Kampfes* (Berlin, 1936).

assume an outward show and falsify the preservation of these values, proclaiming themselves saviors of the world." To every appearance this looked like an attack on both confessions. However, as in so many other cases, when Heydrich homed in on his target, the vituperations were all aimed at the institutions of Catholicism: "[T]he basic party structures (the Center Party and Bavarian People's Party) clearly betrayed their politically secular nature. Those groups founded earlier, with a great deal of foresight, to prepare the way for religious politics, have been transformed into supporters of political parties (Catholic Action, etc)."[98] Only the institutions of Catholicism are being criticized here, not Protestantism. Heydrich maintained that the Catholic Church was fighting Hitler's attempt to bring religious peace through the Concordat, as this would threaten their political prerogatives.[99]

Part of Heydrich's extreme anti-Catholicism was accountable to his rebellion against "an eternally pious" home life. Unlike other Nazis, however, this did not lead Heydrich to a preference for Protestantism over Catholicism. He made no mention of belief in Christ or positive Christianity, instead simply suggesting that "the lens through which he sees his God is a matter of individual concern for each German." Nonetheless, according to his biographer, another factor in his growing detachment from Catholicism was his marriage to a woman who had been "brought up in a particularly north German Protestant atmosphere."[100] It is therefore all the more relevant that, although Heydrich would attempt to curtail the prerogatives of the Catholic Church at every turn, toward the Protestant Church he was less bellicose: "Contacts between the evangelical churches, world Protestantism and leading figures in England were [simply] observed."[101] One of Heydrich's greatest charges against Catholicism was its internationalism; the Protestant Church, known for its national ethos, could not have come in for such attack.

GERMAN LUTHER DAY 1933

An early opportunity for the new Nazi State to display tangibly its comportment toward both confession and religion would soon present itself. The portentous occasion was the *Deutsche Luthertag* 1933, the 450th anniversary of Luther's birth. The fortuitous timing of the event was not lost on the Nazis, who took an active hand in preparing the celebrations. In an announcement to the supreme Reich authorities, Wilhelm Frick proposed that

[98] Ibid., 7.

[99] Ibid., 9.

[100] Deschner, *Heydrich*, 102. Significantly, Deschner suggests this rebellion had something as well to do with his father, who was originally Protestant but converted to Catholicism to please his wife. Heydrich was therefore raised a Catholic in a town (Halle) that was 94% Protestant: "Young Reinhard was thus brought up in an atmosphere of consciously maintained Catholicism. His very father was instrumental in making him an outsider" (ibid., 20). Reinhard's marriage to a Protestant, the author implies, was a further demonstration of his rebellion against Catholicism.

[101] Ibid., 109.

10 November – the actual date of Luther's birth – should be an official holiday, to celebrate "the work of the German Reformation" and serve as "a lively echo in all German Protestantism, indeed directed far across Germany's borders."[102] In a letter to the state governments, Frick also ordered that all Protestant pupils were to participate in the activities surrounding the *Luthertag*.[103] Frick, along with other leading members of the Nazi Party, took part in these celebrations. In a festivity in Wittenberg leading up to the anniversary, Frick spoke of Luther's "ruthless will to truthfulness," "inner modesty," and "uncompromising belief."[104]

The most important state celebration took place on 19 November itself, in Berlin. In attendance were Reich President Hindenburg, non-Nazi Foreign Minister Konstantin von Neurath, historian Gerhard Ritter, Erlangen theologian Werner Elert, and Hans Schemm. More than nine months after Hitler's appointment as chancellor, Hindenburg gave no indication that he disapproved of the direction the Nazis were taking: "This Luther Day 1933 brings the whole world of Protestantism to consciousness of its community and its bond in faith. But this day of thanks summons the German *Volk* in particular to be united in the stewardship of its great historical inheritance, to accomplish the tasks of the present and future in unanimity. Therefore stay firm in the faith of your fathers, be strong in your love of *Volk* and Reich and full of confidence in Germany's destiny!"[105] Neurath invested even more religious meaning into that year's turn of events: "The German *Volk* celebrates the 450th anniversary of Luther's birth at a time when a mighty political event is welding together a great inner unity. An innerly unified *Volk* will know to value the personalities and acts of the great men of their history.... The mighty development of the spiritual life of the German *Volk*, even outside the sphere of the religious, is unthinkable without Luther."[106] Gerhard Ritter, the famous historian and conservative stalwart, took a similar view of the contemporary situation: "The 450th anniversary of Luther's birthday comes at a time of great *völkisch* awakening."[107]

---

[102] *Dokumente zur Kirchenpolitik*, 1: 140–1. The celebrations were eventually held on 19 November, as 10 November was fixed as the date of new Reichstag elections: *VB*, 25 October 1933.

[103] BAP R43 II/168/69 (28 October 1933: Berlin).

[104] *Badische Presse*, 11 September 1933: in BAP R5101/23189/14. Among the others in attendance on this occasion were Reich Bishop Ludwig Müller, Reich Minister of Finance Schwerin von Krosigk – one of the very few non-Nazis to stay in Hitler's cabinet for the duration of the Third Reich – and the Lutheran bishop of Uppsala, Sweden.

[105] BAZ NS 12/808 (10 November 1933: Berlin).

[106] BAZ NS 12/808 (10 November 1933: Berlin).

[107] BAZ NS 12/808 (19 November 1933: Berlin). As Peter Lambert has shown, Ritter's later role as "resister" to Nazism had nothing to do with the Nazis' secular ideology, but only with the disputes surrounding the *Kirchenkampf*: "German Historians and Nazi Ideology: The Parameters of the *Volksgemeinschaft* and the Problem of Historical Legitimation, 1930–45," *European History Quarterly* 25 (1995), 555–82. According to Lambert, the antisemitism of Ritter and his milieu demonstrated their "inability to free themselves of the very same fears and prejudices that motivated the Nazis" (567).

Schemm, who that same year unambiguously upheld the equal value of both confessions for the establishment of a *Volksgemeinschaft*, on this occasion exhibited a love for Luther and appreciation for his religious deeds that only a committed Protestant could make: "So long as the Bible was available to us only in a foreign language, so long as it was only spoken to us in Latin, we could only grasp it as things are grasped through the iron gloves of a knight: he is aware of the shape and weight, but can only feel iron. When Luther made the Bible accessible to Germans in the glorious German language, it was as if we had cast off the iron glove and with the flesh and blood of our German hand were finally able to grasp our unique character [*unser ureigenstes Lebensgut*]."[108] Schemm's comparison of Luther and Nazism on this occasion also brought with it a sanctification of antisemitism: "The older and more experienced he became, the less he could understand one particular type of person: this was the Jew. His engagement against the decomposing Jewish spirit is clearly evident not only from his writing against the Jews; his life too was idealistically, philosophically antisemitic. Now we Germans of today have the duty to recognize and acknowledge this."[109]

Several *Gauleiter* took part in the various activities surrounding the anniversary. Gauleiter Loeper of Braunschweig-Anhalt took part in festivities in Magdeburg,[110] and Christian Mergenthaler, the *Kultusminister* of Württemberg, was asked to be a member of the planning committee of the *Luthertag*.[111] Erich Koch of East Prussia (who was also president of the provincial church synod) took part in festivities in Königsberg. Reflecting his particular commitment to Protestant Christianity, he stated: "Only we can enter into Luther's spirit.... Human cults do not set us free from all sin, but faith alone. With us the church shall become a serving member of the state.... There is a deep sense that our celebration is not attended by superficiality, but rather by thanks to a man who saved German cultural values."[112] Other members of the Nazi leadership participated as well. Rust spoke at a celebration in August, in which he, like other Nazis, drew direct parallels between Luther and Hitler: "Since Martin Luther closed his eyes, no such son of our people has appeared again. It has been decided that we shall be the first to witness his reappearance.... I think the time is past when

---

[108] "Luther und das Deutschtum," BAZ NS 12/808 (19 November 1933: Berlin), reprinted in Gertrud Kahl-Furthmann (ed.), *Hans Schemm spricht: Seine Reden und sein Werk* (Beyreuth, 1935), 126–7.

[109] Ibid., reprinted in Kahl-Furthmann (ed.), *Schemm*, 126. This reference and Walter Buch's in the *Kampfzeit* confirm that Nazis were fully aware of Luther's notorious "On the Jews and Their Lies" and seemed to have gained inspiration from it. Portions of this tract also found their way onto the pages of the *VB*: see "Luther und die Juden," *VB*, 8 September 1933; "Luther und die Judenfrage," *VB*, 18 November 1933.

[110] "Luthergeist im neuen Reich," *Magdeburger Tageszeitung*, 2 November 1933: in BAP R5101/23189/73.

[111] BAP R5101/23189/38 (5 September 1933: Stuttgart). There is no indication whether he accepted the offer.

[112] *Königsberg-Hartungsche Zeitung*, 20 November 1933: in BAP R5101/23189/83.

one may not say the names of Hitler and Luther in the same breath. They belong together; they are of the same old stamp [*Schrot und Korn*]." [113] On a separate occasion, Rust also laid a wreath on Luther's grave. [114]

Broad segments of the Nazi Party participated in Luther Day across Germany. In Coburg on 31 October, celebrations sponsored by the Luther League were held that included the SA, SS, HJ, and League of German Girls (*Bund deutscher Mädel*, or BdM), as well as Schemm and Bavarian State Bishop Hans Meiser. [115] On the same day, the Fighting League for German Culture participated in the Luther festivities in the cities of Eisleben and Wittenberg. [116] This was not the first time such high esteem was held for Luther within the ranks of the *Kampfbund*. Just a few days after the Seizure of Power, Hans Hinkel, the leader of the Berlin chapter and editor of the league's periodical *Deutsche Kultur-Wacht*, gave a speech on Luther. Hinkel later gained influential positions in Goebbels' Reich Chamber of Culture (*Reichskulturkammer*) and Propaganda Ministry, where he became head of both the Jewish section and the film department. [117] On this occasion he spoke of Luther in typically racialist terms: "Through his acts and his spiritual attitude he began the fight which we still wage today; with Luther the revolution of German blood and feeling against alien elements of the *Volk* was begun." However, in a remarkable passage Hinkel plainly demonstrated his belief that the Nazi goal of bridging the gap between the confessions would not be a purely syncretic affair: "To continue and complete his Protestantism, nationalism must make the picture of Luther, of a German fighter, live as an example *above the barriers of confession* for all German blood comrades." [118] The presumption that Luther could somehow stand above the sectarian divide in Germany, when in fact he represented that divide for millions of Germans, clearly demonstrates an implicitly Protestant attitude. Like the NSDAP itself, the *Kampfbund* could also count Protestant pastors among its members. [119]

Such a coupling of Luther and nationalism could not have been a confessionally neutral affair. Such ideas did not find a positive reception among Catholics, who, it must be remembered, felt no less patriotic for rejecting Luther. Inside the party, there is no record of the Catholic Goebbels lauding Luther in these terms. Of course, the same held true for Catholics outside the party. Representing their interests, the Papal Nuncio approached Neurath with his opinion that the Luther Day would become "a kind of nationalist

---

[113] *VB*, 25 August 1933.

[114] *Deutsche Zeitung*, 11 November 1933: in BAP R5101/23189/49.

[115] *Berliner Börsen-Zeitung*, 1 November 1933: in BAP R5101/23189/41. Meiser was a member of the BK.

[116] *Magdeburger Tageszeitung*, 30 September 1933: in BAP R5101/23189/18.

[117] Ralf Georg Reuth, *Goebbels* (New York, 1993), 275, 278, 334; Steinweis, *Art, Ideology and Economics*, 62, 124–5.

[118] *Der Tag*, 17 February 1933: in BAP R5101/23138/7 (emphasis added).

[119] One example was the Badenese pastor Teutsch, an "old fighter" who gave a speech at a *Kampfbund* assembly on "the power of belief in National Socialism": *Karlsruher Tagblatt*, 8 June 1934: in BAP 62 Di 1/75/112e.

celebration": what was involved was "the celebration of an action (the nailing of the theses on the church door in Wittenberg) which had had a plainly hostile tendency towards the Catholic Church." The Nuncio "feared for the ratification of the concordat were this celebration to take place on a large scale and with government involvement." Neurath responded by pointing out that "on the Catholic side as well, festivities were held which in no way were always filled with a friendly spirit towards the Protestant church," and refused to consider the matter further.[120] This response was likely conditioned in part by an event that had occurred four months earlier. Frick had brought to Neurath's attention several anti-Protestant articles that had appeared in the Vatican's semiofficial newspaper *Osservatore Romano*. He objected particularly to an article written by a Jesuit describing Protestantism as a symptom of "advanced decay" and warned that such utterances caused offense to Germans and would undermine the "common defense against the enemies of religion, thereby advancing tendencies destructive to the state." Even though the offending articles concerned only Protestantism in Italy, Frick requested that the German embassy take up the matter.[121] By expressing a traditional anti-Protestant attitude, this Catholic newspaper both demonstrated and reaffirmed the perceived link in many Nazi minds between Protestantism and Germanhood.

Nazis commonly cast themselves as both revolutionary and an extension of the German past: The Luther Day celebrations provided a perfect platform through which to communicate this dual message. The Nazi involvement in the Luther Day was certainly an act of political appropriation, but it would be a mistake to explain it away as a *mis*appropriation or a feigned affection for a historical personality for whom they had no real feeling. As Heiko Oberman points out, "The Nazis did not have to discover or create Luther as a German national reformer – he was already there, rifle at the ready."[122] Protestants as well had long made Luther into both a religious revolutionary and nationalist hero, as both a guarantor of German heritage and beacon for Germany's future.[123] During the festivities, a great many people spoke with a rhetoric almost identical to the Nazis'. A typical example was an article in the *Chemnitzer Tageblatt*, which stated: "The German *Volk* are united not only in loyalty and love for the Fatherland, but also once more in the old German beliefs of Luther [*Lutherglauben*]; a new epoch of strong, conscious religious life has dawned in Germany."[124] The leadership

[120] BAP R43 II/168/46 (7 September 1933: Berlin).
[121] BAP R43 II/161/42-43 (2 May 1933: Berlin). This file contains no information as to any immediate response.
[122] Heiko Oberman, "The Nationalist Conscription of Martin Luther," in Carter Lindberg (ed.), *Piety, Politics and Ethics* (Kirksville, MO, 1984), 70.
[123] During the *Luthertag* celebrations, for instance, the theologian Werner Elert gave a speech on "Luther und der revolutionäre Gedanke": BAZ NS 12/808 (19 November 1933: Berlin). For more on this phenomenon, see Hartmut Lehmann, "Martin Luther as a National Hero in the 19th Century," in J.C. Eade (ed.), *Romantic Nationalism in Europe* (Canberra, 1983).
[124] "Luther weist den Weg," *Chemnitzer Tageblatt*, 1 November 1933: in BAP R5101/23189/65.

of the Protestant League espoused a similar view. Fahrenhorst, who was on the planning committee of the *Luthertag*, called Luther "the first German spiritual Führer," who spoke to all Germans regardless of class or confession. In a letter to Hitler, Fahrenhorst reminded him that his "Old Fighters" were mostly Protestants and that it was "precisely in the Protestant regions of our Fatherland" in which Nazism found its greatest strength. Promising that the celebration of Luther's birthday would not turn into a confessional affair, Fahrenhorst invited Hitler to become the official patron of the *Luthertag*.[125] In subsequent correspondence, Fahrenhorst again voiced the notion that reverence for Luther could somehow cross confessional boundaries: "Luther is truly not only the founder of a Christian confession; much more, his ideas had a fruitful impact on all Christianity in Germany." Precisely because of Luther's political as well as religious significance, the *Luthertag* would serve as a confession both "to church and *Volk*."[126] It was all the more lamentable therefore that the HJ would not take part in the ceremonies, as Baldur von Schirach had designated 19 November as a recruiting day for the WHW. It was feared this would create a conflict of conscience within the Protestant population, especially because the WHW was a Christian activity: "The chief task of Christianity is helpfully to set to work and allow socialism to become reality."[127] Fahrenhorst also expressed concern that, among "liberal" circles in the movement, Nazism was being promoted as a "third confession," and that, thanks to the Concordat, Catholicism was in danger of taking over Germany. Hitler informed Fahrenhorst that arrangements for the HJ had already been made and that he did not want to see the Luther Day pushed back a second time; he made no reference to Fahrenhorst's other concerns. During the entire planning and execution of the event, this was the only moment of discord between the Nazi State and the Protestant organizers.

Opinions expressed that year made it plain that, despite these concerns, many leaders of the Protestant League saw Nazi policies as congruent with their own. Addressing the "Eastern Question," one member of the League argued that Luther and the Reformation had saved the colonization of the German East at the turn of the sixteenth century. In the nineteenth century, liberalism and the Poles brought new dangers to German nationality, but Hitler's National Socialism meant a new start in the east for the "slumbering Protestant and Prussian socialist powers."[128] One of the speakers at the annual assembly of the League in Kurhessen asked: "Upon what is the

---

[125] BAP R43 II/168/41-42 (15 August 1933: Berlin). Citing preexisting commitments, Hitler turned down the invitation.

[126] BAP R43 II/168/70-76 (4 November 1933: Berlin).

[127] Ibid.

[128] "Der Evangelische Bund in Marienburg," *Reichsbote*, 1 October 1933: in BAP R5101/23126/9. Much was made of the "persecution" of the Protestant Church, and therefore Germans also, in Catholic Poland. See, for instance, the article in *Freie Presse* (Lodz), 30 October 1933: in BAP R5101/23189/74, which laments the Slavic domination of German cultural life.

authority of the state and the family grounded? Why is our *Volk* holy to us? Only because these orders were created by God.... We thank God that our Führer clearly recognizes this and draws its conclusions."[129] This reference to *Schöpfungsglaube* also brought the Protestant League to an explicit endorsement of Nazi racialism. At a 1933 meeting in Magdeburg, a League speaker stated: "The Protestant church and every Protestant Christian must participate in the clarification and utilization of the racial and eugenic questions which are so significant for the future of our *Volk*."[130]

RELIGIOUS RIVALRY IN PARTY ORGANIZATIONS

Further evidence of the relative strengths of Christians and paganists in the Nazi movement was their status within party organizations. In the many ancillary organizations of the NSDAP the presence of Christians was affirmed, whereas a distinctly negative attitude was displayed toward paganism. One of the most notable in this regard was the National Socialist Women's Organization (*Nationalsozialistische Frauenschaft*, or NSF), founded in 1931. In an ideological manifesto drafted by the NSF leadership in 1932, all the recognized fundaments of Nazi ideology were affirmed: national rebirth, autarky, purity of race, indoctrination of youth, and the fight against the "Jewish–Marxist spirit." And also Christianity: "*We stand for the preservation of Christian belief. We feel responsible for our acts before our family and our Volk, before ourselves and before God.*"[131] Commemorating the founding of the NSF, Lilli Otto, one of its leaders, wrote in 1933: "Our Frauenschaft flag carries the same colors as the Swastika flag, only in different order. Just as red shines out in the Swastika flag, with our flag black stands out, solemn and worthy. On top shines forth the Christian cross in the color of purity, constantly warning us: 'You women and mothers, be real Christians; protect Christianity in your family, rear your children to love the savior'."[132]

This aspect of the NSF and other *völkisch* women's organizations is one of the few areas in which scholars have recognized a strong Christian element within the NSDAP – usually explained, however, as the Nazis' grudging concession to greater religiosity among women.[133] However, one of the most outstanding examples of a Christian identity in the NSF came from its only male leader, Gottfried Krummacher. Although he did not last long in this position, being replaced with Gertrud Scholtz-Klink within six months,

---

[129] "Evangelischer Bund und nationalsozialistischer Staat," *Kasseler Neueste Nachrichten*, 10 October 1933: in BAP R5101/23126/11.
[130] *Magdeburgische Zeitung*, 26 September 1933: in BAP R5101/23126/8. See Chapter 6.
[131] BAZ NS 44/55 (1 October 1932: Munich) (emphasis in the original).
[132] BAZ NS 26/254 (n.d.[1933], n.p.).
[133] See Claudia Koonz, *Mothers in the Fatherland: Women, the Family and Nazi Politics* (New York, 1987), Chapter 7; Michael Phayer, *Protestant and Catholic Women in Nazi Germany* (Detroit, 1990), Chapters 2, 4.

he revealed a complete commitment to the Nazi agenda.[134] Krummacher's
speeches contained repeated references to God and the role he ordained for
women. Shortly after assuming control of the NSF, Krummacher reminded
women of their maternal task: "Everything is located in God's grace. This
knowledge, which our *Volk* has forgotten in the last years, must be reawak-
ened in them. . . . We expect that our German women will view their work,
their service to the German *Volk*, as a calling, as a command from God, as
our Führer Adolf Hitler time and again stresses how he views his office and
his task as God's calling."[135] The heavily religious tone of this speech, and
others that Krummacher gave as NSF's leader,[136] might be regarded as little
more than calculation, reflecting the Nazis' interest in telling their female followers what they wanted to hear. However, Krummacher was also a member
of the provincial synod of the Protestant Church and the Rhineland leader
of the DC.[137] In fact, he had been recommended to Rudolf Hess for the position by Protestant Reich Bishop Ludwig Müller.[138] His speeches repeatedly
sounded Christian themes, so much so that even some in the NSF complained.
According to one member's protest, "Krummacher cannot talk three minutes without quoting the Bible four times."[139] Josef Grohé, the *Gauleiter* for
Krummacher's home town, similarly lamented that Krummacher could not
give a speech "without citing a whole series of passages from the Bible, even
from the Old Testament."[140]

These complaints notwithstanding, the broader ranks of the NSF emphasized Christian values. Hildegard Passow, one of its leaders, called Christ
the first socialist and Hitler his successor. She also suggested that the NSF's
antisemitism accorded with the Bible's teachings: "At no time does the Lord
God require of us charitable conciliation with the Jew, the mortal enemy of
the Aryan character. Christ himself called the Jews 'the sons of the Devil, a
brood of snakes,' and drove the dealers and moneychangers from the house of
God with a whip."[141] Scholtz-Klink, Krummacher's successor, did not speak
a Christian language as did Krummacher. In fact, Scholtz-Klink is usually
regarded as having been hostile to Christianity.[142] She almost never spoke

[134] Jill Stephenson demonstrates that Krummacher's short tenure as the NSF leader was not
accountable to ideological impurity, but to organizational infighting and the desire among
members of the NSF to have a woman as leader: Jill Stephenson, *The Nazi Organisation of
Women* (London, 1981), 103–5.
[135] *Hamburger Nachrichten*, 29 November 1933: in BStA Sammlung Rehse (hereafter
Rehse)/P3356.
[136] For example, "Die Frau ist die Hüterin deutscher Kultur," VB, 25 October 1933: in BStA
Rehse/P3356.
[137] *Kölnische Volkszeitung*, 19 November 1933: in BStA Rehse/P3356.
[138] Stephenson, *Organisation*, 102.
[139] Koonz, *Mothers*, 160.
[140] BAZ Personalakt Krummacher (28 February 1934: Köln).
[141] BAZ NS 26/254 (n.d.[1933], n.p.).
[142] Koonz, *Mothers*, 231, 249; Stephenson, *Organisation*, 171. Neither, it should be noted,
empirically demonstrate that Scholtz-Klink was anti-Christian. Michael Phayer points

of Christ when she addressed religious themes, but neither did she attack Christianity or its representatives as did Ley or Himmler. At the Women's section of the 1935 National Party Congress, Scholtz-Klink discussed the issue of church leaving: "God is love.... I do not say 'German mothers, stay away from the Church'; I say, 'Be as in olden times the priestess in your own homes'."[143] As we shall see, under Scholtz-Klink the NSF would live up to this claim, not only permitting its members to stay in the church, but also actively cooperating with church organizations well into the Third Reich. The NSF's positive stance toward Christianity could bring it into conflict with Nazi paganists, such as the race theorist Hans Günther, who complained to Rosenberg that, at a 1934 assembly, the NSF had openly propagated a Christian Nazism aimed directly against him.[144]

The NSF tried to extend its influence over the Nazi organization for young women, the BdM; but the BdM ultimately came under the control of the HJ and its leader Baldur von Schirach. Describing a BdM vacation camp in 1935, one girl remarked on the religious education she had received there:

We touched upon the Hauer movement and saw clarity and firmness in Christianity, over against the sincere but uncertain searching of paganism [Deutschglauben]. We did not always solve the difficult questions to everyone's satisfaction; but when we sometimes went to the village church in the evenings, we knew that God's greatness and love would certainly answer our questions and longings.... The last morning we were once again assembled, like so many times before, in front of the Swastika flag. 'Be active Christians [Christen der Tat]! Serve our Führer, serve our God! Give all honor to him who so happily leads our Volk.' These words spoke to us, and accompanied us afterward.[145]

It is not clear whether the "him who so happily leads" was Hitler or God. Given the tenor of the occasion, it was most likely both.

Schirach, head of the HJ and Reich Youth Leader (Reichsjugendführer), had been widely regarded as one of the main exponents of an anti-Christian paganism within the Nazi Party. Even the party leadership expressed concern about him: In a discussion among Hitler, Hans Schemm, and Otto Wagener in the Kampfzeit, Hitler poured his usual derision on paganism: "All that rubbish about the Thing places, the solstice festivals, the Midgard snake." Schemm agreed with Hitler: "I'm very glad to hear you say this.... There is such a lot of nonsense talked about the cult of Wotan and the spirit of the Edda.... These idiotic windbags have no idea what their spouting

to Scholtz-Klink's hostility toward Catholicism: Protestant and Catholic Women in Nazi Germany (Detroit, 1990), 117–18 – but nowhere does he suggest that she was ideologically opposed to Protestantism.

[143] Quoted in Koonz, Mothers, 294. Curiously, Koonz contends this speech "appealed to a panthestic, pagan Germanic faith" (ibid.), even though Scholtz-Klink makes no reference to non-Christian religions.

[144] BAZ NS 8/257/94 (24 March 1934: Jena).

[145] "An der Front," Das Wort, 17 November 1935: in BAP 62 Di 1/75/81.

causes."[146] Referring to these paganistic rites, Wagener pointed out that they were known to happen in the HJ. Hitler suggested that these could have beneficial consequences, as they brought German youth into nature, "to show them the powerful workings of divine creation." They also served a moral purpose by keeping youth out of saloons and "airless dives."[147] Wagener maintained that "the youth leaders must not fall into the error of wanting to turn this into a religion." Hitler reassured him: "Don't worry, they won't."[148]

As a private conversation, this could hardly have allayed the fears of the churches, especially the Catholic Church, which believed that in Schirach they had found a definite enemy of Christianity.[149] Schirach did little to pacify clerical opinion. At a December 1933 speech in Braunschweig, he made a promise: "The newly-enrolled members of the Hitler Youth will not ask of their comrades: 'Are you Protestant?' or 'Are you Catholic?', only 'Are you German'."[150] Taken in isolation, this passage would seem to offer ample evidence that the churches' fears were justified. However, in the same speech, Schirach insisted he was not anti-Christian: "They say of us that we are an anti-Christian movement. They even say that I am an outspoken paganist.... I solemnly declare here, before the German public, that I stand on the basis of Christianity, but I declare just as solemnly that I will put down every attempt to introduce confessional matters into our Hitler Youth." The churches' fears were in one sense well-founded: Schirach made no hesitation to publicly proclaim an anticonfessional and anticlerical position. However, as with so many others in the party elite, Schirach demonstrated his belief that Christianity and the churches were not the same thing. Schirach gave further indication of his religious views in a poem he wrote in 1934 called "Christ" (he considered himself the poet laureate of the Nazi movement, even publishing a collection of his work). In it we see not just the warrior Christ of *völkisch* Christianity, but the suffering Christ of conservative Christian doctrine: "If today he descended from Heaven, the great warrior who struck the moneychangers/ You would once again shout 'crucify!'/ And nail him to the cross that he himself carried/ But he would gently laugh at your hatred/ 'The truth remains even when your bearers are passed/ Faith remains, because I give my life . . . '/ And the fighter of all the world towers on the cross."[151]

In his book of the same year, *The Hitler Youth: Idea and Form*, Schirach made what again appeared to be an anti-Christian statement: "Whoever

---

[146] Turner (ed.), *Memoirs of a Confidant*, 277.
[147] Ibid., 278–9.
[148] Ibid., 277–8. As Turner explains, the "Midgard snake" was supposed to be the adversary of Thor in Nordic religious mythology.
[149] Compare Conway, *Persecution*, 124–5.
[150] *Dokumente zur Kirchenpolitik*, 1: 182–3. In a meeting at the beginning of October, Schirach said of himself: "I belong to no confession. I am neither Protestant nor Catholic, I believe only in Germany" (ibid., 182).
[151] *Evangelium im Dritten Reich*, 1 July 1934: in BAP 62 Di 1/75/122.

works for Germany uncompromisingly is the mortal enemy of every confessional principle in a state organization." Here again was an unrestrained – and public – attack on confessionalism. Although Hitler, among others, suggested that Nazism would respect both confessions equally, in Schirach's view Nazism would respect neither. Such sentiments led some observers to the conclusion that Schirach intended to create a "third confession."[152] At the same time, however, Schirach insisted that his Hitler youths would have every right to worship according to their own beliefs: "In no manner does the HJ restrict the religious activities of its members. Neither in their visits to Sunday services, nor in their contribution to other church festivities, will Catholic Hitler youths be restricted by the leadership of the HJ."[153] Indeed, Schirach made free each Sunday morning and one afternoon during the week for both Protestants and Catholics in the HJ to worship and engage in religious activity. Additionally, the HJ provided support for church educational work, so long as it was of a "purely religious" character.[154] According to Schirach, this granting of religious expression, providing a place for Christianity within one of the most important Nazi organizations, did not contradict the totalizing claims of the Nazi movement: "I hold the view that religious meetings and events in special religious youth gatherings do not contradict the HJ's totalizing claims. Every effort that aims at a deepening and intensification of religious feeling must not only be welcomed, but also led, by any youth leadership with a sense of responsibility. I believe that through the agreement with the Reich Bishop of the Protestant Church, the Hitler Youth has indicated that it is ready to grant the necessary space for religious education."[155] Here Schirach was referring to the 13 December 1933 agreement between him and Müller to incorporate formally the various Protestant youth groups into the HJ. Whereas the Catholic Church sought to maintain its confessionally distinct youth groups, the pro-Müller faction of the Protestant Church had signaled its desire to subsume confessionalism under the "above churches" doctrine of positive Christianity.

Several examples of HJ activity demonstrate that Schirach was sincere in his willingness to permit, seemingly without hindrance, Christian observance and activity. Refuting accusations made by the Protestant Church in Saxony that Schirach was encouraging his officers to leave the church, the Reich Youth Leadership Office informed the party's Reich Leadership Office in private correspondence that "HJ leaders do not have to make a decision between being an HJ leader or being a Christian."[156] A Protestant newspaper observed with approval that pastors were to be found addressing outdoor HJ gatherings. At one such gathering a pastor invited HJ to regard Christ

[152] Compare Charles Macfarland, *The New Church and the New Germany* (New York, 1934), 151.
[153] Baldur von Schirach, *Die Hitler-Jugend: Idee und Gestalt* (Berlin, 1934), 44.
[154] Scholder, *Churches*, 2: 115.
[155] Schirach, *Hitler-Jugend*, 44.
[156] BAP 62 Ka 1/22/184–185 (12 July 1935: Berlin).

as the Lord: "He is our light. Away with all dialecticism and formalistic squabbling! Living faith is what counts. Christ seized upon this: selflessly devote yourself to the community, to your brothers; stand responsible before God, be overwhelmed by him. Be free of dross, be free of oneself! As John said: while he grows, I am diminished."[157] In May 1935, the *Stürmer* reported with consternation that a troop of HJ had greeted representatives of the Inner Mission – the Protestant Church's welfare branch and as such a confessional organization – in "full uniform" at Berlin's Anhalter Bahnhof.[158] Although HJ members were allowed these prerogatives, the same freedom of religious expression was not granted within the HJ to paganist organizations like the DGB. When the DGB attempted to use a passage from one of Schirach's poems in a promotional flier, the leadership of the HJ voiced its disapproval. Writing to the head office of the Gestapo, the Reich Youth Leadership Office complained: "The Reich Youth Leader has never given the German Faith Movement permission to use this poem for its propaganda purposes. That the Reich Youth Leader moreover has forbidden any propaganda activity in the Hitler Youth for the German Faith Movement is proof that the quote has been misused." Schirach's office requested that the Gestapo confiscate all copies of the leaflet.[159]

Christian voices could also be heard within the ranks of the SA, until the Röhm Purge of 1934 the most radical exponent of Nazism.[160] One example from the *Kampfzeit* was an article in an SA organ titled "Christ's Spirit – SA Spirit!": "We interpret in the Gospel not the word, but the spirit. We see in the seed, in the model of our Savior not only that he does good and shuns evil, but also that he struggles. . . . Jesus was not locked up in a church, waiting for the throng. . . . What SA man has not surprised himself with the thought that the orator in a meeting, the man of the people, says exactly what a minister would preach?"[161] Another article, "Under the Cross," engaged even more closely with an evangelizing discourse: "To us Christianity is not an empty phrase, but a glowing life. It lives through us and in us. . . . Thus is the strength of the nation gathered under the sign of the cross. When the red beast threatens us, or the well-behaved philistine [*sittsame Spießer*] . . . sneers at us, we look up to the Cross and receive the doctrine of struggle."[162]

---

[157] "Hitlerjugend hält Gottesdienst zur Sonnenwende," *Evangelium im Dritten Reich*, 1 July 1934: in BAP 62 Di 1/75/122.

[158] "HJ sammelt für konfessionelle Zwecke," *Der Stürmer*, 19 May 1935: in BAP 62 Di 1/75/175.

[159] BAP R5101/23139/360 (16 December 1935: Berlin).

[160] One of the leaders of the purge was Buch. In a postwar interview, Buch claimed it was he who forced Hitler to recognize Röhm's homosexuality as unacceptable and to suggest Victor Lutze – "a man who was the exact opposite of Röhm; married with children, modest" – as his replacement: IfZ ZS 855/34-39 (18 July 1945: n.p.). Donald McKale confirms this, adding that Buch was one of the first to work for Röhm's assassination: *The Nazi Party Courts: Hitler's Management of Conflict in His Movement, 1921–1945* (Lawrence, 1974), 100.

[161] *Der S.A. Mann*, VB supplement, 18 January 1930.

[162] *Der S.A. Mann*, 11 December 1930.

Fig. 9   The SA at prayer. Source: Heinrich Hoffmann, *Das braune Heer* (Berlin, 1932).

Fig. 10   The SA leaving a prayer service. Source: Heinrich Hoffmann, *Das braune Heer* (Berlin, 1932).

Such sentiments were still being expressed after the *Machtergreifung*. 1933 saw a spate of Nazi mass weddings in Protestant churches, such as one held in the Lazarus Church in Berlin. More than forty couples were married on this occasion, with the entire "Horst Wessel *Sturm*" of the SA in attendance.[163] In 1935 a Protestant theology student in the SA insisted that he and fellow Christians were never made to feel outside the community, were always greeted with feelings of comradeship, and were even appreciated as men of "inner conviction." Theologians in the SA, this student continued, "show their comrades that above all else theologians are not enemies of the *Volk*, but men like they, who, precisely because they are Christian, want to serve their *Volk* and Fatherland with body and soul."[164] He was not the only theologian in the SA.[165] Nor would he necessarily have been a German Christian; within SA ranks could be found members of the BK as well. Among other instances, a BK vicar in Silesia was a member, Göttingen members of the BK "routinely belonged to the SA," and in Brandenburg there were several SA men who were active in the BK.[166]

Just as paganists complained of Christian activity in the HJ and the NSF, they also expressed dismay when it occurred in the SA. One paganist newspaper reported on a SA *Sturm* taking part in the hundredth anniversary celebrations of the Young Men's Christian Association (*Christliche Verein Junger Männer*, or CVJM) of 1935 in Bremen. One of the members of this *Sturm*, which had come all the way from Silesia for the event, publicly declared that "the SA is prepared to make its confession to Christ."[167] In the

---

[163] *Evangelium im Dritten Reich*, 3 July 1933. Horst Wessel, an SA man killed in a street brawl and one of the greatest heroes in the Nazi pantheon, was the son of a Protestant pastor, and, according to his sister Ingeborg, a believing Christian: *Evangelium im Dritten Reich*, 4 March 1934. On Nazi activity in other Berlin churches, see Manfred Gailus (ed.), *Kirchengemeinden im Nationalsozialismus: Sieben Beispiele aus Berlin* (Berlin, 1990). An SA *Sturm* was roughly the size of an army company.

[164] "SA-Mann und Theologie Student," *Evangelischer Beobachter*, 8 August 1935: in BAP 62 Di 1/75/88.

[165] The IfZ in Munich contains a file (F 304) devoted to Protestant theologians in the Nazi movement. One of them, a Hans Kipfmüller, was a pastor and *alte Kämpfer*, having entered the NSDAP in 1925 with membership number 9929. In addition to being the local Protestant pastor, Kipfmüller was also SA *Oberscharführer*, local leader of the Nazi People's Welfare Organization (*Nationalsozialistische Volkswohlfahrt*, or NSV) and district leader of the office for cultural policy. In his personnel file, he was listed as a specialist in "race policy." Bearing the party's Golden Badge of Honor, a rare distinction that was conferred only on those who displayed true ideological commitment, rounded out Kipfmüller's credentials as a Nazi (IfZ F 304 [n.d., n.p.]).

[166] Victoria Barnett, *For the Soul of the People: Protestant Protest against Hitler* (Oxford, 1992), 40; Robert Ericksen, "A Radical Minority: Resistance in the German Protestant Church," in Francis Nicosia and Lawrence Stokes (eds.), *Germans Against Nazism: Nonconformity, Opposition and Resistance in the Third Reich* (New York, 1990), 129–30; EZA 14/589 (8 April 1935: Zepernick, Kreis Niederbarnim). In the small Brandenburg town of Zepernick alone, two members of the BK synod were also SA men.

[167] *Flammenzeichen*, 23 February 1935: in BAP 62 Di 1/75/99. The paper reported that this unit had given itself the moniker "Holy *Sturm*."

same year, a rumor had spread that the Rosenberg faction of the party was attempting to expel clergy from the SA. This question was addressed by the Department for Cultural Peace, a small office set up in the *Reichsleitung* in February 1934 to handle religious matters in the Nazi Party. In a letter addressed to the governing board of the BK, the Department assured them that such an order had neither been given nor proposed.[168]

THE GERMAN FAITH MOVEMENT

These organizations were all formally affiliated with the NSDAP. However, in the context of Nazi encounters with paganism, it is also worth exploring the history of an external group of paganists loyal to the Nazi movement. Although it never became a party organization, the DGB represented the main organizational voice for paganism in the Third Reich. Members of the NSDAP could be found in their ranks, even if none in the party leadership were present.

A major DGB rally in June 1934 saw speeches given by both Jakob Hauer and Ernst Reventlow, specifically regarding their views on Christian dogma. As Rosenberg had done, Hauer rejected the notion of Original Sin. Reventlow added that the DGB rejected the biblical concepts of guilt, retribution, and salvation: "Our forefathers knew nothing of these concepts, and they were more pious and reverent than the Jews of the Old Testament." Hauer, the ex–pastor, explicitly rejected "positive Christianity" as irrelevant and even expressed disappointment with Luther: "We will not and cannot stand by Martin Luther's half protest."[169] At the same time, however, they insisted that they were not breaking away from the person of Jesus; they were not propagating racial materialism; and they did not believe that the *Volk* itself was divine. They also insisted that the idea of religion without the Hereafter was "unthinkable." Toward individual Christians they professed no animus: "Whereas the Christian is of the view that the Christian of an alien *Volk* stands closer to him than the 'paganist' of his own *Volk*, we maintain that the Christian of our own *Volk* stands closer to us than the 'paganist' of an alien *Volk*, precisely because he is of our blood. This is the exact foundation of our faith." The defense of Jesus was in line with Hauer's declaration from the month before: "The thousand year history of Christianity in the *germanisch–deutsch* space is only an episode, which today is coming to an end. We do not mean the figure of Jesus – in the future there will always be Jesus congregations [*Gemeinden Jesu*] – but rather the near eastern–semitic form of faith which is alien to the *germanisch–deutsch* world."[170]

---

[168] EZA 50/17/91 (15 October 1935: Berlin). This office merged into a new Reich Church Ministry the following year.

[169] *Deutsche Zeitung*, 12 June 1934: in BAP R5101/23139/12.

[170] "Prof. Hauer über die Deutsche Glaubensbewegung," *Frankfurt Oder-Zeitung*, 18 May 1934: in BAP R5101/23139/2.

Other leaders of the DGB took a similarly differentiated view. One was Herbert Grabert, who edited the paganist monthly *Deutscher Glaube* ("German Faith").[171] He also worked in the Religious Studies section of Rosenberg's Office of Ideological Information. In 1936, Grabert published a book called *The Protestant Mission of the German Volk: Fundamentals of German Faith History from Luther to Hauer*, which provides one of the most detailed expositions on the paganist appropriation, and appreciation, of Protestantism.[172] He suggested that Germanic faith and Christianity were irreconcilable, that his movement was about belief rather than religion, God rather than Christ, *Volk* rather than Church.[173] Luther was a central figure in Grabert's religious history, having begun the long process of German liberation from the stifling Roman Church. But Luther did not, in Grabert's view, found Protestantism. Rather, Luther's struggle against the Roman Church expressed a preexisting Protestant "original force," which Grabert defined as a Nordic–German spirit of the soul (*Seelentum*) aimed against the christianizing forces emanating from the south.[174] Luther went only halfway toward fulfilling the Protestant mission. It was the task of the current age to complete the process: "Never was the Protestant mission of our *Volk* so clear and indispensable as today."[175] Jesus as a person could remain as a friend and traveling companion (*Weggenossen*).[176] However, the "foreign, Jewish" Bible would have to be removed. Hence Grabert advocated a Protestantism with even less Christian doctrine than Rosenberg had retained.

Grabert knew this would prompt a question: "What, then, do we as the German Faith Movement have to do with Protestantism, with this phase of Christian church history?" The answer: "It is precisely a chief concern of this work to show that German Protestantism in its best parts can be regarded as a movement of German blood from the German spirit and German soul."[177] Like Rosenberg, Grabert maintained that contemporary Protestantism, under the influence of Barth, was losing its unique line of thought and returning to Rome. This led Grabert to a paradoxical assertion: "German Protestantism is dead, but the Protestant spirit and mission still live.... The German Faith Movement of today is the heir of the best elements of German Protestantism."[178] In other words, the Protestant *institution* was dead, but not Protestant belief, which expressed itself in four fundamentals: an immediacy to God (*Gottunmittelbarkeit*), trust and belief in God, a faith beholden

---

[171] BAP R5101/23140/273. (Unidentified newspaper clipping, 30 September 1936.)
[172] Herbert Grabert, *Der protestantische Auftrag des deutschen Volkes: Grundzüge der deutschen Glaubensgeschichte von Luther bis Hauer* (Stuttgart, 1936).
[173] Ibid., 9–20.
[174] Ibid., 38–9.
[175] Ibid., 40.
[176] Ibid., 285.
[177] Ibid., 42.
[178] Ibid., 43.

to no one but God, and freedom of conscience before God.[179] When Grabert mapped out his intellectual path from Luther to Hauer, he significantly gave a prominent place to the development of liberal Protestantism in the nineteenth century, which culminated in the works of the "last great Protestant theologian," Adolf von Harnack.[180]

The DGB's insistence that it was *the* religious expression of Nazism was not taken kindly in the NSDAP. Certainly they had their sympathizers. Himmler, for instance, permitted the SS to take part in the official ceremonies of the DGB's Sports Palace meeting in Spring 1935, an occasion that marked the height of their fortunes.[181] In Württemberg, *Kultusminister* Christian Mergenthaler permitted members of the DGB to teach at Protestant schools, much to the displeasure of the Protestant press.[182] At best, such Nazis were willing to tolerate the DGB as a religious community that would remain outside the party. Even Rosenberg, who shared many, if not most, DGB precepts, could not envision them as a formal party organization. In his ideal Nazi State, they would be made a religious community on par with the Christian confessions, which would lose their status as official religions and become independent associations.[183] On the other hand, many other Nazis were far less tolerant and even took an active stand against them. In July 1934, Richard Zwörner, the consultant for religion and churches in the NSLB, suggested that the religious claims of the DGB were spurious and that the NSDAP reject them.[184] In October Hans Schemm banned the DGB in his capacity as *Gauleiter* of Bayerische Ostmark.[185] In Brandenburg the same month, Wilhelm Kube banned the organization after what he regarded to be an inflammatory speech.[186] Another paganist organization, the Nordic Ring, was disbanded by the Nazi authorities altogether, and even the use of Norse names was outlawed for a time.[187] The next year saw even more repressive measures, including the banning of Reventlow's paper *Reichswart* for subversive content in February.[188] Repression of the DGB intensified after the Sports Palace meeting, during which time and again they made claims to being the true voice of Nazi religion. That June the head of the Saxon Gestapo banned a meeting of the DGB in Leipzig, even though it was a private meeting

[179] Ibid., 59.
[180] Ibid., 208. Nowhere did Grabert refer to Harnack's rejection of the Old Testament, which would have presumably enhanced his esteem for this theologian all the more.
[181] BAP R5101/23139/338 (2 May 1935: Berlin).
[182] *Das Evangelische Deutschland*, 2 September 1934: in BAP 62 Di 1/106/349. It was noted with indignation that the Concordat protected Catholics from such infiltration.
[183] "Plan für die NS-Religionspolitik," BAP 62 Di 1/84–2 (n.d., n.p.).
[184] BStA MK/37069a (31 July 1934: Bayreuth).
[185] BAP 62 Di 1/106/34 (16 October 1934: Tübingen).
[186] BAP R5101/23139/253 (30 November 1934: Berlin).
[187] Paul Weindling, *Health, Race and German Politics between National Unification and Nazism, 1870–1945* (Cambridge, 1989), 478.
[188] *Berliner Tageblatt*, 15 February 1935: in BAP R5101/23139/59.

for members only.[189] Members complained when, a short time later, the Saxon Minister of the Interior banned the movement altogether.[190] Finally, in August 1935, Heydrich forbade all rallies and other public meetings of the DGB across the Reich.[191] By contrast, the DC never came under such state restriction.

Even this was not sufficient for some party leaders. Josef Terboven, *Gauleiter* of Essen and Reich Commissioner for Occupied Norway during the war, was opposed to the DGB on the grounds that their activities caused considerable difficulties for him in his overwhelmingly Catholic district. He also expressed indignation when the local DGB speaker maintained that "No Christian can be a National Socialist and no National Socialist Christian." Terboven believed this went against the will of the Führer; furthermore, it was not up to the DGB to decided who could be a Nazi and who not.[192] Further action was taken against the DGB when it was noticed that their newspaper *Reichswart*, which had had its ban lifted, described itself as a "National Socialist weekly." Hanns Kerrl, who as Reich Church Minister was responsible for all religious bodies in Germany, declared this to be a false association of the NSDAP with the DGB, and, on obtaining the backing of Hess and Goebbels, ordered the paper to drop this designation.[193]

The DGB's claims to represent the true face of Nazi religiosity were also resented by the DC. They were especially insulted by Bishop Wurm's contention that the DC stood for the ideology of Rosenberg and the DGB. They insisted that *they* were the true representatives of Nazi religion, who stood "in the middle of the great National Socialist front against all opposed ideologies."[194] Joachim Hossenfelder, one-time leader of the DC and one of its most theologically radical exponents, also rejected comparisons of the DGB with the DC, arguing that not only their theologies differed, but that the DGB contained politically unreliable elements.[195] This was not entirely unwarranted: Among the many religious associations the DGB absorbed in 1933 was the sizable League of Free Religious Communities, which, according to Klaus Scholder "came from the free-thinking Marxist tradition."[196] Even

---

[189] BAP R5101/23139/203 (15 July 1935: Berlin).

[190] BAP R5101/23139/223 (20 July 1935: Lübz).

[191] *Dokumente zur Kirchenpolitik*, 3: 60.

[192] BAP R5101/23139/145 (8 October 1935: Koblenz).

[193] BAP R5101/23139/296 (14 December 1935: Berlin). Starting with the 25 January 1936 issue of *Reichswart*, the subtitle was changed to "Weekly for National Independence and German Socialism": in BAP R5101/23139/295.

[194] BAP 62 Di 1/75/89-90 (2 August 1935: Berlin). Nazi authorities issued an order to the DC two years later, similar to the action taken against the *Reichswart*, forbidding them to use the swastika in their official emblem. However, although the action against the *Reichswart* was taken to assert the party's independence from paganism, their stance toward the DC was motivated by a desire to appear neutral in the Church Struggle: BAP R43 II/150/103–04 (4 May 1938: Berlin).

[195] BAP R43 II/163/145-156 (28 January 1935: Berlin).

[196] Scholder, *Churches*, 1: 452.

Artur Dinter entered the fray. Hauer sued the one-time *Gauleiter*, expelled by Hitler for trying to make the NSDAP into a platform for his religious views, when Dinter publicly accused Hauer and the DGB of being atheistic.[197]

In spite of repeated warnings, Hauer continued to argue that the DGB's religion fit that of the Nazis better than any other. For this reason, Nazi State authorities finally forced Hauer to resign his leadership of the DGB in April 1936. Reventlow left the leadership as well, but voluntarily. Unlike Hauer, he found the repeated attacks on Christianity increasingly disagreeable. As he stated in private correspondence to Kerrl's Ministry: "The struggle which the DG[B] leads against both Christianity and Christian *Volk* comrades is, for me as a National Socialist, highly intolerable. This struggle is not compatible with point 24 of the [party] program."[198] He had always been in favor of religious peace, he wrote, and wanted above all to follow Hitler's dictum that there could be no religious warfare for the sake of the nation. Instead of working for cooperation among Protestants, Catholics, and non-Christians, elements of the DGB were pushing it in a radically anti-Christian course that he had found unacceptable, because anti-Nazi. Reventlow was not simply covering his tracks here. As early as 1927, years before the founding of the DGB or the Seizure of Power, Reventlow had announced his agreement with Hitler's policy of religious neutrality, especially the idea that Protestant and Catholic should be united in common defense against the Jew. Reventlow took his paper *Reichswart* with him, using it to further his own view that the non-Christian German had to respect and tolerate the views of his Christian compatriots.[199]

CONCLUSION

With the conquest of power in 1933, the Nazis were afforded the opportunity to act on the religious convictions they professed in the *Kampfzeit*. The anti-Christians of the party were strikingly honest about their dislike of the Christian religion. Neither Rosenberg nor Himmler affected a Christian stance in public after the Seizure of Power any more than they did behind closed doors. The great clerical hostility that met his *Mythus* did not lead Rosenberg to retract his criticisms in the name of political opportunism; they were instead publicly reaffirmed in his subsequent writings. In the same way, Heydrich publicly derided the Catholic Church as perhaps *the* enemy of the state. Himmler, who might have been expected to lean on his former Christian faith for the sake of propaganda, made no public attempt to do so. He did state publicly that his SS men must believe in God: and this was his private position as well.

---

[197] *Westfälischer Volksblatt*, 7 May 1936: in BAP 62 Di 1/71/33.

[198] "Die nationalsozialistischen Gründe für mein Ausscheiden aus der Deutschen Glaubensbewegung": BAP R5101/23140/39-43 (8 April 1936: Berlin).

[199] Compare "Um die innerliche Geschlossenheit des Volkes," *Reichswart*, 23 October 1937: in BAP R5101/23141/177.

On the other hand, those who upheld positive Christianity before 1933 sustained their allegiance to it afterward. Goebbels and Hitler suggested in public that many of the domestic measures taken by the regime – the destruction of Marxist organizations, the strengthening of the family, the WHW, and other attributes of the *Volksgemeinschaft* – were inspired by the ethical principles of positive or practical Christianity. All who insisted they or their movement were Christian in the *Kampfzeit* maintained this attitude afterward. As Goebbels affirmed in his diary in 1937, even in private Hitler continued to gain inspiration from Christ, who, like Hitler, "was also against Jewish world domination."[200] Just as new voices emerged on the anti-Christian side, especially Himmler's, they emerged on the positive Christian side, most notably with Göring. Their enduring rejection of paganism was equally as public as Rosenberg's endorsement of it. Publicly and privately, the party's elite rejected paganist attempts to claim the mantle of "party religion," whether these came from members of the party or the DGB. Therefore there is little to support the claim that the DGB or its ideology were "widely supported" in Nazi circles.[201] Lower down the ranks of the party, the right of Christians to retain their religious beliefs and practices was affirmed.

Many of these positive Christians celebrated Luther as a national hero, and positioned themselves as his inheritors. But as was demonstrated by the 450th anniversary of Luther's birth, they also showed the limits of their interconfessionalism. Catholic positive Christians were hard to find during Luther Day. Notable in his absence during the festivities was Goebbels, who as propaganda minister might have been expected to say anything deemed advantageous. Although Nazi leaders like Frick, Buch, Koch, Rust, and Schemm all freely associated Luther with Nazism, none of Christianity's antagonists in the party – Himmler and Ley most notably – felt obligated to publicly praise Luther for the sake of expediency. Their private hostility was matched by public silence. Even Rosenberg, who meticulously detached Luther from Lutheran Christianity, made no appearance at the Luther festivities, presumably because he found them too ecclesiastical.

Another limit to the interconfessionalism of positive Christianity was the party's church policy. Relations with the Catholic Church were never warm, despite several points of ideological contact: Whereas Catholics tended to reject Nazi racial theory, in almost all instances Nazis rejected Catholic internationalism. On the other hand, many Nazis proclaimed an affinity for Protestantism. Did this translate into a positive bearing toward its institutions? Was Nazi action against Protestant pastors later in the regime, particularly against Martin Niemöller, the natural consequence of putting idea into practice or the product of contingency? Was it Nazi policy to destroy the Protestant church as an institutional rival, or did the Nazis seek instead to build a relationship with it as an ideological ally?

---

[200] Fröhlich (ed.), *Tagebücher*, entry for 23 February 1937.
[201] Compare Conway, *Persecution*, 109, 122.

5

COMPLETING THE REFORMATION

The Protestant Reich Church

Through me the Protestant Church could become the established church, as in England.

Adolf Hitler[1]

Nazis expressed various degrees of anticlericalism. Although this was often articulated in an undifferentiated manner, it was not applied uniformly to both confessions. Whereas the Catholic Church continued to be attacked for its "internationalism" and doctrinal stand against racialist categories, the Protestant Church was generally treated much more favorably. Particularly revealing in this regard was the plan to unite the twenty-eight Protestant state churches of Germany into one national church – a Reich Church. Conventional historiography regards the Nazi interest in institutional Protestantism as duplicitous. For instance, John Conway believes that the Nazi endorsement of a *Reichskirche* in no sense implied pro-Protestant sentiment. In his view, the Nazis' aim in uniting the state churches was to render Protestantism innocuous, to make the Protestant church "an instrument subservient to the Nazi State. . . . The Church was a pillar of the old order, whose standing, though it might be exploited as a temporary measure, was fundamentally resented by the leading members of the Party."[2] In this chapter, we shall see that the Nazis in fact hoped for a lasting relationship with the Protestant Church, at least until 1937, when the stance of Niemöller and his allies led them to conclude that the church could not be relied on. After this break, actions against Protestant clergymen grew in number, although never becoming comparable in frequency or harshness with the measures that had already been leveled against Catholic clergy. For most Nazis, and certainly nearly all positive Christians, the anticlericalism of the regime toward Protestantism arose only when other policy options had been exhausted and was not planned from the outset.

[1] Albert Speer, *Inside the Third Reich* (New York, 1970), 95.
[2] John Conway, *The Nazi Persecution of the Churches* (London, 1968), 35, 102.

THE MÜLLER ERA

As early as 1927, Hitler discussed the subject of a Protestant *Reichskirche* with the military chaplain of Königsberg, Ludwig Müller.[3] This was not the first time that the idea of a unified national Protestant Church had arisen. It had been on the agenda of large segments of Protestant opinion some time before then; as with so much else of the Nazis' ecclesiological platform, the idea of a *Reichskirche* was most closely, but not exclusively, associated with theologically liberal Protestantism. The liberal Protestant Association was founded in 1863 to promote the idea of a national church, and this became a centerpiece of the German Christian (DC) platform. The idea of a Protestant Reich Church was not, as is sometimes suggested, an imposition of Hitler's Catholic understanding of ecclesiastical structure; nor was it symptomatic of a non-Christian, racialist mania that allegedly infected its advocates.[4] On the other hand, owing to their theological conservatism confessional Lutherans often opposed the idea of a *Reichskirche*, which, it was feared, threatened to transgress the boundaries of doctrine to unite all Protestant Germans.[5] For instance, confessionalist Lutheran August Marahrens, state bishop of Hanover and acknowledged ideological ally of Nazism,[6] nonetheless opposed the Nazi hopes for a national church because this would mean a merger with Reformed and ("Old Prussian") Union churches. The most he could support was a union of the Lutheran state churches of central Germany.[7]

But this does not mean that the Protestant establishment remained a motionless island of conservatism in a surging sea of revolution. As the church historian Jonathan Wright states, "There was a widespread desire among Protestants for a more united church grouped around the different creeds. There was also general hostility to 'parliamentarism' in the church.... In the Spring of 1933 there was a general feeling, especially among young theologians, that a new era had dawned which offered great new opportunities

---

[3] Klaus Scholder, "Die evangelische Kirche in der Sicht der Nationalsozialistischen Führung bis zum Kriegsausbruch," *Vierteljahrshefte für Zeitgeschichte* 16 (1968), 17.

[4] For the former argument, see Klaus Scholder, *The Churches and the Third Reich*, 2 vols. (London, 1987–8), 1: 306; for the latter argument, see Michael Burleigh, *The Third Reich: A New History* (New York, 2000), 259.

[5] Martin Gerhardt, *Zur Vorgeschichte der Reichskirche: Die Frage der kirchlichen Einigung in Deutschland im 19. und 20. Jahrhundert* (Bonn, 1934). The idea of a national Protestant Church had also been propagated by the theologically liberal Protestant League and the Adolf Gustav Association, an organization established to address the concerns of "diaspora" Protestants (mostly *Volksdeutsche*) living outside the borders of the German Reich. On the Protestant League's support for the *Reichskirche*, see *Deutsche Allgemeine Zeitung*, 16 July 1933: in Evangelisches Zentralarchiv in Berlin (hereafter EZA), 7/1296.

[6] Robert Ericksen, *Theologians under Hitler: Gerhard Kittel, Paul Althaus and Emanuel Hirsch* (New Haven, 1985), 167; Eberhard Klügel, *Die lutherische Landeskirche Hannovers und ihr Bischof 1933–1945* (Berlin, 1965), 37.

[7] Klügel, *Landeskirche Hannovers*, 20–1.

after a long period of retreat."[8] If the confessional Lutheran Marahrens was against a Reich Church, others, like Bavarian State Bishop Hans Meiser, supported the idea of a united Reich Church so long as it was "sufficiently" Lutheran. However, the strongest advocates of the national church idea were the DC. This did not mean that the DC were simply the Nazis' "fifth column" in this regard. Hitler for one made no indication that he regarded a unified Protestant Church solely as a tool to aid in the nazification of German Protestants. According to Müller, the lapsed Catholic Hitler confided to him in the *Kampfzeit* that he "longed to have a religious home again."[9] Owing to Hitler's well-established scorn for Rosenberg's ersatz faith, this statement – made to a Protestant pastor – could only have implied Protestantism. The meaning of the episode is conjectural, especially when we consider that Hitler took no tangible steps to find that religious home. Nonetheless, this sentiment was consistent with the favorable remarks he made about Protestantism, not just publicly in *Mein Kampf*, but privately in his circle of confidants.[10] This attitude continued well into the Third Reich.

Almost immediately after the Seizure of Power, a series of events in Mecklenburg provided Hitler the opportunity to reveal his intentions for the Protestant Church. On 22 April 1933 the Nazi State authorities in Mecklenburg announced that the government of the state church, whose head was the confessional Lutheran Rendtorff, had been overthrown and replaced with a commissioner for church affairs. The move was instigated by Richard Walther Darré, who, along with fellow "Blood and Soil" ideologue Walter Bohm and Nazi *Ministerpräsident* of Mecklenburg Walter Granzow planned to replace the "reactionaries" in the state church with those more in line with the Nazi Party. Bohm, appointed as commissioner, appealed to the pious country people of Mecklenburg not to be "humbled under the domination of bishops... [and to dispose] of bishops who want to arrogate to themselves the power of the crosier over against the parishes and the Landeskirchen." Bohm continued with his admonition: "Take over the government of the church for yourselves along with all functions of church government down to community level."[11] After an unsympathetic interview with Granzow, Rendtorff wrote Hitler and Hans Lammers, Hitler's secretary in the Reich Chancellery, to protest the action. Only two days later, Hitler and Frick convened a meeting with Darré, Granzow, and Bohm. Hitler made no reference to the church "revolution" just undertaken – much to the

---

[8] Jonathan Wright, *'Above Parties': The Political Attitudes of the German Protestant Church Leadership, 1918–1933* (Oxford, 1974), 120.

[9] Quoted in Jonathan Wright, *'Über den Parteien': Die politische Haltung der evangelischen Kirchenführer 1918–1933* (Göttingen, 1977), 152. This quote is not in the original English version.

[10] Adolf Hitler, *Mein Kampf*, trans. Ralph Manheim (Boston, 1962), 112–13; Henry Ashby Turner (ed.), *Hitler: Memoirs of a Confidant*, (New Haven, 1985), 19–21, 210.

[11] *Niederdeutsche Beobachter*, 18 April 1933.

consternation of Bohm, who expected to be congratulated on his achievement. Instead they were informed that they were immediately to meet Rendtorff. Frick opened this meeting by declaring that, even though these were revolutionary times, the actions of the Mecklenburg state government were illegal. Rendtorff was reinstated as *Landesbischof*, Bohm resigned three days later, and the *Ministerpräsident* resigned some months afterwards because of the fallout caused by the incident.[12] That some of the highest Nazi officials in a state government lost their positions over this affair – not reprimanded, not furloughed, but removed from office – demonstrated not only Hitler's intentions toward German Protestants, but also how seriously Protestant Church affairs could be taken by the Nazi regime.

This affair precipitated a meeting that Hitler held with the president of the Protestant *Oberkirchenrat*, Hermann Kapler. This was the first meeting between Hitler as head of state and a designated representative of the Protestant Church. In it, Hitler upheld the church's autonomy, but declared himself ideologically for the DC. That day, Hitler also made Frick his official liaison in Protestant Church affairs and Müller his personal advisor. Lammers noted Hitler's keen interest in the effort toward unity in German Protestantism, not least because this could serve as a counterweight to Catholicism.[13] In a meeting with the representatives of the state churches, Müller informed them of Hitler's wishes. Hitler was interested in reaching an agreement with institutional Protestantism, Müller stated. Referring to the Concordat with Rome, Müller suggested that Hitler now wanted a bloc against Rome.[14] Because Hitler's own conception of Nazism was that of a secular movement imbued with religious values, it was logical to seek a relationship of this kind with organized religion. Had the Dinter approach of creating a religious movement prevailed, then organized religion would have been viewed as a rival church literally to be replaced. For the duration of the Third Reich, Hitler never entertained this approach; indeed, he hoped to put the Protestant Church to use. However, conceiving of a unified Protestant Church as a bulwark against Catholicism was not simply the consequence of Hitler's instrumentalism. A "broad middle group" in the Protestant establishment, including Kapler, contemplated the possibility of a Reich Church in exactly these terms.[15] When the Protestant churches were unable to find mutual agreement, owing largely to the doctrinal differences between the DC and those who would eventually merge into the BK (at this point called the "Young Reformers"), Hitler, because of his preference for the former, entered into the power struggle, thereby violating his own party's position of religious neutrality. However, he did so "hesitantly and reluctantly,"[16] not with the enthusiasm to be

---

[12] Carsten Nicolaisen (ed.), *Dokumente zur Kirchenpolitik des Dritten Reiches*, 3 vols. (Munich, 1971–94), 1: 38. The entire episode is recounted in ibid., 1: 37–41.

[13] Ibid., 1: 39.

[14] Bundesarchiv Potsdam (hereafter BAP), R 5101/28/173 (11 July 1933: n.p.[Berlin]).

[15] Wright, *'Above Parties'*, 118–19.

[16] Scholder, *Churches*, 1: 333.

Fig. 11 Reich Bishop Ludwig Müller, a theological moderate among the German Christians. (SV-Bilderdienst)

expected from someone desiring to bend yet another social institution to his totalitarian will. Lower down the ranks, Nazi participation in the Protestant Church lent confirmation to Hitler's position. Two months after the Seizure of Power, the opening session of the new Prussian *Landtag* was celebrated. Wilhelm Kube, as the National Socialist caucus leader in the Prussian *Landtag*, led all the NSDAP delegates on a march through Berlin to the Protestant Christ Church, where they heard a sermon on John 10:12 delivered by the German Christian leader Joachim Hossenfelder.[17]

Hitler's candidate to head a newly created Reich Church in the position of Reich Bishop was Müller. Müller was a member of the DC, but came from their more moderate East Prussian wing, which he also led. Hitler's endorsement of Müller was based on his desire to have the Protestant Church led by a Nazi supporter. He also believed Müller would have the support of the majority of Protestant churchmen. However, there was a rival in the contest for Reich Bishop in the more established Friedrich von Bodelschwingh, head of the charitable Bethel Institution in Bielefeld. Pressed to run against Müller by Union and Calvinist churchmen, in May 1933 Bodelschwingh won in a vote of state church representatives.[18] The vote was split: Whereas the disproportionate representation of Prussia assured that Bodelschwingh would win, Lutheran state bishops, headed by Heinrich Rendtorff, had called for "an unconditional Yes to the National Socialist movement, to the new Reich and therefore to Ludwig Müller."[19] Müller and his allies were outraged by the results, recruiting the SA to harass Bodelschwingh's offices and

---

[17] *Der Angriff*, 22 March 1933.
[18] *Völkischer Beobachter*, 25 May 1933.
[19] Scholder, *Churches*, 1: 330. Wright points out that of the eleven *Landeskirchen* that voted for Müller only one was not Lutheran (132).

having Nazi Party offices send off protest telegrams. In Prussia, *Kultusminister* Rust appointed August Jäger as state commissioner for the church, with the goal of forcing through a "coordination" of the church along DC lines.[20] Feeling his position to be untenable, Bodelschwingh resigned. The path for Müller was once again cleared. Despite the strong-arm tactics against his opponents and rivals, in ecclesiastical matters Müller subsequently took a position considered far too conciliatory for the tastes of most DC opinion. In fact, although the DC backed Müller as their candidate for Reich Bishop, they refused to name him as their leader, giving him instead the largely empty title of "patron."[21] The national leader of the DC remained the more radical Hossenfelder; it was thought that Müller would be too conciliatory with the older church establishment.[22]

Despite their internal quarreling, the DC obtained the personal and institutional support of the rest of the party leadership, even as a strict institutional separation between them and the NSDAP was maintained and even as Nazis argued with each other as to how much the state should intervene in the "Church Struggle" (*Kirchenkampf*).[23] At the first national conference of the DC, held in April 1933, an "honorary committee" was established, made up of Nazi dignitaries with a personal interest in Protestant affairs: Frick; Göring; Graf von Helldorf, Berlin leader of the SA and later the city's chief of police; Hans Hinkel; Hanns Kerrl, President of the Prussian *Landtag* and later Reich Minister for Church Affairs; and Wilhelm Kube.[24] At the behest of Müller, Robert Ley (Strasser's replacement as Reich Organization Leader) told all *Gauleiter* to instruct Protestant party members in their domains – regardless of whether they were active churchgoers – to vote DC in the upcoming church elections, in which the vote for the Reich Bishop would be opened to all Protestant Church members in the country.[25] Such support was not a given: Responding to DC complaints that party offices in the Saar were causing them difficulties, Ley sent a letter to Gauleiter Bürckel assuring him

---

[20] There is no evidence that Hitler or Müller directly encouraged this appointment: Wright, '*Above Parties*', 144.

[21] *Dokumente zur Kirchenpolitik*, 1: 43.

[22] Shelley Baranowski, "The 1933 German Protestant Church Elections: *Machtpolitik* or Accommodation?," *Church History* 49 (1980), 303–4.

[23] Generalist historians still fall under the impression that the *Kirchenkampf* was a war waged by the Nazi State against the Protestant Church. See, for instance, Martyn Housden, *Resistance and Conformity in the Third Reich* (London, 1997), 46–7: "The first significant Nazi crusade in this connection was led by the German Christians *against* Protestantism" (emphasis mine). Although the Nazis certainly took sides in the dispute, this was in fact a struggle between two opposed tendencies *within* Protestantism, not a state-conducted campaign against organized religion: Doris Bergen, *Twisted Cross: The German Christian Movement in the Third Reich* (Chapel Hill, 1996), 12; Conway, *Persecution*, xx.

[24] *Evangelium im Dritten Reich*, 26 March 1933.

[25] Bundesarchiv Berlin-Zehlendorf (hereafter BAZ), Sammlung Schumacher (hereafter Schu), 244/2/24 (17 July 1933: Berlin).

that the DC were supported by the "highest leadership of the party," and were welcomed to use the party organization in their campaigning.[26] Hess later instructed all party members to register their names on the election lists of their parishes because "participation in the election is mandatory."[27] Similarly, all *Gauleiter* were instructing party members to vote DC.[28] Paganists like Rosenberg were powerless to stop this cooperation, observing the party's involvement with deep unease.[29]

As the Reich's chief legal authority, the most important "state Nazi" in church matters was Wilhelm Frick. He generally held to a moderate line, even though he had displayed a personal preference for the DC during his time in Thuringia. He became the first government authority to intervene in the *Kirchenkampf*, but he advised against state intervention on the Müller side. In a meeting with Reich Bishop-Designate Bodelschwingh in June, Frick expressed his opinion that the latter "should certainly remain in and carry on the office, but declare that the final decision on the question of the bishop should be made by the Reich Synod," with either an election or vote of confidence.[30] Even though Frick was willing to work with Bodelschwingh, he was constrained by radicals close to Hitler. The degree of constraint became evident in a meeting among Frick, Hitler, Rust, and Müller later that month, which was prompted by Hindenburg's call for Hitler to find a "statesmanlike" resolution to the growing fractiousness of the Protestant Church situation. Here again Frick argued against state intervention, whereas Rust was strongly in favor of it, on the side of the DC. Rust in fact was one of the staunchest supporters of state intervention. It was he who appointed the radical August Jäger as state commissioner of the Prussian churches. Rust's position on this occasion won out: National elections were planned for late summer, with the full organizational strength of the NSDAP at the DC's disposal. Frick sent a letter to Müller, wishing him "total success and God's blessing."[31] Even though his hand was forced in this issue, Frick hoped that Müller would nonetheless build bridges with his Young Reformer rivals. Rudolf Buttmann, NSDAP leader in the Bavarian *Landtag* and now leader of the Culture Department in Frick's Ministry, also shared this view. In January 1934, Buttmann informed Müller of his and Frick's view that the Nazi State would not endorse a Reich Church that did not represent the entirety of Protestant opinion.[32]

---

[26] BAZ Schu 244/2/26 (24 April 1933: Munich).

[27] Leonore Siegele-Wenschkewitz, *Nationalsozialismus und Kirchen: Religionspolitik von Partei und Staat bis 1935* (Düsseldorf, 1974), 87.

[28] BAP R43 II/161/158-159 (19 July 1933: Berlin).

[29] See Rosenberg's letter of complaint to Göring: BAZ NS 8/167/156 (27 March 1934: Berlin).

[30] Wilhelm Brandt, *Friedrich von Bodelschwingh 1877–1946: Nachfolger und Gestalter* (Bethel, 1967), 134. Bodelschwingh refused this course of action, which many DC had actually agreed to (Wright, 'Above Parties', 136).

[31] *Dokumente zur Kirchenpolitik*, 1: 84.

[32] BAP R43 II/161/279-280 (15 January 1934: Berlin).

Göring, as *Ministerpräsident* of Prussia, also took what appeared to be a position more moderate than Rust's. Citing the ongoing struggle within the ranks of the Protestant Churches in a letter to Rust, Göring insisted: "So long as we have state churches and no Reich Church, in my view we cannot appoint a Reich Bishop." Göring's feelings were not directed against Müller, however. Rather, they had a different motive: "Until the revolution the King of Prussia was the *summus episcopus* of the Prussian State Church. In my view this authority has now passed over to the Prussian *Ministerpräsident*. On this basis an alteration to the state church without our explicit consent is not conceivable."[33] This consent is exactly what Müller tried to obtain. As late as December 1933, Müller and his advisors in the Reich Church tried to get the appointment of Göring as Reich minister *in evangelicis* – an appointed, as opposed to hereditary, *summus episcopus*.[34] According to Müller, Göring was amenable to the idea. For reasons that are unclear, Göring did not pursue his bid to be named secular head of the Reich Church: It is most likely that Hitler vetoed the idea. In any event, Göring was a strong supporter of Müller. Under his control the Gestapo monitored the activities of Müller's opponents. He fully supported the partisan position of his education minister Rust, and informed Hitler that any opposition that Müller and the German Christians encountered was due to the *political* reaction of the Young Reformers. By contrast, Frick and Buttmann blamed the ongoing dissention in the Protestant churches on the incompetence of Müller and his associates.[35]

Whereas Hitler decided to back the DC with the party's organizational support, this did not yet mean that he regarded the opponents of the DC as opponents of Nazism. In a meeting he held with Hitler, the American churchman Charles Macfarland asked what would be "the reaction of the Government towards utterances by pastors who did not agree with the position or actions of the Government on church matters." Hitler responded that "such a reaction on the part of Protestant clergymen was not at all directed against the Government of the Reich."[36] Here Hitler recognized a position that members of the BK would later argue with marked consistency: that opposition to the Nazis' church policy was not opposition to Nazism itself.[37] That Hitler would later take a hostile stand against the BK was due to his growing impression that the political resistance of *some* of its members represented *all* BK opinion. Müller, who portrayed his institutional rivals as Hitler's total ideological enemies, in no small measure encouraged this

[33] Correspondence of 27 June 1933: *Dokumente zur Kirchenpolitik*, 1: 75.

[34] Scholder, *Churches*, 2: 17.

[35] Ibid., 2: 33–4.

[36] Charles Macfarland, *The New Church and the New Germany* (New York, 1934), 52–4.

[37] As Victoria Barnett points out, the majority of BK leaders repeatedly insisted that they were *not* an anti-Nazi resistance group and resented the vocal minority who wished to see the BK take on a political opposition to Nazism: Victoria Barnett, *For the Soul of the People: Protestant Protest Against Hitler* (Oxford, 1992), passim.

impression. In a letter to Hitler shortly before the national church elections Müller falsely asserted that, "in the final analysis, this so-called 'Church Struggle' is none other than a struggle against you and against National Socialism."[38] Whether Hitler accepted Müller's view or not, Hitler instructed that no party disturbances were to occur in the upcoming elections.[39]

At least as important as the organizational support lent to the DC was Hitler's radio address to the nation given the night before the church elections, on 22 July 1933. Hitler spoke to the German people after a performance of Wagner's Christian allegory *Parsifal* in Bayreuth, conducted that evening by Richard Strauss:

Among the congregations of the Protestant confessions there has arisen in the 'German Christians' a movement that is filled with the determination to do justice to the great tasks of the day and has aimed at a union of the Protestant state churches and confessions. If this question is now really on the way towards solution, in the judgement of history no false or stupid objections will be able to dispute the fact that this service was rendered by the *völkisch*-political revolution in Germany and by that movement within the Protestant confessions that clearly and unequivocally professed its allegiance to this national and *völkisch* movement at a time when, unfortunately, just as in the Roman Church, many pastors and superintendents without reason have opposed the national uprising in the most violent, indeed often fanatical, way.[40]

This change in Hitler's attitude toward the DC's opponents (now called "Gospel and Church") was almost certainly due to Müller's appeal, regardless of how much Hitler himself really believed it. In reality, few in this group were "fanatical" opponents of the regime.

Just how little the members of Gospel and Church contemplated resistance to Nazism was demonstrated the next day. In several states, such as Braunschweig, the Gospel and Church lists voluntarily withdrew "under the impact of the Chancellor's speech and out of loyalty to Adolf Hitler," as one announcement put it.[41] In many states there was simply no election: In light of Hitler's endorsement, lists were joined into one, thereby precluding the need for elections. Synods in Baden, Württemberg, the Palatinate, Schleswig-Holstein, Hanover, Saxony, Frankfurt, and Hamburg were mostly formed by agreement, all with DC majorities. In the Old Prussian Union Church, in which opposition to the DC was strongest and in which elections were still necessary, the DC won 75% of the vote, with all the church provinces save Westphalia returning DC majorities.[42] Any lingering question of anti-Nazi activity within Gospel and Church was laid to rest when it was discovered

[38] *Dokumente zur Kirchenpolitik*, 1: 120.
[39] BAP R43 II/161/161 (21 July 1933: Berlin).
[40] As reported in *Volksparole*, 24 July 1933: in Bayerisches Hauptstaatsarchiv (hereafter BStA), Presseausschnittssammlung 929. For a slightly different translation see Peter Matheson (ed.), *The Third Reich and the Christian Churches* (Grand Rapids, 1981), 28.
[41] Quoted in Scholder, *Churches*, 1: 447.
[42] Günther van Norden, *Kirche in der Krise: die Stellung der evangelischen Kirche zum national-sozialistischen Stat im Jahre 1933* (Düsseldorf, 1963), 83–8.

that party members themselves had voted for it. To be sure, this was limited to isolated cases in the lower ranks of the party, but it happened often enough that the Reich Interior Ministry began to take note.[43] Party authorities took action against these Nazis, many of whom protested loudly. Eventually the party reversed itself, as Hitler wanted to return to a position of religious neutrality as soon as the elections were over. In October this stance was affirmed by Rudolf Hess in a circular to all party offices, guaranteeing the religious freedom of party members.[44] Thereafter, some who had been expelled from the NSDAP because of their opposition to the DC were readmitted.[45]

The fortunes of the DC vacillated greatly in the next months. Their initial successes were impressive. Overall, the DC received over two-thirds of the national vote. The Reich Synod that met in September to select a Reich Bishop consisted of 229 delegates, only 75 of whom were from the Gospel and Church party. This time Müller was easily elected. However, when the synod voted to make the Aryan Paragraph (the new law forcing all civil servants and their spouses to be "free of Jewish blood") applicable to the Protestant Church, the Gospel and Church delegates walked out.[46] The following November came the national DC conference in the Berlin Sports Palace. The rift in German Protestantism was widened even more when one of the Berlin DC leaders, Reinhold Krause, formally called for the removal of the Old Testament.[47] The outrage that ensued led Martin Niemöller to found the Pastors' Emergency League (*Pfarrernotbund*, or PNB), the direct institutional forerunner of the BK, as a counterpoint to the DC and their scriptural position. Such outrage was not confined to PNB members, however; even within the ranks of the DC there was indignation. Many left the DC, and the Bavarian section went so far as to voluntarily disbanded itself in protest.[48]

In spite of, or perhaps because of, this growing opposition, Hitler's endorsement of Müller became increasingly uncertain. When reports emerged of the immense revolt against Krause's speech at the Sports Palace meeting, Müller's position began to weaken. He tried to stem the tide by stripping Krause of all his church positions. Even Hossenfelder, the more radical leader of the DC, agreed to this action. However, this did not serve to placate the opposition. Müller attempted a further step toward conciliation by

---

[43] See EZA 7/1296 (18 August 1933: Berlin) and EZA 7/1296 (25 August 1933: Berlin), which document several cases of members of the NSDAP voting Gospel and Church.

[44] On the existence of Gospel and Church and later BK supporters within the NSDAP, see Barnett, *Soul*, 39–44, who points out that some BK members could count themselves *alte Kämpfer* of the Nazi movement.

[45] Like Wilhelm Niemöller, brother of Martin, who fought to stay in the party "as a matter of honor" and won: ibid., 42.

[46] Ibid., 34.

[47] This episode, which caused a scandal even within DC ranks, is well documented in the literature; cf. Bergen, *Twisted Cross*, 103, 145; Matheson (ed.), *Third Reich*, 39–40.

[48] Ian Kershaw, *Popular Opinion and Political Dissent in the Third Reich: Bavaria 1933–1945* (Oxford, 1983), 160.

withdrawing the Aryan Paragraph on 16 November 1933. That same day, Müller even entered into negotiations with Niemöller, offering to disband the DC immediately if the PNB would do the same. Müller's offer was rejected by Niemöller, who refused to acknowledge that both groups had equal rights in the church.[49] This, plus Frick's and Buttmann's preference for neutrality vis-à-vis the DC, made Hitler reconsider his previous loyalty to Müller. Following his usual pattern of maintaining a "wait-and-see" attitude in such internecine rivalry, Hitler allowed himself to be convinced by Frick of the need for "strict neutrality" in the Church Struggle.[50]

When Müller met with Hitler on 29 November 1933, he no longer found the Hitler who had previously expressed such faith in him. Instead, Hitler told Müller that the government would in no way intervene on his behalf, and that "he would have to cope with the difficulties himself."[51] Müller made further attempts to recover his position by withdrawing his patronage of the DC and, in his capacity as Reich Bishop, replacing the radical Hossenfelder as DC leader with the more moderate Christian Kinder. (It was this action that precipitated Rosenberg's formal exit from church membership.) Meanwhile, Frick immediately instructed the state governments that they were to remain uninvolved in the church dispute. Any police activity against Protestant clerics, including protective custody and confiscation of mail, was to be stopped. Furthermore, the DC were no longer permitted to enlist party or state offices for their purposes.[52]

The Nazi State therefore backed away from a *Gleichschaltung* of the Protestant Church. While every other institution in German society was being ruthlessly "coordinated," the Protestant Church was now being left unassailed. As Klaus Scholder states, "this decision brought into being – amidst the ideological totalitarianism of the Third Reich – a kind of free space, a place where things could be said that could be uttered *nowhere else* in the Third Reich."[53] It was a stark reversal of the Nazis' earlier policy of

---

[49] Wilhelm Niemöller, *Der Pfarrernotbund: Geschichte einer kämpfenden Bruderschaft* (Hamburg, 1973), 178. Niemöller's intransigence did not impress Karl Barth, who often expressed his opinion that Niemöller was no better than Müller. In private correspondence, Barth wrote of the "whole anthill of agitated pastors ready for action under the dictatorship of the U-boat commander Niemöller, who was all set to turn the Sports Palace scandal into a 'Tannenberg' for the German Christians and in the name of 'fellowship' forbade any theological misgivings.... If sooner or later there is a catastrophe for the German Christians, and if then the so-called Council of Brethren of the Pastors Emergency League should become our future conference of bishops, my dear pastor, we shall then be in no better shape than at present under the rule of the German Christians..." (quoted in Scholder, *Churches*, 1: 555). The next month – December 1933 – Barth wrote to another pastor: "All the trouble and anxiety that this year has cost will have been in vain if the only difference is that the future Reich Bishop is – for example – called Niemöller" (quoted in ibid., 556).

[50] Walter Conrad, *Der Kampf um die Kanzeln: Erinnerungen und Dokumente aus der Hitlerzeit* (Berlin, 1957), 58–60.

[51] Ibid.

[52] *Dokumente zur Kirchenpolitik*, 1: 181.

[53] Scholder, *Churches*, 1: 566–7 (emphasis mine).

intervention. However the fact that the Nazis were now permitting the unhindered existence of a supposed resistance group while the enemies of Nazism were being rounded up everywhere else in Germany brings into sharp relief the fundamentally positive attitude of the Nazi State toward the Protestant Church as a whole. As Martin Broszat observes: "it came about that under a regime which was otherwise so strict, pastors who were dismissed from office, like Niemöller, were confirmed in office by their parishes, continued to carry out their duties and in May 1934 even set up a formal rival organization to Müller's church rule with the Barmen Confessional Synod."[54] This does not mean that the Church Struggle ceased. Its continuation after this point was based on the desire of the DC faction *within* the Protestant Church to conquer their opposition, not on Nazi Party pressure.

In spite of Hitler's new caution, Müller recovered considerable ground after an audience of dignitaries of the Protestant Church, including Niemöller, held by Hitler on 25 January 1934, five days before the first anniversary of the *Machtergreifung*. These churchmen were all Müller's opponents, who had taken further offense when Müller handed over all Protestant youth organizations to Baldur von Schirach in December. In a vain attempt to silence the protests that emerged from this transfer, Müller then placed a "muzzling decree" on the entire pastorate. These church leaders hoped that the meeting would be an occasion for them to voice their concerns by a direct appeal to Hitler. However, the audience with Hitler ended as a total defeat for them and a total success for the Müller camp. It was also useful for demonstrating the views of the Nazi leadership. This encounter has almost always been cast as a classic example of Hitler's hatred for Christianity. According to John Conway, the episode betrayed Hitler's innate hostility toward the Protestant Church,[55] a view shared by several other church historians.[56] As one of the most analyzed events in the history of church–state relations in the Third Reich, it warrants attention here. Hitler's suspicion that the anti-Müller camp was directed against the state, and not just Müller, was certainly strengthened after this meeting, but a close examination of the episode reveals that Hitler was largely innocent of Conway's and others' charges.

Before his reception, Hitler held a conversation with President Hindenburg, who as head of state and a religious Protestant had taken an interest in the Church Struggle. Hindenburg took the side of Müller's opponents, asserting that Müller "stood in the way of an agreement, that the unity of the church cannot be allowed to be broken on a personal question." Hitler responded that the "shameful" picture of division within Protestantism was the issue, not the person of Ludwig Müller. He assured Hindenburg that he

[54] Broszat, *Hitler State*, 227.
[55] Conway, *Persecution*, 76.
[56] Victoria Barnett also suggests, although in more qualified terms, that this meeting displayed Hitler's preexisting hostility: *Soul*, 51. See as well Kurt Meier, *Kreuz und Hakenkreuz: Die evangelische Kirche im Dritten Reich* (Munich, 1992), 50.

would work for an understanding. However, the PNB was "more active in politics than in the church." Hitler made his position entirely transparent when he concluded: "If the Pastor's Emergency League does not stop its activity the government will have to act against it to maintain its own authority."[57] Hitler did not defend Müller, but at the very least he still accepted Müller's characterization of Niemöller's activities as political.

The reception of the Protestant dignitaries took place in the afternoon. Before any of them could begin, however, Hitler had Göring read out the transcript of a taped telephone conversation between Niemöller and Walter Künneth held just that morning. The very fact that Niemöller's phone had been bugged betrayed the Nazis' lack of faith in him. However, the contents of the conversation largely confirmed Hitler's suspicion that the PNB, or at least its leader, was actively engaging in politics: "The Reich President will receive Hitler in his dressing room. The last oiling [*letzte Ölung*] before the discussion! Hindenburg will receive him with our memorandum in his hand. Things have also gone well in the Ministry of the Interior. I am glad that I have got [Bodelschwingh] here and that we have engineered everything so well.... If things go wrong – which I do not anticipate – we have a simple step to the Free Church."[58] Niemöller's description of the preparations for the meeting demonstrated his attempt, in an almost conspiratorial fashion, to play off the authority of Hindenburg against Hitler. His disdain for Hitler's political abilities ("letzte Ölung" also means "last rites") was a view commonly shared by the conservative elites of the time, who believed they could use Hitler for their own ends.[59] Hitler's audience was stunned by this revelation. However, rather than complain about how closely they were being watched, either to Hitler or to each other afterward, they instead tried to undo Niemöller's work, insisting on their nationalism and loyalty to the state.[60]

When asked by Hitler if he in fact had had this conversation, Niemöller, as a former U-boat commander, took a step forward in military fashion and declared that he had. He defended himself by referring to the hardships the PNB were experiencing at the hands of Müller and Jäger, adding that the Church Struggle was being carried on not only out of a concern for the church, but also out of a concern for the *Volk* and the state as well. For Hitler, this signaled the political engagement that he had suspected. He shouted back: "You leave concern for the Third Reich to me and look after the

---

[57] Quoted in Scholder, *Churches*, 2: 40.

[58] BAP R43 II/161/326-327 (24 January 1934: Berlin). In spite of suggestions that Göring changed the text to make Niemöller appear more treacherous – for instance Kurt Meier, *Der Evangelische Kirchenkampf*, 3 vols. (Göttingen, 1976–84), 1: 162 – Scholder amply demonstrates that this was not the case: *Churches*, 2: 302 n. 108.

[59] As Broszat points out, Niemöller's services in Dahlem "were demonstratively attended by the leading conservative circles of Berlin" (*Hitler State*, 229).

[60] Barnett, *Soul*, 52; Conway, *Persecution*, 74; Scholder, *Churches*, 2: 41: "...none of the churchmen present even remotely thought of protesting against pressure applied in this way."

church!"[61] Then, drawing on examples from Göring's Gestapo reports, he detailed anti–government statements that had been made by other Protestant pastors associated with the PNB.[62] He then added that Müller had in fact been chosen as Reich Bishop by the church, not by him. This was somewhat disingenuous, given Hitler's considerable patronage of Müller; but it was nonetheless an accurate statement. Hitler also added that, although he was born a Catholic, "Inwardly he stood closer to the Protestant Church."[63] The current "politicizing" of the PNB was all the more disappointing therefore because Hitler expected from Protestant pastors "a different attitude to that of the Catholics."[64]

When the other church leaders finally had a chance to speak, they insisted that isolated expressions of political discontent did not reflect the views of the pastorate as a whole. They stated that their complaint rested solely with Müller, who lacked leadership ability and who opened himself up to ridicule by associating himself with the DC.[65] When Hitler asked whether a Reich Bishop from any other camp could guarantee an end to the Church Struggle, Bishop Meiser of Bavaria replied that no one could make such a guarantee.[66] Hitler's question was not rhetorical; he demonstrated that he was willing to give up on Müller if it meant peace in the church. Given Meiser's answer, however, Hitler could only conclude by stating that all segments of the Protestant Church had to attempt a conciliation. Müller should therefore be given another chance. Before he left, he shook hands with each of the churchmen, including Niemöller.[67]

The assembled churchmen had expected to prevail over Müller at this meeting; instead, they left totally dejected. They had been thrown on the defensive by Hitler's "opening shot," and thereafter fought simply to prevent further loss. However, instead of accusing Hitler of having laid a trap, they blamed the failure of the meeting on Niemöller. In a letter he sent to Rudolf Buttmann, Bishop Wurm stated: "From the beginning the whole thing was utterly devastating. And it was also abominable for you and the minister to appear in this light." Here Wurm meant Niemöller's reference to the Interior Ministry – implying that Frick and Buttmann, as Nazis more sympathetic to Müller's opponents, would now look complicit in Niemöller's scheming.

[61] According to some accounts, Niemöller then responded by telling Hitler that "neither you nor any nor any other power in the world is in a position to take from us Christians and from the Church responsibility for our people that God has placed upon us": Arthur Cochrane, *The Church's Confession under Hitler* (Philadelphia, 1962), 130. However, among the many recountings of this meeting printed in *Dokumente zur Kirchenpolitik* (2: 20–33), including Niemöller's, not one shows that he made this remark.

[62] BAP R43 II/161/326-327 (24 January 1934: Berlin).

[63] *Dokumente zur Kirchenpolitik*, 2: 24; Matheson, *Third Reich*, 43.

[64] Ibid.

[65] Matheson, *Third Reich*, 43–4.

[66] *Dokumente zur Kirchenpolitik*, 2: 22 (for Meiser's recounting), 28 (for Niemöller's).

[67] According to Niemöller's account, Hitler did not shake his hand with aggression or hostility, but simply "gave me his hand, as any German man gives his hand" (ibid., 29).

Wurm stated his opinion that "this time the U-boat commander has torpe-
doed not his opponents but his friends and himself."[68] Nowhere did Wurm
lay responsibility for the outcome on Hitler. Neither did any of the other
participants' accounts blame Hitler for the turn of events.[69]

Hitler displayed no preexisting animosity toward the Protestant Church
or its representatives at this meeting. He left the meeting more suspicious of
Niemöller than before, but there is no indication that he presumed the others
in the audience were behind Niemöller. Nonetheless, the meeting provided
Müller and the DC with nothing less than a new lease on life. Putting to
rest any possible suspicion of their politics, Müller's opponents (excepting
Niemöller) signed a declaration two days later swearing "their unconditional
fidelity to the Third Reich and its Führer," and rejected "most sharply all in-
trigues or criticism of state, *Volk* and movement." Their declaration added:
"The assembled church leaders stand firmly behind the Reich Bishop and
are determined to carry out his measures and decrees in the way in which
he desires."[70] The decree not only undercut opposition to Müller, it also
weakened the PNB. In the Lutheran *Landeskirchen* of Bavaria, Württemberg
and Hanover, 1,500 pastors resigned from the PNB. Encouraged by Wurm,
the Württemberg PNB elected to disband itself altogether a few days later.[71]
Müller quickly seized the initiative and resumed the course he had taken before the Sports Palace debacle. He reintroduced the Aryan Paragraph into the
Reich Church constitution. His associates, most importantly Prussian State
Commissioner August Jäger, aggressively reasserted their prerogatives, incorporating one provincial church after the next into the Reich Church.[72] The
remaining members of the PNB refused to recognize their new DC bishops.
Hitler received Müller again in February but, as before, requested that the
Reich Bishop go about his business in unity and peace.[73] Heydrich ordered
his police forces "to avoid any action that might disturb the work of unity
and growth of a united Evangelical Church.... The authorities must take
great care not to mix themselves in purely theological questions."[74]

---

[68] As quoted in Scholder, *Churches*, 2: 42. As Barnett points out, Bishops Wurm, Meiser, and
Marahrens – the most powerful non-"German Christian" Lutheran state bishops – continually accused Niemöller and the BK of being too political (*Soul*, 49, 57, 69, 90, 200). Even
within the BK, the political activities of a minority were a constant source of infighting (ibid.,
55, 57–8, 89–92, 174–5).

[69] *Dokumente zur Kirchenpolitik*, 2: 21–33.

[70] Quoted in Johannes Gauger, *Chronik der Kirchenwirren: Gotthard Briefe*, 3 vols. (Elberfeld,
1934–36), 1: 138.

[71] Niemöller, *Pfarrernotbund*, 58–9.

[72] Within the boundaries of the Prussian state existed not only the Prussian State Church (Old
Prussian Union), but also other churches – such as the Hanover and the Schleswig-Holstein
Landeskirchen – that were established before the territories they served were annexed by
Prussia in 1866. The Old Prussian Union Church covered only those areas that were part of
Prussia *before* 1866. As a *state* official, however, Jäger had authority over all churches within
the state boundary of Prussia as it existed after 1866.

[73] Scholder, *Churches*, 2: 51.

[74] Conway, *Persecution*, 75.

Frick backed this up by cautioning Müller to proceed in an orderly fashion.[75] Given Hitler's renewed confidence in Müller, Frick could curb him only
this far. However, he was opposed to the ruthless Jäger. Rust and Göring,
on the other hand, remained on Jäger's side. This was both a conflict between personalities and between governments: Frick's authority was at the
level of the Reich government, whereas Rust's and Göring's authority was
limited to *one* state government, although it was by far the most important
one. Whereas state governments outside Prussia left their churches relatively
untouched – the Reich government having ordered that "it is not the task of
the National Socialist state to intervene with its forces in purely church controversies"[76] – within Prussia Göring used Gestapo reports to cast the PNB
as a political, reactionary group.[77] The Gestapo was not practicing universal
anticlericalism, however. At the same time the PNB was being surveilled, the
Gestapo was expressing interest in helping emigrant German pastors with
their overseas mission work.[78]

As a result of this forced coordination, in March Meiser and Wurm –
both of whose churches were still "intact" – requested another audience
with Hitler. In their letter to him, they also stated that they were publicly
withdrawing the promise of support to Müller they had made two days after
their disastrous January reception. With the help of Neurath and Lammers,
they were able to get an audience with Hitler within a week.[79] In their meeting, Hitler stated that, although he found the continued dissention within
Protestant ranks a growing source of irritation, he still hoped for a strong
and united Reich Church. Although he wished that the DC would cease
their theological bickering and "forego all quarrels over doctrinal matters,"
he claimed that, if Luther were alive, he would have stood behind them. He
acknowledged Müller's shortcomings as a leader, but was still prepared to
back him in his efforts to bring unity to the Protestant churches. Hitler also
added that the church should come to terms with the realities of "blood
and race," otherwise "developments will simply pass them by." Finally, he
warned that, if pastors wanted to declare resistance, this would not make
them his "most loyal opposition," but rather "Germany's destroyers."[80]

[75] *Dokumente zur Kirchenpolitik*, 2: 59–60.
[76] Ibid., 60.
[77] See Göring's reports of Gestapo activities to the Reich authorities: *Dokumente zur Kirchenpolitik*, 2: 70–8.
[78] BAZ NS 26/1240 (16 February 1934: Berlin).
[79] *Dokumente zur Kirchenpolitik*, 2: 79. For Neurath's involvement in the Church Struggle, see
John Heineman, *Hitler's First Foreign Minister: Constantin Freiherr von Neurath, Diplomat and
Statesman* (Berkeley, 1979), 75–7.
[80] *Dokumente zur Kirchenpolitik*, 2: 80–1. Both Scholder (*Churches*, 2: 70–1) and Conway
(*Persecution*, 76–7) claim that Meiser and Wurm declared *themselves* to be Hitler's "most
loyal opposition," on which Hitler, "in a fury of rage," is supposed to have told the bishops
"You are not my most loyal opposition, but traitors to the people, enemies of the Fatherland
and the destroyers of Germany." Both Scholder and Conway use the same source for this
quote: Heinrich Schmid, *Apokalyptisches Wetterleuchten: Ein Beitrag der Evangelischen Kirche*

Here Hitler raised the threat of an attack on the church, indicating that his respect for the institutional independence of the pastorate had definite limits. By rejecting the notion of a "loyal opposition," Hitler also betrayed his belief that opposition to any one Nazi policy was opposition to Nazism as a whole.

In spite of this episode, the comportment of the Nazi State remained positive for the time being. Even the famous Barmen Synod, which formally founded the BK and unambiguously attacked the theology of the DC, did little to harm church-state relations. Frick, for one, made no objections to the synod, whereas the Gestapo similarly made no moves against its members. The chief of all German police decided in this instance to leave matters as they were, to "guarantee [...] religious freedom of conscience" as one report put it.[81] This did not mean that BK members were left unhindered elsewhere. At the behest of the many church governments now under the control of the DC, the state authorities confiscated the declarations of the Barmen Synod and in several places took pastors into protective custody. The strongest state action took place in Schwerin, where three BK pastors were given between three and six months in prison for "political resistance."[82]

The most important litmus test for the attitudes of the Nazi leadership toward institutional Protestantism came with Jäger's attempt at a forced coordination of the "intact" state churches of Bavaria and Württemberg, seen as the last bastions of a non-German Christian ethos. The events surrounding Jäger's actions marked the height of the Church Struggle for the entire period of the Third Reich. Here Müller's allies would come across unparalleled popular reaction and were finally confronted with the limits of their power. Although they would receive the support of many powerful Nazis in their coordination campaign, as will be demonstrated, wide segments of Nazi opinion, much of it no less powerful, stood against them.

Even before Müller turned his sights on the southern *Landeskirchen*, Nazis were beginning to express wariness with his and Jäger's ruthless actions and began to wonder how much their party was involved. The head of ideological training for a Bavarian SA unit, who was also a Protestant pastor, noted in March 1934 that "Many evangelical ministers have prepared the ground for the Third Reich with dogged passion and even today know no other political goal. Is all that already forgotten . . . ?"[83] The government president for Upper and Middle Franconia believed that the *Kirchenkampf* was an ecclesiastical rather than a political affair, but that it posed a political danger because of

---

zum Kampf im 'Dritten Reich' (Munich, 1947), 61–3. However, in Meiser's version of events used here, no mention is made that either he or Wurm described themselves as a loyal opposition, that Hitler called them traitors or enemies, or that Hitler shouted in a fury of rage. Meiser was one of only four people at this meeting (the others being Hitler, Wurm, and Franz Pfeffer von Salomon), thereby making his account the more reliable one.

[81] Heinz Boberach (ed.), *Berichte des SD und der Gestapo über Kirchen und Kirchenvolk in Deutschland, 1933–1944* (Mainz, 1971), 60.

[82] As Conway himself admits, it was Müller, and not officials of the Nazi Party or state, who put these few Protestant pastors into concentration camps: *Persecution*, 416 n. 12.

[83] Quoted in Kershaw, *Opinion*, 163.

its potential for broadening into a mass protest by the religiously Protestant: "In particular the religiously inclined evangelical circles, which stand behind their Bishop Meiser, could and still can be counted among the most loyal supporters of National Socialism. It is a tragedy that precisely these people have to be upset in the conflict between Reich Bishop and Provincial Church by the State they most gladly acclaimed."[84] The president not only pointed to the reality that the state was once again behind Müller, but also demonstrated that Nazis like himself made no confusion between a church dispute against the DC and a political dispute against the Nazis.

Other Bavarian Nazis failed to make this distinction. Hans Schemm was no less insistent of the party's foundation on Christian principles when he declared that there could be no opposition to the Reich Church: "We wish for nothing as ardently as a powerful Protestant Church which stands on the foundations prepared by the great Reformer Martin Luther.... It is not possible for a church to stand apart or against the *Volk*. Rather the church must stand in service to the *Volk*. The great Nazarene did not stand apart in a quiet corner." Although Schemm did not mention the BK by name, his conclusion made it clear that this was his target: "I warn the pastors who spoke out against the Reich Church government last Sunday that we know your struggle is aimed not so much against the Reich Bishop as against National Socialism!"[85] This attitude was shared by deputy *Gauleiter* of Franconia, Karl Holz, who wrote in the local Nazi paper (which he also edited) that Meiser displayed disloyalty to Hitler through his refusal to acknowledge Müller as Reich Bishop.[86]

Local authorities increased their pressure on the "intact" churches. When Holz followed up his article two days later with a mass meeting to be held in Nuremberg's Market Square, Meiser went to Nuremberg to hold rival meetings in nearby Protestant churches. After he arrived, "the crowds streamed away from the meeting in the Market Place and packed the churches." When crowds started to gather after Meiser's service, the authorities, rather than dispersing the celebrants, stood at attention as "Deutschland über alles" was sung.[87] So it was that the ensuing struggle between Nazis state and provincial church should have started in a town – Nuremberg – and region – Franconia – that was a stronghold of both the Nazi movement and the Protestant faith. This did not go unnoticed by the Nazis themselves: As a local Nazi leader pointed out, "the great majority of Meiser's supporters in Franconia are to be regarded as loyal National Socialists who often include the old Party members."[88] Following this episode, in October Jäger attempted a forced coordination of the Württemberg church, placing Wurm under house arrest. The next day Meiser went to a Bavarian town along the border with

[84] Quoted in ibid., 165.
[85] BStA MK/37069a (n.d.[1934], n.p.[Bayreuth]).
[86] Kershaw, *Opinion*, 165.
[87] Ibid., 166.
[88] Scholder, *Churches*, 2: 251.

Württemberg, and addressed a huge audience made up of laity from both states. Meiser told the congregation to remain loyal to the church and resist the machinations of the Reich Church authorities. In conclusion, two songs were sung: "A Mighty Fortress is our God" and the "Horst Wessel Song," the Nazi Party anthem.

Four days later Meiser was also put under house arrest, with Jäger declaring that the state church would be divided into two regional churches.[89] Immediately the Protestant population began public protests in the tens of thousands, and started petitions demanding Meiser's restoration. Nuremberg's churches were packed as service after service was given in solidarity to Meiser. Within a week, Julius Streicher met with leading church dignitaries and published a ban on party attacks on the church. Schemm followed a similar route in Bayreuth.[90] Another high-ranking Nazi now stepped in on Meiser's side: the *Ministerpräsident* of Bavaria, Ludwig Siebert. Siebert presided over the inauguration of Meiser as Bavarian State Bishop in June 1933. On that occasion Siebert expressed his desire to work with Meiser, as "church and state must discuss and promote the same questions.... 1) The awakening of a sense of sacrifice; 2) The creation of the new social ethic; 3) Leading our youth to *Volk* and God, to Fatherland and Christianity."[91] Having been made aware of the plans of the Reich Church government, Siebert advised Müller to avoid any action against Meiser.[92] Now, with Meiser's arrest, Siebert wrote to Frick, stating that party members who held the Golden Badge of Honor, Nazi *Kreisleiter* ("district leaders" of the NSDAP, one step below *Gauleiter*), and long-standing Nazi supporters among the Protestant pastorate all warned of the political consequences for the party if things did not change.[93] Over the period of a week Meiser received several deputations from Franconian citizens, including one which stated that even Nazis with the Golden Badge of Honor were close to rebellion.[94] After several such meetings, in which it was made clear that the attacks on Meiser were being associated not only with the Reich Church but also with the party, Siebert wrote again to Frick, urging that Hitler be comprehensively informed of the situation. The attitude of Siebert and other Nazis demonstrates that not all in the party – or even most – were in favor of Meiser's arrest. This was also true for the Reich Governor of Bavaria, Franz Ritter von Epp, who wrote: "What interests us is the question: who has ordered all this? Who is master in the front – who is master in the back?"[95] According to Klaus Scholder, the only

---

[89] Helmut Baier, *Die Deutschen Christen im Rahmen des bayerischen Kirchenkampfes* (Nuremberg, 1968), 128–31.

[90] Ibid., 147–8.

[91] *Dokumente zur Kirchenpolitik*, 1: 61–2.

[92] Ibid., 2: 187.

[93] Ibid., 2: 182.

[94] Kershaw, *Opinion*, 171.

[95] BStA MK/37069a (22 October 1934: Munich). Epp added that "in Berlin no one understands the structure of Protestantism in Bavaria and Württemberg."

Nazi leaders in Bavaria to have unequivocally supported Meiser's arrest had been Streicher and Adolf Wagner, *Gauleiter* of Munich and Bavarian Minister of the Interior. Even the leader of the DC, Christian Kinder, began to work for Jäger's fall "with all the means at his disposal."[96]

Jäger's activities had repercussions as well in the BK, which held its second synod in Berlin-Dahlem at the same time. On this occasion, even more than at Barmen, considerable division was displayed. Under the leadership of Niemöller, the radical wing of the BK insisted on a statement that the BK was the only legitimate representative of the Protestant Church in Germany and that between them and the DC there was no common faith: "We are not leaving this our church for a free church; rather, we *are* the church."[97] Lutherans, even those whose bishops were under arrest, found this provision unacceptable, as it entirely shut out one part of the church. As one delegate complained, the BK had rejected "the freedom and the willingness to preach to the supporters and followers of the National Socialist Movement." On the day of the vote, almost half the delegates were absent; of those present, 52 voted in favor, 20 against.[98] Others in the BK began referring to the radicals as the "Dahlemites." These were the first signs of the eventual breakup of the BK.

The political repercussions of Meiser's arrest could be felt not only outside Bavaria, but even outside Germany, and would soon bring Hitler into the decision-making process. Foreign Minister Neurath had received reports from the embassy in London that English churchmen, led by the Archbishop of Canterbury, were planning a conference for 24 October at which a statement on the German church situation would be made. Neurath received news of this on the 17th, and immediately delivered it to Hitler. Two days later Hitler postponed the reception planned for Müller and other leaders of the Reich Church from the 23rd to the 25th.[99] Although it would seem from this that Hitler chose to react only under foreign pressure, in fact he had been unaware of the near rebellion taking place. Josef Bürckel, the *Gauleiter* of the Palatinate, provided proof of this. His jurisdiction was in Bavaria, but he had also been appointed by Hitler as the plenipotentiary for the Saarland, a part of Germany broken off under the Versailles Treaty, that was soon to vote on reincorporation into the Reich. Bürckel had never liked Müller, fearing that the anti-Catholic comments he made at public gatherings could only damage the Nazis' prospects in the Saar. In his view, the current events in Bavaria made matters worse still, so on the 22nd he went directly to Hitler to press for the dismissal of Müller and Jäger. And significantly, he found that Hitler

---

[96] Scholder, *Churches*, 2: 260. Scholder states the DC believed that Jäger's continued presence made it "impossible to reach an agreement with the opposition in the Evangelical Church," implying that the DC desired a sincere dialogue (ibid.).

[97] Barnett, *Soul*, 65.

[98] Ibid., 66. As Barnett puts it, "Other delegates at Dahlem worried that the Confessing Church was assuming a power it did not really have" (67).

[99] Neurath had warned Müller the previous month about the possible foreign relations repercussions of his actions, but to no avail: BAP R43 II/162/274-276 (20 September 1934: Berlin).

had received almost no detailed information on the state of affairs in Bavaria: According to a report written by one of Bürckel's Saar officials, "up until now the Führer was not informed of events."[100] The Reich Church authorities had been acting with the general authority over church affairs provided by Hitler, without reporting back to him. On hearing of the demonstrations – as Hitler would report later in a closed meeting of Reich Governors – he asked a Munich *Standartenführer* whether such demonstrations were in fact taking place (the *Standartenführer* indicated he had not heard of any).[101] In the meantime, Siebert and Epp attempted to lift Meiser's house arrest, but both Frick and Hess declared that they did not have the authority. As Hess told Siebert on the 22nd, because he had been "left out of the game, he did not want to give the orders." He would, however, meet with Hitler to discuss the matter the next day.[102]

Three days later, the scheduled date for Müller's reception, Hitler personally ordered that Meiser and Wurm be immediately released.[103] The next day Jäger was relieved of all his duties, thereby ending his damaging engagement in church affairs. This was also a victory for Frick, who had consistently advocated a policy of moderation. Frick now ordered that party members were no longer to involve themselves in the internal disputes of the Protestant Church.[104] Having cancelled his meeting with Müller and the Reich Church leaders, Hitler instead received Meiser, Wurm, and Marahrens on 30 October, and assured them that the state would not again interfere in Protestant Church affairs.[105] In the entire period of the Third Reich, this marked the climax of the Protestant *Kirchenkampf* and the effective end of Müller's career. Although he continued in the post of Reich Bishop, he lost Hitler's confidence.

The public protest that arose from Meiser's arrest constituted the Nazis' greatest domestic setback to date. As Ian Kershaw puts it, "It was a spectacular display of what popular protest could achieve even in the restrictive conditions of a repressive police state."[106] As much as the Nazi Party smarted from their public embarrassment, it appears that only a minority of Nazis actually endorsed the radical actions taken by Müller and his associates. The majority, including Hitler, were sincerely interested in avoiding any kind of open conflict with the Protestant Church. At the same time, those most responsible for the attacks on the BK and their allies were not agents in Rosenberg's employ, but rather a rival group of Protestants. The Protestant Church in Bavaria drew no political conclusions from the affair.

---

[100] *Dokumente zur Kirchenpolitik*, 2: 193.
[101] "Niederschrift über die Reichsstatthalterkonferenz am 1. November 1934": BAP R43 II/1392/49-50 (1 November 1934: Berlin).
[102] *Dokumente zur Kirchenpolitik*, 2: 189.
[103] Ibid., 192.
[104] BAP R43 II/163/74 (6 November 1934: Berlin).
[105] *Dokumente zur Kirchenpolitik*, 2: 197–8.
[106] Kershaw, *Opinion*, 174.

As Kershaw states, the affair "touched on no other aspect of Nazi policy or ideology and could come to the boil ironically in a region with a very high level of long-standing avid Nazi support." Even though opposition to the enforced coordination of the Protestant State Church was so high, Franconia continued to be a "hotbed of vicious popular antisemitism," and displayed "intense pro-Hitler feeling."[107] Throughout this period, the majority in the BK similarly never translated their protest against Nazi church policy into any other domain of Nazi governance. On the contrary: They approved of all Nazi measures in foreign and domestic affairs. For instance, when the Nazis pulled Germany out of the League of Nations, the PNB leadership, instead of suggesting that such a move worked against the brotherhood of nations, expressed their joy in a letter to Hitler, "in the name of over 2500 Protestant pastors who do not belong to the 'German Christians'."[108]

Although Hitler was exasperated by the turn of events, this rebuff did not turn him into an enemy of Protestantism, as he demonstrated in a closed meeting he held with the Reich Governors and members of the party elite (Hess, Frick, Göring, Lammers, and Bormann) just a few days after his reception with Meiser, Wurm, and Marahrens. His impatience with the turn of events was clear: "In his short reception Bishop Meiser indicated that the confession must be free. If the confession must be free, then the state must also be free. The churches can collect their taxes themselves!"[109] Hitler then immediately pulled back from this position, declaring: "The Reich Bishop must be given time to bring the situation under control. He, the Führer and Reich Chancellor, wanted to create a united, strong Protestant Church." As Hitler told Albert Speer, "Through me the Protestant Church could become the established church, as in England."[110] Hitler knew that the BK comprised a significant portion of that church and that seeking unity in German Protestantism meant accommodating them in some way. Whatever he may have thought of Niemöller, he was not yet ready to cast off the BK itself as an enemy of the state. By contrast, Hitler's attitude towards Germany's other great confession left no room for ambiguity: "the Catholic Church has always been an enemy of a strong form of government."[111]

Although always ready to spot anti-Nazi activity, Himmler's Gestapo was not yet convinced that the BK was anti-Nazi. In a confidential memorandum from February 1935, the Gestapo reported that the BK's fight with the DC remained "above all an internal church fight, in which each of the two parties has assured its loyalty to the state." At the same time, there was a feeling that *some* in the BK were potentially anti-Nazi: "Both sides must be granted that, at least as far as their genuine adherents are concerned, they do not stand opposed to the state. Nevertheless, there is no doubt that, on the part

[107] Ibid., 176–7.
[108] Quoted in Siegele-Wenschkewitz, *Nationalsozialismus*, 138.
[109] BAP R43 II/1392/49-50 (1 November 1934: Berlin).
[110] Speer, *Inside*, 95.
[111] BAP R43 II/1392/49-50 (1 November 1934: Berlin).

of the Confessing Movement, the number of inner opponents of National Socialism is large, simply because here the church is more important than the state."[112] The reference to "genuine adherents" suggests that the Gestapo did not necessarily view the political activity of some within the Confessing Church as representative of the whole group.

THE KERRL ERA

Despite Hitler's statements on 1 November 1934, Müller finally fell out of favor with Hitler. The incompetence of the Reich Bishop was proving a danger to the stability of the regime. But despite his growing impatience and disappointment with the course of the Church Struggle, Hitler did not throw out the baby of the Protestant Church with the bathwater of Müller. Hitler's interest in maintaining institutional Protestantism in Germany was confirmed seven months later by the creation of a Reich Ministry for Church Affairs under Hanns Kerrl. Kerrl, president of the Prussian *Landtag* before the Seizure of Power, was a close associate of Göring's, becoming Prussian Justice Minister when the latter was made Prussian *Ministerpräsident*. In this capacity Kerrl faithfully enacted antisemitic and racialist legislation and purged the legal system until the amalgamation of his portfolio with that of Reich Justice Minister left him temporarily out of a job.[113] When he was given the position of Reich Church Minister, it was not because he was known to be especially Christian.[114] He was simply at the right place at the right time – namely, in Hitler's entourage on a tour of inspection when Hitler was pondering the Church Struggle. Kerrl immediately suggested himself, and he was without hesitation made head of the new ministry in July 1935.[115] Rosenberg was resentful of what he regarded as a pro–church measure and blow to his own position. In his diary, he assured himself that Kerrl's appointment must have been the work of the "old bureaucracy," and wrote off the new minister as "primitive."[116]

It was hoped that Kerrl could do what Müller could not: bring a peace to the church that would be amenable to the Nazi State while uniting the contesting factions within Protestantism. Witnessing the damage that resulted

---

[112] Boberach, *Berichte des SD*, 63–4.

[113] Saul Friedländer, *Nazi Germany and the Jews: The Years of Persecution, 1933–1939* (New York, 1997), 29.

[114] Kurt Meier suggests otherwise, pointing to Kerrl's "affinity for Church and Christianity": Meier, *Kirchenkampf*, 2: 68. Conway goes further, suggesting that Kerrl was the only one in the party leadership who actually believed that Nazism was related to Christianity: *Persecution*, 204–7. Had such a belief been the only criterion, however, Nazis like Koch, or Buch, to mention just a few, would have been strong candidates. Schemm would also have been ideal for the job, had he not died in a plane crash the previous March. Conway makes no mention of Buch, Koch, or Schemm in his book.

[115] *Dokumente zur Kirchenpolitik*, 3: xvi–xvii.

[116] Reinhard Bollmus, *Das Amt Rosenberg und seine Gegner: Studien zum Machtkampf im nationalsozialistischen Herrschaftsystem* (Stuttgart, 1970), 115–16.

Fig. 12 Hanns Kerrl. Before
becoming Reich Church Minister
he had served as Prussian Justice
Minister. (SV-Bilderdienst)

when the Reich Bishop drove a particular agenda through the church –
instead of staying above the theological and political fray – Nazi functionaries came to the conclusion that the Church Struggle could be better resolved
through governmental means. Pivotal in this regard was a memorandum
written in January 1935 by the jurist Wilhelm Stuckart, formerly state secretary in the Reich Education Ministry and soon state secretary in the Reich
Interior Ministry. Stuckart was more famous as coauthor and promoter of
the Nuremberg racial laws, which he and Hans Globke wrote a few months
later. His infamy grew further in January 1942 when he took part in the
Wannsee Conference on the "Final Solution of the Jewish Question." In this
memorandum, which was personally delivered to Hitler, Stuckart called for
the creation of a "central authority for all church questions." The DC had
been unable to unify the church, and the BK represented nothing more than
"German National reaction."[117] In contrast to the disarray that had so far
marked church policy, it was necessary to impose a unified will. Instead of
allowing the church to reshape itself under Müller and the DC, Stuckart
suggested that the state should take the reins and reshape the church from
above. Goebbels voiced much the same opinion in a speech he gave at the end
of March: "When we call for the unification of the Protestant Church, we
do so because we do not see how, in a time when the whole Reich is unifying
itself, twenty-eight *Landeskirchen* can persist. . . . In the interpretation of the
Gospel one may hold the command of God higher than human commands.
In the interpretation of political realities, we consider ourselves to be God's

---

[117] BAP R43 II/163 (21 January 1935: Berlin). "German National" here means the right-wing
German National Peoples' Party (DNVP), a coalition member of the first Hitler cabinet in
January 1933.

instrument."[118] A few months later, the Reich Church Ministry came into being.

Almost immediately after taking up his new appointment, Kerrl convened representatives of the *Länder* to assess the church–political situation throughout Germany and to solicit the views of the Nazi regional leadership. The proceedings therefore represent an invaluable cross section of Nazi elite opinion after two and a half years of party rule. Both proclerical and anticlerical *Gauleiter* expressed their opinions. Martin Mutschmann, *Gauleiter*, Reich Governor, and *Ministerpräsident* of Saxony, was the most anticlerical of all, suggesting that the Jews were behind the Church Struggle. The Catholic Church, he added, wanted nothing less than to create a "state within a state."[119] Several other leaders, such as *Kultusminister* Mergenthaler of Württemberg, as well as Mutschmann and representatives from Hesse and Baden, suggested a separation of church and state, especially with regard to ending the church tax.[120] Kerrl interjected at this point, suggesting that separation would be very complicated legally. Furthermore, he added, "The *Führer* wants to protect positive Christianity; this must be maintained. It is necessary, therefore, to seize upon the powers of the Christian confessions which affirm the state and National Socialism, and to maintain church life."[121] Leaders from Thuringia, Mecklenburg, Schaumburg-Lippe, and Westphalia all agreed with this position, noting that either one faction or the other was so strong in their areas that there was no Church Struggle. The Oldenburg representative noted that there was a definite fight between the BK and the DC in his region, but wanted to take no state action for fear of creating martyrs.[122] The leaders of Braunschweig, Anhalt, and Hesse-Nassau stated their belief that behind the activities of the BK in their areas stood the Catholic Church.

At this point Wilhelm Kube made a startling statement: He considered the Church Struggle "unbearable" and declared that "National Socialism is religious but not confessional. The organizations within the Church must be banned, that means both the German Christians and the Confessing Front."[123] For one of the founders of the DC, this was an incredible

---

[118] *Hannover Kurier*, 29 March 1935: in EZA 50/428/50.

[119] "Protokoll einer Besprechung des Reichkirchenministers mit den Oberpräsidenten und Vertretern der Länder," 8 August 1935: *Dokumente zur Kirchenpolitik*, 3: 41. Mutschmann had elsewhere indicated his allegiance to "Deutsche Glaube": BAP 62 Ka 1/22/272-74 (15 April 1935: Berlin).

[120] *Dokumente zur Kirchenpolitik*, 3: 41–2.

[121] Ibid., 3: 42–3.

[122] Ibid., 3: 44.

[123] Ibid. The Nazis, unwilling to accept the claims of the BK that they represented a "church," used the more pejorative "Confessing Front" instead. Kube found the struggle "unbearable" especially because of his fighting with Otto Dibelius, general superintendent in his domain of Brandenburg: BAZ NS 26/1240 (19 January 1934: Berlin). Later that year, Kube would involve himself in a dispute between Dibelius and pastor Falkenberg of the DC: BAP R43 II/164/44-47 (20 September 1935: Berlin). Kerrl advised Kube to not get involved.

reversal. Kube was nonetheless prepared to endorse such a position if it meant peace in the church. This did not signify, however, that Kube viewed both parties in the same light. He insisted that only "the Confessing Front is today the political enemy of the state." Although Kube suggested changes should be made to the legal relationship between church and state, he did not endorse separation. Erich Koch's representative from East Prussia stated that the region's Catholic bishop was "unreliable from a nationalist viewpoint." However, he made no mention of separation. As his representative put it, it was Koch's personal view that "through the encouragement of the patriotic (*staatstreu*) elements of the Protestant Church, Protestantism must be made stronger vis-à-vis Catholicism." Even though he was no longer president of the provincial church synod, Koch evidently retained an interest in the fortunes of his church.[124] The representatives of Hamburg, Bremen, and Lübeck – Northern city-states where separation took place before the Nazis came to power – all reported that no Church Struggle existed in their areas.

The assembled regional leaders concluded by acknowledging two religious camps within Nazi ranks: "the followers of Rosenberg's *Mythus*, and those who unreservedly stand on the foundation of Point 24 of the Party Program."[125] The minutes of the meeting show that Kerrl had the last word: "It is untenable to have within the movement an official standpoint (Point 24 of the Party Program) and an unofficial standpoint (Rosenberg's direction) towards Christianity." In his opinion, it was necessary to "eliminate" the unofficial standpoint.[126]

To demonstrate the party's commitment to its platform, Kerrl went about the work of attempting to bridge the theological and political gaps that divided the DC and the BK. As he had done with Müller, Hitler stepped back to await results. Kerrl began in September 1935 by restoring the authority of the *Landeskirchen*, stripping the rival DC and BK church bodies of their power and issuing a general amnesty for all pastors charged by the police for opposing Müller's administration.[127] In October Kerrl instituted "church committees" for the churches that Müller coordinated, designed to effect an accommodation among the DC, the BK, and the substantial number of neutral churchmen in the middle. These committees oversaw the administrative and financial operations of the churches and were not state bodies as such. Kerrl also established a central "Reich Church Committee," which was chaired by the leader of the Lutheran Church in Westphalia, Wilhelm Zoellner, and populated by moderates from both factions.[128] Kerrl purposely chose committee members who had avoided the Church Struggle, as he hoped to mediate between the contesting parties; Zoellner, for

---

[124] *Dokumente zur Kirchenpolitik*, 3: 46–7.
[125] Ibid., 3: 49.
[126] Ibid., 3: 50.
[127] Conway, *Persecution*, 135.
[128] R 5101/23756/35 (15 October 1935: Berlin).

instance, enjoyed the confidence of "moderates" in the BK.[129] Whereas Müller was kept away from the proceedings, Bodelschwingh, the victim of Müller's and Jäger's machinations, was invited to participate, but declined.[130] Finally, for the duration of the negotiations, Kerrl ordered that the Gestapo take no coercive measures – arrests, expulsions, prohibitions or confiscations – against BK pastors.[131] As before, the "totalitarian" Third Reich would allow a degree of freedom of expression that existed no where else in Germany.

Kerrl's gesture caused a rift within the BK. Among the strongest proponents of cooperation with the new church committees were the Lutheran bishops Wurm, Meiser, and Marahrens of the "intact" churches.[132] The Dahlemites, mostly from the Old Prussian Union, were opposed. Their treatment at the hands of Müller helped them become permanent enemies of the DC. However, the Dahlemites were also disturbed by BK displays of loyalty to the regime, such as holding services of thanksgiving for Hitler when the Saarland was reincorporated into the Reich.[133] Their opposition grew when the Reich Church Committee affirmed their allegiance to "the National Socialist *Volk* on the foundation of race."[134] At their annual synod in Bad Oeynhausen in February 1936, the BK formally split, with the Lutherans going their own way in a "Council of Evangelical-Lutheran Churches." The Lutheran churches accused the "Council of Brethren," the Dahlemite governing body of the BK, of politically motivated intransigence, whereas the Dahlemites professed to be interested only in the Word of God.[135] In fact, the minority Dahlemites were rigidly opposed to any suggestion that members of the DC, who like them confessed faith in Christ, had a right to be in

[129] Broszat, *Hitler State*, 228.
[130] *Dokumente zur Kirchenpolitik*, 3: 92–8.
[131] BStA Epp 621/1 (5 September 1935: Berlin).
[132] Once the DC ceased to be a threat to his church, Marahrens was enthusiastically behind most Nazi policies: Klügel, *Landeskirche Hannovers*, passim. Wurm actually went so far as to blame the Dahlemites, rather than the Nazi regime, for the difficulties between church and state. In his view, they "did not merely fight the intrusions of the state into church territory: rather, as a power from below that assumed inappropriate authority, they fought the state as such.... They were too convinced that an arrangement with the state would drive the church to ruin" (ibid., 223).
[133] For these declarations, see Nikolaus Preradovich and Joseph Stingle (eds.), *'Gott segne den Führer!': Die Kirchen im Dritten Reich* (Leoni, 1986), 86–94.
[134] Klaus Scholder, "Kirchenkampf," in *Evangelisches Staatslexikon* (Stuttgart, 1975), reprinted in idem, *A Requiem for Hitler and Other New Perspectives on the German Church Struggle* (Philadelphia, 1989), 105.
[135] Shelley Baranowski points to additional differences between the confessional Lutherans of the "intact" churches and the BK of the Prussian Old Union: "The disproportionately Prussian composition of the Pastors' Emergency League disturbed the bishops, who could never entirely suppress their ingrained anti-Prussian regionalism and Lutheran confessionalism": Shelley Baranowski, "The Confessing Church and Antisemitism: Protestant Identity, German Nationhood, and the Exclusion of the Jews," in Robert Ericksen and Susannah Heschel (eds.), *Betrayal: German Churches and the Holocaust* (Philadelphia, 1999), 97.

the church.[136] Hermann von Detten, the former head of the Department for Cultural Peace now working in Kerrl's ministry, noted how leaders of the BK had rejected his suggestion that the BK share church space with the DC in smaller parishes.[137]

A further sign of their position came when the Dahlemites wrote the "Hitler Memo," sent directly to the Führer in May 1936 above the head of the church minister. Oblivious to the removal of Jakob Hauer as leader of the DGB just a month earlier, or the banning of their public meetings the year before, the authors of the letter wondered if paganism was the official religion of the party. They suggested that positive Christianity was theologically unsound, criticized state actions to curtail the Dahlemites, and refuted antisemitic measures as contrary to "love one's neighbor."[138] However outraged Hitler may have been by the letter, he chose to ignore it. Nothing more would have resulted from it had the foreign press not published a copy they received from individuals within the BK. It was roundly rejected by the Lutheran state bishops, who declared some months later: "We stand with the Reich Church Committee in support of the Führer in the struggle for the life of the German *Volk* against Bolshevism."[139] Regardless of the rectitude of their position, the Dahlemites faced new repressive measures at the hands of Kerrl's ministry. Three of their members were arrested and put into concentration camps, including Friedrich Weißler, a lawyer who had authorized the publication. Weißler was arrested by the Gestapo and sent to Sachsenhausen concentration camp, where he was killed. Weißler was the first member of the BK to be killed by the Nazis. However, this was not a simple matter of Christianity now facing its "Final Solution."[140] Under the Nuremberg Laws, Weißler was a Jew. Two other members of the BK implicated in the matter were also sent to Sachsenhausen, but were immediately separated from Weißler and eventually released unharmed.[141]

---

[136] Protestant churchmen outside of Germany noted this intransigence with some dismay. As one foreign theologian observed: "That natural theology of creation which characterizes the 'German Christians' can also be found in Anglicanism, in modern world Protestantism and in American activism. But the theology of the Confessing Church, above all its strictly dialectical version, is not fully shared either in the Lutheran north or in the Anglican and American west" (quoted in Scholder, *Churches*, 2: 235). Scholder himself refers to "the danger to which even the Confessing Church readily succumbed, of declaring one's own cause without further ado to be God's cause and thus limiting or even doing away with the freedom of the word of God" (ibid., 2: 87).

[137] BAP 62 Ka 1/22/202–205 (2 July 1935: Berlin).

[138] Wilhelm Niemöller, *Die bekennende Kirche sagt Hitler die Wahrheit* (Bielefeld, 1954), 9-18.

[139] Quoted in ibid., 18. Scholder argues that the reference to Bolshevism was provided by Germany's involvement in the Spanish Civil War: "Politik und Kirchenpolitik im Dritten Reich: Die kirchenpolitische Wende in Deutschland 1936/37," reprinted in idem., *Requiem*, 150.

[140] As implied by Conway, *Persecution*, 164.

[141] Barnett, *Soul*, 84–5. Wolfgang Gerlach notes with dismay how the Dahlemite leadership did little to come to Weißler's defense. He also demonstrates that, although the memo criticized the Nazis for their antisemitism, it hid the antisemitism present in the BK: *Als die Zeugen schwiegen: Bekennende Kirche und die Juden* (Berlin, 1993), 169.

By the beginning of 1937, the church committees were no closer to forging links between the BK and the DC than they had been a year before. Rapprochement was not helped by a series of orders that had placed various difficulties on the radicals within the BK: the banning of certain periodicals, increasing state control over theological exams, and the censure of clergy for political speeches.[142] At the same time, the Church Ministry responded positively to some complaints. When the BK pointed out with dismay that at Nazi assemblies religious songs were being sung to secular texts and that in some churches Nazi songs were being sung to religious texts, the ministry ordered a halt to this practice.[143] The BK leadership also tried to get in touch with ministers in Hitler's cabinet who in various ways displayed a commitment to the Protestant faith. Aside from Kerrl, they addressed their pleas to the Nazis Wilhelm Frick and Bernhard Rust. Additional letters were sent to Werner von Blomberg, war minister and commander-in-chief of the Wehrmacht, Foreign Minister von Neurath, Finance Minister Lutz Schwerin von Krosigk, Labor Minister Franz Seldte; and Hjalmar Schacht, president of the Reich Bank and economics minister.[144]

Kerrl's actions against the Dahlemites, although far from persecution, were sufficient harassment to make the work of the church committees impossible. In February 1937 the Reich Church Committee resigned because of the irreconcilable differences between the BK and the DC and in protest of the measures taken by the Gestapo against select Protestant pastors.[145] The very purpose of Kerrl's ministry was therefore threatened with collapse. Kerrl immediately convened the state and the provincial church committees in a desperate attempt to reassert his authority. He assured the assembly that there would be no chance of new church elections and threatened that the state would take direct control over the administration of the Protestant Church, since taxes continued to be used for "revolts against the state." The regulations, he promised, had already been sent to the newspapers for publication.

Two days later, however, Hitler again intervened. Annoyed that Kerrl had been as unable as Müller to overcome the divisions in the church, Hitler gathered the party leadership to discuss the church situation. As Goebbels noted in his diary: "A great dilemma about Kerrl's planned decree in the church question. Kerrl has given this to the press without the knowledge of the Propaganda Ministry. Kerrl, Frick, Hess, Himmler and I were ordered

---

[142] *Dokumente zur Kirchenpolitik*, 3: 185, 188–9, 191–2, 276–7. In June 1936, Heydrich ordered that BK pastors were not to be placed under censure for "purely ministerial activities" (ibid., 3: 199).

[143] BAP NS 6/224/40-42 (21 October 1936: Munich).

[144] EZA 50/136/10 (17 November 1936: Berlin); EZA 50/136/12 (16 November 1936: Berlin). Of the conservative fellow travelers on Hitler's cabinet, Blomberg, Neurath, and Schacht were out of office by 1939. Schwerin von Krosigk and Seldte, on the other hand, stayed in the cabinet for the duration of the Third Reich. It is not known whether any of these men responded to the letter.

[145] *Dokumente zur Kirchenpolitik*, 3: 318.

to Obersalzberg for a conference on the church question. The Führer wants to issue a clear policy. Kerrl made a serious mistake going over our heads.... One cannot solve the Church Struggle in this way; one will only create martyrs."[146] Hitler directly contravened Kerrl by announcing that new church elections were to be held for a general synod that would write a new constitution for the Reich Church.[147] Just as Hitler reversed the work of Müller in 1934, so too was he willing to give up on the path chosen by Kerrl. This signaled a decisive break with Kerrl's futile policy of state intervention. Most church historians agree that Kerrl had sincerely hoped for a resolution to the Church Struggle, even if his own actions had undermined that goal. As Kerrl would later remember, Hitler's decision for an election meant that "my authorization as Reich Minister for Church Affairs comes to an end: I no longer carry out church policy on my own responsibility to the best of my knowledge and conscience."[148] For the third time since 1933, Hitler acted in the hope that the Protestant Church, left to its own devices, would voluntarily coordinate itself with National Socialism. And for the third time, he was disappointed.

The reaction in the BK was again mixed. As one observer noted, the moderates greeted the announcement in a way "comparable to the reaction that must have greeted Moses' announcement to the children of Israel that Pharaoh had promised to let them depart from Egypt. However, it was Kerrl who was Pharaoh and Hitler who was Moses. The Führer's prestige actually rose, because it was he who had countermanded Kerrl's orders by decreeing new synodical elections."[149] But the Dahlemites took a different position. Otto Dibelius sent an open letter to Kerrl at the end of February, which indicated his objections: "When children are told in their morning religious instruction that the Bible is the word of God which speaks to us in the Old and New Testament, and when in the afternoon they must learn 'What is our Bible? Our Bible is Hitler's *Mein Kampf*' – who has to change his teachings?" According to Dibelius, if the state were aware of its limits, it could rely "on the readiness of the Protestant Christians of Germany for sacrifice." If not, however, then they would "offer resistance in God's name. And we shall do that!"[150] The Council of Brethren issued a similar statement in March: "Today the Church is called upon to allow the Word of God and a human worldview to stand together and to combine them in its preaching. The Church must reject this demand."[151] Here was a rejection of *Heilsgeschichte*, of the theological notion that one could detect the will of God in human history.

[146] Elke Fröhlich (ed.), *Die Tagebücher von Joseph Goebbels: Sämtliche Fragmente* (Munich, 1987), entry for 15 February 1937.
[147] BAP R43 II/160/105 (17 March 1937: Berlin).
[148] Quoted in Scholder, *Requiem*, 155.
[149] Quoted in Conway, *Persecution*, 207.
[150] Joachim Beckmann (ed.), *Kirchliches Jahrbuch für die evangelische Kirche in Deutschland 1933–1944* (Gütersloh, 1948), 160.
[151] Ibid., 163–4.

This was an unmistakable rebuff to the totalitarian *style* of Nazism. It was not, however, a rebuff to aspects of its ideological *substance*. Even Dahlemites did not refute Nazi policy lying outside the direct sphere of the church, including the policy of antisemitism. Dibelius for one had prided himself on being an antisemite even before the Nazis took power. Long after 1945 he congratulated himself on his refusal to help Jews convert to Christianity in the Third Reich: "I therefore became increasingly firm and exact in my demands. This gradually became known, and in the end I was spared such externally motivated requests for baptism."[152] Such a position represented a flirtation with racialist antisemitism. Flirtation became active endorsement three years after his letter to Kerrl, when Dibelius recommended that the Aryan Paragraph – the original source of conflict between the BK and the DC – be formally instituted in the pastorate.[153]

Niemöller also displayed no real opposition to Nazi antisemitism. In 1935, the year of the Nuremberg Laws, Niemöller told his congregation that "the Jews have caused the crucifixion of God's Christ.... They bear the curse, and because they rejected the forgiveness, they drag with them as a fearsome burden the unforgiven blood-guilt of their fathers."[154] Up until the war, when he volunteered for military service from his prison cell, Niemöller made no apparent sign of rejecting this position. A similar attitude was displayed when members of the BK attacked Rosenberg's *Protestantische Rompilger*. Responding to the claim that the Protestant establishment had become Judaized, one angry member of the BK, Dean Kornacher of Kempten, protested that "0.3% of the pastorate, by definition of the current law, is non-Aryan. Which other profession (lawyers, doctors) has been kept so pure?"[155] The persistent antisemitism evident within BK circles lasted even after the *Kristallnacht*. Whereas BK members voiced public disapproval of the Nazis' lawlessness and wanton destruction of property, they remained silent regarding its victims.[156] Outside the BK, clerical antisemitism could take even greater strides in the direction of racial antisemitism. One example is an official statement issued by seven Lutheran state churches in

---

[152] Otto Dibelius, *In the Service of the Lord: The Autobiography of Bishop Otto Dibelius* (New York, 1964), 95.

[153] Bergen, *Twisted Cross*, 57. On the greater issue of antisemitism in the BK, see Gerlach, *Zeugen*, passim; Uriel Tal, "On Modern Lutheranism and the Jews," *Leo Baeck Institute Year Book 1985* (30), 203–13.

[154] Quoted in Ruth Zerner, "German Protestant Responses to Nazi Persecution of the Jews," in Randolf Braham (ed.), *Perspectives on the Holocaust* (Boston, 1983), 63.

[155] "'Protestantische Rompilger' (einige Vorwürfe und Antworten)": BAZ NS 8/151/159 (Reformationsfest 1937: Kempten). This tract goes on to refute Rosenberg's other accusations, for instance, that the Protestant pastorate is pacifist: "7000 theologians have marched in the fields; 2400 of those have fallen. That's 36.3%. Of doctors, 14.6% have fallen, lawyers 25.5%. Only the officer corps has overtaken the pastorate in the number of victims. Is that pacifism??"

[156] See especially Heinz Eduard Tödt, "Die Novemberverbrechen 1938 und der deutsche Protestantismus: Ideologische und theologische Voraussetzungen für die Hinnahme des Pogroms," *Kirchliche Zeitgeschichte* 2 (1989), 14–37.

December 1941, which flatly rejected those "Protestant Jews" who had been at the heart of the doctrinal dispute between Confessing Christians and DC. Fondly recalling Luther's command that Jews should be banished from German lands, the statement went on to claim that "From Christ's crucifixion to the present day, the Jews have fought against Christianity, or have misused or falsified it for their selfish aims. Christian baptism does not alter the racial character of the Jew, his affiliation with his people, or his biological essence."[157] As Victoria Barnett states: "The troubling historical evidence suggests that the churches refrained from criticizing the regime, not just because they wanted to remain 'apolitical' but because they often agreed with it."[158]

Institutional arguments within Protestantism persisted however. Realizing that the elections would do nothing to accomplish a unanimous assent to Nazi ecclesiology, Hitler soon developed second thoughts. Only now, in 1937, were his hopes for a Protestant Reich Church beginning to fade. Up until this point Hitler apparently believed that all of German Protestantism could rally around him unequivocally. The Dahlemites, however, no matter how small their numbers, held sufficient power to frustrate that hope. The election was delayed first until April 1937 and then for an additional six months. Finally, at the end of June, all further preparations for an election were halted. Instead, a new wave of repression was launched against the Dahlemites. Within the week Dibelius was put on trial for his letter of February and eight members of the Council of Brethren were arrested by the Gestapo. This was quickly followed by the detention of forty-eight additional BK pastors, including the most persistent thorn in the side of Hitler's church policy, Martin Niemöller.[159] At the same time that Hitler was unleashing the coercive power of the state, he wanted these actions to be controlled and measured. He therefore ordered that all *Reichsleiter* and *Gauleiter* take no measures against pastors unless explicitly permitted by him.[160] Further action was taken in August with the so-called "Himmler Decree," which forbade the administering or taking of BK theological exams and declared separate BK seminaries illegal. These were henceforth criminal activities punishable by imprisonment.[161] The repressive nature of these measures and the human suffering they caused are undeniable. Nevertheless, it is worth noting that they were taken almost exclusively against the BK of the Old Prussian Union, where the Dahlemites were strongest. By contrast, members of the BK outside the Union Church experienced almost no repression. As one

[157] Beckmann (ed.), *Kirchliches Jahrbuch*, 481.
[158] Barnett, *Soul*, 72. See also Robert Ericksen, "A Radical Minority: Resistance in the German Protestant Church," in Francis Nicosia and Lawrence Stokes (eds.), *Germans Against Nazism: Nonconformity, Opposition and Resistance in the Third Reich* (New York, 1990).
[159] Conway, *Persecution*, 209.
[160] BAZ Schu 245/1/153 (30 June 1937: Munich).
[161] Barnett, *Soul*, 87.

Berlin pastor noted, 206 pastors from Berlin-Brandenburg alone had been imprisoned that year, compared with two from Hanover and one each from Württemberg and Bavaria.[162]

Niemöller's trial was perhaps the most notorious case of Nazi anticlericalism vis-à-vis the Protestant Church. Ironically, Rosenberg was against the trial, as he believed it constituted state interference in church–theological matters. Believing Kerrl had led the charge against Niemöller in the hopes of recovering his position, Rosenberg wrote to Hess that "Here only cold *state* machinery governs, which has lost sight of the *Volk* and its members – Niemöller is also a member of the *Volk* and before the law *not one dot less* than Kerrl."[163] Niemöller, like Dibelius, was found not guilty of the charges laid against him in court; in February 1938, he was released from prison. Unlike Dibelius, however, Niemöller was rearrested by the Gestapo on Hitler's personal order and, as a political prisoner, was sent to Sachsenhausen concentration camp. Short of capital punishment, Nazi repression could not have been more severe. However, Niemöller's experience in the concentration camps was far from typical. As the commandant of Sachsenhausen informed the Reich Chancellery, Niemöller's creature comforts were carefully attended to, including treatment for illness and permission to go on walks.[164] Although Else Niemöller failed in her efforts to have her husband released, Hitler personally granted permission for Niemöller to leave Sachsenhausen for a day to visit his dying father.[165] If this typified the Nazis' persecution of the Protestant Church, compared with their other persecutions it was exceedingly mild.[166]

The idea of a Reich Church was now definitely abandoned. When Kerrl made intermittent attempts to pursue unity in the Protestant Church, Hess continually countermanded him.[167] As Hess wrote to Göring: "The Führer has not only abandoned the originally much-prized plan of creating a Reich Church; he now opposes it absolutely."[168] Even though Hitler had now given up on institutional Protestantism, he had not yet given up on Christianity. In a March 1938 meeting he held with Fürst von Bentheim, the marshal

---

[162] EZA 399/19 (6 October 1937: Berlin).

[163] BAZ NS 8/179/138-140 (14 February 1938: Berlin) (emphasis in the original).

[164] BAP R43 II/155/236-237 (6 March 1939: Oranienburg). This was confirmed by Niemöller himself in a letter he sent to his wife Else: BAP R43 II/155/238 (6 March 1939: Oranienburg).

[165] BAP R43 II/155/260 (18 March 1941: Berlin).

[166] Comparison with the Catholic clergy is revealing. In Dachau, the primary destination for priests and pastors, 447 German clergymen were interned: 411 were Catholic, 36 Protestant. When the numbers are further broken down, the disparity becomes even greater: 8 Catholic clergymen executed, 0 Protestant; 3 Catholic sentenced to death, 0 Protestant; 47 Catholic "deported in KZ," 2 Protestant; 99 Catholic "imprisoned," 8 Protestant; 163 Catholic "detained," 24 Protestant. Konrad Repgen, "German Catholicism and the Jews, 1933–1945," in Otto dov Kulka and Paul Mendes-Flohr (eds.), *Judaism and Christianity under the Impact of National Socialism* (Jerusalem, 1987), 211–12.

[167] See, *inter alia*, BAP R43 II/169/186-187 (17 May 1938: Munich).

[168] BAZ NS 8/184/211–215 (18 April 1940: Munich).

of the German Association of Nobles (*Deutsche Adelsgenossenschaft*), Hitler continued to maintain that he rejected Rosenberg's *Myth* and affirmed positive Christianity. When Heydrich caught wind of this, he wrote to Lammers, wondering if this was really Hitler's view.[169] Lammers responded that this was indeed Hitler's position and that furthermore Hitler was of the opinion that "Church and Christianity are not identical."[170]

CONCLUSION

There is no empirical evidence to support the claim that the Nazis tried to gradually extinguish the Protestant Church in Germany or that they secretly held off a final showdown until they were secure in their control of the state. To the contrary: The creation of a unified Reich Church would have meant a stronger church organization, as the Nazis realized. The ranks of the Protestant churches were indeed purged, but this was an intra–church affair conducted by the DC; the Nazis supported DC actions, but did not instigate them. Hitler demonstrated a consistent desire to bring unity to the ranks of German Protestantism. For much of the Third Reich, he correctly understood the BK per se to be a theological opponent of the DC, not a political opponent of the Nazis themselves. There is no proof that Müller and Jäger were executing Hitler's secret will in their arrest of Wurm and Meiser. Through a careful reconstruction of the time line of events in those crucial weeks in Autumn 1934, we can see that Hitler did not seek to destroy the church, either from without or within. The claim that "the Führer must not have known," essential to maintaining Hitler's prestige in the face of unpopular party actions, seems to have been the case here.

In the same way, the creation of a Reich ministry with the sole purpose of ending the Church Struggle cannot be taken as an anti-Christian act. Had the Nazis wanted to destroy Christian institutions, they would have handed control of the Reich Church Ministry to a paganist or not created such a ministry at all. Had Hitler been resolutely hostile to Protestantism, he would not have even pondered the idea of church elections four years after every other vestige of democracy in Germany had been wiped out. Only when Hitler understood the permanent impossibility of bringing unity to the fractured ranks of Protestantism did he finally give up on the idea of a Reich Church and dispense with Kerrl. Hitler's turn against the Protestant Church was signaled not by his attempt to "coordinate" it into a unified body, but by his acceptance of its disparate ecclesiastical structure. Only when Hitler gave up on the Reich Church did he give up on institutional Protestantism once and for all. This was the most important watershed for relations between the Protestant establishment and the Nazi State: After it, a spate of Nazis left the Protestant Church, and the DC gradually lost favor.

[169] BAP R43 II/150/127-130 (7 March 1938: Berlin).
[170] BAP R43 II/150/133 (26 July 1938: Berlin).

Nazi attempts at "coordination" have traditionally been viewed as an act of defilement or, at the very least, disrespect. To the Nazis, however, coordination of an institution was more often acknowledgement that something was *worth* coordinating. Hitler could not have come to power had he not "coordinated" the various splinter parties of the radical right into a unified movement. Likewise, the Nazis' determined effort to coordinate the Protestant churches suggests that they were seen as compatible – in a particular institutional form – with the Nazi order. This was true as well for the secular institutions and activities of the church. The practical Christianity exercised by church bodies for the health of the nation was of paramount interest to the Nazis. As we have seen, many Nazis proclaimed that their worldview largely revolved around ethical and social precepts found in Christianity. They therefore claimed the same ideological and institutional space as the churches in their efforts to answer the "social question." In the next chapter, we explore the process whereby the Nazis and the churches, through the implementation of practical Christianity, became institutional rivals. There we explore the possibility that the Nazis and the churches found themselves in an antagonistic position not in spite of, but because of, their ideological proximity.

6

PUBLIC NEED BEFORE
PRIVATE GREED

Building the People's Community

If positive Christianity means...the clothing of the poor, the feeding of the hungry...then it is we who are the more positive Christian. For in these spheres the people's community of National Socialist Germany has accomplished prodigious work.

Adolf Hitler[1]

Both before and after the Seizure of Power, leading Nazis claimed that "practical" or "active Christianity" guided them in defining the ethic of the *Volksgemeinschaft*. As Point 24 of the Party Program stated, "public need comes before private greed." A whole range of social policy was upheld as the palpable effect of neighborly or brotherly "love," in which the brother was defined – as we have seen – in terms of his racial belonging. However, as with any other aspect of Nazi discourse, we must ask whether such professions, especially when made in public, were anything more than propaganda. Were these declarations mendacious, meant purely to co-opt potential dissent? Or, aside from their acknowledged propaganda value, could they have been based on a belief that Nazism put forward a kind of Christian ethic? One way to answer this question is to explore the social policies of the churches and their relation to Nazi social policy. It was the churches and their ancillary institutions that had been defining and practicing active Christianity decades before the Nazis. If Nazis claimed their actions were the result of practical Christianity, did practical Christians agree? How similar were the ethical beliefs and practices of these Christian bodies and those of their Nazi rivals? How close were relations between them? We have already explored the ideological relationship with regards to antisemitism: three additional areas of particular centrality in Nazi ideology that are usually treated discretely – eugenics, women, and youth – can help uncover the ideological and institutional relationships between certain Nazi and Christian conceptions of "the social."[2]

[1] Hitler speaking to an assembly of *Alte Kämpfer* in Munich: *Völkischer Beobachter* (hereafter VB), 26 February 1939.

[2] Conceptualizations of the social in the German context are discussed in George Steinmetz, *Regulating the Social: The Welfare State and Local Politics in Imperial Germany* (Princeton, 1993).

EUGENICS

Lutheran Protestants were more likely to endorse the basic contours of Nazi ideology than Calvinists or Catholics were. This was evident not only in their conceptualization of the Marxist or Jewish "dangers" – which Catholics often feared as much as Protestants – but in a theological valorization of the *Volk* as an order of God's creation. Whereas the Catholic establishment was wary of *völkisch* theology and its practical consequences, large segments of the Protestant establishment felt more comfortable with the racialist precepts that underlay Nazi eugenicism. In fact, more than simply accommodating eugenics, many of these Protestants actively advanced its cause through their own institutions, most notably the Inner Mission, the Protestant welfare organization founded in the nineteenth century. These Protestants did not passively accept eugenics as a *fait accompli* of Nazi governance; rather, they were among the primary advocates of racial science before the Seizure of Power.

How could these Christians endorse eugenics from a theological standpoint? Since the Theology of the Orders of Creation (*Schöpfungsglaube*) relegated the value of the individual to that of the communal (the family, the estate, and latterly the nation), the status of the sick and suffering was similarly demoted: "Charitable institutions which had been designed to alleviate suffering" in the view of *Schöpfungsglaube* theologians "had been transformed into their antithesis.... in practice, [such institutions] actually favored evil over good and sickness over health."[3] The pronatalist struggle against a declining birthrate and secular "evils" like abortion, contraception, and loose morality presupposed the sanctification of a morally and physically healthy population.[4] Therefore the procreation of the physically and "morally" sick came to be viewed as a sin against God. Although Catholics opposed abortion and contraception with no less determination, Protestants far more than Catholics were disposed to view physical abnormality as an index of sin, as a sign of moral and social degeneration. Therefore, as long as this sin existed in the world, the "blessings of science" would be needed to combat it.[5]

Symptomatic of the interest in racial science was the establishment of the Research Center for the Study of Worldview (*Forschungsheim für Weltanschauungskunde*) in 1927. Headed by Pastor Otto Kleinschmidt, it was associated with the Martin Luther University and housed in the old elector's palace in Wittenberg. Its aim was to synthesize the supposed dialectic between

---

[3] Young-Sun Hong, *Welfare, Modernity, and the Weimar State, 1919–1933* (Princeton, 1998), 256.

[4] Compare Cornelie Usborne, *The Politics of the Body in Weimar Germany: Women's Reproductive Rights and Duties* (Ann Arbor, 1992).

[5] Claudia Koonz, "Eugenics, Gender, and Ethics in Nazi Germany: The Debate about Involuntary Sterilization 1933–1936," in Thomas Childers and Jane Caplan (eds.), *Reevaluating the Third Reich* (New York, 1993), 77.

belief and science and undo the common assumption that scientists needed no belief system. Explaining the mission of the center, General Superintendent Schöttler of Magdeburg asked his readership: "What are we doing to our sons? Just as his religion instructor is an orthodox theologian, so is his physics teacher an orthodox monist. The first becomes indignant with the second; the second mocks the first. The student bears the consequences, since he will perpetually be driven back and forth between two intellectual directions, only to be spiritually destroyed in the end." The Center's mission was to bridge the gulf between rationalist science and nonrationalist faith, "especially with regard to heredity and race."[6] As both a pastor and trained zoologist, Kleinschmidt was promoted as the personification of this synthesis.

After a year's work, one Protestant commentator could remark with satisfaction that, in place of the antagonism between science and religion, strides were being made toward their reconciliation. Natural sciences could be pursued without threat of apostasy. Especially commendable was the interest in race, which as a "new clear concept, is of enormous worth, especially in the field of worldview."[7] By reinserting religion into science, the Center was working to counteract the image of God as a deistic spirit who simply initiated earthly existence "and then slept." In scientific circles, this article proclaimed, God could once again be considered the living Lord of history. The scientist seeks truth, but, as this observer put it, "truth alone is like light without warmth." Scientific truth needed the warmth of a religious worldview, but not just any: "The Christian one is simply the most valuable.... It is important not just for the theologian, but for every man." At the same time, Protestantism was especially commendable because it "knows no dogmatic coercion [Dogmenzwang].... The Protestant church does not stand aside from things, but rather [is] in the center of life as builder and guardian."[8]

This same attitude to racialist science was evident in the work of the Inner Mission. In the 1920s a growing number of theologians advocated eugenics legislation, including Reinhold Seeberg, Schöpfungsglaube theologian and, after 1923, chairman of the Inner Mission's Central Committee.[9] Some theologians were advocating eugenic answers to the problems of mental and physical "defectives" as early as 1920.[10] Seeberg was especially noteworthy in this regard, having "converted" the eugenically minded scientists Baur, Gruber,

---

[6] *Deutsche Allgemeine Zeitung*, 27 December 1927: in Bundesarchiv Potsdam (hereafter BAP), R5101/23135/21.

[7] Kleinschmidt detailed his racialist views in *Blut und Rasse: Die Stellung der evangelischen Christen zu den Forderungen der Eugenik* (Berlin, 1933).

[8] *Reichsbote*, 9–11 September 1928: in BAP R5101/23135/22–23.

[9] Daniel Borg, *The Old-Prussian Church and the Weimar Republic: A Study in Political Adjustment, 1917–1927* (Hanover, NH, 1984), 170; Kurt Nowak, 'Euthanasie' und Sterilisierung im 'Dritten Reich': Die Konfrontation der evangelischen und katholischen Kirche mit dem 'Gesetz zur Verhütung erbkranken Nachwuchses' und der 'Euthanasie'-Aktion (Göttingen, 1980), 91.

[10] Paul Weindling, *Health, Race and German Politics between National Unification and Nazism, 1870–1945* (Cambridge, 1989), 383.

and Fischer to the idea of a broad eugenic front.[11] Other Protestant Christians who took up the cause of eugenics included Heinrich Wichern, the grandson of the founder of the Inner Mission, and the scientist Bernhard Bavink. Like Kleinschmidt, both were deeply concerned with reconciling faith and science.[12] Both welcomed the Nazis, especially the passage of the Law for the Prevention of Hereditarily Diseased Offspring in 1933. Countering the objections to eugenics in some Christian circles, especially from the papal encyclical *Casti connubii* of 1930, Bavink argued that "The mistake of many Christians is that they do not or cannot see that populations and races have the same standing in God's creation as individuals and therefore have the same claim to existence and protection from extermination.... God's creation obliges us with all our might to protect the well being of that whole to which we as individuals are subordinate: our *Volk*."[13]

The single most important personality in the Inner Mission's engagement with racialist science was Hans Harmsen, the chairman of its Working Committee on Eugenics. He was at the forefront of eugenics not only in the Protestant milieu, but in Germany as a whole. His interweaving of racial and moral categories was illustrated by the great success he achieved in campaigning for a German Mother's Day, meant both as a pronatalist celebration of racial hygiene and the family and an attack on abortion, contraception, and "decadence." Harmsen's vision was finally brought to fruition under the Nazis, who made Mother's Day an official holiday.[14] Harmsen also fervently supported the Nazi sterilization laws of 1933.[15] In 1930, three years before the Nazis came to power, Harmsen called for a reorientation in the welfare system, suggesting that "the interests of the individual must retreat further behind those of society."[16] At a meeting of the Inner Mission in August of that year, Harmsen suggested that Protestant charities had to limit the procreation of the socially inferior through compulsory sterilization.[17]

The most important policy statement for the Inner Mission as a whole came at a January 1931 conference in Treysa, under the chairmanship of Harmsen, who called on the assembly to recognize the "natural inequality

[11] Ibid., 315; Michael Schwartz, "Konfessionelle Milieus und Weimarer Eugenik," *Historische Zeitschrift* 261 (1995), 421. These four came out with a popular eugenic journal, *Das kommende Geschlecht* ("The Coming Generation"), in 1920.

[12] Heinrich Wichern, *Sexualethik und Bevölkerungspolitik* (Schwerin, 1926); Bernhard Bavink, "Die moderne Rassenhygiene und ihre Beziehung zum sittlich-religiösen Standpunkt," *Unsere Welt* 18 (1926); idem, "Eugenik und Protestantismus," in Günter Just (ed.), *Eugenik und Weltanschauung* (Berlin, 1932); idem, *Die Naturwissenschaft auf dem Wege zur Religion* (Frankfurt a.M., 1933).

[13] *VB*, 17 August 1933.

[14] Karen Hausen, "Mother's Day in the Weimar Republic," in Renate Bridenthal et al. (eds.), *When Biology Became Destiny: Women in Weimar and Nazi Germany* (New York, 1984), 131–2.

[15] Weindling, *Health*, 526.

[16] Quoted in Hong, *Welfare*, 257.

[17] Jochen-Christoph Kaiser, *Sozialer Protestantismus im 20. Jahrhundert: Beiträge zur Geschichte der Inneren Mission 1914–1945* (Munich, 1989), 316.

of all human beings." Whereas the conference as a whole avoided an endorsement of euthanasia, the participants agreed that "the artificial prolongation of life which is in the process of being extinguished" represented "an interference in God's creative will."[18] One of the most eminent participants in the conference was Friedrich von Bodelschwingh, head of the Bethel institutions and Reich Bishop-designate in 1933. At this conference, it was his opinion that "In service to the Kingdom of God we have received our body.... God gave man responsibility for the body. If [the body] leads to evil and the destruction of the Kingdom of God in this or that member of the community, then there is the possibility or even duty for elimination [*Eliminierung*] to take place."[19] The public statement issued by the participants was almost identical to this opinion. It proclaimed that the 30,000 patients in their institutions were "the victims of guilt and sin." The statement concluded that the need for assistance should therefore be curtailed by sterilization, with substantial help given only to those who could regain their productive status in the community.[20] The statement added that there was "a moral obligation to sterilization on the grounds of charity and the responsibility which has [been] imposed upon us not only for the present generation, but also for future generations." Even though the statement rejected sterilization and eugenic abortion, within the Inner Mission's clinics and hospitals many such procedures had already been conducted.[21]

The Inner Mission was not simply one voice among the chorus of eugenics advocates in Weimar: It actually constituted part of the eugenics vanguard. The Inner Mission supported the November 1932 draft law providing for the decriminalization of eugenic sterilization, but proposed expanding its scope from the genetically inferior to include the "asocial" as well. In addition, whereas the law would have been based on the voluntary assent of the individual, the Inner Mission proposed that sterilization be dependent solely on the consent of a legal guardian.[22] When the Nazis passed a much stronger version of the law in 1933 against the wishes of the Catholic Franz von Papen (then in Hitler's cabinet as vice chancellor), the Inner Mission welcomed it. The Inner Mission proceeded to voluntarily sterilize inmates in its own asylums, free from coercion by the Nazi State.[23] As Michael Burleigh puts it, "The annual reports of [Inner Mission] asylums such as Schwäbisch Hall or Stetten were positively self-congratulatory in tone regarding how the

[18] Sabine Schleiermacher, "Der Centralausschuß für die Innere Mission und die Eugenik am Vorabend des 'Dritten Reiches'," in Theodore Strohm and Jörg Thierfelder (eds.), *Diakonie im 'Dritten Reich': Neuere Ergebnisse zeitgeschichtlicher Forschung* (Heidelberg, 1990), 70.

[19] Quoted in Schleiermacher, "Centralausschuß," 70; Kaiser, *Protestantismus*, 330.

[20] Ernst Klee, *'Euthanasie' im NS-Staat: Die 'Vernichtung lebensunwerten Lebens'* (Frankfurt a.M., 1983), 32; Hong, *Welfare*, 258.

[21] Ernst Klee, *'Euthanasie'*, 32–3. The Treysa conference is discussed at length in Kaiser, *Protestantismus*, 324–32.

[22] Kaiser, *Protestantismus*, 338–9.

[23] Nowak, *'Euthanasie'*, 96–7, 101–6; Michael Burleigh, *Death and Deliverance: 'Euthanasia' in Germany 1900–1945* (Cambridge, 1994), 41–2.

staff had coped with the extra workload involved, or the diplomatic skill they displayed in persuading patients to 'volunteer' for sterilisation."[24]

Historians have rightly pointed out that eugenics found an audience in many political tendencies in Weimar and that acceptance of some or most of its tenets did not necessarily constitute a move toward Nazism.[25] However, the attention the Inner Mission paid to eugenics was not simply part of a larger *Zeitgeist* transcending party lines. Congruence with Nazi ideas could be found on a larger scale. As Burleigh points out, the organization "welcomed the advent of a National Socialist Government."[26] Young-Sun Hong similarly contends that "most members of the Inner Mission enthusiastically greeted the Nazi Seizure of Power."[27] As one non-Nazi eugenicist wrote after a course he gave for the Inner Mission in 1931, "among many pastors strongly National Socialist tendencies prevailed, making them convinced that the Jewish problem was the central problem."[28] Pastor Johannes Wolff, head of the *Stephansstift*, went so far as to encourage members of his staff, among them SA men, to work as guards in the neighboring Papenburg Concentration Camp.[29] Outside the ranks of the Inner Mission as well, established Protestant theologians welcomed the Nazi emphasis on eugenics. One of the most prominent was none other than Paul Althaus, one of Germany's leading *Schöpfungsglaube* theologians.[30]

If these representatives of social Protestantism were favorably inclined toward the Nazis and their eugenics policies, what were the Nazis' views of social Protestantism? This question can be answered through an examination of a parallel welfare organization set up by the Nazis in 1932, the National Socialist People's Welfare (*Nationalsozialistische Volkswohlfahrt*, or NSV). Headed by *alte Kämpfer* Erich Hilgenfeldt, it grew into a mass organization, reaching 3.4 million members within two years. True to form as a Nazi organization, it experienced polycratic infighting over control of welfare activity with Ley's German Labor Front, Schirach's HJ, and Scholtz-Klink's NSF.[31] Whereas each of these organizations had their own welfare

---

[24] Michael Burleigh, "Between Enthusiasm, Compliance and Protest: The Churches, Eugenics and the Nazi 'Euthanasia' Programme," *Contemporary European History* 3 (1994), 254; idem, *Death*, 51.

[25] For eugenics within Social Democracy, for instance, see Michael Schwartz, "Sozialismus und Eugenik: Zur fälligen Revision eines Geschichtsbildes," *Internationale wissenschaftliche Korrespondenz zur Geschichte der deutschen Arbeiterbewegung* 25 (1989).

[26] Burleigh, "Enthusiasm," 254.

[27] Hong, *Welfare*, 227.

[28] Quoted in Weindling, *Health*, 477.

[29] See Christoph Mehl, "Das Stephansstift im Jahr 1933," in Strohm and Thierfelder (eds.), *Diakonie*, 153–5.

[30] Nowak, *'Euthanasie'*, 122–3.

[31] See Herwart Vorländer, *Die NSV: Darstellungen und Dokumentationen einer nationalsozialistischen Organisation* (Boppard, 1988), especially 29 for intraparty conflicts; idem, "Erich Hilgenfeldt – Reichswalter der NSV," in Ronald Smelser et al. (eds.), *Die Braune Elite II: 21 weitere biographische Skizzen* (Darmstadt, 1993).

programs, they eventually gave up their competency in this field to the NSV. More than just a platform for orations about the *Volksgemeinschaft*, the NSV took tangible action, providing approximately sixteen million Germans with additional winter income to supplement unemployment insurance in the first years of the regime.[32] The NSV grew enormously by the beginning of the war, taking over many aspects of social policy in the Third Reich.

Whereas the NSV had little to do with the Nazis' sterilization and euthanasia programs, it nonetheless performed many of the functions – notably welfare and Winter Relief – that also fell within the domain of the Inner Mission.[33] Referring to the necessity of cooperation between the NSV and its Christian counterparts, Reich Interior Minister Wilhelm Frick took a positive view of the work of the Inner Mission. In June 1933 he denounced the expansion of public, secular welfare during Weimar, which confessional organizations had resented as an invasion and secularization of their domain. Emphasizing that welfare could never do without a Christian sense of charity and love of neighbor, Frick promised that church organizations would be called on to help build the new *Volksgemeinschaft*.[34] That same month, Göring issued a similar statement, proclaiming that the Nazi State should seek active cooperation with Christian welfare organizations.[35] Hilgenfeldt, as the leader of a mass organization, wanted the NSV to become the sole body responsible for welfare in the new Germany. He sought cooperation with Christian welfare organizations in the short run, but had little interest in seeing rival bodies competing with his.[36] At the same time, true to the doctrine of positive Christianity, he insisted that, whereas the NSV was not confessional, it was Christian. In a September 1933 meeting with the Inner Mission leadership, Hilgenfeldt declared that the NSV firmly stood on the basis of Christianity, that it indeed encompassed both of the confessions by effecting their practical agenda.[37] As well as emphasizing the ideological affinity between the NSV and Christian welfare, Hilgenfeldt here pointed to the potential for institutional rivalry.

In a similar meeting in 1934, in which the president of the Central Committee greeted Hilgenfeldt as the "Führer" of all German welfare, Hilgenfeldt and his deputy Hermann Althaus pointed to a shared ideology between the NSV and the Inner Mission: belief in the biblical God, the state, and the

---

[32] Thomas de Witt, "'The Struggle against Hunger and Cold': Winter Relief in Nazi Germany, 1933–1939," *Canadian Journal of History* 12 (1978), 364–5.

[33] Although the Nazis' WHW was *de jure* a separate organization from the NSV, both were headed by Hilgenfeldt – the latter as an independent organization, the former as a subsidiary of Goebbels' Propaganda Ministry; Herwart Voränder, "NS-Volkswohlfahrt und Winterhilfswerk des Deutschen Volkes," *Vierteljahrshefte für Zeitgeschichte* 34 (1986), 342.

[34] Vorländer, *NSV*, 204–5.

[35] Eckhard Hansen, *Wohlfahrtspolitik im NS-Staat: Motivationen, Konflikte und Machtstrukturen im 'Sozialismus der Tat' des Dritten Reiches* (Augsburg, 1991), 73.

[36] Hong, *Welfare*, 232–3; Vorländer, *NSV*, 20–43.

[37] Hong, *Welfare*, 236; Kaiser, *Protestantismus*, 282.

Volk as part of God's creation. Hilgenfeldt rightly pointed out that, unlike Catholicism, Protestantism neither needed nor desired a concordat with the state. This comment was aimed primarily against the Catholic counterpart to the Inner Mission, the Caritas Association, which was much less willing to endorse Nazi policies.[38] Referring to his audience as his "co-workers," he applauded the Inner Mission's positive stand on sterilization, adding that artificially sustaining the lives of the spiritually dead ran against God's order of creation and stood "in opposition to Christian ethics and worldview."[39] In spite of the inherent potential for rivalry, the NSV supported these assertions by seeking active cooperation with the Inner Mission in the drafting of new legislation. A top priority was the National Youth Welfare Law, promulgated in 1922 with the aim of overtaking Christian welfare with a secular, republican ethos. In contrast to the NSV's nonconfessional Christian approach to altering the law, the Caritas Association wanted an explicit maintenance of confessionalism in welfare. However, unknown to Caritas, the NSV had already obtained the consent of the Inner Mission for their own draft, which would eventually win out. In that draft, the NSV proclaimed its vision of welfare in the new Germany: to cultivate "a bodily and psychically healthy, morally firm, spiritually developed, vocationally skilled German person, who is rooted... in a racially conscious manner and, borne by the living forces of Christianity, is committed and bound to *Volk* and state."[40]

This was not only an overlap of ideas; personnel from the Inner Mission found their way into the NSV as well. The most important among them was Hermann Althaus, pastor's son and cousin of theologian Paul Althaus. Originally active in the Berlin city missions during the Weimar Republic, Althaus was made deputy director of the NSV by 1934, having joined the NSDAP just two years earlier.[41] His long involvement in the Inner Mission and relation to Paul in no way made him suspect to Hilgenfeldt. Other NSV leaders to come from the Inner Mission included Bertha Finck, who would become the spokeswoman of the NSV's "Mother and Child" aid service, and Werner Betcke, who had worked as Reinhold Seeberg's assistant in the Inner Mission's Institute for Social Ethics and Science.[42] By contrast, no one from the Caritas made their way into the NSV leadership.

With the progress of "coordination," the Nazi intolerance for rival organizations grew. However, this was not primarily the product of ideological

---

[38] Kaiser, *Protestantismus*, 294; Vorländer, *NSV*, 213. Only a minority of those involved in the delivery of Catholic welfare in Germany endorsed any kind of sterilization, and even this small number was presented with a major obstacle after the papal encyclical *Casti connubii* of 1930. See Donald Dietrich, "Catholic Eugenics in Germany, 1920–1945," *Journal of Church and State* 34 (1992), 575–600.

[39] Kaiser, *Protestantismus*, 295.

[40] Quoted in Hong, *Welfare*, 237.

[41] Kaiser, *Protestantismus*, 194.

[42] Ibid., 280.

difference on the issue of eugenics, as demonstrated by the regime's view of Kleinschmidt's Research Center. In 1937 the Gestapo started to contemplate action against the Center, claiming that Kleinschmidt's work was not built on the foundation of the Nazi *Weltanschauung*. In a letter it sent to Church Minister Kerrl, the Gestapo declared the scientific contributions of the Center to be of dubious value and suggested that Kleinschmidt had demonstrated his unreliability by accepting a monetary gift from a Masonic lodge.[43] The Gestapo also took note of a comment Kleinschmidt made about blood mixing – that a white man who receives a blood transfusion from a black man becomes no more black than someone eating blood sausage made from pigs becomes a pig or a sausage.[44] The Gestapo, taking this as an attack on Nazi science, called for the Center to be closed. As soon became evident, however, the real bone of contention was that the name of Kleinschmidt's Center included the phrase *Weltanschauung* – an expression that the Nazis were anxious to appropriate as their intellectual property. In his defense, Kleinschmidt submitted testimonials to the authorities. One was from the anatomical department of the Halle-Wittenberg University, which confirmed Kleinschmidt's status as a scientist and race scholar of world renown who was doing Germany and the Nazi State a great service.[45] Even more significant was a letter from Wilhelm Schneider, the head of the party's own Race Policy Office for *Gau* Halle-Merseburg, which praised Kleinschmidt for his work on science and worldview.[46] Kerrl himself had written the previous year that the Center was known "in broad circles" for its great value and that he was happy to continue supporting it financially, as Frick had done when the Interior Ministry was responsible for funding.[47] When it was discovered that Kleinschmidt's Center was in fact well regarded by race scholars, and could even rely upon the patronage of Göring,[48] no more threats arrived from the Gestapo. In the final analysis, it was declared that the Center's primary aim – of proving that religion and racial science, Protestantism and Nazism, were compatible – was in no way aimed against the regime. As long as the Center dropped *Weltanschauung* from its title, it could continue its work with financial support from the state.[49]

A similar attitude was apparent toward the Inner Mission. As a consequence of the NSV's drive to take over their welfare activities, the Inner Mission and Caritas found their state subsidies increasingly diminished with time. Whereas they were offered reimbursements equal to their WHW collections in the first years of the Third Reich, these amounts were gradually

[43] BAP R5101/23135/152-153 (21 February 1938: Berlin).
[44] BAP R5101/23135/154-156 (13 December 1937: Halle).
[45] BAP R5101/23135/40 (29 January 1934: Halle).
[46] BAP R5101/23135/172 (3 December 1934: Halle).
[47] BAP R5101/23135/120 (9 November 1936: Berlin).
[48] BAP R5101/23135/166 (30 August 1938: Berlin).
[49] BAP R5101/23135/192 (18 January 1939: Berlin).

reduced and finally ended in 1936.[50] However, although the NSV wished for the total removal of confessional groups from these activities, its ambition was stymied by other Nazi offices, particularly the Labor and Finance Ministries, which showed a more sympathetic attitude by maintaining the Inner Mission's state subsidies.[51] When Hilgenfeldt asked that the Protestant League be excluded from the WHW in 1935, Church Minister Kerrl turned him down, pointing out that their participation that year would help mark the League's fiftieth birthday.[52] Even as late as 1937/38, most Protestant state churches were participating in the WHW.[53] Confessional welfare was therefore maintained, even if in reduced form. Michael Burleigh's assertion that "the Churches were excluded from collecting for charity" is therefore incorrect.[54] Although the NSV was able to curtail their activities by receiving the lion's share of welfare subsidies from the state, it was unable to entirely remove the Inner Mission and Caritas from these fields.

If welfare was becoming slowly deconfessionalized, was the NSV becoming concomitantly dechristianized? In a 1937 article, Walter Schäfer, the head of the NSV for Kurhessen, insisted that it was not. In his view, Christian charitable love was aimed at the entirety of the *Volk* and not the individual. The focus on the individual was not the product of Christianity, this author stated, but of a secular philosophy.[55] In October 1937, Hitler himself insisted that "Winter Relief is in the deepest sense a Christian work.... This is the Christianity of an honest confession, because behind it stand not words but deeds."[56] Even when the Inner Mission began to take aim at the NSV for restricting its activities,[57] leaders of the NSV continued to maintain that their work accorded with positive Christianity. The NSV's main goal, its leaders suggested, was to coordinate all German welfare efforts under one authority. As Hermann Althaus insisted, the goal was not a dechristianization of welfare, but a rationalization of welfare activity under national leadership.[58] Even in areas run by piously Catholic *Gauleiter*, such as Josef Wagner of Silesia, the NSV appropriated the functions of confessional welfare.[59] This points both to the generalized nature of deconfessionalization as an institutional practice and to the fact that this process was not of itself an anti-Christian act, as it could take place even under the auspices of Nazis like

[50] Thomas de Witt, "The Economics and Politics of Welfare in the Third Reich," *Central European History* 11 (1978), 268.

[51] Ibid., 269.

[52] BAP R5101/23126/32-33 (27 November 1935: Berlin) for Hilgenfeldt's request; BAP R5101/23126/39-40 (9 December 1935: Berlin) for Kerrl's response.

[53] VB, 22 December 1937: in BAP 62 Di 1/75/33.

[54] Michael Burleigh, *The Third Reich: A New History* (New York, 2000), 260.

[55] Kaiser, *Protestantismus*, 423.

[56] *Frankfurter Zeitung*, 7 October 1937.

[57] Kaiser, *Protestantismus*, 424-5.

[58] Ibid., 427. De Witt suggests that this was in fact the primary goal of the NSV: "The Struggle against Hunger and Cold"; "The Economics and Politics of Welfare," passim.

[59] Hansen, *Wohlfahrtspolitik*, 249.

Wagner – who took his own children to parochial Catholic schools instead of to the Adolf Hitler Schools favored by party functionaries (see Chapter 7).

There were NSV polemics that criticized Christian charity as "Bolshevik," as it supposedly led to the "reign of *Untermenschen*" and the propagation of the racially inferior. However, these were aimed primarily against Catholic charities like Caritas, which neither subscribed to *Schöpfungsglaube* nor defended sterilization in the name of the larger community.[60] When it carried over to Protestant organizations, Nazi leaders quickly retracted. After the Protestant deaconess mother house of Gunzenhausen was attacked as "un-Nazi" by the rival Nazi Nursing Organization (*NS-Schwesternschaft*), the local *Kreisleiter* wrote to Hilgenfeldt, testifying that the deaconesses were firmly behind Hitler, "in word and above all in deed." They gave material and monetary assistance to the NSDAP during the *Kampfzeit* and actively sought to work with the *NS-Schwesternschaft*. In short, according to the *Kreisleiter*, they were a "bulwark of National Socialism."[61] Hilgenfeldt, on hearing of this complaint, visited the deaconess house shortly thereafter to assure them personally of his high esteem.[62]

If sterilization met with general approval in the ranks of the Inner Mission, euthanasia was given a mixed response. Many church leaders, especially those with BK leanings such as Bodelschwingh and Wurm, came out firmly against the Nazis' euthanasia program. Shortly before the war, both men would make attempts to curtail this program, also known as the infamous "T-4" Action. However, this picture of opposition has to be weighed against the fact that fully half of all victims of the Nazis' euthanasia action came from church institutions.[63] This figure alone testifies to the muted nature of such church opposition. However, it is also attributable to the fact that some Protestants were actually in favor of euthanasia. One was Ewald Meltzer, head of the Protestant Katherinenhof Home. After the Seizure of Power, he admitted that he had permitted sterilizations to take place at a time when they were still illegal. In 1937, at an Inner Mission conference on racial hygiene, he stated that there were certain conditions under which the "patient too must pay his duties to the fatherland" through "mercy killing." Such circumstances included food shortages or urgent care for military personnel. Meltzer specifically referred to "idiots" as the target group, thereby excluding others like the elderly.[64]

If Meltzer's was only a qualified endorsement of euthanasia, there were more outspoken proponents. One was Rudolf Boeckh, chief doctor of the

---

[60] Kaiser, *Protestantismus*, 427–8.

[61] BAP R43 II/180/47 (26 June 1935: Gunzenhausen).

[62] The rector of the house, Pastor Keupp, noted that he had already received a visit from the area *Gauleiter*, Julius Streicher, assuring him of the Nazi's regard for the house's work: BAP R43 II/180/48 (13 September 1934: Munich).

[63] Burleigh, *Death*, 166.

[64] Burleigh, "Enthusiasm," 256; Ernst Klee, *'Die SA Jesu Christi:' Die Kirche im Banne Hitlers* (Frankfurt a.M., 1989), 97.

Lutheran Neuendettelsau Asylum in Central Franconia.[65] In a 1937 address to the local NSDAP *Ortsgruppe*, he advocated the elimination of "life unworthy of life." His theological justification for this course of action acknowledged that "the Creator had certainly imposed illness upon the destiny of mankind." However, "the most severe forms of idiocy and the totally grotesque disintegration of the personality had nothing to do with the countenance of God. . . . we should not maintain these travesties of human form through an exaggerated, and therefore false, type of compassion; rather, we should return them to the Creator."[66] Rector Hans Lauerer, head of Neuendettelsau, disagreed that there was such a thing as "life unworthy of life." This was not quite a refutation of biological determinism, however, as Lauerer immediately added that "naturally there exists life of lesser value." He then added that, because the Nazi State was "an order of God," it was contingent on good Lutherans to affirm the state in its actions.[67] In 1941, 1,911 of Neuendettelsau's 2,137 patients were removed in the T-4 Action and killed.

Such active support for euthanasia was rare within the Inner Mission. The same director of Stetten who had so glowingly approved of sterilization found himself opposed to the measures being taken to kill his patients. When he was ordered by T-4 personnel to round up 92 inmates for transportation, he flatly refused to cooperate, going so far as to complain to the Württemberg Interior Minister (with the help of a doctor on staff, the patients were rounded up nonetheless).[68] Overall, however, reactions to the T-4 Action tended to be substantially more ambiguous. One case was the Protestant asylum of Mariaberg in Württemberg, where, instead of blocking Nazi attempts to euthanize patients, the staff went over the list of transferees to determine who were the more physically productive. Far from countering the Nazis' work, this asylum facilitated it, determining the value of their patients by their productive abilities instead of leaving it up to the Nazi authorities, who had not bothered to discern between "loyal and willing workers" and "those needing constant care."[69]

Even some of the Protestants at the forefront of protest exhibited a paralyzing ambivalence toward euthanasia. Egged on by the objections of Pastor Gerhard Braun, vice president of the Central Committee of the Inner Mission and head of the Lobetal asylum, Bishop Wurm decided to state his personal position to the Nazis. He did so privately, so as to spare the regime public embarrassment – a very charitable gesture, given that his release from Jäger's

[65] Christine-Ruth Müller and Hans-Ludwig Degener, *Warum sie sterben mußten: Leidensweg und Vernichtung von Behinderten aus den Neuendettelsauer Pflegenstalten im 'Dritten Reich'* (Neustadt/Aisch, 1991).

[66] Hans Rössler, "Die 'Euthanasie'-Diskussion in Neuendettelsau 1937–39," *Zeitschrift für bayerischen Kirchengeschichte* 55 (1986), 208; Klee, *'Euthanasie' im NS-Staat*, 244.

[67] Rössler, "'Euthanasie'-Diskussion," 202.

[68] Klee, *'Euthanasie'*, 269–72.

[69] Quoted in Burleigh, *Death*, 140.

house arrest six years before was precipitated on *public* protest. Writing to Wilhelm Frick, he presented the evidence he had compiled from laity whose relatives had been killed and denounced the euthanasia action. However, he also displayed a willingness to see things from the regime's point of view. He was careful to distinguish his criticism of Nazism on this one issue from any thought of disloyalty to the regime itself, even stating that he had prayed for the recent defeat of France. Even more significant – given that Wurm had once been a pastor in a state asylum – was his opinion: "Naturally, the thought has crossed the minds of those who have seen such regrettable people: 'Wouldn't it be better to put an end to such an existence'?"[70]

Bodelschwingh's position was even more ambivalent, as he had been a strong supporter of sterilization before the Nazis. He was initially against the T-4 Action, refusing to carry out the registration of his patients. Even the head psychiatrist at Bethel, an *alte Kämpfer* who joined the Nazi Party in 1931 and served during the *Kampfzeit* as Martin Bormann's physician, worked against the euthanasia program by falsifying medical records.[71] Like Wurm, Bodelschwingh kept his concerns private, never contemplating a direct challenge to the regime. However, Bodelschwingh began to change his position after he talked with Pastor Constantin Frick, the president of the Inner Mission's Central Committee. Bodelschwingh now reversed himself and approved of the euthanasia program, as long as it would affect only "patients no longer capable of any human contact." He would not allow his staff to be involved, but would instruct them to not obstruct the work of state authorities or refuse access to medical records.[72] Bodelschwingh then went a step further by ordering his own doctors henceforth to categorize patients according to their productive abilities, easing the work of the Nazis.[73] As Burleigh acerbically puts it, "'Aktion T-4' stopped before the efficacy of Bodelschwingh's brand of decentralised opposition through apparent accommodation could be tested."[74] In fact, not one *public* protest against euthanasia was ever launched by a Protestant churchman. This would be left to Catholic Bishop Clemens August Graf von Galen, whose fiery denunciation of euthanasia from the pulpit in August 1941 sent shock waves through the Nazi regime. Whereas most Protestant churchmen could not be called active supporters of euthanasia, their ability to work actively against it was undermined from the start by *Schöpfungsglaube* and its racialist implications.

---

[70] Klee, '*Euthanasie*', 213–14.
[71] Jörg Thierfelder, "Karsten Jaspersens Kampf gegen die NS-Krankenmorde," in Strohm and Thierfelder (eds.), *Diakonie*, 229–31 (Bormann reference: 234).
[72] Klee, '*Euthanasie*', 281. Constantin Frick had entered into secret negotiations with Leonardo Conti, the Reich Health Leader, consenting to the voluntary completion of registration forms so long as the euthanasia program "would proceed more circumspectly": Burleigh, *Death*, 168.
[73] Klee, '*Euthanasie*', 320–1.
[74] Burleigh, *Death*, 169.

WOMEN

The ideological and institutional affinities between Nazism and certain types of Christianity became even more apparent regarding the issue of women. As we have already seen, Christian ideologies played a particularly important role in mediating the message of Nazism for women, both in a positive sense for many Protestants and in a negative sense for most Catholics. As with welfare and eugenics, the experiences of Catholics and Protestants under Nazism revealed sharp differences in their relationship with the regime and its ideology. Indeed, the nature of the relationship revealed itself in great measure over the issue of welfare, one of the very few areas within the public sphere traditionally open to the influence of women.

Protestant women were attracted to Nazism in a way that Catholic women were not. As Wilhelm Zoellner, chairman of the Protestant Reich Church Committee, wrote to Reich Women's Leader Gurtrud Scholtz-Klink in 1936, Protestant women "put themselves at the disposal of the party" when it rose to power, whereas liberal and Catholic (and he might have added Jewish) women stayed away.[75] These women were attracted to Nazism by a mutual loathing of Weimar and appreciation of the cultural role of women as the center of the German family. They shared remarkably similar notions about the position of women in society – out of politics and the workplace and into the home as wives and mothers.[76] In addition, as with so many other voices within German Protestantism, a large portion of Protestant women subscribed to *Schöpfungsglaube*. As Michael Phayer puts it, "As far as most churchgoing women were concerned, belief in Protestantism and support of the National Socialist revolution went hand in hand."[77]

As with the Inner Mission, Protestant women's groups were in the forefront of advocating social policies that the Nazis would later adopt as their own. In 1927, hundreds of thousands of Protestant women signed a petition opposing educational reforms that would have given girls the same curriculum (including science and mathematics) as boys.[78] One particularly noteworthy organization in this regard was the Protestant Mothers' Association, founded by Klara Lönnies. She was committed to the fight against

---

[75] Michael Phayer, *Protestant and Catholic Women in Nazi Germany* (Detroit, 1990), 67. Zoellner's language clearly indicated his belief that one could not be both Protestant and liberal.

[76] Some historians have contended that women had no positive place in the Nazis' conceptual universe, even going so far as to suggest that women were victims of Nazism and stood in opposition to it: See Gisela Bock, *Zwangssterilisation im Nationalsozialismus: Studien zur Rassenpolitik und Frauenpolitik* (Opladen, 1986). For a convincing dissection of this argument, see Atina Grossmann, "Feminist Debates about Women and National Socialism," *Gender and History* 3 (1991), 350–8.

[77] Phayer, *Women*, 81 (for quote); 81–2, 84 (on women and *Schöpfungsglaube*).

[78] Doris Kampmann, "'Zölibat – ohne uns!' Die soziale Situation und politische Einstellung der Lehrerinnen in der Weimarer Republik," in Frauengruppe Faschismus Forschung (ed.), *Mutterkreuz und Arbeitsbuch: Zur Geschichte der Frauen in der Weimarer Republik und im Nationalsozialismus* (Frankfurt a.M., 1981), 99.

the falling birthrate and asserted that "mothers are the most worthwhile part of the *Volk*."[79] The same year Lönnies started publication of *Mutter und Volk*, a racialist, pronatalist magazine that supported eugenics from its inception. It advocated such practical measures as marriage loans and subsidies for large families, initiatives that were adopted after the Nazis came to power.[80] Lönnies' organization, among other Protestant women's groups, actively supported Nazi legislation that increased penalties for abortion, pornography, prostitution, and homosexuality.[81] Among their ranks could also be found support for eugenics. Lönnies suggested that individual women should not have the right to decide if and when to have children. As one Protestant woman put it, there was a need for "a new morality, a new will for purity, healthy marriages and healthy families – together with physically, spiritually, and psychologically healthy children."[82]

Another Protestant women's leader whose ideas foreshadowed much of the Nazi program was Guida Diehl, who in 1919 founded the ultraright New Land League (*Neulandbund*). A disciple of Adolf Stöcker, Diehl did battle with the alleged enemies of Christianity and the Fatherland: Judaism, Marxism, materialism, and mammonism.[83] Hitler recognized Diehl's ideological value, having paid her a visit at her headquarters in Thuringia as early as 1925.[84] She finally joined the NSDAP in 1930 and shortly thereafter made a bid to take over the NSF. Leaders in the party administration, particularly Gregor Strasser, were willing to accept her, together with others, into the party leadership; but she wanted nothing less than exclusive control. She was made its "cultural advisor" in 1931, but soon fell out with her rivals, refusing to accept the authority of those above her. When she revealed that she would not cooperate with others or bring her New Land League into the Nazi movement, she was expelled from her office the next year.

The differences between her and Nazi women were not ideological, but rather were more often concerned with "ambition and place-seeking."[85] Even after she was removed from office, Diehl's vision for the NSF – to reestablish women's place in the community and family, making women upholders of the German *Volk* and German culture – formed the basis of its activities until the beginning of the war. Diehl and the Nazis remained close enough that she campaigned for the NSDAP in the November 1932 elections.[86] There were other organizations besides the *Neulandbund* to support

[79] Quoted in Phayer, *Women*, 87.
[80] Claudia Koonz, *Mothers in the Fatherland: Women, the Family and Nazi Politics* (New York, 1987), 240–1.
[81] Ibid., 241.
[82] Ibid., 240.
[83] Jill Stephenson, *The Nazi Organisation of Women* (London, 1981), 27, 77.
[84] Koonz, *Mothers*, 81.
[85] Stephenson, *Organisation*, 78.
[86] Ibid., 79–81.

the Nazis. The members of the largest Protestant women's organization, the Protestant Women's Auxiliary (*Evangelische Frauenhilfe*), were "among Hitler's most avid supporters at the polls," and counted many *alte Kämpfer* of the NSDAP among their ranks.[87] The German Protestant Women's League, headed by Paula Müller-Otfried, similarly embraced Nazism. Just weeks before the Seizure of Power, Müller-Otfried wrote: "Are we on the brink of collapse? Is the *Volk* to become extinct? ... We must remain faithful and pray, confident that God is at the controls."[88] As Michael Phayer puts it, "the fascination of Protestant women with *völkisch* renewal antedates national socialism [sic]. ... Protestant women liked to view themselves as the precursors of the *völkisch* renewal under the National Socialists."[89]

As with the NSV regarding the Inner Mission, we must ask: if these Protestant women's organizations were so favorably inclined toward the Nazis, was the feeling reciprocal? One of the first leaders of the NSF, Gottfried Krummacher, was not only positively inclined toward Protestant women's organizations, but was actively Protestant himself. However, Krummacher's tenure as head of NSF was brief. Much more important for the development of relations between Protestant and Nazi women was his successor, Gertrud Scholtz-Klink. Scholtz-Klink was brought in to calm the dissent that arose from having a man as NSF leader. (Because Krummacher had also proven himself a poor administrator, Erich Hilgenfeldt was put in charge of the NSF's day-to-day operations. The NSF was formally made a subsidiary of Hilgenfeldt's NSV.[90]) Scholtz-Klink provided little indication of a personal Protestant religiosity. Nonetheless she sought active cooperation with these Protestant groups. She complimented the maternal aid services of Protestant groups as "immeasurably fruitful."[91] The NSV's "Mother and Child" aid service also cooperated with the Protestant Women's Auxiliary ("Mother and Child" *Referentin* Bertha Finck had come out of the Inner Mission). Throughout Germany, members of the Women's Auxiliary cooperated with the NSV in collections for the WHW. In some areas the level of cooperation reached the stage at which officers in the Women's Auxiliary simultaneously served as heads of local NSF branches.[92]

Perhaps the most significant instance of cooperation between Nazi and Protestant women was the founding of a new Protestant women's umbrella organization, the Women's Bureau (*Frauenwerk*) of the German Protestant Church. Established in 1933 by Pastor Hans Hermenau, it claimed a

---

[87] Phayer, *Women*, 157. Phayer translates *Evangelische Frauenhilfe* as "Protestant Ladies' Auxiliary" whereas Koonz translates it as "Ladies' Aid."

[88] Quoted in Claudia Koonz, "The Competition for Women's *Lebensraum*, 1928–1934," in Renate Bridenthal et al. (eds.), *Biology*, 222.

[89] Phayer, *Women*, 87.

[90] Stephenson, *Organisation*, 105–6.

[91] Quoted in Phayer, *Women*, 53.

[92] Ibid., 90.

membership that year of 2.5 million women. It was lead by Agnes von Grone, who was given the title of Reich Women's Leader (*Reichsfrauenführerin*), an appellation that did not yet apply to Scholtz-Klink.[93] Von Grone was both very active in the Women's Auxiliary, having been the head of its Braunschweig branch since 1925, and a member of the Nazi Party. She was offered an immediate pretext for revealing her intentions when, in early 1934, Nazi authorities began to take measures against Protestant women's organizations. In conjunction with Hilgenfeldt's NSV, Reich Bishop Müller worked to have Klara Lönnies expelled from her position as head of the Mothers' Association. Furthermore, party leaders in Saxony declared that Women's Auxiliary activities would henceforth be outlawed. Scholtz-Klink similarly banned the formation of new branches of Women's Auxiliary.[94] As offended as Protestant women were by Nazi measures, their complaints were not ideological in nature. Instead, they had been motivated by organizational ambition; if branches of the Women's Auxiliary continued to spring up, it was feared, the NSF would be unable to establish its own network.[95] The expulsion of Lönnies was similarly based on institutional rivalry, not ideological opposition.[96]

Von Grone successfully worked to have these measures reversed. She was aided by the fact that she had already proven her credentials as a Nazi. Without pressure from above, she had already purged the Women's Bureau leadership of anti-Nazis and could boast that her entire family as well were active in Nazi organizations.[97] Von Grone succeeded in getting the NSF to order its branches not to restrict the work of Protestant organizations. Even though new Women's Auxiliary branches could still not be founded, Scholtz-Klink announced that double membership in her organization and von Grone's would be permitted and that active cooperation would be sought between the two in their common areas of interest, such as education and maternal assistance. Von Grone even got the NSV to overrule the orders of the Saxon authorities regarding organizational activity.[98]

Part of the reason for the NSF's retreat was the realization that it was not sufficiently developed institutionally to take over all the tasks of its

---

[93] Phayer translates *Frauenwerk* in this context as "Women's Work Front." For a biographical overview see Fritz Mybes, *Agnes von Grone und das Frauenwerk der Deutschen Evangelischen Kirche* (Düsseldorf, 1981). Koonz considers this work apologetic (*Mothers in the Fatherland*, 254).

[94] Jochen-Christoph Kaiser, "Das Frauenwerk der Deutschen Evangelischen Kirche: Zum Problem das Verbandsprotestantismus in Dritten Reich," in Heinz Dollinger et al. (eds.), *Weltpolitik, Europagedanke, Regionalismus* (Münster, 1982), 491.

[95] Phayer explicitly points *away* from ideological differences in explaining this premature attempt at "coordination": *Women*, 91–3.

[96] Jochen-Christoph Kaiser, *Frauen in der Kirche: Evangelische Frauenverbände im Spannungsfeld von Kirche und Gesellschaft 1890–1945* (Düsseldorf, 1985), 196–206.

[97] Koonz, *Mothers*, 237.

[98] Phayer, *Women*, 93.

Protestant counterparts. As much as they wished to gain exclusive control of all Women's Auxiliary competencies, Nazi women did not want to do so at the expense of the services being rendered. However, another reason was the realization that, by attacking Protestant women, the Nazis would burn ideological bridges they could not afford to lose. The most portentous sign of this ideological connection came in the summer of 1934, when von Grone and Scholtz-Klink agreed that the NSF could use Protestant facilities for open courses in racial ideology.[99] By contrast, Catholic women's organizations unequivocally rejected a similar offer made by Scholtz-Klink.

If imitation is the sincerest form of flattery, then Protestant women had every right to feel flattered. For as the NSF developed its organization, it systematically adopted one feature after another of its Protestant counterpart: Scholtz-Klink named her bureau the *Frauenwerk*; Scholtz-Klink began to call herself *Reichsfrauenführerin*; and the NSF copied exactly the format and logo of the Protestant mother's magazine *Mutter und Volk*, eventually taking it over outright.[100] The NSF also took on the exact tasks that the Women's Auxiliary performed: marriage counseling, maternal education, and the building of maternal-aid centers. With the growing membership and increasing budgets of Scholtz-Klink's *Frauenwerk* and its parent organization NSV, renewed attempts were made to forcibly "coordinate" Protestant women. Slowly, the members of the Women's Auxiliary were once again curtailed in their actions and often told by regional authorities that they could not hold double membership in Protestant and Nazi organizations. Whereas the NSF had earlier relied on the Women's Auxiliary homes for their own work, with the increased funding that came from the regime, it withdrew from these arrangements.[101]

The *Kirchenkampf* raging between the BK and the DC also played a role in the growing rift between Nazi and Protestant organizations. Much as Bishop Meiser of Bavaria simultaneously fought Reich Bishop Müller while swearing unconditional loyalty to Hitler, so too did von Grone oppose Müller's aggressive attempts to place her organization under Nazi control, even as she affirmed the Nazi State. Many Protestant women, especially in BK strongholds like Westphalia, were alarmed by Müller's handing over of Protestant Youth to the HJ, fearing a similar fate awaited them. Even though von Grone was not a member of the BK and displayed no particular attachment to its cause,[102] she was concerned for the autonomy of the organization she headed. When she fought with Müller over the *Frauenwerk*'s forced coordination with the NSF, he fired her and replaced her with Hermenau. However, because the leaders of the *Frauenwerk* refused to recognize Hermenau's authority, he set up a rival *Frauendienst* (Women's Service),

---

[99] Ibid., 94.
[100] Koonz, *Mothers*, 239.
[101] Phayer, *Women*, 187.
[102] Ibid., 143.

made up of DC women in line with Müller and the Reich Church.[103] Von Grone continued to offer resistance to these machinations, even after Bishop Marahrens indicated that he backed Scholtz-Klink's efforts at "coordination."[104] Shortly afterward, von Grone was expelled from the Nazi Party by local authorities in September 1935 – a decision she immediately appealed to Buch's party court. Zoellner, by then chair of the Reich Church Committee, faulted not Scholtz-Klink but von Grone and worked for the latter's removal as *Reichsfrauenführerin* of the Protestant Women's Bureau.[105]

In an attempt to break her power, in 1936 Hermenau's Women's Service, Hilgenfeldt's NSV and Scholtz-Klink's NSF worked together to have von Grone defeated in the party court.[106] The party, represented by Hilgenfeldt, specifically accused von Grone of continuing to establish new Women's Auxiliary branches, leading her organization into the Church Struggle and making cooperation with the NSF impossible. Although attacks on her became personal, the real aim was not to do away with Grone, but to get her to stay on while conceding Scholtz-Klink's supremacy. Because von Grone refused to do this, her expulsion was upheld.[107] Shortly thereafter the *Frauenwerk* was finally incorporated into the NSF.[108] Church authorities, seemingly taking Scholtz-Klink's side, ordered von Grone to sever all ties with women's organizations.[109]

The NSF's attempts to cut away at the *Frauenwerk* were undertaken in cooperation with DC churchmen, state bishops among them; this was more than just a party act. All the leaders of the Women's Service sided with Scholtz-Klink. One of the Service's leaders, Eleanor Liebe-Harcourt, discussed the relationship of her organization with Scholtz-Klink, who assured her that they would continue to work closely together. Scholtz-Klink also provided evidence of a DC leaning when she stated: "For National Socialism there can be no division of religious and *völkisch* interests."[110]

It would be a mistake to characterize the conflict between Protestant and Nazi women as exclusively institutional. Many members of Women's Auxiliary took the BK side of the Church Struggle, rejecting the Aryan Paragraph

---

[103] Fritz Mybes, *Geschichte der evangelischen Frauenhilfe in Quellen unter besonderer Berücksichtung der Evangelischen Frauenhilfe im Rheinland* (Gladbeck, 1975), 106–9. Koonz suggests that approximately 10% of Protestant women joined the German Christians: *Mothers*, 246. Hermenau's organization was much smaller than von Grone's, comprising only 32 regional associations out of a nationwide total of 704 for all Protestant women: Mybes, *Geschichte*, 110.

[104] Phayer, *Women*, 161.

[105] Mybes, *Agnes von Grone*, 55–63.

[106] Kaiser, *Frauen*, 233.

[107] Koonz, *Mothers*, 253.

[108] Carsten Nicolaisen (ed.), *Dokumente zur Kirchenpolitik des Dritten Reiches*, 3 vols. (Munich, 1971–94), 3: 277.

[109] Kaiser, *Frauen*, 223.

[110] Kaiser, "Frauenwerk," 495.

on ideological grounds. These women were strongest where the BK itself was strongest: Westphalia and the Rhineland.[111] Dissension between them and their Nazi counterparts reached such levels that in some cases Nazi women were forced out of Protestant organizations. As Liebe-Harcourt put it, "This really hurts when our National Socialist women, early fighters for our cause, receive no gratitude for their service during the hard times when they had encountered ridicule and rebuff." In some cases, wives of Nazi leaders were known to resign from Protestant organizations because of increased hostility.[112] There was also growing dissension over the place of eugenics and racialism in Protestant women's organizations. Many women social workers began to complain of the dire impact of sterilization on the victim as well as on the larger society. Among those who had always supported eugenics came concerns over its practical implementation.[113] Fighting between Nazi and Protestant womens' organizations was not entirely over ambition and place seeking.

However, this dissension was not typical of relations between Protestant and Nazi women. Although they were dismayed with the curtailing of their activities and the progressive appropriation of their programs one by one into the rival NSF, Protestant women rarely reached the stage of outright ideological opposition. More typical was the attitude of von Grone herself, who never wavered in her support for Nazism, even as she came under attack from fellow party members: "Not only as a party member but also as a Protestant woman I stand in the most thoughtful, respectful and most faithful obedience in our work behind our Führer."[114] Consistent with her earlier position, she never turned against the eugenicist thrust of her organization.[115] Whereas it might be claimed that some women's break with eugenicism represented a true ideological split with the Nazis, even here institutional rivalry played a role. Protestant women still resented their own eugenicist magazine *Mutter und Volk* being rudely taken over by the Nazis. Claudia Koonz even argues that institutional rivalry was primary: "When they believed they would control eugenics programs, Protestant women approved; but when Nazi programs excluded them from influence and left them to repair the social and psychological damage, they objected."[116]

The Nazis themselves maintained a distinction between institutional conflict and ideological opposition. Although Scholtz-Klink was eager to monopolize women's activities and attempted to suppress those organizational branches that backed the BK, she did not attack all Protestant women equally. Right up to its forced "coordination" in 1936, there were many branches of the Protestant Women's Auxiliary that remained politically acceptable

[111] Mybes, *Geschichte*, 96.
[112] Koonz, *Mothers*, 256.
[113] Mybes, *Geschichte*, 257.
[114] Quoted in Phayer, *Women*, 163.
[115] Kaiser, *Frauen*, 218.
[116] Koonz, *Mothers*, 258.

to Scholtz-Klink.[117] Even after she precluded them from maternal-aid activities, Protestant and Nazi women very often continued to cooperate in pronatalist work.[118] Relations between Protestant and Nazi organizations varied from region to region, with many branches of the Women's Auxiliary continuing to work peacefully with their Nazi counterparts up until the war. Some Protestant women were actually pleased to see the NSF take over these programs, as centralized authority and control meant greater efficiency and increased funding.[119] The specifically religious activities of women's organizations, such as Bible study programs and the establishment in 1936 of a Bible Institute in Potsdam, went on without interference from either the NSF or the state.[120] The Christian mien of the NSF itself was upheld well into the process of "coordination," even while challenged by paganists and anticlericals. At a December 1938 meeting of the local NSF in Neuruppin, a speaker caused considerable dissension when she quipped: "The real unemployed in Germany are the pastors. Only on Sundays between 9 and 10 have they anything to do." In a letter of complaint to the NSF head office, a branch official expressed her rejection of this position, "since among the audience a great number have been members of Christian congregations and since all the local pastors' wives are members of the *Frauenschaft*."[121] If the NSF attacked institutional Protestantism in the shape of the Women's Auxiliary, its members still affirmed Protestantism as ideology and religion.

YOUTH

Rivalries in associational life between Christian and Nazi organizations arose in a third area held especially dear to both: youth. For the confessions and the Nazi Party alike, the inculcation of a belief system into coming generations of Germans was the best guarantee of their perpetuity; therefore the institutional battles waged here were just as heated as elsewhere. Again, however, questions of institutional and ideological conflict should not be conflated. Here, as with eugenics and women, confessional responses to the lure of Nazism varied considerably. And as far as Protestants were concerned, the struggle that emerged between them and Nazi groups – particularly the NSLB and HJ – was largely institutional in nature.

Immediately after the Seizure of Power, a new intraconfessional parents' association was established, the Christian Parents' League (*Christliche Elternbund*, or CEB). Although it aspired to be an ecumenical organization representing both confessions equally, its strongest representation came from the

[117] Kaiser, *Frauen*, 236.
[118] Phayer, *Women*, 201.
[119] Ibid.
[120] Ibid., 193–7, 201–2.
[121] Evangelisches Zentralarchiv in Berlin (hereafter EZA), 14/590 (6 December 1938: Berlin).

Protestant Reich Parents' League, and it was set up in conjunction with the Inner Mission. Its view toward the new regime was made abundantly clear in a manifesto from 1933: "The most important task in the new Germany is to educate the coming generation in Germandom based on Christian foundations. The state safeguards Christianity, so the churches must serve the state in order to preserve and develop it. They may not behave as rulers of the state, or create a state within a state. The various confessions may not struggle against one another, but rather must meet one another with respect in the spirit of Christian charity. . . . The objective is the creation of a strong, unified *Volk* in a Christian, National Socialist state."[122] Here the major tenets of positive Christianity were affirmed: a unified *Volk* seeking common ground and a state ruling supreme in temporal affairs, without the threat of clerical interference. Most significant of all, no mention was made of the confessional school.

At precisely the same time, a rival Nazi organization was established. The NSLB, having sponsored the ancillary Working Group of National Socialist Pastors in the *Kampfzeit*, flexed its organizational muscle again by erecting a new group, the National Socialist Parents' League (*Nationalsozialistische Elternbund*, or NSEB). Growing out of a prefatory Saxon organization called the National Socialist Working Group for the Rights of the Parent and the Strengthening of the German Family, the NSEB's professed aim was to restore parental authority in the education and schooling of German children. Its goal was the elevation of the "German State School" as the sole medium of education in the new Germany. It would be in service of the German parent, but nonetheless completely under state control. Only children of German blood would be permitted as pupils. Regarding religion, the NSEB's manifesto stated that "The German State School is a confessional school only in the sense [that it confesses] the German state and the *Volksgemeinschaft* in the spirit of positive Christianity. The liberation of the German State school from the shackles of the Concordat is to be effected as soon as possible."[123] Even though the ideological thrust of education would be nationalist, it was specifically added that this would not be at the expense of the "various Christian religious communities." Finally, the NSEB plainly stated that it worked for the dissolution of all confessional youth groups into the HJ.

Whereas rivalry between confessional and Nazi organizations took some time to emerge in welfare and women's fields, here there was almost immediate confrontation. In Saxony, as they attempted to cooperate together, the possibility of formally merging the CEB and the NSEB was raised almost immediately. The members of the local CEB, with one exception, voted to enter *en masse* into the NSEB.[124] However, disagreement soon arose as to

---

[122] Bundesarchiv Berlin-Zehlendorf (hereafter BAZ), NS 12/822 (n.d.[1933]: Berlin).
[123] BAZ NS 12/822 (24 May 1933: Munich).
[124] BAZ NS 12/822 (18 July 1933: Leipzig).

whether they would merge under the aegis of the Inner Mission or the Nazi Teachers' League.[125] The NSEB had no interest in bowing to the authority of the Inner Mission, using the argument that the Inner Mission was not an educational organization, whereas this was the NSLB's exclusive concern. The leader of the Leipzig NSEB was ready to compromise, however: The churches themselves could establish a pastors' committee within the NSEB in order to ensure a "strong union" of Christian and Nazi interests.[126] Intersecting loyalties were made harder to disentangle when the Saxon state bishop, the German Christian Friedrich Coch, entered the fray as both a member of the Inner Mission and the Nazi Party. The debate was cut short, however, when Rudolf Buttmann, leader of the Cultural Policy section of the Reich Interior Ministry, ordered the NSLB to abandon the project of creating a parents' league altogether. Such a league, Buttmann proclaimed, would be superfluous, as the state itself was now taking over the responsibilities that were left to parents' associations in the days of the "liberal state."[127] Buttmann assured the NSLB that it could seek cooperation with parents in individual schools, but that it was to disengage itself from any formal relationship with parents' associations. This was an unusual setback for the process of "coordination," all the more so because the Nazi State had ordered it.

Other organizational rivalries of much greater scope would emerge that year. One of the greatest concerned youth organizations. Protestant youth were represented in several groups with a total membership of approximately 700,000: the Reich Association of Protestant Young Men's Leagues, Youth Leagues for Determined (*entschiedenes*) Christianity, the League of Christian–German Youth, Christian Boy Scouts of Germany, the League of German Bible Circles, the Christian Young Men's Association, and the League of Protestant Young Women's Associations.[128] By comparison, Catholic youth groups in Weimar were far more centralized, having been brought together in 1928 under one umbrella organization, the Catholic Youth of Germany, with a membership of 1.3 million.[129] Here again, there were stark confessional differences in attitudes toward Nazism and the HJ. Catholic Youth, as might be expected, stayed away, having been warned by one of its leaders that no member "who stands by the banner of Christ and by the young Catholic Peoples' Front can belong to [this] movement."[130] There were only isolated cases of Catholics belonging to the

[125] BAZ NS 12/822 (12 August 1933: Dresden).
[126] BAZ NS 12/822 (18 July 1933: Leipzig).
[127] BAZ NS 12/822 (7 September 1933: Berlin).
[128] Arno Klönne, *Jugend im Dritten Reich: Die Hitler-Jugend und ihre Gegner* (Düsseldorf, 1982), 164; Manfred Priepke, *Die evangelische Jugend im Dritten Reich 1933–36* (Hanover, 1960), 237; Peter Stachura, *Nazi Youth in the Weimar Republic* (Santa Barbara, 1975), 116.
[129] Stachura, *Youth*, 115.
[130] Quoted in Hans Müller (ed.), *Katholische Kirche und Nationalsozialismus: Dokumente 1930–35* (Munich, 1963), 6.

Kampfzeit HJ. In fact, before 1933 the HJ was weakest in precisely those areas where Catholic religiosity and membership in Catholic Youth was strongest: Bavaria, the Rhineland, and parts of Silesia.[131] This is accountable both to institutional centralization of Catholic youth and to ideological opposition to Nazi racial thought.

By comparison, Protestant youth groups were far more favorably inclined toward the Nazis. The League of Bible Circles in particular was supportive of Nazism, with many *alte Kämpfer* among its ranks.[132] As one observer stated, "In 1931 it could be affirmed . . . that the young mens' association of the entire *Bündische* and Protestant youth . . . belong either to the NSDAP and its youth or combat organizations, or at least . . . they stand very close to them."[133] As part of the religious renewal that took place that year, Protestant youth groups actually saw an increase in their numbers for most of 1933.[134] Immediately after the Seizure of Power, the various Protestant youth groups began to centralize their organization, eventually unifying themselves into the Protestant Youth of Germany, under the leadership of Erich Stange and the patronage of Reich Bishop Müller. One of the first acts of the unified Protestant youth was to issue this statement: "Germany's destiny has once again been pulled back from the abyss of Bolshevism. A strong leadership of the state calls upon all Germans to their responsibility. The God-ordained foundations of Heimat, *Volk* and state are once again newly recognized. . . . Therefore the position of Protestant Youth in these days can be nothing other than a passionate participation in the destiny of our *Volk*."[135]

The HJ rejected confessional organizations even as they insisted they were Christian or at least favorably disposed to Christianity. Headed by the ambitious and aggressive Baldur von Schirach, the HJ – like the NSV and NSF – aimed at nothing less than the total incorporation of all preexisting confessional groups into his own. This did not mean, however, that Christian religiosity was removed from the HJ. Throughout 1933, Protestant field services were frequently conducted within the HJ.[136] Many HJ units collectively attended Protestant services and began meetings with such services. Pastors even took up office in the HJ.[137] Well into the Third Reich, HJ continued to receive religious instruction from Protestant clergy, in which the juvenile audience was instructed to receive Christ, not Wotan, into their hearts.[138] The

[131] Stachura, *Youth*, 106.
[132] Priepke, *Jugend*, 11.
[133] Quoted in Stachura, *Youth*, 108.
[134] Priepke, *Jugend*, 52.
[135] "Erklärung der 'Evangelischen Jugend Deutschlands' ": EZA 50/420/2 (30 March 1933: n.p.).
[136] Werner Klose, *Generation im Gleichschritt: Ein Dokumentarbericht* (Oldenburg, 1964), 50–1.
[137] Klönne, *Jugend*, 165.
[138] "Hitlerjugend hält Gottesdienst zur Sonnenwende," *Evangelium im Dritten Reich*, 1 July 1934: in BAP 62 Di 1/75/122.

HJ even participated in purely confessional ceremonies, such as a reception for the Inner Mission in Berlin.[139]

Members of both Catholic and Protestant youth groups wished to retain their institutional autonomy; but the reactions from the Catholic Church were once again starkly different from those of the Protestant Church. Catholic youth organizations strenuously fought to maintain their existence independent of the HJ, whereas Protestant youth organizations were incorporated into the HJ in December 1933 by decree of Reich Bishop Müller. Segments of the Protestant establishment protested Müller's action, especially those opposed to the DC.[140] Bishop Wurm, for instance, decried Müller's action, which did nothing to ease relations between him and the local Nazi authorities.[141] However, this was largely due to questions of institutional autonomy, not ideological difference. In an October 1933 meeting, in which the HJ and the Protestant youth discussed how to effect a working relationship with each other, the most important Protestant youth leaders and youth pastors stated "virtually unanimously [that] Protestant youth unconditionally supported National Socialism."[142] Stange declared that the Protestant youth wanted to remain independent. Nonetheless, he sought close relations between his organization and the HJ. Discussions were held on making Protestant Youth a "corporate member" of the HJ, in which political and military training of their youth would be left to the HJ in exchange for the ability to conduct mission work among HJ members. Whereas most Protestant youth leaders were eager to work closely with the HJ, others, like Udo Smidt of the Bible Circle, were more wary of these negotiations.[143] Schirach, satisfied with nothing less than total "coordination," rejected the proposal. Schirach was prepared to honor the Christian religiosity of individual Hitler youths, but was not willing to enter into such an arrangement with Stange. Far from contemplating organizational cooperation, Schirach raised the stakes by prohibiting double membership in the HJ and confessional youth groups.[144]

Proclaiming his desire to "carry the Savior to the *Volk*," Reich Bishop Müller was eager to incorporate the Protestant youth into the Hitler Youth. This was the product both of Müller's attempt to ingratiate himself with the Nazi State and of DC doctrine, which called for the state – once imbued with a Christian spirit – to take over the social network of the churches. Protestant youth leaders, much like Agnes von Grone in the case of Protestant women, were opposed to the dissolution of their own groups into a rival Nazi

---

[139] "HJ sammelt für konfessionelle Zwecke," *Der Stürmer*, 19 May 1935: in BAP 62 Di 1/75/175.
[140] Klaus Scholder, *The Churches and the Third Reich*, 2 vols. (London, 1987–8), 1: 576–7.
[141] BAP R43 II/161/303-308 (22 January 1934: Stuttgart). Later that year Wurm would come under house arrest on the orders of Müller and his adjutant Jäger.
[142] Scholder, *Churches*, 1: 574.
[143] Mattias von Hellfeld, *Bündische Jugend und Hitlerjugend: Zur Geschichte von Anpassung und Widerstand 1930–1939* (Cologne, 1987), 84–6.
[144] Klönne, *Jugend*, 165.

organization. When Stange complained about Müller's ongoing negotiations with Schirach despite his objections, Müller dismissed him from office.[145] In December 1933, Müller handed over leadership of the Protestant youth to the HJ. This action largely precipitated the crisis that Müller encountered not only with Niemöller's PNB, but with the Nazis themselves. However, if youth leaders and the PNB were against the "coordination" of a major part of the Protestant establishment, the DC were very pleased. State Bishop Peter of Magdeburg, himself a league pastor for the Protestant Young Mens' Association, applauded this merging.[146] Others in the ranks of the DC, notably Joachim Hossenfelder, shared the sense of joy in the "coordination" of youth. However, the later BK, remaining opposed, would continue to defy the order, setting up local branches of their own youth groups, often based on original groups whose local leaders were committed to the BK.[147] The HJ, in turn, made life difficult for BK youth groups. Whereas the HJ promised to allot certain times of the week for religious observance and activity, these rights were curtailed for the BK. To receive permission to conduct youth outings, for example, these groups had to submit months in advance a list of participants with their birthdates, how long and where the outing would take place, and a detailed description of the planned activities. Those who did not receive written permission from their HJ leader were not allowed to participate.[148]

In spite of these curtailments, however, Schirach continued to instruct his HJ groups not to schedule activities during hours of Sunday church services. Special gatherings of Protestant youth were permitted. Bible study hours were allowed in the Hitler Youth without restriction. In 1937, a high point of Nazi coordination, 108 Bible studies were held attracting some 6,000 participants.[149] Even a new office of Reich Youth Pastor was created within the HJ and given to one Karl Zahn.[150] As Schirach himself insisted, "we all believe in an almighty God. We are all, even the youngest among us, witnesses to the wonderful transformation that the *Volk* has experienced through His help, the transformation from impotence and destruction to strength and harmony. The Hitler Youth wants nothing less than to secure this strength and harmony for all time."[151] It is most likely that Schirach would have continued permitting Christian activity within the HJ had he not been reprimanded in 1938 by Martin Bormann, one of the Nazi Party's

---

[145] Priepke, *Jugend*, 196.
[146] *Magdeburgische Zeitung*, 6 March 1934: in BAP 62 Di 1/75/112i.
[147] As was the case, for instance, with the West German Young Mens' League of the Christian Young Mens' Association: Klönne, *Jugend*, 168.
[148] Victoria Barnett, *For the Soul of the People: Protestant Protest against Hitler* (Oxford, 1992), 78.
[149] Heinrich Riedel, *Kampf um die Jugend: Evangelische Jugendarbeit 1933–1945* (Munich, 1976), 230.
[150] Priepke, *Jugend*, 123–4.
[151] *Märkische Volkszeitung*, 3 June 1935: in BAP 62 Di 1/106/271.

most powerful functionaries and greatest anticlericals.[152] Schirach's positive attitude toward religious observance in the HJ was further confirmed by his brief tenure as *Gauleiter* of Vienna after the *Anschluß* of 1938. Schirach advised the HJ in his domain not to snub the clergy and even went so far as to give military inductees a gift of religious pictures and texts, which included one of his own poems.[153]

CONCLUSION

The Nazi coordination of Christian organizations has usually been viewed as proof of the regime's anti-Christian posture. However, in a totalitarian state – no alternative to such coordination existed. The Nazis maintained that it was not enough to be in a religious organization: One had to serve *Volk* and Führer in the new Germany by joining the NSV, NSF, or HJ. This points to the exclusivist claims of the Nazi State. However, just as Nazis freely admitted that their worldview was a totalizing one, they also believed they could take credit for protecting the *Volk* and its religious sensibilities from the threat of liberalism, Judaism, communism, and atheism. The exploration of organizational relations between the churches and Nazism illustrates the need to differentiate the substance of Nazi ideology – which made constant and direct reference to Christian traditions – from the style of Nazi discourse, which permitted no institutional "dual allegiance" in the new regime. Nazism was anticlerical in the sense that it could not tolerate church involvement in secular life. However, this says very little about Nazi ideology. Indeed, it was the consistent overlap of certain Nazi and Protestant conceptions of "the social" that led to the systematic appropriation of the Protestant programs and groups discussed here. Some Protestants advocated a voluntary coordination into Nazi organizations; others fought for institutional autonomy. For the latter, however, the fight was largely institutional; even as they argued for their continued existence, they maintained that they still worked for goals congruent if not identical with those of the Nazis. Just as importantly, many Nazis maintained that their actions were predicated on the same beliefs, the same ethical values, as those of their Protestant counterparts. Catholic organizations, with a different social theory, pursued policies more at odds with those of the regime and came into greater conflict with it.

For still other Nazis, as we shall see in the next chapter, the process of coordination was freighted with more ideological baggage. Old "paganists" persisted in their hostility, and an extreme anti-Christian figure emerged in Martin Bormann. As time went on, the Nazi Party seemed to align itself, not only against the churches, but increasingly against Christianity itself. After

---

[152] Jochen von Lang, *The Secretary – Martin Bormann: The Man who Manipulated Hitler* (New York, 1979), 127. For more on Bormann, see Chapter 7.

[153] Ibid., 250. Although von Lang does not mention the name of this poem, it could very possibly have been "Christus," the poem von Schirach had published in 1934.

the collapse of the planned Reich Church, distinctions between anticlericalism and anti-Christianity were increasingly overlooked. Was this the gradual unfolding of a tactically delayed offensive against an ideological enemy? Or was it a contingent process, based on more immediate factors? As we look to the last years of the Reich, do we see leaders who had formerly been friendly toward Christianity start to turn against it? Did the party have in mind a "Final Solution" for Christianity itself?

7

GOTTGLÄUBIG

Assent of the anti-Christians?

National Socialist and Christian conceptions are incompatible.... Christianity has inalterable foundations, which were established almost 2000 years ago and which have stiffened into dogmas alien to reality.

> Martin Bormann[1]

I've nothing against Christianity in itself.

> Heinrich Himmler[2]

With the breakdown in relations with the Protestant Church in 1937 came a reorientation in Nazi thinking. Whereas the party had previously welcomed the participation of Protestant pastors in the movement and counted church-friendly elements even among the party leadership, with the cancellation of church elections in 1937 emerged a new tenor in Nazi religious attitudes and relations between party and church. The position of churchmen in the party became more tenuous, and individual party members detached themselves from the churches in increasing numbers. Along with this growing separation came what appeared to be a heightened ideological enmity between Christianity and Nazism. Over time, Nazi hostility to Christianity seemed to increase, as new anti-Christian voices, particularly Martin Bormann's, began to be heard. By the start of the war, Hitler himself was taking a more antagonistic stance. As we survey the religious views of Nazi leaders for the latter years of the regime, we must ask the following questions: Did the regime itself become more anti-Christian with time? Did party anti-Christians gain greater power? Did Nazi leaders still distinguish between anticlericalism and hatred for Christianity itself? Or was Christianity now rejected as well? Answering these questions will also help us to unveil the many tensions that arose between party offices over the continuing place of Christianity in the movement, particularly the contentious relationship of party leaders with Bormann, whose hold on power brought him close to sole responsibility for many of the anticlerical and anti-Christian measures taken late in the regime.

[1] Bundesarchiv Potsdam (hereafter BAP), NS 6/336/18-22.
[2] *The Kersten Memoirs*, 155.

THE SEPARATION OF CHURCH AND PARTY

Starting in late 1936, many Nazis began a movement within the party known as *Kirchenaustritt* ("leaving the church"). There was no directive from the party leadership ordering *Kirchenaustritt*; the evidence suggests that it arose as a spontaneous movement within the NSDAP. Whereas no single event triggered it, a general worsening of relations with the churches was the operative factor. Many (nominally) Protestant Nazis left their churches after the *caesura* of 1937; but some of the first Nazis to leave their church, in 1936, were Catholics. Those who withdrew their church membership were designated *Gottgläubige*, "believers in God." In a statement issued to Reich authorities, Interior Minister Frick explained that the phrase was meant as a replacement for the designation "dissident," whose original meaning of not belonging to a designated religious community had been transformed in the public imagination into someone "without belief" (*glaubenslos*). To rectify this problem, one's religious status could henceforth be designated in three ways: member of a religious community, believer in God, or unbeliever.[3] In a letter to the chief of the Reich Chancellery, Heinrich Lammers, Frick pointed out that several technical issues had been weighed in making the decision, including the fact that now Jews would be able to designate themselves *gottgläubig* if they so desired.[4] Another issue was the collection of church taxes, a particular concern for the Reich Finance Ministry. Changes to the tax laws were contemplated, but in the end were not enacted.[5]

Rosenberg was the first party leader to leave the church, in November 1933. For the next three years no Nazi leaders withdrew from their churches. In 1936 there came a flood, however, beginning with Himmler and Heydrich leaving the Catholic Church early that year.[6] This was followed by announcements of the *Austritt* of several *Gauleiter*, including the anti-Christian Mutschmann of Saxony, Röver of Oldenburg, and Robert Wagner of Baden.[7] Whereas paganists uniformly opted for the status of *gottgläubig*, not all *Gottgläubigen* were paganists. Those who had established their faith in Christianity could also be counted among their ranks. For instance, in 1937 Walter Buch had left the church, whereas Silesian Gauleiter Josef Wagner – who was actually expelled from the party in 1941 for taking his own children

---

[3] BAP NS 6/232/136 (16 November 1936: Berlin).

[4] BAP R43 II/150/70 (30 July 1937: Berlin). This would not have posed a threat to the integrity of Nazi antisemitism, however, as Jews would still carry the racial designation of "non-Aryan."

[5] BAP R43 II/150/74-75 (30 July 1937: Berlin).

[6] *La Libre Belgique*, 4 March 1936: in BAP 62 Di 1/106/146; Günther Deschner, *Reinhard Heydrich: A Biography* (New York, 1981), 103.

[7] For Mutschmann, see *Deutsch-Evangelische Korrespondenz*, 21 October 1936: in BAP 62 Di 1/106/209; for Röver, see *Die christliche Welt*, 19 December 1936: in BAP 62 Di 1/106/260; for Wagner, see *Reichspost*, 4 January 1937: in BAP 62 Di 1/106/336.

to Catholic confessional schools – defended those who did.[8] By 1943 Erich Koch had also declared himself *gottgläubig*.[9] This phenomenon reflected the growing institutional tensions between church and party; but the *Austritt* of known Christians gives reason to doubt a move against Christianity per se. Further evidence of this is provided by a 1936 speech by Fritz Sauckel, *Gauleiter* of Thuringia and leader of Germany's slave labor program during the war. Sauckel aggressively attacked those clergy who accused Nazism of deifying Adolf Hitler or the blood of the *Volk*, calling them "jackals and hyenas." The *Gottgläubige* could not be compared to atheistic Bolshevists or paganists. Sauckel insisted that "just as we protect the true clergyman on his altar, we also protect ourselves from the pitiable defamation of atheism or the deception of the concept of paganism."[10] In a secret 1939 memorandum defending *Kirchenaustritt* within the party, the anticlerical Bormann proclaimed that the clergy were not servants of God but of the church. In the context of the church situation in the newly annexed Austria, Bormann claimed that the clergy were hypocritical because they could not possibly know more about the hereafter than anyone else. Church service was not the same as service to God. One therefore had to distinguish between "ecclesiastical" and "religious," between the Christian confession and the Christian worldview.[11] If by 1939 Bormann was already a sworn enemy of Christianity as well as the churches, it seems he was not yet prepared to state so, even in confidential correspondence.

Within the party, *Kirchenaustritt* was not compulsory: Gauleiter Florian of Düsseldorf, in private party correspondence, denied accusations that he was fomenting church leaving in his district.[12] Indeed, in some quarters of the Nazi Party remaining *in* the church was compulsory. Rosenberg expressed dismay when his paganist ally Richard Walther Darré explicitly forbade his peasant leaders from leaving their churches. Rosenberg complained that this went against the individual Nazi's right to choose his religious affiliation.[13] Darré informed Rosenberg that, after consultations with his *Unterführer*, he decided to keep the ban in place, adding cryptically that "it is best to leave these things in peace."[14] However, if leaving the church was not compulsory, holding office in church bodies, especially for higher-ranking Nazis,

[8] In a 1937 form, Buch lists himself as *"gottgläubig"*: Bundesarchiv Berlin-Zehlendorf (hereafter BAZ), Personalakt Buch; for Wagner, see *Westfälische Landeszeitung*, 6 December 1934: in Bayerisches Hauptstaatsarchiv (hereafter BStA), Sammlung Rehse/P5049.
[9] Kurt Meier, *Der Evangelische Kirchenkampf*, 3 vols. (Göttingen, 1976–84), 1: 287.
[10] *Mitteldeutsche Zeitung*, 12 October 1936: in BAP R5101/23126/76.
[11] BAP NS 6/232/134-36 (2 February 1939: Munich).
[12] Evangelisches Zentralarchiv in Berlin (hereafter EZA), 14/708 (14 December 1936: Düsseldorf).
[13] BAZ NS 8/173/119 (12 November 1938: Berlin).
[14] BAZ NS 8/173/117-118 (18 November 1938: Munich). This could have meant either that leaving the church was unpopular with Darré's *Unterführer* or that it would have received a hostile reception from the German peasantry, an especially pious segment of the German population.

was made practically impossible. As the Church Ministry pointed out in a 1937 memo, it was deemed necessary for Nazi leaders from the rank of *Ortsgruppenleiter* upward not to hold office in or serve as speakers for church bodies in order to ensure that the party as such would not get entangled in church–political disputes. This symbolized an indisputable worsening of institutional relations between the Nazis and the churches, particularly the Protestant Church. At the same time, it was pointed out that this held true for all religious bodies, including the DGB, and not simply Christian organizations.[15] However, this stipulation was not always adhered to. For instance, in September 1938, notice was made of *Ortsgruppenleiter* in *Gau* Kurmark sitting on local church councils. As the Protestant Consistory reminded the Nazi *Kreisleiter* for the area, this was now forbidden.[16]

The highest percentage of *Kirchenaustritt* took place in the SS. A secret 1939 report on the confessional makeup of SS members showed that Protestants, Catholics, and *Gottgläubigen* made up 60.0%, 21.1%, and 18.7% of SS members in 1937, respectively; by 1938, those figures had changed to 51.4%, 22.7%, and 25.7%, respectively.[17] The 1.6% rise in the Catholic population of the SS was attributed in the report to the annexation of Catholic territory in 1938. In spite of the sharp 8.6% drop in Protestant confessionalists, the report emphasized that Protestants were overrepresented in the ranks of the SS vis-à-vis Catholics, adding that "one can be certain that the Protestant portion of the population displays greater appreciation for the struggle and the task of the SS, and hence is more readily recruited from than the Catholic [portion]."[18] That the authors of the report would essentially argue against their own evidence shows how capable a positive conception of Protestantism within the Nazi movement still was on the eve of World War II.

Ironically, Himmler viewed the increase in the number of *Gottgläubige* with some trepidation. As we have already seen, for a radical anticlerical, he demonstrated a remarkable degree of flexibility, continually insisting that SS men who chose to remain active Christians had every right to do so.[19] In a 1937 speech he showed equal leniency on the question of *Kirchenaustritt*: "As you know, personally I have chosen to leave the church. But I do not wish for this to become a sport for lower-level leaders.... I would rather have a *Sturm* in which only 10 percent have left, with the remaining 90 percent remaining just as good National Socialists.... To me it is truly preferable

[15] EZA 14/590 (20 December 1937: Berlin).
[16] EZA 14/590 (23 September 1938: Berlin).
[17] "Die Konfession der SS-Angehörigen": BAZ Sammlung Schumacher (hereafter Schu), 245/2/156-57 (2 June 1939: Berlin).
[18] Ibid., 160.
[19] Himmler's earlier warnings that Christian SS be respected were repeated in 1938: See "Bekenntnis der Angehörigen der uniformierten Ordnungspolizei zu religions- und Weltanschauungsgemeinschaften und Teilnahme an Veranstaltungen derselben": BAZ Schu 245/1/163-167 (13 June 1938: Berlin).

if someone takes one, two or five years to leave the church, thus leaving it out of true conviction, than for someone to follow a fashion, and do it only externally."[20] Bormann took a similar position. In a confidential circular to *Gauleiter*, he advised that *Kirchenaustritt* was to be undertaken only by those truly and inwardly lost to the church and was not to be seen as a matter of opportunity.[21] Bormann revealed ambivalence in his own attitude, however, when he defended the rights of those who had left the church to have church bells rung at their funerals: He seems not to have realized that such a request on the part of those supposedly liberated from their church would have signified an incomplete apostasy. It was within the rights of the church to refuse such a service to those who were no longer church members; but Bormann nonetheless ordered churches to ring bells at the funeral of any *Gottgläubiger* who requested it.[22]

Kirchenaustritt outside the party, as a larger phenomenon in German society, was not a striking success. In 1936, when *Kirchenaustritt* became a discernible tendency within the NSDAP, many reports indicated that statistics for people entering the church actually exceeded the numbers for those leaving it. For the first half of 1936, the number of people entering the Thuringian Protestant Church exceeded the number leaving it by 300.[23] Württemberg registered an equal number of those reentering the church as those leaving it.[24] Hamburg, on the other hand, was already registering more church leaving than church entering by 1934: The rise in church participation after the *Machtergreifung* was particularly short lived here.[25] This discrepancy between urban areas like Hamburg and rural areas like Thuringia points to the paradox that this new initiative within the Nazi Party found its greatest popular appeal in precisely those geographic areas where voters most consistently stayed away from the NSDAP at the polls. This was confirmed in a statistical report released by Martin Bormann in 1941, which gave the percentages of those listed as *gottgläubig* in each *Gau* for 1939. The top five were Berlin with 10.2%, Hamburg with 7.5%, Vienna with 6.4%, Düsseldorf with 6.0%, and Essen with 5.3%.[26]

At the same time that some members of the NSDAP were leaving the churches, attempts were being made gradually to force pastors to give up their membership in the NSDAP. The first signs of clerical *Parteiaustritt* were made precisely the same week in February 1937 as Kerrl's confrontation with the Reich Church Committee, which had precipitated the call for new elections. In a circular, Martin Bormann indicated to party officials that they

[20] Institut für Zeitgeschichte (hereafter IfZ), MA 311 (18 February 1937: Tölz).
[21] BAP NS 6/334/48 (15 March 1941: Munich).
[22] BAP NS 18/149 (1 July 1941: Munich).
[23] *Bayerische Volkszeitung*, 15 October 1936: in BAP 62 Di 1/135/31.
[24] *AELKZ*, 11 September 1936: in BAP 62 Di 1/135/28.
[25] *Paulinusblatt*, 5 April 1936: in BAP 62 Di 1/135/34.
[26] Stadtsarchiv München NSDAP/178 (15 August 1941: Führerhauptquartier). Of course, Vienna was not part of the original electoral map of the NSDAP in the *Kampfzeit*.

should "refrain" from admitting members of the clergy into the ranks of the party, "in order to prevent church controversies from entering the movement."[27] This was not a compulsory order, however, and furthermore made no reference to pastors already in the NSDAP. The position of pastors grew more dire in June 1937, when they were required to leave the SA. Once more, the timing of the order – shortly before church elections were called off that same month – is highly revealing. The order met with strong protest by Protestant clergymen, many of whom were long-standing *alte Kämpfer* who sent letters of appeal to Hitler.[28] Bormann followed this action in July 1938 with another circular that indicated that pastors were now forbidden to be "political leaders" or "holders of high rank" in the party.[29] This meant above all their engagement as local leaders or in higher-level offices. This latest move served to limit clerical influence; but pastors were still not barred from membership in the NSDAP. Nor was it entirely prejudicial – at least in the Nazi imagination – for the party leadership to ensure that those who held another institutional allegiance did not hold positions of responsibility, especially because among the ranks of party members could be found members of the BK. As a corollary to the banning of pastors from positions of influence, Bormann also prohibited high-ranking party members from holding leading positions in a "religious community." The kinds of church involvement that Nazis displayed early in the regime, most notably Erich Koch's tenure as president of the East Prussian Synod, were now expressly forbidden. However, this held true as well for explicitly anti-Christian paganist groups like the Tannenberg League and Fighting Ring of German Faith (*Kampfring Deutsche Glaube*).[30] The order was therefore as much anti-paganist as it was anti-Christian. In January 1939, Bormann continued the incremental separation of church and party, prohibiting party *Unterführer* from holding office in church or religious organizations. However, Bormann explicitly exempted regular party members from this prohibition, who apparently could continue their ecclesiastical duties unhindered.[31] The wearing of party uniforms at church services or the activities of other religious communities was also forbidden, with exception made for Christian funerals.[32]

In May 1939 came the single most significant step, when pastors as well as "those *Volk* comrades who are strongly committed confessionally" were told that they were no longer permitted in the party. It was further ordered that

---

[27] Copy of original of 9 February 1937: BAZ NS 8/182/260-261 (14 June 1939: Munich).

[28] Compare BAP R43 II/155/6 (8 June 1937: Eisenach); BAP R43 II/155/14-15 (13 March 1939: Berlin). The records provide no indication that Hitler responded.

[29] BStA Epp/621/1 (27 July 1938: Munich).

[30] BAP NS 6/229/38-39 (1 June 1938: Munich).

[31] BAP R43 II/155/8-10 (28 January 1939: Munich). Kerrl intended to take action against Bormann's order, but without any apparent success.

[32] This issue had been raised the year before in Bavaria, in which the church funeral of SS General Heinemann had been attended by Hess, several Reich leaders, and other leading party members: "Kirchliche Beerdigung von Parteigenossen, Verhalten der uniformierten Teilnehmer hiebei": BAZ NS 19/2242/6 (10 March 1938: Munich).

those party members who entered the clergy or studied theology would be forced from party membership.[33] This order, finally expelling all pastors from the NSDAP, aroused great indignation. In a 1940 letter, Friedrich Wieneke, one of the leaders of the DC, asked what effect this would have on the front, stating: "I can scarcely believe that this is happening in wartime."[34] Similar letters came from other pastors of the Reich.[35] The DC, who had always imagined themselves to be the only true religious voice of the Nazi movement, were deeply disappointed by the party's unilateral action. The expulsion order can be interpreted only as a sign of the Nazis' deep frustration with and final rejection of the Protestant Church as a whole.

Some of the loudest protests came from Austrian pastors. For years, while the NSDAP was banned in Austria, Protestants had stood in the forefront of support for Nazism and Austria's reintegration into Germany. As in the case of Georg von Schönerer, this tendency fit in with an historical understanding of the nation that German nationalists in the Habsburg Empire associated with Protestantism.[36] This held true as well in the 1930s. After 1933, the number of conversions from Catholicism to Protestantism in Austria increased dramatically, reaching 20,000 in the first half of 1934 alone. Since 1898, the highest number of Protestant converts in one year had been only 6,000.[37] Konrad Henlein, the Sudeten Nazi leader who later became *Gauleiter* of the annexed Sudetenland, had been a convert to Protestantism out of "conviction and love for his *Volk*," as one pastor put it.[38] Even Hitler acknowledged the strongly nationalist element of Austrian Protestantism. Long after he gave up on the Reich Church, he told Rosenberg that he "previously had certain impressions which he had brought from his Austrian background, where the Protestants had been a national church."[39]

The German *Anschluß* of Austria was greeted by the Austrian Protestant Church as a "gift from God," as the salvation of the *Volk* from materialism through the hands of the Führer.[40] The Protestant Church in Austria even agreed with the Nazis' abolition of the confessional school, which for Protestants was associated with the long-endured dominance of the Catholic Church and the privileged status it enjoyed in the Austrian state.[41] In

[33] "Aufnahme von Geistlichen und Theologiestudenten in die NSDAP und deren Gliederungen": BAZ NS 8/182/260-261 (14 June 1939: Munich).
[34] BAP R43 II/155/25 (6 April 1940: Berlin).
[35] Compare BAP R43 II/155/70 (22 June 1940: Berlin).
[36] Even Rosenberg's Office of Ideological Information acknowledged the role played by Protestants in German–Austrian nationalism. See *Mitteilungen zur weltanschaulichen Lage*, Nr. 11/ 4. Jahr (6 May 1938): in BAP 62 Di 1/Film 3851 P/20143–20156.
[37] Doris Bergen, *Twisted Cross: The German Christian Movement in the Third Reich* (Chapel Hill, 1996), 107.
[38] Ibid., 52.
[39] Hans-Günther Seraphim (ed.), *Das politische Tagebuch Alfred Rosenbergs 1934/35 und 1939/40* (Göttingen, 1956), entry for 19 January 1940.
[40] *Der Alemanne*, 2 April 1938: in BAZ NS 22/542.
[41] *Deutsch-Evangelische Korrespondenz*, 13 July 1938: in BAP 62 Di 1/124-1/19.

GOTTGLÄUBIG

January 1939 the *Deutsch-Evangelische Korrespondenz* reported with great pride on the place of Protestant pastors in the Austrian Nazi movement: Of the 127 Austrian pastors who responded to an inquiry, 73 were members of the NSDAP. Before the *Anschluß*, the paper reported, pastors' homes often served as meeting places for the party. Pastors could be found holding party office as school leaders, organization leaders, cultural experts, and up the chain of command to *Ortsgruppenleiter*.[42] The paper went on to point out that, because of their involvement in Nazism, several of these pastors suffered state action against them, including seventeen imprisoned or placed under house arrest.

Given their devotion to the Nazi cause and the consequences they endured at the hands of the Austrian authorities, these pastors could only receive the news of their expulsion with great indignation. One letter, written by a Protestant theology student, expressed fairly typical sentiments. As a Protestant Christian, this student was a convinced National Socialist and "true follower of the Führer" during the time of illegality. His fellow theology students were some of Austria's most ardent Nazis. This student pointed out that Hitler himself was aware of this, as he had received an official deputation of the Protestant Church in Vienna on 9 April 1938, shortly after the Nazis entered the city.[43] Others protested as well, all pointing out how they suffered legal and social consequences for joining what was then an illegal organization. One Pastor Kühne of Vienna boasted that he had been clandestinely supporting the movement since 1920.[44]

Reactions to these protests varied. The deputy *Gauleiter* for Vienna wrote that the expulsion order had to be implemented to maintain the party's neutrality in confessional affairs and was not meant as a sign of disrespect to those who had faithfully served the movement under severe conditions. Nor was it to be interpreted as an act hostile to Christianity.[45] Walter Buch, interviewed immediately after the war, stated that "Protestant ministers were dismissed from the party without prejudice as 'Kirchengebunden.' They continued to preach and suffered no disadvantages."[46] Bormann, Buch's son-in-law and the originator of the order, took a more antagonistic view. He acknowledged that *alte Kämpfer* could be found among the Austrian Protestant clergy, but diminished its significance, suggesting that this was simply because the preexisting regime was a Catholic clerical dictatorship (which it was).[47] In a June 1941 memorandum, Bormann argued that Austrians who had converted from Catholicism to Protestantism in the Austrian *Kampfzeit*

---

[42] The *Ortsgruppenleiter* was directly below the *Kreisleiter* and the *Gauleiter*: "Die evangelischen Pfarrer der Ostmark und die NSDAP," *Deutsch-Evangelische Korrespondenz*, 18 January 1939: in BAP 62 Di 1/75/18.
[43] BAP R43 II/155/63 (21 February 1940: Vienna).
[44] BAP R43 II/155/71 (29 August 1940: Berlin).
[45] BAP R43 II/155/36-38 (22 April 1940: Vienna).
[46] IfZ ZS 855/34-39 (18 July 1945: n.p.).
[47] BAP R43 II/157/149-153 (13 and 20 September 1940: Berlin).

225

Fig. 13   Heinrich Lammers, chief of the Reich Chancellery. Like Martin Bormann, his mastery of a central office in the Nazi bureaucracy made him one of the most powerful Nazis in the later years of the regime. (SV-Bilderdienst)

were now leaving Protestantism to declare themselves *gottgläubig*, thereby implying that the move to Protestantism had been motivated by little more than expediency, since under Austrian law one had to have a confession.[48] Bormann would continue to take a view of the Protestant clergy, and of Christianity in general, that was far more antagonistic than that of most other Nazi leaders, including even the paganists.

Church Minister Kerrl was against the attempted expulsion of pastors from the NSDAP. Suspecting that primarily Bormann was behind it, Kerrl asked Heinrich Lammers, the head of the Reich Chancellery, if this order had come from Hess (to whom Bormann was nominal chief of staff) and what Hitler's personal view was.[49] Lammers sought out Hitler's attitude and, in a letter to Hess, indicated that "for the time being, the Führer absolutely does not wish any actions to be taken against the churches. . . . The Führer declares that he – independent of the question of whether pastor membership in the NSDAP is correct – finds the [expulsion] actions of the *Ortsgruppen* to be entirely inopportune in time of war."[50] Apparently the vigorous protests on behalf of Protestant clergy were beginning to have an impact. Ever sensitive to the morale of the German population, Hitler took a position against Bormann on this issue. It would not be the last time that Hitler personally intervened to override Bormann in religious matters. A few weeks later, in June 1940, Lammers wrote to Bormann, expressing displeasure that pastors were still being expelled from the party on his authority and stating that he expected a letter from the Führer's Deputy that would counteract that

48 BAP NS 6/334/162–69 (25 June 1941: Munich).
49 BAP R43 II/155/26 (17 April 1940: Berlin).
50 BAP R43 II/155/27 (23 April 1940: Berlin).

order.[51] The files of the Reich Chancellery do not indicate whether Bormann was formally overridden; but the fact that pastors continued to be found in the ranks of the NSDAP even after 1940 suggests that in practice he was.[52] The continued presence of members of the BK in the NSDAP was also a matter of concern, and segments of the party sought to have them expelled. However, even here their continued presence in the Nazi movement was ultimately affirmed. One case involved a Professor Anrich of Bonn. Anrich's situation was rather unique: The son of a pastor, he had studied at Tübingen and had founded there the Ernst Wurche Academic Guild, whose members came out of the Bible Circle and who were closely associated with the BK. As the judge for his case reported, Anrich had also been active in the Nazi Party, having been its caucus leader in the Bonn Student Chamber in 1930. He entered into the leadership ranks of the NSDStB shortly thereafter, but almost immediately came into conflict with Baldur von Schirach, then its head. As a result of an intrigue against Schirach, Anrich was expelled from the party the next year. After the Seizure of Power he attempted to regain his membership without success. He tried once more, however, after he had been invited to the tenth anniversary of the NSDStB as one of its cofounders. This time he succeeded, and within a few months was made deputy leader of the Bonn branch of the Nazi Lecturers' League. His judge pointed out that he was solidly National Socialist. His affiliation with the BK was noted, but it was not regarded as grounds for denying his readmission into the party.[53]

Another, more complicated, case was that of the school teacher Walter Hobohm of Halberstadt. Like Anrich, Hobohm was a member both of the NSDAP and the BK. In June 1937 he denounced Rosenberg's teachings to party authorities, declaring that they led to "a sort of racial materialism" (something Rosenberg would have strongly denied).[54] The responsible party bureaucrats in the Reich Education Ministry began proceedings to have him expelled from his post, stating that "unreserved support for the National Socialist state and National Socialist ideology cannot be expected" of Hobohm. The case was forwarded to the Reich Chancellery in January 1939, where Lammers, consistent with his attitude toward the expulsion of

---

[51] "Ausscheiden von Pfarrern aus der NSDAP": BAP R43 II/155/32 (5 June 1940: Berlin).

[52] See, for example, the personnel file of one Hans Kipfmüller, a minor official in the NSDAP who was simultaneously a local leader of the SA, the local NSV, and Protestant town pastor past 1940, by which time he would have presumably been forced to choose between party and pastorate: IfZ F 304 (n.d., n.p.). As well, see the statement by Konstantin Hierl, head of the Reich Labor Service (like Ley's German Labor Front, an ancillary NSDAP organization), that theologians and theology students could remain in his organization. Although they would be accorded no special status, neither would they suffer any discrimination for their Christian convictions: BAP NS 6/340/92-95 (24 February 1943: Berlin). In a subsequent memorandum, Hierl explicitly forbade members of the Labor Service to attack the churches or churchgoers: BAP NS 6/341/65-66 (9 May 1943: Führerhauptquartier).

[53] IfZ MA 1160 (5 April 1939: Düsseldorf).

[54] Martin Broszat, *The Hitler State: The Foundation and Development of the Internal Structure of the Third Reich* (London, 1981), 231.

pastors, sought out a second opinion. Whereas one branch of the Chancellery supported the recommendation, a constitutional expert in the Chancellery argued that the only reason to come to this decision "would be the fact that the official in question rejects Rosenberg's conceptions in so far as these conflict with the Christian faith. It does not seem feasible to retire officials ... solely on this ground.... Such a decision would not be without considerable objections in view of Article 24 of the Party Program and the guarantee of freedom of worship." Lammers also sought the council of his personal advisor von Stutterheim, who believed that "belonging to the Confessing Church is also in my opinion no reason for imposing retirement according to Article 71" of the German legal code.[55] Lammers agreed with this opinion, and approached Bernhard Rust with the matter. Eventually Hobohm was reinstated in his post, with the condition that he could no longer teach history.

The separation of church and party, then, was a tenuous and contested affair. There was nonetheless one region under Nazi control that proved the exception to the rule. In the territory conquered from Poland, Nazi anticlericals fashioned a *tabula rasa* that, unhampered by the legal and social restrictions felt back home, presented a canvas on which to paint the ideal Nazi society. Known as the Warthegau or Reichsgau Wartheland, it is generally regarded as the testing ground for the implementation of a pure Nazi utopia. Unhindered by state authorities, Bormann's Party Chancellery was given a free hand to shape the Warthegau in association with its *Gauleiter* and Reich Governor, Arthur Greiser.[56] In November 1940, Bormann ordered that Kerrl's authority as Church Minister was not to reach into the Wartheland: Instead, Greiser and Bormann would handle jurisdiction over ecclesiastical matters.[57] In spite of objections from the Reich authorities, including Frick, no state authorities from Germany proper (the *Altreich*) would be included in the decision-making process. Ecclesiastical authorities, too, were denied jurisdiction over Warthegau's churches.

What exactly Greiser had in mind for religious life in his *Gau* was revealed in a memorandum written the next month. In thirteen points he laid out the new church situation in Wartheland. Most importantly, the churches were no longer state churches, but voluntary, independent church societies. As well, these churches were to have no institutional relationship with churches outside the *Gau*, and no legal or financial connection with the Protestant Church in Germany or with the Vatican. No church taxes would be collected, with financial backing coming only from member contributions. Only adults who gave their consent could become members of a church body. All secular organizations of the churches, such as youth and welfare groups,

[55] Ibid., 232.
[56] Ibid., 127; John Conway, *The Nazi Persecution of the Churches* (London, 1968), 311–12; Georg Denzler and Volker Fabricius (eds.), *Christen und Nationalsozialisten: Darstellung und Dokumente* (Frankfurt a.M., 1993), 108; Jochen von Lang, *The Secretary – Martin Bormann: The Man who Manipulated Hitler* (New York, 1979), 191.
[57] BAP R43 II/150a/97 (1 November 1940: Berlin).

were dissolved. Germans and Poles were to use separate churches. Church property was to be limited to church buildings. All monasteries and cloisters were to be abolished because they "worked against German morality." Only those native to the region, who furthermore had an additional occupation, could be clergy.[58]

These measures were finally made legal in an ordinance of September 1941, which also listed the new churches constituted for the area: the Posen Protestant Church of German Nationality in Wartheland; the Litzmannstadt Protestant Church of German Nationality in Wartheland; the Protestant–Lutheran Church of German Nationality in Wartheland West; and the Roman Catholic Church of German Nationality in Reichsgau Wartheland. There was no provision for any Polish churches.[59] Greiser added to this ordinance a decree that all government officials in the *Gau* had to withdraw from the churches. In January 1942, this order was extended to all party members moving into the *Gau*, who were even compelled not to rejoin the church should they return to the *Altreich*. Bormann was proud to claim coauthorship of this last clause with Greiser, which caused considerable protest within the party.[60] Rosenberg's voice was among them: Under the banner of religious tolerance, which he exhibited as well in the Niemöller trial, Rosenberg told Bormann that he thought it impossible to "require someone never to join a church organization again."[61] This portion of the law was withdrawn in July 1944.[62]

The blank slate of the Warthegau suggests what the fate of the churches would have been in a "pure" Nazi State, or at least Bormann's vision of one, unsullied by the forces of political "reaction" or public opinion. The Wartheland churches were restricted in a way unknown in any other part of Nazi Germany. The seizure of Catholic Church property in particular was consistent with the well-established animosity the Nazis showed toward this institution, one noticeably milder when aimed at Protestantism, as well as the degree of anticlerical zeal that the most extreme Nazis would engage in given the chance. Just as noteworthy as the stringent prohibitions taken by Nazis, however, is the simple fact that the churches were allowed in: They were given a place in the Nazi paradise. In contrast to the razing of churches or their conversion to museums of atheism in the neighboring Soviet Union, here church life continued, although in greatly reduced form and totally separated from the state. Greiser explained his church policy in a lecture to party members in Kiel in 1942, making specific reference to only the Catholic Church: "If we have taken away the property of the Polish Church, this is not to punish faithful Catholics, but rather because economic resources for the political struggle against the German people were derived from this property.

---

[58] Denzler and Fabricius (eds.), *Christen*, 311–12.
[59] BAZ Schu 245/1/4-5 (13 September 1941: Posen).
[60] BAZ NS 8/187/122-23 (27 July 1942: Führerhauptquartier).
[61] BAZ NS 8/187/150 (15 July 1942: Berlin).
[62] Conway, *Persecution*, 453, n. 95.

That is why there are no more monasteries and no more church properties left in the Reichsgau Wartheland."[63] Carefully precluding any proclerical forces from adding their brushstrokes to the Wartheland palette, Bormann and his associates still painted the Christian churches, even if in minimal form, into their picture.

TOWARD CONFRONTATION

Tensions over the presence of Christians in the Nazi movement were felt not just in the party rank-and-file. They were a source of conflict in the party leadership as well. One of the starkest examples was the case of Catholic Josef Wagner, who had been prominent in the *Kampfzeit* as a spokesman for his party's economic platform. Being the only *Gauleiter* with two *Gaue* (Westphalia and Silesia after 1935), and having been appointed the Reich Commissioner for Price Setting (*Preisbildung*) in 1936, he had established his ideological reliability in the eyes of the party leadership. His unapologetic adherence to Christianity, which he had always publicly proclaimed, seems not to have diminished his credentials. Wagner barred all anticlerical measures in his own areas and went so far as to criticize such measures among other party leaders.[64] This too might have gone unnoticed were it not for Wagner's personal religious practices, which caused offense to Bormann and Himmler in particular. First, Wagner and his wife had forbidden their daughter Gerda to marry a member of the SS because the prospective groom had left the church. Second, and certainly more damning, Wagner sent his own children to a convent school in Breslau and did not enroll them in the local SA.[65] These and other disturbing facts – Wagner's wife had genuflected to the Pope at a Vatican reception – were taken very poorly by Bormann, who worked to have Wagner expelled in November 1941. Wagner appealed his case to Buch's party court, defending himself by referring to Point 24 of the Party Program and insisting that he had known nothing of his wife's conduct toward the Pope. Buch and the six members of the party jury, all of them *Gauleiters*, accepted Wagner's defense and reversed the expulsion order. Hitler, however, refused to ratify the decision, thereby upholding Wagner's expulsion. Buch believed that it was his son-in-law Bormann who was really responsible.[66]

If Wagner's case constituted an attack against Christians in the party, other *Gauleiter* no less friendly to Christian institutions continued in their offices unhindered. One who was especially contemptuous of Bormann in this regard was the *Gauleiter* of Schwaben, Karl Wahl. Raised a Protestant, he had married a Catholic and had had his children baptized Catholic. He may not

[63] Quoted in ibid., 319.
[64] Lang, *Secretary*, 244.
[65] IfZ MA 327 (14 April 1942: Führerhauptquartier). Himmler was firmly convinced that Wagner's wife was the driving force behind these acts.
[66] Lang, *Secretary*, 245–6.

have sent his own children to convent schools, but Wahl did have a remarkably close relationship with the Catholic diocese of Augsburg, specifically Bishop Eberle. Augsburgers could observe the two openly walking together "deep in conversation."[67] When Wahl received an emissary from Bormann, who complained that not enough had been done against the churches in *Gau* Schwaben, Wahl responded by asking whether Bormann was "out of his mind" for wanting to damage public morale in wartime. The emissary responded that the attack on the churches was Bormann's "hobby horse," and Wahl quietly let the matter drop.[68] He chose to mitigate Bormann's orders whenever possible until, he reported, "one day I just cut loose and threw everything that had Bormann's name on it into the fire, unread."[69]

Aside from the case of Josef Wagner, whose particular attachment to confessionalism was highly unusual in the party leadership, there was a continuing adherence to an unconfessional Christianity, noted by paganistic party members with dismay. The most notable leader in this regard was Göring, who did not leave the church and displayed no sign of rupture in his religious feelings. Indeed, for the duration of the Third Reich, his convictions appear to have continued unabated. On several public occasions Göring demonstrated an unapologetic adherence to Christianity. In one instance, party paganists expressed alarm when Göring presided over the February 1939 consecration of a nondenominational church in Faßberg, a town on the Lüneberg Heath. As one unhappy official in *Gau* Düsseldorf wrote to Rosenberg in his monthly report: "Now that the excitation caused by the baptism [of Göring's daughter] in the Karinhall has died down, *Volk* comrades have something new to talk about.... In wide circles of party members there is little understanding for the action of the General Field Marshal.... From the circles of *Gottgläubigen* one hears the question: 'Why a church, why not a festal hall or a community house?' It will be increasingly difficult to reject an alien Christianity when, on the other side, Christianity is promoted by the highest powers of state."[70] Had Göring's participation at this event been purely for propaganda purposes, this party official would have been duly informed not to take it seriously. Given that this was not the case, Rosenberg could only file away such complaints.

Further evidence of Göring's position was found the year before, in 1938, when a photo of Hermann and Emmy Göring was published, showing them at the dining room table at Karinhall with a cross hanging prominently above them in the corner. The *Völkischer Beobachter* published it with the following caption: "All ornamentation, arranged with artistic good taste,

---

[67] Edward Peterson, *The Limits of Hitler's Power* (Princeton, 1969), 349.
[68] Ibid., 352.
[69] Lang, *Secretary*, 242. This picture of Wahl's disregard for Bormann, seemingly without consequence, is confirmed by Peterson, *Hitler's Power*, 350–4.
[70] "Die Stiftung einer Kirche durch den Generalfeldmarschall": BAP 62 Di 1/106/104 (February 1939). A similar complaint came from Gau Hessen-Nassau: BAP 62 Di 1/106/111 (March 1939).

is German folk art [*Volkskunst*]."[71] In Rosenberg's office, a clipping of the photo had a question mark penciled in next to the cross. The Christian *Kommende Kirche* also published the photo, stating: "As this true paladin of the Führer modestly demonstrates in his home, Christianity and National Socialism are not opposites."[72] This was not just wishful thinking on the part of the Christian press. In his memoirs Baldur von Schirach wrote: "Of the leading men of the party whom I knew, everyone interpreted the Party Program differently; ... Rosenberg mythically, Göring and some others in a certain sense Christian."[73] Even Rosenberg, who was prone to delusions of grandeur about his place in the movement, made no mistake about Göring's attitude. In August 1939, Göring confronted Rosenberg point blank, asking him: "Do you believe that Christianity is coming to an end, and that later a new form created by us will come into being?" When Rosenberg said he did think this, Göring replied he would privately solicit Hitler's view.[74] No record exists of Göring's asking Hitler this question, but there is little doubt Hitler would have rejected Rosenberg's contention.

Goebbels, too, exhibited little change in his religious attitudes. In an October 1937 speech, he stated unambiguously:

The churches still preach today what their master said 2000 years before. We deal with the same principles, with that great ideological structure which has passed through history. We therefore assemble the *Volk* around us again and again, we preach again and again the ideals through which we became great, not only in order to keep our generation National Socialist, but rather to keep generations centuries after us National Socialist. We do nothing to harm the churches. On the contrary: We accept from them the work which they truly must manage themselves.[75]

Here Goebbels flatly stated that, even if the churches failed in their work, the Nazis' goals were synonymous with theirs. He touched on this point again later in the speech: "They no longer have a proper relationship with the *Volk*, because they no longer understand how to speak to them. A *Volk* that has gone through four years of war and fifteen of Marxism can no longer muster the energy to follow theological hair-splitting. It wants to see an active Christianity, and sees it better embodied in something like Winter Relief than in the theological disputes of the so-called Confessing Front." Although we can raise serious doubts about Goebbels' estimation of church unpopularity, what he said is nonetheless important because it displays a consistent attitude: low regard for the churches and high regard for Christianity. Consistency also characterized Goebbels' low regard for the mysticism enjoyed by many anti-Christians. In June 1941, Goebbels banned all public performances of an occultist, telepathic, astrological, or "supernatural"

[71] *VB*, 13 January 1938: in BAP 62 Di 1/106/103.
[72] *Kommende Kirche*, 30 January 1938: in BAP 62 Di 1/106/102.
[73] Baldur von Schirach, *Ich glaubte an Hitler* (Hamburg, 1967), 87.
[74] Seraphim (ed.), *Tagebuch*, entry for 22 August 1939.
[75] *VB*, 11 October 1937: in BAZ NS 22/542.

nature – exactly the sort of religious expression Himmler dabbled in.[76] Whatever Goebbels believed about the church losing members, it did not apply
in his case: He stayed in the church. Beyond this, however, according to his
aide Werner Stephan, Goebbels told his staff not to leave the church either.
He always emphasized his continuing church membership to other party
members and, like Göring, had his children baptized.[77]

During the war, and right up to its end, Himmler continued to exhibit
the puzzling mix of an unrelenting anticlerical and a highly ambivalent anti-
Christian that had marked his prewar attitude. At a 1942 speech delivered to
the SS and German police leadership, Himmler spoke of the struggle of the
races and the need to fight off the Asiatic horde. Even while he attacked the
"perversity" of Christian morality, he took a favorable view of the Catholic
teaching that a childless marriage was the "greatest sin of all." Himmler
stated his belief that "the decline in our birthrate around 1900 coincided
with the time when the German people began to inwardly free themselves
from their very keen commitment to the churches." This aspect of Christian
orthodox teaching, Himmler declared to the assembled party members, "we
can only welcome from a biological and racial point of view."[78] Besides
the declining birthrate, Himmler credited the Catholic Church with fighting
another nemesis of Nazi ideology: Freemasonry. As he put it in 1940 to
his confidant Felix Kersten, "Only *one* power has not allowed itself to be
deceived, the Catholic Church. She is the inexorable enemy of all Masonry. It
is certainly known to you that any Catholic is automatically excommunicated
the moment he becomes a Mason." In this same eulogy, Himmler was less
charitable to the Protestants: "Only the foolish Evangelical parsons have
still not realized what is at stake. They join the Masons without realizing
that they are digging their own graves."[79] Having heard this, and possibly
being aware of his other felicitous remarks about certain aspects of Christian
ideology, Kersten asked Himmler point blank: "Why have you at one and the
same time made implacable enemies of the Jews and Masons on the one side,
and their professed enemy, the Catholic Church, on the other . . . ?" On this
occasion, Himmler was evasive, simply responding that this was a matter
"which the Führer alone had to decide. To talk about it, now that the die
has been cast, is quite pointless."[80]

Kersten would have opportunity to once again confront Himmler with
his own ambiguity. In 1942 he heard of something incredible from an SS
leader who had been invited to Himmler's house: "Himmler's small daughter
said grace before lunch in his presence. He [the SS leader] had gazed at the
Reichsführer in astonishment, not being able to understand how he – so

[76] BAP NS 6/334/122 (3 June 1941: Munich).
[77] Werner Stephan, *Joseph Goebbels: Dämon einer Diktatur* (Stuttgart, 1949), 138.
[78] IfZ F 37/3 (16 September 1942: Feldkommandostelle Rußland-Süd).
[79] Felix Kersten, *The Kersten Memoirs 1940–1945* (New York, 1957), 31 (emphasis in the original).
[80] Ibid., 32.

hostile to the Church – could allow prayers to be said in his own house. It argued some discrepancy in Himmler's outlook."[81] Kersten prodded Himmler to discern his real attitude. When he asked how the Catholic Church could best be described, Himmler answered: "As a joint-stock company from which the chief shareholders – since its foundation and for nearly two thousand years – draw a hundred or a thousand percent profit and give nothing in return. Insurance companies which always say that it's not in the contract whenever you make a claim are mere novices in the art of deception compared with this gigantic swindle."[82] Here was a vituperative hatred for the institution of Christianity, but nothing as yet on the religion itself.

Kersten knew of Himmler's dabbling in non-Christian forms of religion and interest in mysticism and went so far as to read Eastern religious texts himself to better parry Himmler's religious thrusts. As he told Himmler: "I've read the Bhagavad-Gita, which you so prize, and other Indian writings and found in them much the same teaching as Christianity offers in the Sermon on the Mount. The Ten Commandments recur in a slightly different form in Buddhist doctrine, in the Vedas and Rig-Vedas. There's no doubt that the spirituality is the same, except that Christianity adds belief in a personal God who judges men after their death. It's the actual putting into practice of this teaching which would really make the difference." To this Himmler responded: "That's true enough, and I've nothing against Christianity in itself; no doubt it has lofty moral ideas." Himmler then proceeded to disclose the real reasons for his enmity: "We have to be on our guard against a world power which makes use of Christianity and its organization to oppose our own national resurrection by methods of which we're everywhere conscious."[83] Confronted with the distinction between hatred of Christian institutions and Christian ideology, Himmler stated that he was really anticlerical, not anti-Christian. When Himmler let loose with an apparently anti-Christian statement, "Then we'll unfrock these priests – neither their God nor their Virgin Mary will be able to do a thing for them then," Kersten immediately took him to task: "But you're surely not opposed to the Virgin Mary, Herr Reichsführer?" Again, Himmler conceded the distinction: "No, not at all. To link womanhood with religion is a noble idea. It suits our Germanic outlook."[84]

There was even less ambiguity in Himmler's attitude toward Luther and Protestantism. In a secret speech to assembled SS leaders in May 1944, Himmler lectured on German history: "Only when the picture of history is placed before our eyes," he claimed, "does our mission for the future become clear." Himmler touched on one of his favorite subjects, the churches, and indicated that his hatred was really aimed at the temporal power of Catholicism: "[If] the Christian Catholic Church had remained what it was,

[81] Ibid., 148.
[82] Ibid., 149.
[83] Ibid., 155.
[84] Ibid., 155–6.

fulfillment of the soul, the mediary to the Lord . . . that would have been fine." However, the church acquired temporal ambitions, and came into constant conflict with emperor and state. In Himmler's view, Germany suffered for centuries from this dilemma, especially because the Jews had infiltrated the church in order to dominate the German *Volk*. However, after a long period of oppression and persecution at the hands of this power, the German spirit rose up in defiance: "A Luther, a Zwingli, a Calvin rose up, individual voices in this conflict of the spirit. The Germanic spirit protested, and for their newly founded confession they took the name Protestant. [Such struggle] has always been a hallmark of Germanic blood or German blood."[85] As a signifier of nationhood, both in blood and spirit, Protestantism remained exalted even at this late stage. This is especially evident when Himmler tellingly referred to the Frenchman Calvin as "Germanic." As with Günther's earlier reference to the "blondes" of La Rochelle, Himmler here not only revealed his belief that to be Protestant is to be Germanic, but also that to be Germanic is to be Protestant.

This attitude was revealed on other occasions as well. For instance, when discussing the BK, Himmler explicitly detached Niemöller from Protestantism. As he wrote sardonically but nonetheless revealingly to Walter Buch, "It is Niemöller's intention to convert to the Catholic faith."[86] Just as Protestantism was a marker of national feeling, Catholicism was a marker of national betrayal: If a Protestant pastor stood against the Nazis, Himmler intimated, he must no longer be Protestant. Himmler had high regard for Luther as well. In March 1940, shortly before the beginning of the Final Solution, he held a conversation on the "Jewish problem" with Kersten. Himmler the historian proclaimed that Judaism had infected Catholicism, that in Luther's day the Vatican had been run by "Jew-Popes." But whereas the Catholic Church was blind, Luther saw and understood the Jewish peril: "You should read, moreover, what Luther said and wrote about the Jews. *No judgment could be sharper.*"[87] Here Himmler reveals that he read Luther's notorious "On the Jews and their Lies" and believed that it sanctioned Nazi antisemitism.[88] Himmler held Luther in such esteem that in January 1941 his personal secretary wrote: "The Reichsführer-SS wishes to be remembered at the Luther Archive in Wittenberg after the war."[89]

---

[85] "Rede des Reichsführers-SS am 24.5.44 in Sonthofen vor den Teilnehmern des politisch-weltanschaulichen Lehrgangs (Generale)": BAZ NS 19/4014/10-33 (24 May 1944: Sonthofen), here 10–13.

[86] IfZ MA 327 (14 April 1942: Führerhauptquartier).

[87] Kersten, *Kersten Memoirs*, 35 (emphasis added).

[88] Himmler's claim that "no judgement could be harsher" could have been a reference only to the following passage in Luther's tract "On the Jews and their Lies": "We are at fault in not slaying them." Because Himmler freely admitted to reading this at a time when genocide against the Jews was in its conception, Luther's impact on the later development of the Holocaust cannot completely be discounted.

[89] BAZ NS 19/712/2 (10 January 1941: Berlin[?]). What form this remembrance would take is not indicated in the files.

THE CONTEST FOR IDEOLOGY

The expulsion of pastors from positions of power in the party, together with the withdrawal of party members from the churches, paints an unambiguous picture of increased hostility between Nazism and Christian institutions after 1937. On the other hand, both Christian and paganist party leaders persisted in their beliefs and behaviors, in most cases unhindered. However, this should not leave us with the presumption that a *modus vivendi* between positive Christians and paganists was agreed on within the movement. Quite the opposite: The late 1930s and early 1940s brought something of a showdown between these two factions. This ongoing struggle is documented at the institutional level through the repeated contests that arose over religion between the rival Nazi offices that staked various claims over worldview. Nearly all these disputes pitted Rosenberg's Office for Ideological Information against not only Goebbels' Reich Propaganda Office (*Reichspropagandaleitung*, or RPL) (distinct from the Reich Ministry of Propaganda), but also against a commonly overlooked office: the Party Examination Commission for the Protection of National Socialist Literature (*Parteiamtliche Prüfungskommission zum Schutze des NS-Schrifttums*, or PPK). Philipp Bouhler, the Chief of the Chancellery of the Führer, headed the PPK. These disputes also brought in other high-ranking Nazis, such as Bormann and Kerrl. As we shall see, the quarrels that took place directly addressed the continued presence of Christians and Christian belief in the movement.

A man with literary ambitions, Bouhler apprenticed with several publishers after the war while studying philosophy at the University of Munich. In 1922 he joined the staff of the *Völkischer Beobachter* and after 1925 took

Fig. 14   Philipp Bouhler, head of the Nazi "euthanasia" program and Rosenberg's rival for the oversight of Nazi ideology. (Scherl)

on the distinctly unliterary job of business manager of the NSDAP. After the Seizure of Power, Bouhler refocused on his intellectual ambitions, attempting to acquire control over the policing of Nazi literature. Named the Delegate for Culture to the Führer's Deputy in January 1934, Bouhler approached Goebbels and Max Amann, head of the Nazis' Eher Publishing House and President of the Reich Press Chamber, with the idea of expanding his competence. Three months later he was made head of the newly established PPK, which was invested with the power to inspect all political, economic, cultural, historical, and biographical works for ideological purity.[90] (Ultimate power to censure books remained in the hands of the Propaganda Ministry.) Hitler's confidence in Bouhler's abilities as a Nazi were confirmed when he was put in charge of the T-4 Action, the euthanasia campaign that, in its bureaucratic and administrative élan, served as a precursor to the "Final Solution."

Bouhler's office brought him into direct competition with Rosenberg over the domain of ideological protection. It is no coincidence that Bouhler received the backing of Goebbels, who appointed the head of the literature department in his Propaganda Ministry, Karl Hederich, as deputy director of the PPK.[91] However, the antagonism between Bouhler and Rosenberg was not purely a rivalry over "turf." They also had real differences of opinion, above all on questions of religion. This became evident when Bouhler discussed boundaries of competence with Rosenberg in 1936. Rosenberg was eager to see Bouhler's office absorbed into his own, contending that his authority outweighed Bouhler's in this sphere, as he was the Führer's Delegate and Bouhler only the Führer's Deputy's Delegate. Bouhler responded by suggesting that if Rosenberg were to take over main responsibility for the protection of literature, "in confessional camps this would be considered the beginning of a *Kulturkampf*, simply because through your work, you are strongly considered to be a stumbling block for the Christian worldview."[92] That Bouhler had no intention of being a stumbling block himself was made evident in his assessment of a book called *The Goal of Religious Education in the National Socialist School*, written in 1936 by a party member named Elbertzhagen. The author argued in the positive Christian vein that a religious renewal of the *Volk* had to take place on the foundation of an unconfessional Christianity. Nazi education, this author contended, should start with the personality of Jesus and should regard Martin Luther not simply as the reformer of the Church, but as the reformer of the religious education of the *Volk*.[93] Whereas Rosenberg's office stated that an

[90] Hans-Walter Schmuhl, "Philipp Bouhler – Ein Vorreiter des Massenmordes," in Ronald Smelser et al. (eds.), *Die Braune Elite II: 21 weitere biographische Skizzen* (Darmstadt, 1993), 42–3.
[91] See the biographical sketch of Hederich in "NS-Schrifttum im Kampf," *Bremer Zeitung*, 19 May 1935: in BStA PAS 946.
[92] BAZ NS 8/178/84-85 (3 March 1936: Berlin).
[93] See the appraisal of Elbertzhagen's *Das Ziel der religiösen Erziehung in der nationalsozialistischen Schule*: in BAP 62 Di 1/23/6-11 (19 December 1941: Berlin).

endorsement of its contents was "not justifiable," Bouhler's PPK approved the work for publication.[94] Rosenberg and Bouhler parted company once again over a 1938 book by Friedrich Andersen, whose earlier work, *The German Savior*, was a signal contribution to DC theology during Weimar. Now Andersen received Bouhler's stamp of approval for his new book, *Geschichte des Meisters von Nazareth ohne Legende und theologische Zusätze* ("The History of the Master of Nazareth without Legends or Theological Amendments"). As far as Rosenberg was concerned, such a book had nothing to do with the Nazi *Weltanschauung*. Rosenberg complained to Hess that, by endorsing this book, Bouhler was infringing on his own domain of ideological oversight.[95] These differences of opinion lasted well into the war.[96] Even though Bouhler's office had nominally been subsumed into Rosenberg's Ideology Office by 1943, Bouhler retained and even strengthened his control over the supervision of literature. When Rosenberg complained about this, he was told by Bormann that this had been Hitler's own decision, adding that Rosenberg's new post as Reich Minister for the Occupied East (which provided him with as little real power as his other positions) "was itself a lifetime occupation."[97]

Rosenberg also took Bouhler to task for the relationship he was developing between his PPK and Kerrl's Church Ministry. In 1938 Rosenberg learned to his horror that Kerrl wished to have a representative from the Church Ministry work in the PPK to assist in the evaluation of religious literature and complained about it to Hess. Bouhler explained that he tackled the problem of religious literature "with the greatest restraint," but did not believe that "one can refuse party member Kerrl participation in the literary work that falls within the boundaries of his jurisdiction.... I have therefore granted to the Reich Church Minister his wish that his representative be appointed."[98] Rosenberg protested in "the strongest terms" against this cooperation, claiming it was not the task of Bouhler's office to determine the "church-ideological" position of the movement, but rather that of his own Office of Ideological Information. In a letter to Hess, he made plain his opposition to Kerrl and his ministry and suggested that polycratic infighting in this sphere would undermine party unity. Rosenberg considered Bouhler's actions "sabotage" and warned Hess that he would go straight to the Führer if Bouhler were not reminded of Rosenberg's ultimate authority in ideological matters.[99] Bormann wrote Bouhler, asking that he refrain from appointing a

---

[94] BAP 62 Di 1/23/39 (21 August 1936: Berlin).

[95] BAZ NS 8/182/139-140 (21 August 1939: Berlin).

[96] See the case of Hermann Schwartz, whose book *Ehre, Volksgemeinschaft, Vaterland* was considered too Christian for Rosenberg's officials (it denounced racialist "biologism"), but which received the PPK's approval: BAP 62 Di 1/23/67 (3 June 1943: Berlin).

[97] Lang, *Secretary*, 175.

[98] BAZ NS 8/180/70-71 (4 November 1938: Berlin).

[99] BAZ NS 8/180/40-41 (23 November 1938: Berlin).

member of Kerrl's ministry to the PPK, adding that Rosenberg was the one to address the party's position on religion. He furthermore asked Bouhler to henceforth send all books touching on the relationship between party and church to Rosenberg's office for examination.[100]

Bouhler ignored this order, as was demonstrated the next year when Hanns Kerrl was preparing to publish a manuscript titled *Weltanschauung und Religion – Nationalsozialismus und Christentum* ("Worldview and Religion – National Socialism and Christianity"), which not only suggested a strong ideological relationship, *contra* Rosenberg, but also upheld the idea of a Protestant Reich Church. Anticipating certain hostility, Kerrl neglected to have the book evaluated by Rosenberg's office, but did get approval from Bouhler's office. Rosenberg and Bormann were immediately opposed, with the latter sending an angry letter to Kerrl instructing him to postpone publication until the Führer gave his decision.[101] Given his rejection after 1937 of a Protestant Reich Church, Hitler banned the book. In October Rosenberg's office sent a letter to Goebbels – whose ministry oversaw censorship – informing him to halt all advertising.[102] No apparent action was taken, and two months later Bormann wrote to Goebbels, complaining that Kerrl's book had made its way into the Christmas catalogue of a Protestant bookstore in spite of Hitler's wishes.[103] Rosenberg for one could not have viewed this as a mistake. In a letter to Hess the year before he had described as "grotesque" the acquiescence of Bouhler and Goebbels (and their go-between Hederich) in the proliferation of literature friendly to the Catholic Church.[104] Bouhler defended his position in a letter to Bormann, stating that he did not believe that the questions raised by Kerrl's book could not be asked.[105]

Rosenberg and Bouhler confronted each other again when Rosenberg learned that Bouhler intended to set up an office for the handling of complaints, as a type of party ombudsman. This episode also brought the direct intervention of Göring against Rosenberg. In October 1939, Rosenberg and Göring agreed that, because the war amounted to a "spiritual struggle" against Germany's enemies, they needed to do all they could to secure the inner unity of Nazism. Both men agreed that the time had come to bury their differences.[106] Only two months later, however, over Bouhler's latest enterprise, Rosenberg wrote angrily to Göring, who, as Chairman of

---

[100] BAZ NS 8/180/17 (8 December 1938: Munich).

[101] Lang, *Secretary*, 391-2.

[102] BAZ NS 8/182/84 (25 October 1939: Berlin).

[103] BAZ NS 8/182/9 (19 December 1939: Munich). Goebbels replied that this could not be helped, as catalogues came out before Hitler's ban: BAZ NS 8/183/133 (8 January 1940: Berlin).

[104] BAZ NS 8/180/63-65 (21 November 1938: Berlin).

[105] BAZ NS 11/10/29-31 (13 December 1939: Berlin).

[106] BAZ NS 8/167/104 (2 October 1939: Berlin).

the Ministerial Council for Defense of the Reich, had given Bouhler his commission. Rosenberg conceded that this office would most likely handle economic and social complaints, but he worried that it would serve the churches as a "wailing wall" against him. Rosenberg therefore requested that Göring notify Bouhler in writing that his office could not handle concerns relating to worldview, that this was his jurisdiction alone.[107] Bouhler completely disregarded Rosenberg's counsel, however, and began taking on complaints from Christian organizations. One such group, the "League for Determined Christianity" (*Bund für entschiedenes Christentum*), sent a letter of complaint about anticlerical activity in the Hitler Youth (HJ) to Bouhler. Rosenberg wrote to Göring, reminding him again that affairs touching on ideological or confessional disputes went through him alone and were not included in Bouhler's competency.[108] Bouhler assured Göring that he would no longer take on such cases.[109] Göring then wrote to Rosenberg: "In ideological matters I have proceeded in accordance with your wishes." However, through a legalistic caveat, he reserved for himself one area of immense importance to the churches, "namely in those cases in which somebody in acute circumstances complains to me, as Chairman of the Ministerial Council, about the Church Minister or police actions or the actions of the Education Minister. For example: the police dissolve a confessional association, and this association complains about it to me. In this case, which concerns the administrative actions of the police, naturally only I can make a direct decision."[110] This was a classic instance of the Nazi Party's polycratic duplication of competency, since in this fashion presumably all religious organizations could be saved from Rosenberg's jurisdiction. By dint of complaining to the police, the positive Christian Göring would have his pretext for intervening in their defense. Those powers given to Rosenberg with one hand were effectively taken away with the other.

Suffering continual challenges to his authority as the Führer's Delegate for Ideological Training, Rosenberg sought to reinforce his authority – and in the process seek reassurance from Hitler – by attempting to elevate his position from a purely party office to a more imposing state office. A circular of 19 December 1939 stated the parameters of Rosenberg's proposed authority. Kerrl, whose book had been rejected for publication just a few days earlier, saw an opportunity for revenge and immediately protested, pointing out the damage this would do to the morale of the German people, especially in wartime: "Over the past years the name of Rosenberg has become for broad sectors of the people – rightly or wrongly I will not say – a type of symbol for hostility to Church and Christianity."[111] Rust also stood

[107] BAZ NS 8/167/95 (8 December 1939: Berlin).
[108] BAZ NS 8/167/73 (25 June 1940: Berlin[?]).
[109] BAZ NS 8/167/68 (25 July 1940: Berlin).
[110] BAZ NS 8/167/70 (14 July 1940: Berlin).
[111] IfZ Fa 199/47/75-76 (23 December 1939: Berlin).

opposed to such an appointment, because he felt it would essentially elevate Rosenberg to the position of a minister, thereby infringing on his own domain.[112] He was careful to protect his power, but was also interested in preserving the "positive Christianity" he helped shape. Another source of opposition was Baldur von Schirach.[113] Rosenberg's hopes were diminished as more voices against him were heard. In January, Lammers conducted a straw poll of the party leadership. Of the twelve who responded, five supported Rosenberg: Reich Health Leader Leonardo Conti; Reich Armaments Minister Fritz Todt; Adolf Hühnlein, head of the National Socialist Motor Corps; Fritz Wächtler, who on Hans Schemm's death in a plane accident in 1935 was made head of the NSLB; and Viktor Lutze, Röhm's replacement as SA chief of staff. With the exception of Wächtler, none of them had an official interest in ideology. As Lammers' notes put it, Goebbels, Frick, and Himmler "voiced criticisms and desired changes." Rust and Walter Schultze, the Reich Leader of University Teachers (*Reichsdozentenführer*) were "substantially more reserved." Bouhler and Robert Ley, the man who provided Rosenberg with his Führer's Delegate title in the first place, were totally opposed.[114] Rosenberg's opponents not only included defenders of Christianity: More important was the fact that all of them, to varying degrees, staked their own claim to ideological oversight. Ley was no friend of Christianity, but he was active in the erection of Adolf Hitler Schools. Even Himmler, who of any party leader was the most in tune with Rosenberg's ideas, was apprehensive.

To resolve the question of Rosenberg's appointment, Hitler convened a meeting on 9 February 1940. Present were Rosenberg, Lammers, Goebbels, Rust, Kerrl, Ley, Bouhler, Heydrich, and a representative from Ribbentrop's Foreign Ministry. The most persistent opponent was Kerrl, who noted that: "The Third Reich needs Christianity and the churches because it has nothing to replace the Christian religion and Christian morality.... His appointment will result in marked unrest among the *Volk*, which is precisely what we must avoid during the war under all circumstances." Goebbels raised unspecified concerns, and the Foreign Ministry pointed to the impact such an appointment would have in relations with the Vatican.[115] In the following days, Hitler mulled over his decision. Significantly, he cited Kerrl's concerns as the most compelling for canceling Rosenberg's new post. As Lammers wrote, "The Führer did not share the foreign policy objections of the Reich Foreign Minister. With the objections raised by the Reich Church Minister the Führer reluctantly agreed."[116] When Hitler explained his decision to

[112] Reinhard Bollmus, *Das Amt Rosenberg und seine Gegner: Studien zum Machtkampf im Nationalsozialistischen Herrschaftssystem* (Stuttgart, 1970), 131.
[113] Ibid., 131–2.
[114] IfZ Fa 199/47/81-82 (January 1940: Berlin).
[115] IfZ Fa 199/47/85-89 (10 February 1940: Berlin).
[116] IfZ Fa 199/47/95-96 (21 February 1940: Berlin).

Rosenberg, he professed that "Mussolini asked him three times to undertake nothing against the Church."[117] However, Rosenberg indicated in a letter to Lammers that he suspected Kerrl was behind the decision.[118]

A victim once more of the party's internal social Darwinism and confined to his preexisting offices, Rosenberg continued to do battle with his opponents. Almost from the start, one particularly hostile adversary had been Goebbels. If Goebbels on past occasion had found countless opportunities to pour derision on Rosenberg, he now directly contested Rosenberg's authority as the Führer's Delegate through his power to prohibit publication. One particularly noteworthy case concerned a short book by Hans Blöthner entitled *Gott und Volk* ("God and People"). It was a strongly anti-Christian book and was published anonymously. Almost as soon as it came out, party members began to complain about it. One letter addressed to Rosenberg attacked the book on the grounds that "the power source of our belief in the Führer, in Germany, in the victory of truth and righteousness...is the positive Christian faith in the sense of Point 24 of the Party Program, but never the dogmatic beliefs of the confessions and other international sects falsified by the Jews." Revealing himself to be a member of the DC, this party member asked that the book be withdrawn.[119] Another party member, describing himself as a "Christian and National Socialist," regretted that the book had received the endorsement of Ley's organization. As much as he agreed with some of the attacks made against the churches, he counseled against "pouring the baby out with the bath water [*dem Kind mit dem Bade auszuschütten*]." At the very least, this Nazi estimated, it would offend the religious sensibilities of 95% of the German population.[120]

In August 1941, Rosenberg's Office of Ideological Information appraised the book. The reviewer noted the following passage as particularly relevant: "We respect this Jesus of Nazareth. But we do not love him. As our leader [*Führer*] we reject him." The reviewer disagreed with another passage, "How should we educate our children? As if they had never heard of Christianity," adding that one can fight an enemy only by knowing him. The book was nonetheless certified "acceptable" for the party's educational work.[121] Soon free copies were made available to soldiers of the Wehrmacht. A flood

---

[117] Seraphim (ed.), *Tagebuch*, entry for 3 March 1940.

[118] IfZ Fa 199/47/98-99 (9 March 1940: Berlin). There is some uncertainty surrounding Bormann's role in this episode. Conway claims that Bormann was particularly favorable to Rosenberg's quest for state power and makes no mention of the fact that Rosenberg actually lost this battle: John Conway, *Persecution*, 250–1. On the other hand, Jochen von Lang states that Bormann was against Rosenberg, and furthermore contends that Bormann carefully manipulated events to ensure Rosenberg's defeat: Lang, *Secretary*, 132. However, neither the primary sources nor the two main Rosenberg biographies, Cecil's *Myth of the Master Race* and Bollmus' *Das Amt Rosenberg*, make any reference to Bormann's opinion or his role in the decision-making process.

[119] BAP 62 Di 1/37-1/128 (24 June 1941: Dresden).

[120] BAP 62 Di 1/37-1/116 (15 August 1941: Neustadt i.Sa.).

[121] BAP 62 Di 1/37-1/76–78 (19 August 1941: Berlin).

of complaints written by non–party members soon surfaced, one of them complaining that Roosevelt's comments about Nazism being anti-Christian looked to be coming true.[122] By December 1941, Goebbels had the book banned. In June 1942, an official from the Propaganda Ministry informed Rosenberg's office that the book could be reissued only if large sections were rewritten and the manuscript sent over to his offices for inspection.[123] The Office of Ideological Information complained that this was an infringement on their territory.[124]

The activities of the RPL also point to a positive attitude toward Christianity and the continuing presence of Christians in the party. One such example was the case of Kurt Lehmann, a party speaker who worked for the office. In 1938 Lehmann wrote a short book titled *Deutschtum und positives Christentum* ("Germandom and Positive Christianity"). Conforming to the basic contours of DC theology, it upheld the need to reject the Old Testament, firmly defended the New Testament against attacks from paganists, and argued that Jesus was an Aryan.[125] Shortly after the book was published, however, an officer in the RPL revoked the author's speaking privileges. Lehmann immediately began to defend himself, pointing out that approval to publish the book had been granted by Bouhler's PPK, adding that both the deputy *Gauleiter* of Berlin, Arthur Görlitzer, and the *Gau* propaganda leader had found nothing objectionable in the book.[126] His case was discussed further and Goebbels' personal views solicited: Lehmann was given his job back.[127]

Martin Bormann, although never a "paganist," emerged as the leading anticlerical and anti-Christian in the later years of the Third Reich. As a party functionary working almost entirely behind the scenes, he was totally unknown to the German public. For most of the Third Reich he was chief of staff for Rudolf Hess, the Führer's Deputy. Hess, although nominally behind only Hitler and Göring in the party hierarchy, was largely uninfluential. Acting only in accord with Hitler's wishes, he represented no particular tendency and had no ideological agendas himself. As someone largely uninterested in power politics, Hess left the field to Bormann, who was interested in little else. Through his personal control of increasing portions of the bureaucratic machinery of the party, Bormann was able to accrue more and more power to himself. After Hess' flight to England in 1941, Bormann became head of the newly created Party Chancellery, a position that increased his power further. As Hitler's secretary, Bormann had control over Hitler's appointments, deciding who could see the Führer and who could not. One of Bormann's biographers has gone so far as to suggest

[122] BAZ NS 8/204/165 (12 November 1941: Munich[?]).
[123] BAP 62 Di 1/37-1/19-20 (15 June 1942: Berlin).
[124] BAP 62 Di 1/37-1/21-22 (n.d.[1942]: Berlin)
[125] BAP NS 18/94 (7 October 1942: Berlin).
[126] BAP NS 18/94 (10 October 1942:Berlin).
[127] BAP NS 18/94 (8 February 1943: Berlin).

that it was Bormann, and not Hitler, who ran Nazi Germany in its last years.[128]

Bormann, an ideological dilettante even by Rosenberg's standards, undertook to fulfill his vision of Nazi religious policy. Many of the anticlerical policies initiated by the party after 1937 were conceived by him. He took part in the removal of Josef Wagner from office, and he was intimately involved both in the banning of party leaders from holding office in religious organizations and in the attempted expulsion of pastors from the party. He is almost universally regarded as one of Nazism's most extreme opponents of the churches.[129] As Albert Speer recalled, "He was the driving force behind the [anti-church] campaign, as was time and again made plain at our round table."[130] While still Hess' chief of staff, Bormann led the campaign to seize Catholic Church property, most notably the monasteries that lay in the newly annexed territories such as Austria. These measures then reached into the *Altreich*, including Bavaria and the Rhineland.[131] Bormann was also in the forefront of attacks on religious instruction. By incremental measures he sought to remove Christian influence. As he wrote to Rosenberg in February 1940, "Christianity and National Socialism are phenomena that originated from entirely different causes. Fundamentally both differ so strongly that it would not be possible to conduct a Christian teaching which would be completely compatible with the point of view of the National Socialist ideology."[132] When Adolf Wagner, Schemm's successor as Bavarian Minister of Education and Culture, attempted in 1941 to remove religious iconography from the schools in the famous "Crucifix Affair," Reich Governor Epp noted that "Wagner wanted in his way to give visible effect to the teaching handed down by Reich Leader Bormann, that National Socialism and Christianity are irreconcilable opposites."[133] For Wagner it was an incredible blunder; the action provoked such unrest that Hitler personally interceded to reverse the order, threatening Wagner that he would send him to Dachau "if he should do anything so stupid again."[134]

[128] See the rather sensationally titled biography of Jochen von Lang, *The Secretary – Martin Bormann: The Man who Manipulated Hitler* (New York, 1979). Von Lang relies in good part on the characterizations of Bormann found in Albert Speer, *Inside the Third Reich* (New York, 1970).

[129] Besides Lang, *Secretary*, 125–132, 182–191, see Joachim Fest, *The Face of the Third Reich: Portraits of the Nazi Leadership* (New York, 1970), 132–3; Conway, *Persecution*, 188–9, 255–8; Speer, *Inside*, 95.

[130] Speer, *Inside*, 125.

[131] E.D.R. Harrison, "The Nazi Dissolution of the Monasteries: A Case-Study," *English Historical Review* 99 (1994), especially 325–27.

[132] BAZ NS 8/183/54-57 (22 February 1940: Berlin).

[133] Quoted in Ian Kershaw, *Popular Opinion and Political Dissent in the Third Reich: Bavaria, 1933–1945* (Oxford, 1983), 353. The Crucifix Affair is covered in detail in idem., 340–57 and Peterson, *Limits*, 216–21. For a similar episode in Northern Germany, see Jeremy Noakes, "The Oldenburg Crucifix Struggle of November 1936: A Case of Opposition in the Third Reich," in Peter Stachura (ed.), *The Shaping of the Nazi State* (London, 1978).

[134] Peterson, *Limits*, 219.

Just a month after taking over from Hess and being named head of the new Party Chancellery, Bormann wrote a secret circular on his view of the Christian religion, distributed only to *Gauleiter*. In it he made clear that he is justly regarded as the leading anticlerical force in Nazism:

National Socialist and Christian conceptions are incompatible. The Christian churches build on peoples' uncertainty and attempt to maintain this fear in the widest possible section of the population, since only in this way can the Christian churches keep their power. By contrast National Socialism rests upon *scientific* foundations. Christianity has inalterable foundations, which were established almost 2000 years ago and which have stiffened into dogmas alien to reality. On the other hand, National Socialism, if its task is to be fulfilled, must always be geared towards the newest findings of scientific research.... It follows from the incompatibility of National Socialist and Christian concepts that we are to reject a strengthening of existing Christian confessions. A distinction between the various Christian confessions cannot be made. For this reason the thought of creating a Protestant Reich Church through a union of the various Protestant churches has definitely been given up, because the Protestant church is just as hostile to us as the Catholic church.... the church must never again be permitted to influence the guidance of the *Volk*.[135]

According to Joachim Fest, "Before the ideology of National Socialism [Bormann] was as helpless as before intellectual matters in general.... National Socialism meant to him not so much a faith as an instrument of his ambition.... It was this will to power too, and not any ideological opposition, that made him one of the most extreme opponents of the churches."[136] It is true that Bormann displayed no particular animus against the churches early in the party's history. He married into a particularly pious family and, unlike Rosenberg, did not leave the Protestant Church until *Kirchenaustritt* became fashionable. Bormann seems to have been unaware of the vast range of attitudes toward science among the Christian confessions and toward modernity in general. If he made life difficult for many Christians in the party, and perhaps unsurprisingly counted Himmler among his few friends, he was also on very good terms with Erich Koch.[137] However, regardless of his true motives or what he thought he knew about Christianity, he remained the most active opponent of clerical influence. In addition, his battles against the party's positive Christians constituted the most heated moments in the contest for ideology.

That Bormann was by far the most radical of anti-Christians in the NSDAP is revealed in his institutional combat with other leading Nazis, including Rosenberg himself. Whereas he often overruled nominal colleagues in forcing through his agenda, more adept party leaders were effectively able to obstruct his anticlerical and anti-Christian zeal. A case of the former

[135] BAP NS 6/336/18-22 (9 June 1941: Munich). Also reprinted in Conway, *Persecution*, 383–6.
[136] Fest, *Face*, 132.
[137] Lang, *Secretary*, 170–1, 318–19. Nowhere in his book does Lang mention Koch's church activities.

was Bormann's involvement in education. Before the Seizure of Power, the Nazis made no pretense that they were in favor of confessional schools. Some Nazis displayed a preference for the Protestant over Catholic school, but this was only in relation to those areas of Germany, like Bavaria, with a strong Catholic majority. In Bavaria particularly, Nazi authorities saw to it that Protestants gained control over the school system. Against this background it is no accident that Hans Schemm became the first Protestant ever to hold the portfolio of Bavarian *Kultus* Minister. At the same time that they forced through "deconfessionalization," party leaders insisted that the "German State School" would retain a Christian element. Leading school policy-makers, such as Rust and Schemm, were equally insistent that the new school in Germany, if no longer confessional, would still be positive Christian. Even after Schemm's death, when his offices were taken over by more anticlerical comrades, there was agreement that Christian instruction would retain its presence.[138]

Bormann, however, contested the qualified Christian mien of the Nazi school and did battle with Rust in the process. Rust in turn tried to forestall Bormann's measures where he could. For instance, in November 1938 the NSLB declared that the murder of Ambassador Rath in Paris at the hands of a young Jew had filled them with a desire for revenge. This event was used throughout Germany as a pretext for *Kristallnacht*; the members of the NSLB reacted by "spontaneously" deciding they would no longer conduct Christian religious instruction in school, thereby indicating that they considered Christianity equivalent to Judaism.[139] Given their history under Schemm, this seemed like an incredible step for the NSLB to take. Even its new head, Wächtler, had rejected the idea of removing religious instruction from the curriculum when the DGB had suggested it two years before.[140] Rust, asked by Kerrl to look into the matter, was informed by Gauleiter Kaufmann of Hamburg that the "spontaneous" action had in fact been ordered by Bormann.[141] A few days later Rust countermanded Bormann and ordered that religious instruction in the schools was to continue as before.[142] Bormann tried again the next year, when he informed Rust that he wanted to see theological faculties at universities phased out. If legal obstacles got in the way, preventing such faculties from being eliminated altogether, Bormann instructed that they at least be cut back substantially.[143] Bormann's power had already grown since the murder of Rath, and Rust found it harder to fight him off this time. He tried through negotiations and bureaucratic

[138] For Adolf Wagner's *Gau*, see "Das Ende der Konfessionsschule im Gau München-Oberbayern: in Zukunft nur mehr christliche Deutsche Volksschule," *VB*, 21 June 1937: in BAZ NS 26/1323.
[139] BAP R43 II/157/83-85 (26 November 1938: Berlin).
[140] BAP R5101/23139/443 (2 February 1936: Bayreuth).
[141] BAP R43 II/157/103-104 (2 December 1938: Berlin).
[142] BAP R43 II/157/105-6 (2 December 1938: Berlin).
[143] BAZ NS 8/184/208 (27 April 1940: Berlin).

red tape to delay this action, and he knew that Göring, for one, was on his side, as was Goebbels to a certain extent.[144]

There were similar confrontations with other Nazi leaders. Bormann attacked Baldur von Schirach for leaving Sundays open in the HJ for church services and later for being too friendly with clergy in his new office as *Gauleiter* of Vienna. Albert Speer also ran afoul of Bormann's anticlericalism. Undertaking the remodeling of Berlin according to Hitler's grandiose plans, Speer approached Protestant and Catholic authorities to discuss the location of churches in what would be the new sections of the capital. Bormann reprimanded him, instructing him that there were to be no new churches in the rebuilt areas.[145] Speer found a way around Bormann's animosity after church buildings started to receive damage in bombing raids. Certain *Gauleiter* wanted to take the opportunity to raze such churches as "citadels of reaction." Speer was able to preserve them, however, by stating that they were "historically and artistically important monuments." It was an argument that worked again when Bormann criticized Speer for devoting material to the repair of these buildings.[146]

Astonishingly, even Rosenberg came in for Bormann's criticism. We have seen that Rosenberg's hostility to Christianity was far from consistent. Nonetheless, judging from his own battles with other leaders and offices, he could hardly be seen as too soft. Several enlightening exchanges between Bormann and Rosenberg demonstrate how Bormann went beyond the pale of conventional paganist thinking on this subject. In January 1940, Rosenberg had described as "excellent" a new book written by Reich Bishop Müller for German soldiers. A few days later, he received a testy letter from Bormann: "I feel differently, since, through this book, soldiers who were lost to Christianity will be reacquainted with partially disguised Christian ideas." He then went on to suggest that Rosenberg's office was not doing its job properly.[147] Rosenberg defended himself by reminding Bormann that it was written, after all, by a Protestant cleric: Had a Reich or *Gau* Leader written it, then his reaction would have been more justified.[148] A month later, Rosenberg received another chilly letter from Bormann, this time accusing him of inviting Müller to help him develop a party plan for religious education in the schools. Bormann rejected this as an attempted synthesis with Christianity.[149] Rosenberg wrote back, assuring Bormann that at no point had he approached Müller with such an idea.[150] Rosenberg took the opportunity to return fire the next year after Bormann came out with his confidential

---

[144] Lang, *Secretary*, 130. See BAP R43 II/157/143 (26 April 1940: Berlin) for the plan, which specifically mentions Göring's approval.
[145] Speer, *Inside*, 177.
[146] Ibid., 314–15.
[147] BAZ NS 8/183/153 (18 January 1940: Berlin).
[148] IfZ MA 544 (20 January 1940: Berlin).
[149] BAZ NS 8/183/54-57 (22 February 1940: Berlin).
[150] BAZ NS 8/183/43-45 (27 February 1940: Berlin).

anti-Christian tract. Almost immediately after it was released, Hitler suppressed it, ordering Bormann to retract his statements and recover all the copies he had sent out. Others in the party, particularly Goebbels, castigated him for writing such an inopportune attack on the churches.[151] Rosenberg added his voice as well, insisting as usual that any discussion of religious matters was his responsibility alone, but adding with unusual derision that the piece "contains several misconceptions."[152]

This mild setback notwithstanding, Bormann did not relent in his attempts to outdo Rosenberg. One occasion concerned a body established by the Protestant Church called the Institute for the Study and Eradication of Jewish Influence on German Church Life. Founded in Eisenach under the leadership of New Testament scholar Walter Grundmann, the institute was run in conjunction with both Protestant Church and Reich governments.[153] Even though Grundmann had been critical of Rosenberg in a book published in 1933,[154] Rosenberg supported the work of the Institute. In 1942, three years after the Institute was founded, Bormann wrote to Rosenberg, suggesting that he was getting himself unduly involved in church affairs.[155] Bormann also wrote to the Church Ministry, suggesting that state authorities should cut their formal association with the institute, as it was a purely ecclesiastical undertaking.[156] Bormann also criticized and undercut Rosenberg's actions in the field of religion as Reich Minister for the Occupied East. Looking for ways to endear the Slavic population to Nazi rule, in February 1942 Rosenberg suggested that religious tolerance be reintroduced into the conquered territories.[157] This was part of Rosenberg's larger scheme to create a system of satellite states under Nazi suzerainty. Nearly all other Nazis, however, wished to exploit the occupied east ruthlessly, and, viewing Slavs as *Untermenschen*, had little regard for their religious liberties. Bormann voiced objections to Rosenberg's plan, specifically the idea of resurrecting the Orthodox Church, as this would likely turn into a locus of resistance. Instead, Bormann suggested that religious bodies would remain local in scope, undercutting the potential of a united front. He furthermore suggested that local Nazi potentates sign the decree, and not Rosenberg, as his signature on the document would give encouragement to the churches back in the *Altreich*.[158]

---

[151] Lang, *Secretary*, 189.
[152] IfZ MA 545 (8 September 1941: Berlin).
[153] See Susannah Heschel, "Nazifying Christian Theology: Walter Grundmann and the Institute for the Study and Eradication of Jewish Influence on German Church Life," *Church History* 63 (1994), 587–604.
[154] Walter Grundmann, *Gott und Nation: Ein evangelisches Wort zum Wollen des Nationalsozialismus und zu Rosenbergs Sinndeutung* (Berlin, 1933).
[155] BAZ NS 8/187/160 (1 June 1942: Führerhauptquartier).
[156] BAZ NS 8/187/52-54 (25 September 1942: Führerhauptquartier).
[157] Robert Cecil, *The Myth of the Master Race: Alfred Rosenberg and Nazi Ideology* (London, 1972), 205–6.
[158] Ibid., 206.

The two Nazis who could effectively obstruct Bormann on matters of Christianity and the churches were Goebbels and his aide Walter Tiessler, the head of the "Reich Ring" for National Socialist Peoples' Enlightenment and Propaganda within the RPL. As the contact person between Goebbels and Bormann, Tiessler was well placed to act as Goebbels' *agent provocateur* in heading off Bormann's extremism. One of the first such opportunities arose with the strong denunciation of euthanasia that came from Bishop Galen's sermon of August 1941. On 13 August, ten days after Galen spoke, Bormann declared that Galen deserved the death sentence. The local *Gauleiter* suggested that he be imprisoned for the rest of the war. There was a general feeling among party radicals that, if Galen did not receive punishment in some way, the prestige of the party and state would suffer.[159] However, Goebbels intervened against this group, warning that "if anything were done against the bishop, the population of Münster could be regarded as lost to the war effort, and the same could confidently be said of the whole of Westphalia."[160] Goebbels prevailed: Nothing was done against Galen.

Of the many party voices to be heard against Galen, Tiessler's was perhaps the most damning; he recommended that Galen should be hanged. Scholars usually regard this sentiment as the most radical of any that were expressed over the affair.[161] In fact, Tiessler, working with Goebbels, had an entirely different motive for making this statement. In a postwar interview, he maintained that "Goebbels' method was one of involving very sensitive and timely psychological devices to corner Bormann, by pushing, even forcing him to retreat from his radical positions on [church] questions." According to Tiessler, Goebbels knew that the most radical voice against Galen would be Bormann's, who had little sense of restraint when it came to attacking the churches. To prevent his views and influence with Hitler from prevailing, "Goebbels then set Tiessler loose with his cat and mouse ruse by having his man express the most radical opinion possible, thus forcing Bormann to back down. Bormann answered that there was no sense in taking this matter to the Führer, he would never agree."[162] In this way, according to Tiessler, Goebbels was able to outmaneuver Bormann and prevent a public relations disaster.

Because Tiessler's version of events was given in a postwar interview, there is good reason to suspect his interpretation. Like many fellow party members interested in salvaging their reputations, he professed himself innocent of any malevolence during the Third Reich. However, there is ample proof from the contemporary documentation that Tiessler and Goebbels truly sought to

---

[159] Conway, *Persecution*, 281. See as well Friedrich Löffler (ed.), *Bischof Clemens August Graf von Galen: Akten, Briefe und Predigten 1933–1946*, 2 vols. (Paderborn, 1996).

[160] Quoted in Jeremy Noakes and Geoffrey Pridham (eds.), *Nazism 1919–1945: A Documentary Reader*, 3 vols. (Exeter, 1983–8), 3: 1039.

[161] Conway, *Persecution*, 281; Michael Burleigh, *Death and Deliverance: 'Euthanasia' in Germany 1900–1945* (Cambridge, 1994), 178.

[162] IfZ ZS 2327 (30 July 1970: Munich) (original report in English).

undo Bormann's agenda. Claiming that the burdens of war brought a special need for lightness in popular entertainment, in Autumn 1942 Bormann ordered that the performance of religious music should cease for the time being. In place of performances of Christian music, "many more concerts with beloved, beautiful German music" should be performed.[163] Just a few months before, Goebbels had revealed his own view on the issue when he granted permission for church music to be played over state radio.[164] It was Tiessler's opinion that church music had to be respected and valued as "our cultural and musical inheritance." Goebbels, he noted, also wanted this music to be respected, for instance totally rejecting one Nazi's suggestion that the "Matthew Passion" be abolished. Tiessler was even able to evoke Hitler's listening habits in his argument: "Goebbels points out that he finds the Führer in full agreement with him.... If the Führer as a non-Christian nevertheless possesses enough piety to go to the Bayreuth *Festspielhaus* every year and listen for six hours to *Parsifal*, a completely 'Christian' work, then we as National Socialists need be no more negative [about religious music] than the Führer himself."[165] Another officer in the RPL pointed out that Bormann's reference to church music as "heavy" left open the question of what constituted "light" music. In the end Bormann's idea was rejected.[166]

Perhaps the most revealing case of how far removed Bormann's religious ideas were from those of the rest of the party leadership concerned the publication of a book called *Unser Glaube* ("Our Faith"), written by an SS man named Greismayr. As one officer in the RPL noted, the publisher, Nordland Verlag, was owned by Himmler. The book itself took the form of a religious catechism for Nazi ideology. Among other things, its author maintained that in National Socialism there could be no belief in a hereafter. Pointing out that only a "small circle within the party" believed this and that Germans "since the old Teutons" have believed in a hereafter, this officer inquired as to whether the book should be banned.[167] Tiessler passed this matter on to Bormann, who stated that it was not the task of the party to ban the book. Because Germany was a land of "religious freedom," in which everyone could find fulfillment in their own fashion, he had nothing to say against such beliefs. Bormann told Tiessler not to overlook the fact that it was the Christian churches, after all, that had always strongly emphasized belief in the hereafter.[168] Tiessler then solicited the views of Goebbels' long-standing enemy, Rosenberg. He informed Rosenberg that Goebbels wanted the party to make a declaration as to whether a German could still be a National Socialist while believing in a hereafter.

[163] BAP NS 18/529 (16 December 1942: Berlin).
[164] BAP R43 II/151/38 (14 September 1942: Berlin).
[165] BAP NS 18/529 (3 December 1942: Berlin).
[166] BAP NS 18/529 (n.d., n.p.).
[167] BAP NS 18/140 (24 November 1941: Berlin).
[168] BAP NS 18/140 (14 January 1942: Führerhauptquartier).

As Tiessler saw it, two issues in particular needed to be addressed: "Is it un-German to believe in a Hereafter? Is it the task of National Socialism to determine the answer to this question, or is it more correct to let everyone find salvation in his own way?" He warned that "if National Socialism demands of every German that he not believe in any kind of Hereafter, then I see this as an incredibly great danger for the future." Nazism was concerned only with matters of earthly existence, Tiessler insisted, and had no prerogative to cast judgment on the existence of an afterlife. He added that if the party formally declared that members could believe in a hereafter if they wanted to, it would rob the churches of one of their most important arguments against certain elements of Nazism, and therefore expose their real – political – opposition to it.[169] In a subsequent letter, Tiessler also pointed out that Hitler himself had proclaimed in *Mein Kampf* that "a religion in the Aryan sense cannot be imagined which lacks the conviction of survival after death in some form."[170] Rosenberg responded, unambiguously stating that belief in a hereafter was up to the conscience of the individual National Socialist and that denying this right would only lend credence to propaganda about Nazism wanting to destroy religion.[171] Because Bormann as head of the Party Chancellery had the final word, however, no such decree was issued.

The evidence suggests that Bormann was indeed motivated not by a committed ideological opposition to Christianity, but by an attempt to outdo other Nazis, to shame them and thereby bring them under his control. His extremism transgressed the views of radicals like Rosenberg and even Hitler himself and seemed at times to flirt with atheism. In his attempted forays into ideology, he never mentioned Jesus, Luther, or positive Christianity. He seems to have outdone the party's anti-Christians at their own game. Given the many attempts within the party to curb him, it is safe to conclude that, without Bormann, Nazism would not have received quite the same anti-Christian reputation. He remained a party functionary first and foremost. His obsession with the churches, although very real, was as much about asserting his position in the party than it was about a true ideological commitment to Nazism. The singularity of this obsession, most likely based on a febrile need for Hitler's affection and a mounting hatred for his in-laws, arguably constituted a departure from Nazism as much as its most radical expression.

Reinhard Heydrich was, along with Bormann, one of the regime's most adamant anti-Christians. When two Free Czech agents killed Heydrich in Prague in 1942, Nazi anticlericalism lost one of its most effective partisans. However, his hatred of the churches was not regarded as a necessary precondition to succeed him as head of the Reich Security Main Office.

---

[169] BAP NS 18/140 (16 January 1942: Berlin).
[170] BAP NS 18/140 (12 February 1942: Berlin); Adolf Hitler, *Mein Kampf*, trans. Ralph Manheim (Boston, 1962), 306.
[171] BAP NS 18/140 (21 February 1942: Berlin[?]).

Ernst Kaltenbrunner, the head of the Austrian SS, took over this position in 1943. He considerably relaxed Heydrich's anticlerical campaign, already toned down for the sake of the war. This was not just a strategic consideration: According to one of his former associates, Kaltenbrunner did not understand how Heydrich "could harbor such a deadly hatred of the [Catholic] Church."[172] If Kaltenbrunner was not a practicing Catholic, neither had he left the church. In fact, of all his brothers – all involved in the Nazi movement as he was – he was the only one *not* to leave the church. Although Kaltenbrunner persecuted clergy who attacked the Nazi State and professed his opposition to "political Catholicism," he had no patience for Heydrich's anticlerical schemes. At the same time that he was busily doing his best to bring the "Final Solution of the Jewish Question" to its genocidal climax, he disbanded Department IVB ("religious opponents") within the Gestapo, established by Heydrich headed by Albert Hartl, an ex–priest who had turned against his church. Hartl's activities included penetration of Catholic circles and the collection of intelligence. As part of his resentment for being defrocked, he also conjured up schemes for infiltrating the Catholic Church, including sending Nazis into the priesthood to nazify the clergy from within. Kaltenbrunner dismissed the plan as "ridiculous."[173]

REREADING HITLER'S *TABLE TALK*

Hitler's own religious views underwent significant change in the latter half of the Third Reich. He gave up on the Protestant Church after three failed attempts to achieve unity within its ranks. It is only in the period after this failure that we begin to see some of the anti-Christian remarks for which he is so famous. In October 1937, Hitler commented privately: "I have been freed, after an intense inner struggle, from the still living and childish imaginings of religion. . . . I now feel as liberated as a foal in the pasture."[174] Although he did not say so explicitly, the personalistic tone of the comment reveals that this was primarily a reference to his original Catholic faith, not to all religion per se. Whereas Hitler insisted as late as 1938 that he still believed in the party's positive Christianity, on other occasions his tone was very different. In December 1939, for example, Goebbels noted in his diary that "The Führer is deeply religious, but entirely anti-Christian. He regards Christianity as a symptom of decay."[175] As unambiguous as this statement appears, it raises an important question: What was Hitler's religion by this time if

---

[172] Quoted in Peter Black, *Ernst Kaltenbrunner: Ideological Soldier of the Third Reich* (Princeton, 1984), 146.

[173] Ibid., 148. On Kaltenbrunner's furtherance of the Final Solution, see ibid., 149ff.

[174] Max Domarus (ed.), *Hitler: Reden und Proklamationen 1932–1945*, 2 vols. (Würzburg, 1962–4), 1: 745.

[175] Elke Fröhlich (ed.), *Die Tagebücher von Joseph Goebbels: Aufzeichnungen 1923–41* (Munich, 1998), entry for 29 December 1939. Goebbels indicated that he agreed with Hitler on this occasion.

not Christianity? Had Hitler finally converted to Himmler's paganism? Just the day before, Goebbels wrote: "The Führer rejects any thought of founding a religion. He does not want to become a Buddha." On the one hand, Hitler professed to reject Christianity: On the other, he was still religious and adamantly opposed to a replacement faith. It could be that Hitler was no closer to finding a religious home than he had been all those years before in conversation with Ludwig Müller: But it is also possible that he meant "Catholicism" when saying "Christianity."[176]

Publicly as well as privately, Hitler's anticlericalism grew. In a Reichstag speech on 30 January 1939, the sixth anniversary of the Seizure of Power, Hitler warned that "the National Socialist state is at any time ready to undertake a clear separation of church and state, as is already the case in France, America and other countries.... The National Socialist state has not closed a church, nor has it prevented the holding of a religious service, nor has it ever exercised any influence upon the form of a religious service.... But on one point there must be no uncertainty: the German priest as servant of God we shall protect, the priest as political enemy of the German state we will destroy."[177] Even though he threatened potential violence against clergy in this speech, this did not extend to religion itself. Furthermore, the "real" servant of God, the one who presumably preached political quietism if not outright enthusiasm for the state, would find his affections reciprocated.

Hitler's *Table Talk*, a series of wartime conversations he held with his immediate circle of confidants, is widely regarded as *the* source of Hitler's true wartime feelings about Christianity. Whereas the reliability of these conversations is coming under increasing scrutiny – one historian going so far as to suggest that portions of the Trevor–Roper version are actually fraudulent – I will examine *Hitler's Table Talk* due to the importance attached to it by that school which argues that Hitler's "true feelings" about Christianity are to be found here.[178] In contrast with other sources for Hitler's "confidential" views, notably Otto Wagener's memoirs, Hitler's "secret conversations" seem to reveal an unmistakable rupture with his previous religious attitudes. This change from the 1920s and early 1930s is attributable to Hitler's feeling of rage at having been defeated in the arena of Protestant church policy, and with it the belief that the Protestant Church *in toto* could not be counted on to support Nazism. If the Niemöllers of the world were the true representatives

[176] Ibid., entry for 28 December 1939. When attacking Christianity, Hitler contended that both it and Judaism had "comparable religious rites," which would have been truer of Catholicism than of Protestantism.
[177] *Frankfurter Zeitung*, 1 February 1939.
[178] Ian Kershaw alludes to the questionable nature of *Table Talk* as a historical source: see his *Hitler 1889–1936: Hubris* (London, 1998), xiv. Richard Carrier goes further, contending that certain portions of *Table Talk*, especially those regarding Hitler's alleged hatred of Christianity, are outright inventions: see his "*Hitler's Table Talk*: Troubling Finds," *German Studies Review* 26:3 (forthcoming 2003). However, although Kershaw recommends treating the work with caution, he does not suggest dispensing with *Table Talk* altogether. My thanks to Diethelm Prowe for bringing Carrier's forthcoming article to my attention.

of Christianity, Hitler possibly concluded, then Christianity itself must be guilty. In July 1941 he allegedly condemned the religion he had previously esteemed: "The heaviest blow that ever struck humanity was the coming of Christianity; Bolshevism is Christianity's illegitimate child. Both are inventions of the Jews."[179]

Hitler took aim at specific aspects of Christianity. He was particularly severe in his view of Paul, who "transformed a local movement of Aryan opposition to Jewry into a supra-temporal religion, which postulates the equality of all men amongst themselves, and their obedience to an only god. This is what caused the death of the Roman Empire."[180] In June 1942 Hitler apparently rejected Luther's translation of the Bible because "the whole of the German people should have thus become exposed to the whole of this Jewish mumbo-jumbo."[181] Toward the churches, Hitler was never more abusive. For instance, in February 1942 he made the following prophecy: "The evil that's gnawing our vitals is our priests, of both creeds. . . . The time will come when I'll settle my accounts with them."[182] In short, Hitler seemed to have rejected Christianity once and for all: "Pure Christianity – the Christianity of the catacombs – leads quite simply to the annihilation of mankind. It is merely whole-hearted Bolshevism, under a tinsel of metaphysics."[183]

Nevertheless, as in so many other documented instances of Nazi hostility to Christianity, there are notable moments of ambivalence and outright contradiction in the *Table Talk*, moments overlooked in the secondary literature partly because they are buried in conversations on other topics. Most significantly, and consistent with his previous attitudes, Hitler continued to hold Jesus in high esteem. On one such occasion, he proclaimed: "The Galilean, who later was called the Christ, intended something quite different. He must be regarded as a popular leader who took up his position against Jewry. . . . He set Himself against Jewish capitalism, and that is why the Jews liquidated Him."[184] This interpretation of Jesus – as the messenger of a new belief who had been betrayed by a corrupt establishment – was remarkably consistent with the remarks Hitler made about the churches in the *Kampfzeit*.[185] Hitler showed no willingness to give up on the figure of Jesus, whose status as an Aryan remained unquestioned: "It is certain that Jesus was not a Jew."[186]

---

[179] Adolf Hitler, *Hitler's Table Talk 1941–1944: His Private Conversations*, trans. Norman Cameron and R. H. Stevens, introduction by Hugh Trevor-Roper (London, 1953), 7 (11–12 July 1941). Bormann was in attendance on all occasions. Other members of the audience are listed below when noted in *Table Talk*.

[180] Ibid., 78 (21 October 1941).

[181] Ibid., 513 (5 June 1942).

[182] Ibid., 304 (8 February 1942). Speer and Himmler are indicated as being in the audience on this occasion.

[183] Ibid., 146 (14 December 1941). In attendence were Rosenberg, Bouhler, and Himmler.

[184] Ibid., 76 (21 October 1941).

[185] Otto Wagener, *Hitler: Memoirs of a Confidant*, Henry Ashby Turner (ed.) (New Haven, 1985), 139–40.

[186] *Hitler's Table Talk*, 76 (21 October 1941).

Hitler's conception of Jesus' relevance did seem to change; Jesus' alleged antisemitism was increasingly emphasized at the expense of other qualities Hitler had previously evoked, such as his "socialism." However, even as late as November 1944, just a few months before his death, he stated that "Jesus was most certainly not a Jew. . . . Jesus fought against the materialism of His age, and, therefore, against the Jews."[187]

There are other indicators of ambivalence. No matter how much he vituperated against Christianity or the churches, Hitler gave no indication that he was now agnostic or atheistic: He displayed a continued attachment to a belief in God. In one revealing passage, he actually compared the religious policy of Nazi Germany with that of the Soviet Union:

It's senseless to encourage man in the idea that he's a king of creation, as the scientist of the past century tried to make him believe. . . . The Russians were entitled to attack their priests, but they had no right to assail the idea of a supreme force. It's a fact that we're feeble creatures, and that a creative force exists. . . . it's better to believe something false than not to believe anything at all. Who's that little Bolshevik professor who claims to triumph over creation? People like that, we'll break them. Whether we rely on the catechism or on philosophy, we have possibilities in reserve, whilst they, with their purely materialistic conceptions, can only devour one another.[188]

Hitler's readiness to rely on the catechism in his assault against Marxism brings into question his alleged insistence earlier that Christianity and Marxism were equidistant from Nazism. Hitler's language here makes no specific reference to any kind of personal Christian attachment, striking instead a distinctly theistic note. However, Hitler gave no indication that he ceased believing in an active, providential God in favor of the rationalist, watchmaker God typical of deistic thought.

Other moments in the *Table Talk* reveal a more direct attachment to Christianity. Referring to the Spanish, Hitler said: "What a queer sort of Christianity they practice down there! We must recognize, of course, that amongst us, Christianity is coloured by Germanism. All the same, its doctrine signifies: 'Pray and work'!"[189] Here Hitler echoes the motif of positive Christianity – a positive appraisal of Christianity, contingent on its compatibility with "Germanism." In *Mein Kampf*, Hitler stated his belief that Protestantism had already achieved this goal: "Protestantism will always stand up for the advancement of all Germanism as such, as long as matters of inner purity or national deepening as well as German freedom are involved, since all these things have a firm foundation in its own being."[190] At that point, Hitler already believed that a variety of *preexisting* Christianity held up to his racialist scrutiny. Whereas Hitler clearly rejected the Protestant Churches by 1941, it

---

[187] Ibid., 721 (29–30 November 1944).
[188] Ibid., 86–87 (24 October 1941). In attendance was Lieutenant General von Rintelen.
[189] Ibid., 46 (27–28 September 1941).
[190] Adolf Hitler, *Mein Kampf*, trans. Ralph Manheim (Boston, 1962), 112–13.

is not clear how much of the Protestant religion itself was to be rejected along with it. On another occasion, he commented positively on one of the basic cornerstones of Christian belief: "The Ten Commandments are a code of living to which there's no refutation. These precepts correspond to irrefragable needs of the human soul; they're inspired by the best religious spirit, and the Churches here support themselves on a solid foundation."[191] Hitler's positive reference here is all the more surprising given that Christianity shares the Ten Commandments with Judaism, a fact that seems to have troubled Hitler not at all.[192]

A particularly noteworthy example of Hitler's ambivalence is provided in a rant against Roosevelt. Hitler derides Roosevelt on several grounds throughout *Table Talk*. On this occasion he responds to Roosevelt's recent claim that Nazism was anti-Christian. In particularly striking form, Hitler revealed the limits of his apostasy: "What repulsive hypocrisy that arrant Freemason, Roosevelt, displays when he speaks of Christianity! All the Churches should rise up against him – for he acts on principles diametrically opposed to those of the religion of which he boasts."[193] Hitler makes no claim here to be Christian. However, he is nonetheless irritated that his enemy Roosevelt should call *himself* Christian. There is no record of Hitler's expressing irritation when Stalin spoke of himself as a Marxist. Had Hitler truly given up on Christianity and demoted it to the level of Judaism and Bolshevism, as he professed to do elsewhere, he would have felt no compulsion to protect it from Roosevelt's "repulsive hypocrisy." Hitler revealed outright contradiction when he spoke of Luther and his achievements. In July 1941, he hailed Luther and his translation of the Bible as revolutionary: "Luther had the merit of rising against the Pope and the organisation of the Church. It was the first of the great revolutions. And thanks to his translation of the Bible, Luther replaced our dialects by the great German language!"[194]

Aside from the *Table Talk*, other sources point not just to ambivalence, but to a continuing positive Christian attitude in Hitler. As Albert Speer recalled, "Even after 1942 Hitler went on maintaining that he regarded the church as indispensable in political life. He would be happy, he said in one of those teatime talks at Obersalzberg, if someday a prominent churchman turned up who was suited to lead one of the churches – or if possible both the Catholic and Protestant churches reunited."[195] If true, Speer's observation

---

[191] *Hitler's Table Talk*, 85 (24 October 1941). Von Rintelen in attendance.

[192] This sharply contradicts Rauschning's contention that Hitler had rejected the Ten Commandments, allegedly quoting Hitler as saying "The Ten Commandments have lost their validity": Hermann Rauschning, *The Voice of Destruction* (New York, 1940), 24. On the unreliability of Rauschning as a primary source, see Chapter 1.

[193] *Hitler's Table Talk*, 125 (11 November 1941).

[194] Ibid., 9 (21–22 July 1941).

[195] Speer, *Inside*, 95.

would contradict the picture of Hitler's anticlericalism obtained from other sources. Speer suggested that Hitler often tailored his remarks to suit his audience, something that a host of historians has also argued.[196] However, pointing to a Janus-faced Hitler no more proves the deceitfulness of pro-Christian remarks than it does the sincerity of anti-Christian remarks.[197] Speer himself made the following observation: "If in the course of such a monologue Hitler had pronounced a more negative judgment upon the church, Bormann would undoubtedly have taken from his jacket pocket one of the white cards he always carried with him."[198]

Regardless of the question of *Table Talk's* authenticity, Hitler's capacity for self-contradiction is well documented. Nonetheless, on some subjects he remained consistent. He never demoted Jesus, regardless of his audience. And, whether in the back rooms of his Berlin headquarters or in teatime chats at Obersalzberg, Hitler remained consistent in his negative assessment of paganism. In Obersalzberg he said: "A new party religion would only bring about a relapse into the mysticism of the Middle Ages. The growing SS myth showed that clearly enough, as did Rosenberg's unreadable *Myth of the Twentieth Century*."[199] By comparison, the private Hitler stated: "I must insist that Rosenberg's 'Myth of the Twentieth Century' is not to be regarded as an expression of the official doctrine of the Party. . . . It is interesting to note that comparatively few of the older members of the Party are to be found among the readers of Rosenberg's book, and that the publishers had, in fact, great difficulty in disposing of the first edition."[200] Not once did Hitler have anything positive to say about paganism. At Obersalzberg as well as "in secret," Hitler indicated that he still approved the idea of a Christian state church, even though he had given up on its practicability in the German case. Publicly he proclaimed: "Through me the Protestant Church could become the established church, as in England"[201]; and privately, in December 1941,

---

[196] See *inter alia* Timothy Mason, "Intention and Explanation: A Current Controversy about the Interpretation of National Socialism," in Gerhard Hirschfeld and Lothar Kettenacker (eds.), *Der 'Führerstaat': Mythos und Realität* (Stuttgart, 1981), 33. Mason's observation is made in the context of Hitler's military strategy.

[197] For instance, of the five anti-Christian passages quoted from *Table Talk* above, two were uttered in the presence of Himmler, who was not in Hitler's audience in any of the passages favorable to Christianity. Himmler was present neither for the pro- nor the anti-Luther comments Hitler made. Bormann, however, was present on all occasions.

[198] Speer, *Inside*, 95. Speer's book has been critiqued for myth making, but this critique has been limited to Speer's justification of his own role in the Nazi State. None of the authors who convincingly point to the fallacies found in Speer's memoirs dispute the pictures he paints of other Nazis, and none specifically refer to the portrayal of Hitler's religious views as spurious. See Gitta Sereny, *Albert Speer: His Battle with Truth* (New York, 1995); Matthias Schmidt, *Albert Speer: The End of a Myth* (New York, 1984); Dan van der Vat, *The Good Nazi: The Life and Lies of Albert Speer* (London, 1997).

[199] Speer, *Inside*, 95.

[200] *Hitler's Table Talk*, 422 (11 April 1942).

[201] Speer, *Inside*, 95.

"Against a Church that identifies itself with the State, as in England, I have nothing to say."[202]

The continued inspiration Hitler professed to gain from Christ as the "original antisemite" points to the possibility as well of an ongoing Christian element in Hitler's antisemitism. In *Table Talk*, Hitler makes no direct statement that his antisemitism was religious rather than racial. However, his political testament, written just a few days before his death, contains a highly relevant passage about the nature of his hatred: "We speak of the Jewish race only as a linguistic convenience, for in the true sense of the word, and from a genetic standpoint, *there is no Jewish race*. . . . The Jewish race is above all a community of the spirit. Anthropologically the Jews do not exhibit those common characteristics that would identify them as a uniform race. . . . A spiritual race is harder and more lasting than a natural race."[203] With one stroke Hitler apparently discarded the flimsy discursive apparatus he and his movement had used with such regularity to prove that Nazi antisemitism, unlike previous forms of Jew hatred, was "scientific." Rejecting the notion that the Jews were a biological race implicitly meant that the idea of biological antisemitism – never a clean category in the first place – was also to be rejected.[204] In this instance, at least, we see not an interweaving or cohabitation of racial and religious categories of the Jew, but a simple denial of the racial category altogether. As Hitler stated in his secret conversations, Christ understood the danger of the Jews and led an inspired struggle against them. If Hitler made no explicit statement that killing the Jews was revenge for the death of Christ or for the refusal of Jews to recognize Christ as the Lord, he nonetheless believed that Christ "fought" the Jews and that they "liquidated" him. Christ's affirmative example was returned to again and again, throughout the period of the Final Solution.

What do we make of the conflicting evidence? In previous years Hitler had always been able to detach Christianity from the churches. Several passages of *Table Talk*, however, reveal no such distinction. We can conclude therefore that between these later "conversations" and earlier ones lies at least a difference of degree. But we can see considerable equivocation in Hitler as well. Hitler rejected the German churches in the end. Nonetheless, he indicated more than once that he would have preferred a different outcome – on his own terms. Had the Protestant Churches fallen into line in the way

---

[202] *Hitler's Table Talk*, 143 (13 December 1941). In attendance were Ribbentrop, Rosenberg, Goebbels, Terboven, and Bouhler.

[203] Adolf Hitler, *Politisches Testament: Die Bormann-Diktate vom Februar und April 1945* (Hamburg, 1981), 68–9 (emphasis added).

[204] This goes against the argument of Gavin Langmuir, who, like many other scholars of antisemitism insists that "When Hitler thought of 'Jews,' he thought about an imaginary race whose members' horrifyingly evil moral and social ideas and characteristics could not be changed because they were inescapably determined by biological characteristics that might be diluted but could not be changed." Gavin Langmuir, "Continuities, Discontinuities and Contingencies of the Holocaust," in Jonathan Frankel (ed.), *The Fate of the European Jews, 1939–1945: Continuity or Contingency?* (Oxford, 1997), 25.

Hitler had hoped, his wartime rhetoric would very likely not have been so hostile. Totally absent, besides Hitler's vague ranting, is any firm evidence that Hitler or the Nazis were going to "destroy" or "eliminate" the churches once the war was over. Hitler may have come to hate them, but he was consistent enough in his concern for German public opinion and his dismissal of paganism that he would have kept the churches in some form. And whereas Ludendorff rejected Christ along with the churches, Hitler consistently refused to go this far. No degree of apparent hostility toward Christianity could turn him to atheism. Hitler's personal religion probably approached theism near the end of his life. However, even assuming that the portion of *Table Talk* concerning Christianity are authentic, Hitler could not have been unaware of contradictions found in many of his statements. For instance, in rejecting Luther's translation of the Bible, Hitler would also have had to reject Luther's creation of the German language, which he looked on as a seminal moment in the birth of German nationhood.

If we read Hitler's comments on religion against the grain, we see a view of Christianity fraught with tension and ambiguity. When Hitler raged against Christianity and the churches, he mobilized the full fury of Nazism's totalizing discourse. Never accepting the concept of a "loyal opposition," he apparently chose to interpret the resistance of *some* churchmen to *some* Nazi policies as total opposition to all Nazi policies. But, in moments when he spoke on other issues, whether it was Spain, Roosevelt, or Bolshevism, he revealed that he was not ready to destroy his former faith.

CONCLUSION

In the latter years of the regime, many Nazi leaders expressed antagonism to Christianity. In addition to the paganists who had always expressed their hostility, there emerged a new opponent in Martin Bormann. Largely because of his increasing hold on power, Bormann was able to effect increasingly bold anticlerical actions as the war drew closer. Such measures were largely halted in wartime, but there was little doubt that the Nazi regime had definitively turned against the institutions of Christianity. The mass exodus from the church and the attempted expulsion of clergy from the party demonstrate a fundamental rupture in party–church relations.

As firmly anticlerical as the regime became, there was real and persistent disagreement as to the continuing place of Christians and their religion in the movement. As rival party offices fought with Rosenberg on the terrain of ideological protection, they revealed a more positive assessment of Christianity than did the Führer's Delegate for Ideology. Their differences over religion played an important role in the polycratic struggle for Hitler's favor. Rosenberg, always blocked in his quest for power, was defeated in his final bid for ideological hegemony precisely on the question of Christianity. Party Christians, both prominent and unknown, continued their religious practices, while certain paganists – most notably Himmler – revealed in startling fashion that their hatred of Christianity had less to do with Christian teachings than with the perceived manipulation of religion by institutional enemies. The "blank slate" of the Warthegau, the testing ground for the unhindered implementation of Nazi ideology, revealed that church institutions, although totally severed from the state and strongly curtailed in their activities, would nonetheless find a place in the future Nazi utopia. If the failure of the Reich Church had closed Nazi minds to clerical involvement in the state, it did not lead to an effort to destroy or dismantle the churches. Their basic right to exist was ultimately affirmed.

Bormann was the most radical of Nazism's anti-Christians. More than just initiating most anticlerical and anti-Christian actions in the later years of the Reich, Bormann came into direct conflict with other party members – no less committed to Nazism than he – over the escalating campaign against Christianity. Nazi anticlericalism would have existed without extremists like Bormann, but it very likely would not have taken the same shape or been as harsh. The example of Ernst Kaltenbrunner, in no way as anticlerical as his predecessor Heydrich, shows how the actions of a few Nazi anti-Christians were not necessarily representative of their movement as a whole. Had the "persecution" of the churches been as important to the regime as the persecution of Jews, Marxists, or other *Reichsfeinde*, Kaltenbrunner's tolerance toward them would have been entirely unacceptable.

The contradictions and inconsistencies found in *Table Talk* on many issues make it impossible to claim to know Hitler's mind. Nonetheless, certain tendencies in his thought are discernible. Even though he never converted to paganism, Hitler nonetheless became increasingly opposed to Christian institutions and, on the face of it, to the Christian religion as well. However, the process was not as clear as historical analysis generally suggests. In fact, Hitler's professed hatred of Christianity was shot through with ambiguity and contradiction. Even as he accused Christianity of being Jewish and Bolshevik, at all times he carefully protected the Jew Jesus from his attacks. According to Hitler, Christ's "original message" could still be detached from what was later called Christianity. In other words, Hitler continued his long-held belief that the unfettered ideas of Christ were different from the ideas of the churches. Elsewhere, Hitler went further, indicating an appreciation for aspects of Christian teaching and even a remorse that the churches had failed to back him and his movement as he had hoped. Although increasingly anticlerical, Hitler put limits on his apostasy.

8

THE HOLY REICH

Conclusion

...whoever kills you will think he is offering a service to God.
John 16:2

Looking to the Holocaust as the ultimate expression of Nazi practice, the sociologist Zygmunt Bauman suggests that Nazism should not be viewed as the failure of civilization, but rather its product: "We suspect (even if we refuse to admit it) that the Holocaust could merely have uncovered another face of the same modern society whose other, more familiar, face we so admire. And that the two faces are perfectly comfortably attached to the same body. What we perhaps fear most, is that each of the two faces can no more exist without the other than can the two sides of a coin."[1] Bauman continues by adding that "often we stop just at the threshold of the awesome truth . . . that every ingredient of the Holocaust – all those things that rendered it possible – was normal."[2] This study has attempted to interrogate the role of Christian belief as one ingredient of that normalcy. Christianity, in the final analysis, did not constitute a barrier to Nazism. Quite the opposite: For many of the subjects of this study, the battles waged against Germany's enemies constituted a war in the name of Christianity. The dualism Bauman alludes to was itself predicated on a dualistic understanding of human behavior hegemonic in Western, Christian civilizations. Nearly all the Nazis surveyed here believed they were defending good by waging war against evil, fighting for God against the Devil, for German against Jew. They were convinced that their movement did not mean the death of God, but the preservation of God.

Two main currents of religious thought, each with their internal nuances and variations, existed in the Nazi movement. One of them, "positive Christianity," proclaimed that Nazism was compatible with, even derived from, varieties of Christian ideology. Positive Christians suggested that Nazism was predicated on a Christian understanding of Germany's ills and their cure. In the eyes of these Nazis, the Jew was an enemy of Christianity as well as of Germany and the Aryan. Marxists and liberals were not simply

---

[1] Zygmunt Bauman, *Modernity and the Holocaust* (Ithaca, 1989), 7.
[2] Ibid., 8–9.

the exponents of rival social theories, but embodied dangers to the moral and ethical beliefs of Aryan/Christian Germans. For the positive Christians of the party, radical upheavals of war and revolution in German society required new, radical solutions. In many ways, the extreme answers these Nazis provided went beyond the previous bounds of Christian practice in Germany. Whereas past forms of Christian politics were known to embrace nationalism, antisemitism, anti-Marxism, or antiliberalism, the Nazis took these ideologies to new levels. For this reason the Nazis represented a departure from previous Christian practices. However, this did not make them un-Christian. Whereas millions of Catholics and Protestants in Germany did not think Nazism represented their interests or aims, there were many others who regarded Nazism as the correct Christian response to what they saw as harsh new realities.

The other principal current of religious thought in the Nazi movement was paganism. One finds distinctions and nuances here as well. Nonetheless, the basic ingredient of paganist belief was the determination to create a new religion that would link the individual directly to God, unfiltered by intermediary, worldly authorities. Proponents of this new religion sought to move Germans' spiritual center from Jerusalem or Rome to Germany and to introduce new objects of worship to the *Volk*. However, even as these paganists professed their detachment from Christianity and rejection of its "stiffened" dogmas, with marked consistency they appropriated Protestantism as a barometer of Germanism. If they rejected Jerusalem, like many positive Christians they hailed Wittenberg. If they dispensed with Christianity as Jewish, they went to considerable lengths to make the Jew Jesus into an Aryan. If they despised Christian meekness and humility, they nonetheless found praise for a Christian social ethic. If they rejected most of Christian dogma, they elevated past Christian figures as the intellectual forefathers of their new system. In these ways, they demonstrated an ambiguous, partial, and often contradictory detachment from Christianity. Rosenberg in particular, convinced that he had successfully outlined a new religious belief system, salvaged many dimensions of the Christian worldview for his new, un-Christian faith.

These two religious strands were not simply window dressing for what was really a secularizing or atheistic movement. Although many Nazis left no record of a religious sensibility one way or the other, positive Christianity and paganism expressed bona fide religious feelings within the party. Professions of Christian feeling were not the product of Nazi mendacity. Nazi actors on the public stage would profess the same Christian sentiments to each other even after the curtain came down. Concomitantly, no paganist who rejected Christianity before the curtain went up appeared on the public stage as anything else. More importantly, both these religious streams found theological and philosophical precedence dating back to before Nazism was founded. Positive Christianity was essentially a syncretic mix of the social and the economic tenets of confessional Lutheranism and the doctrine and ecclesiology of liberal Protestantism. Liberal Protestantism is of particular importance in understanding the racial antisemitism the Nazis would perfect. It represented a Christian response to the theological challenges posed both by secular modernity and the perceived danger of the acculturated and assimilated German Jew. The attempt to meet this challenge came through a theological accommodation with science, one that still preserved the relevance of the Gospels. The growth of Jewish emancipation and conversion to Christianity in the nineteenth century, under the auspices of politically liberal regimes, powerfully determined a racialist reaction within certain nationalist Protestant circles. Not only did racialist antisemitism find a warmer reception among liberal Protestants than among confessional Lutherans, in many ways racialist antisemitism was born of the theological crisis that liberal Protestantism represented.

The racialist departure is displayed not only through the lineages of positive Christian thought, but also through the lineages of overtly anticlerical paganism. A more diffuse set of artists and intellectuals, still pivotally concerned with the preservation of Christ for the modern age, gave rise to a great deal of later paganist thinking. This is especially evident in a racialism and denial of Christ's Jewishness that went beyond what *Kulturprotestanten* had sanctioned. Their own insistence notwithstanding, we should not take at face value Nazi paganist claims that their ideological "program" originated in Nordic legends or other forms of mystical esoterica. These were simply window dressing for an ideology rooted in a different source. That Himmler or Rosenberg proclaimed a new faith based on Wotan, sundials, or mystic runes tells us a great deal about how they spent their spare time, but nothing about the substance of Wotan belief. Despite their insistence that they were basing their new faith on Germany's misty past, Nazi paganists found much of their doctrine in the philosophies of a much more recent past.

Once in power, the ranks of the positive Christians and paganists remained largely stable. The Nazis' gradual acquisition of power in the Third Reich did not mean that the anti-Christians only now revealed their true colors; they had already done so before 1933, and continued to do so afterward, with no regard for public opinion as a stabilizing force for the regime. In just the same way, the party's positive Christians continued to maintain their own positions, both publicly and privately. Never were paganist ideas hegemonic in the movement, as was displayed in the attitudes of the party elite, who heaped public scorn and private ridicule on party comrades who dreamed of implementing the new Nordic religion. The marginality that paganists faced was also displayed in the infighting between them and Christians lower down the ranks of the party's organizations. Particularly revealing was the notable misfortune of the German Faith Movement, the paganist counterpart to the German Christians that never came close to imprinting their own beliefs on the movement as a whole.

In the Third Reich, Nazis undertook to coordinate all aspects of national life into the all-embracing topos of the Nazi worldview. As their totalizing agenda gradually and partially came to fruition, institutional rivals came under increasing attack. The enduring hope among leading Nazis for a Protestant Reich Church – when all other autonomous sources of power in German society were rapidly being suppressed or banned – demonstrates the Nazi leadership's desire to cooperate with a variety of institutional Christianity in the building of a new Germany. Those Nazis who sought such a relationship were attempting both to enter into and to extend an historical coupling of Germanness and Protestantism embedded in nationalist ideology and discourse. The amount of effort the Nazis put into the *Deutsche Christen* early on (in spite of Rosenberg's hostility) and Hitler's creation of a ministry designed to deal with a fractured church situation, was not the product of hostility toward the Protestant Church but an interest in building bridges with it. In this even Rosenberg took part, rejecting the Catholic Church as irredeemably "Judaized," while the Protestant Church's greatest offense was "losing opportunities" to cooperate.

The rival social institutions of the Nazis and the Christian establishment also demonstrated ideological affinities. Whereas incompatible social theories prohibited a close cooperation between Catholic institutions and the Nazi regime, for many Protestant organizations the ideological proximities were numerous and promising. Institutional cooperation quickly gave rise to rivalry as the Nazi State attempted the coordination of German public life, which they had never denied would take place. For many Protestants who had already been working toward these goals, this came as a serious and disillusioning blow. However, many of the same disillusioned Protestants broadly welcomed the general path on which German society under Nazism was traveling. It was not primarily out of ideological or moral opposition to Nazi social policy, but rather the desire to implement that policy, that Protestants found themselves simultaneously hopeful and disheartened. Some Protestants squared this circle by joining Nazi institutions, even in leadership roles. Such a move was usually marked more by ideological continuity than ideological break. By contrast, Nazi organizations attracted no members from rival Catholic institutions.

Even as Christian social organizations were being gradually but forcefully eliminated through coordination, the Nazis still hoped for a united, and institutionally strengthened, Protestant Church. By 1937, however, the split within Protestantism was recognized both by church leaders and leading Nazis as precluding the possibility of a Reich Church. Only then did the Nazis turn their wrath against all forms of institutional Christianity. Seen in this light, the anticlericalism of the Nazis was not simply the product of an ideological opposition to all Christian religion. When the regime turned against the Protestant Church, the DC often came under attack as well. They were not simply the agents of Nazism within the church, but represented an autonomous trend within Protestantism – which makes the proposal of 1933, to make voting for the DC in the church elections of that year mandatory for all party members, even more remarkable in its implications. If plans for destroying Christianity and replacing it with a new political religion were hatched long before the Seizure of Power, then Nazi participation in church affairs and close relations with a church group originating outside the party was certainly an odd way to go about it.

More enigmatic is the change in Hitler's attitude. During the *Kampfzeit* and into the first years of the Third Reich, he maintained – both publicly and privately – that the movement bore some fundamental relationship to Christianity, as witnessed by his repeated intonations of positive Christianity and his repeated reference to the relevance, even priority, of Christian social ideas to his own movement. Then we see an apparent total rejection of those same ideas near the end. Did this mean that, for Hitler, the ideological basis of the Nazi movement had changed? Did he feel that Nazism became something later on that it had not been before? Did Hitler's condemnation of Christianity as Jewish mean that he had been unaware of its religious origins when praising it? Or might there be another explanation for his seeming about-face? Hitler's estimation of Christianity undoubtedly changed near the end. But even while he claimed to be unambiguously opposed to Christianity, he revealed considerable ambivalence and even contradiction in his views on certain Christian precepts. As well, he betrayed a persistent affection for Christianity's founder. Especially evident in Hitler's case, the Nazis' consistent association with the person of Jesus and his message reveals a religious dimension to Nazi antisemitism, which coexisted with and in some ways even informed the racist dimension. The change that we do see, especially in the war years, is a growing vituperation in Hitler's language. However, this vituperation does not necessarily tell us a great deal about a fundamental change in Nazi ideology. Any institution or individual that did not perform up to expectations – whether the Protestant Church, the Foreign Ministry, or his own army officer corps – became the subject of Hitler's increasingly abusive ranting. On the face of it, this ranting often took the form of a total rejection. Any failure on the part of his underlings was more and more likely to be seen as abetting the Judeo–Bolshevik cause. What Hitler's vituperation reveals is not, however, a nihilist bent on destroying friend and foe alike, or a defection of previously reliable forces to Judeo–Bolshevism, but an increasingly isolated megalomaniac who blamed others for his own mistakes and failures. That Hitler's vituperation against Christianity signaled an actual rejection of the religiously associated ideas he had previously acclaimed is highly dubious.

The Nazi Party was not a clerical party run by churchmen, even though churchmen were present in its membership. Many of its members expressed clear hostility to Christianity, although frequently this hostility was fraught with tension and ambivalence. Nazism chose to take the form of a secular party instead of an explicitly religious movement, as some of its earliest members had wanted. Nevertheless, among wide circles Nazism was infused with key elements of Christian belief. Many Nazi leaders, paganist and Christian alike, revered Jesus as someone whose personal "struggle" against the Jews served as inspiration for their own struggle. Among paganists and Christians both, Luther was cast as a great national hero *and* religious reformer: as the first German, the first Protestant, and implicitly the first Nazi. Many party leaders demonstrated their belief that Christianity was deeply relevant to Nazi ideology. They did so in their private conversations, their writings, and their actions, both before 1933 and after.

It is apparent that certain presumptions about Nazism will never fully disappear. If for no other reason, Nazism serves as a useful foil, a way of gauging good and evil in the world. We are given to presuming that the things we tend to dislike in modern society must have reigned triumphant in Nazism. In fact, what we suppose Nazism must surely have been about usually tells us as much about contemporary societies as about the past purportedly under review. The insistence that Nazism was an anti-Christian movement has been one of the most enduring truisms of the past fifty years. It started as a preconception even before the movement gained power and only gained strength after the war. For Western societies intent on rebuilding themselves after the worst devastation in world history and facing a new atheistic "menace," it could be argued that preserving this truism was a political necessity. The unprecedented polarity in which the postwar world found itself and the almost crusadelike mentality of the Western establishment at the time hardly provided a warm home for critical self-examination. Exploring the possibility that many Nazis regarded themselves as Christian would have decisively undermined the myths of the Cold War and the regeneration of the German nation that the metaphor of the *Stunde Null* (zero hour) so precisely represented.

Even as other preconceptions of Nazism – either as capitalist smoke screen or medieval anachronism – have fallen under the weight of empirical scrutiny, this particular preconception seems as firmly entrenched as ever. In one sense this is entirely understandable. Nearly all Western societies retain a sense of Christian identity to this day. Moral boundaries are still in some measure drawn by biblical stricture and other forms of Christian social ethic. That Nazism as the world–historical metaphor for human evil and wickedness should in some way have been related to Christianity can therefore be regarded by many only as unthinkable. Christianity is not just a theological system; it is also a byword for moral and upstanding behavior of any kind. This is especially evident in the contemporary United States, where acts regarded as immoral, improper, or unethical are sanctioned as un-Christian, no matter how Christian the perpetrator or the motivation. This pedestrian usage of the phrase "Christian," no less significant for being ill defined, serves to reinforce the theological argument that the evil of Nazism surely bears no relation to the beauty and magnificence of the Christian religion in whatever form.

But men of God have been responsible for numerous acts of aggression and murder born of prejudice. The Crusades, Inquisition, and Apartheid, to name only the most obvious historical episodes, are generally regarded as "un-Christian" moments, even though it was piously Christian men who devised them and carried them through. Of course in a Christian society, the best way to attack intolerance of any kind, most particularly antisemitism, is to argue that it is anti-Christian. However, although the ethical value of this stance is self-evident, when it is transposed onto historical analysis problems emerge. Moral instruction quickly becomes historical apologia. The desire to shape a morally upstanding populace too often implies the suppression of difficult truths. By detaching Christianity from the crimes of its adherents, we create a Christianity above history, a Christianity whose teachings need not ultimately be investigated. Seen in this light, those who have committed such acts must have misunderstood Christianity, or worse yet purposefully misused it for their own ends. "Real Christians" do not commit such crimes. "Real Christianity" is about loving one's neighbor and the righteousness of the meek. But there is another side of the coin. As the theologian Richard Rubenstein puts it, "The world of the death camps and the society it engenders reveals the progressively intensifying night side of Judeo–Christian civilization. Civilization means slavery, wars, exploitation, and death camps. It also means medical hygiene, elevated religious ideas, beautiful art, and exquisite music."[3] Christianity, in other words, may be the source of some of the same darkness it abhors.

There is a danger in depicting any aspect of Nazism as "normal." However, the corollary to such an admission is not that Nazism is somehow redeemable, but rather that it is that much closer to us than we dare allow ourselves to believe. The discovery that so many Nazis considered themselves or their movement to be Christian makes us similarly uncomfortable. But the very unpleasantness of this fact makes it all the more important to look it squarely in the face.

[3] Richard L. Rubenstein, *The Cunning of History* (New York, 1978), 91.

PRIMARY SOURCES

UNPUBLISHED

BUNDESARCHIV POTSDAM (BAP)

R 43, Reichs-Kanlzei: II/ 149–52, 154–5, 157–65a, 168–9a, 170a–1, 173a, 177, 180, 909b, 951a, 1378, 1393a, 1503, 1569.

R 5101, Reichsministerium für die kirchlichen Angelegenheiten: 20, 25, 28, 30–1, 33, 23126, 23138, 23189, 23762.

NS 6, Partei-Kanzlei der NSDAP: 84, 98, 133, 166, 216, 220, 222–5, 229–30, 232, 334, 336, 340–1, 348–9, 382, 386, 497, 820.

NS 10, Persönliche Adjutantur des Führers und Reichskanzlers: 29, 31, 35–6, 106, 109, 112.

NS 18, Reichspropagandaleiter der NSDAP: 6, 93–4, 140–1, 148–9, 151, 529, 595.

NS 44, Reichsfrauenführung/ Nationalsozialistische Frauenschaft und Deutsches Frauenwerk: 9.

62 Di 1, Dienststelle Rosenberg: 23, 37/1, 51/1, 71, 75, 82, 84/2–3, 100, 106, 124/1–3, 126, 128, 135.

62 Ka 1, Dienststelle Bouhler: 22.

BUNDESARCHIV BERLIN-ZEHLENDORF (FORMERLY BERLIN DOCUMENT CENTER) (BAZ)

NS 8, Kanzlei Rosenberg: 130, 151, 167, 173, 178–84, 187, 204, 238, 256–7, [265], 280.

NS 11, Parteiamtliche Prüfungskommission zum Schutze des Nationalsozialistische Schrifttums: 10, 33.

NS 12, Nationalsozialistische Lehrerbund: 8, 14, 327, 638–9, 808, 817–20, 822, 824–5, 861, 1499.

NS 15, Der Beauftragte des Führers für die Überwachung der gesamten geistigen und weltanschaulichen Schulung und Erziehung der NSDAP: 307, 346, 349, 363, 365, 367–8, 370.

NS 19, Persönlicher Stab Reichsführer-SS: 140, 387, 593, 712, 860, 1202, 1333, 2241–2, 2620, 3134, 3409, 3564, 3944, 4014.

NS 22, Reichsorganisationsleiter der NSDAP: 410, 415, 446, 542, 565, 689–90, 736, 911, 1063–5, 1068–9, 1071.

NS 26, NSDAP Hauptarchiv: 55, 254, 487–9, 922, 1240, 1323, 1344, 1361, 1374–5, 1466–7, 1795, 1799.

PRIMARY SOURCES

NS 51, Kanzlei des Führers des NSDAP: 3.
Sammlung Schumacher (Schu): 205, 244, 245.
Personalakten: Walter Buch, Friedrich Cornelius, Artur Dinter, Franz Ritter von Epp, Joachim Hossenfelder, Erich Koch, Gottfried Krummacher, Friedrich Wieneke.

EVANGELISCHES ZENTRALARCHIV IN BERLIN (EZA)

7, Evangelischer Oberkirchenrat
14, Konsistorium Berlin-Brandenburg
50, Archiv für die Geschichte des Kirchenkampfes.

GEHEIMES STAATSARCHIV PREUßISCHER KULTURBESITZ (GStA)

Rep. 77, Innenministerium; Tit. 4043, Materialen der politische Polizei: 188, 392, 423.

BAYERISCHES HAUPTSTAATSARCHIV (BStA)

Innenministerium (Minn): 81630.
Kultusministerium (MK): 37069a.
Reichstatthalter Epp (Epp): 619–620, 621a, 644.
Sammlung Rehse (Rehse): 3356, 3428, 3436, 5049.
Presseausschnittssammlung (PAS): 929, 946.

STAATSARCHIV MÜNCHEN (StAM)

Polizei Direktion München (Pol Dir): 6686–7.
NSDAP: 178.

INSTITUT FÜR ZEITGESCHICHTE (IfZ)

MA (Mikrofilmarchiv), **MC** (Mikrokopienarchiv), **F, Fa** (Fotokopienarchiv), **ED** (Einzeldokumente), **Db, NG, NO, ZS** (Zeugenschriftum).

PUBLISHED

Althaus, Paul, *Die deutsche Stunde der Kirche* (Göttingen, 1934).
———— *Evangelium und Leben: Gesammelte Vorträge* (Gütersloh, 1927).
———— *Kirche und Volkstum* (Gütersloh, 1928).
———— *Theologie der Ordnungen*, 2nd ed. (Gütersloh, 1935).
Andersen, Friedrich, *Der deutsche Heiland* (Munich, 1921).
Baeumler, Alfred, "Der weltgeschichtliche Wendepunkt des Mittelalters," *Der Schulungsbrief* 3 (Oct–Nov 1936).
———— *Studien zur deutschen Geistesgeschichte* (Berlin, 1937).
Beckmann, Joachim (ed.), *Kirchliches Jahrbuch für die evangelische Kirche in Deutschland 1933–1944* (Gütersloh, 1948).
Boberach, Heinz (ed.), *Berichte des SD und der Gestapo über Kirchen und Kirchenvolk in Deutschland, 1933–1944* (Mainz, 1971).
Brunstäd, Friedrich, *Deutschland und der Sozialismus* (Berlin, 1927).
Chamberlain, Houston Stewart, *Die Grundlagen des 19. Jahrhunderts* (Munich, 1899).

Dannemann, Arnold, *Die Geschichte der Glaubensbewegung 'Deutsche Christen'* (Dresden, 1933).

Darré, Walter, *Das Bauerntum als Lebensquell der nordischen Rasse* (Munich, 1929).

—— *Neuadel aus Blut und Boden* (Munich, 1930).

Dibelius, Otto, *Nachspiel* (Berlin, 1928).

Dinter, Arthur, *Die Sünde wider das Blut* (Leipzig, 1919).

—— *197 Thesen zur Vollendung der Reformation* (Leipzig, 1926).

Domarus, Max (ed.), *Hitler: Reden und Proklamationen 1932–1945*, 2 vols. (Wiesbaden, 1973).

Elert, Werner, *Bekenntnis, Blut und Boden* (Leipzig, 1934).

—— *Morphologie des Luthertums*, 2 vols. (Munich, 1931).

Feder, Gottfried, *Das Programm der NSDAP und seine weltanschaulichen Grundgedanken* (Munich, 1927).

Fröhlich, Elke (ed.), *Die Tagebücher von Joseph Goebbels: Sämtliche Fragmente* (Munich, 1987).

—— *Die Tagebücher von Joseph Goebbels: Aufzeichnungen 1923–41* (Munich, 1998).

Gauger, Johannes, *Chronik der Kirchenwirren: Gotthard Briefe*, 3 vols. (Elberfeld, 1934–6).

Gerhardt, Martin, *Zur Vorgeschichte der Reichskirche: Die Frage der kirchlichen Einigung in Deutschland im 19. und 20. Jahrhundert* (Bonn, 1934).

Goebbels, Joseph, *Michael: Ein deutsches Schicksal in Tagebuchblättern* (Munich, 1929).

Grabert, Herbert, *Der protestantische Auftrag des deutschen Volkes: Grundzüge der deutschen Glaubensgeschichte von Luther bis Hauer* (Stuttgart, 1936).

Grossmann, Constantin, *Deutsche Christen – Ein Volksbuch* (Dresden, 1934).

Günther, Hans F.K., *Kleine Rassenkunde des deutschen Volkes* (Munich, 1922).

—— *The Racial Elements of European History* (London, 1927).

—— *Frömmigkeit nordischer Artung* (Jena, 1934).

Harnack, Adolf von, *Marcion: The Gospel of the Alien God*, trans. John Steely and Lyle Bierma (Durham, NC, 1990 [orig. 1920]).

Heiber, Helmut (ed.), *Goebbels-Reden*, 2 vols. (Düsseldorf, 1971–2).

Heydrich, Reinhard, *Die Wandlungen unseres Kampfes* (Berlin, 1936).

Hirsch, Emanuel, *Deutschlands Schicksal: Staat, Volk und Menschheit im Lichte einer ethischen Geschichtsansicht* (Göttingen, 1921).

Hitler, Adolf, *Mein Kampf* (Munich, 1925–7).

—— *Hitler's Table Talk 1941–1944: His Private Conversations*, trans. Norman Cameron and R.H. Stevens, introduction by Hugh Trevor-Roper (London, 1953).

—— *Politisches Testament: Die Bormann-Diktate vom Februar und April 1945* (Hamburg, 1981).

Hoefler, Konrad, *Protestantismus und Völkische Bewegung* (Nuremberg, 1924).

Iwand, Hans, *Briefe an Rudolf Hermann*, edited by Karl Steck (Munich, 1964).

Jäckel, Eberhard and Albert Kuhn (eds.), *Hitler: Sämtliche Aufzeichnungen 1905–1924* (Stuttgart, 1980).

Kahl-Furthmann, Gertrud (ed.), *Hans Schemm spricht: Seine Reden und sein Werk* (Beyreuth, 1935).

Kersten, Felix, *The Kersten Memoirs, 1940–1945* (New York, 1957).

Klagges, Dietrich, *Das Urevangelium Jesu: Der Deutsche Glaube* (Wilster, 1925).

Klotz, Leopold (ed.), *Die Kirche und das Dritte Reich: Fragen und Forderungen deutscher Theologen*, 2 vols. (Gotha, 1932).

Kremers, Hermann, *Nationalsozialismus und Protestantismus*, 3rd ed. (Berlin, 1931).

Künneth, Walter, Werner Wilm, and Hans Schemm, *Was haben wir als evangelische Christen zum Rufe des Nationalsozialismus zu sagen?* (Dresden, 1931).

Leffler, Siegfried, *Christus im Dritten Reich der Deutschen: Wesen, Weg und Ziel der Kirchenbewegung "Deutsche Christen"* (Weimar, 1935).

Lehmann, Kurt, *Deutschtum und Positives Christentum* (Berlin, 1939).

Leutheuser, Julius, *Der Heiland in der Geschichte der Deutschen: Der Nationalsozialismus, vom Evangelium aus gesehen* (Weimar, 1933).

Ludendorff, Erich, *Vom Feldherrn zum Weltrevolutionär und Wegbereiter Deutscher Volksschöpfung: Meine Lebenserinnerungen von 1919 bis 1925* (Munich, 1941).

Ludendorff, Mathilde, *Deutscher Gottglaube* (Munich, 1932).

Macfarland, Charles, *The New Church and the New Germany* (New York, 1934).

Maser, Werner, *Hitlers Briefe und Notizen: Sein Weltbild in Handschriftliche Dokumenten* (Düsseldorf, 1973).

Micklem, Nathaniel, *National Socialism and the Roman Catholic Church* (Oxford, 1939).

Nicolaisen, Carsten (ed.), *Dokumente zur Kirchenpolitik des Dritten Reiches*, 3 vols. (Munich, 1971–94).

Renan, Ernest, *The Life of Jesus* (Boston, 1907).

Reuth, Ralf (ed.), *Joseph Goebbels: Tagebücher 1924–1945*, 4 vols. (Munich, 1992).

Rosenberg, Alfred, *Der Mythus des 20. Jahrhunderts: Eine Wertung der seelisch-geistigen Gestaltenkämpfe unserer Zeit* (Munich, 1931).

———— *An die Dunkelmänner unserer Zeit* (Munich, 1935).

———— *Protestantische Rompilger: Der Verrat an Luther und der Mythus des 20. Jahrhunderts* (Munich, 1935).

Schirach, Baldur von, *Die Hitler-Jugend: Idee und Gestalt* (Berlin, 1934).

Schmidt, Kurt-Dietrich (ed.), *Die Bekenntnisse und grundsätzlichen Äußerungen zur Kirchenfrage*, 3 vols. (Göttingen, 1934–6).

Seraphim, Hans-Günther (ed.), *Das politische Tagebuch Alfred Rosenbergs* (Göttingen, 1956).

Smith, Bradley and A.F. Peterson (eds.), *Heinrich Himmler: Geheimreden 1933 bis 1945* (Frankfurt, 1974).

Speer, Albert, *Inside the Third Reich* (New York, 1970).

Stark, Johannes, *Nationalsozialismus und Katholische Kirche* (Munich, 1931).

Tyrell, Albrecht, *Führer befiehl . . . Selbstzeugnisse aus der 'Kampfzeit' der NSDAP: Dokumentation und Analyse* (Düsseldorf, 1969).

Wagener, Otto, *Hitler: Memoirs of a Confidant*, edited by Henry Ashby Turner (New Haven, 1985).

Wieneke, Friedrich, *Christentum und Nationalsozialismus* (Küstrin, 1931).

———— *Die Glaubensbewegung 'Deutsche Christen'* (Soldin, 1932).

SECONDARY SOURCES

Abele, Christina and Heinz Boberach (eds.), *Inventar Staatlicher Akten zum Verhaltnis von Staat und Kirchen 1933–1945*, 3 vols. (Cassel, 1987–8).

Ackermann, Josef, *Heinrich Himmler als Ideologe* (Göttingen, 1970).

Albertin, Lothar, "Nationalismus und Protestantismus in der österreichischen Los-von-Rom Bewegung um 1900," Ph.D. dissertation, Cologne, 1953.

Allen, William S., *The Nazi Seizure of Power: The Experience of a Single German Town*, 2nd ed. (New York, 1984).

Altgeld, Wolfgang, *Katholizismus, Protestantismus, Judentum: Über religiös begründete Gegensätze und nationalreligiöse Ideen in der Geschichte des deutschen Nationalismus* (Mainz, 1992).

———"Die Ideologie des Nationalsozialismus und ihre Vorläufer," in Karl Dietrich Bracher and Leo Valiani (eds.), *Faschismus und Nationalsozialismus* (Berlin, 1991), 107–36.

Angress, Werner and Bradley Smith, "Diaries of Heinrich Himmler's Early Years," *Journal of Modern History* 31 (1959), 206–24.

Aschheim, Steven, *Culture and Catastrophe: German and Jewish Confrontations with National Socialism and Other Crises* (New York, 1996).

———*The Nietzsche Legacy in Germany: 1890–1990* (Berkeley, 1992).

Baier, Helmut, *Die Deutschen Christen Bayerns im Rahmen des bayerischen Kirchenkampfes* (Nuremberg, 1968).

Baldwin, Peter, "Social Interpretations of Nazism: Renewing a Tradition," *Journal of Contemporary History* 25 (1990), 5–37.

Baranowski, Shelley, "Consent and Dissent: The Confessing Church and Conservative Opposition to National Socialism," *Journal of Modern History* 59 (1987), 53–78.

———"The 1933 German Protestant Church Elections: *Machtpolitik* or Accommodation?," *Church History* 49 (1980), 298–315.

———"The Sanctity of Rural Life: Protestantism, Agrarian Politics and Nazism in Pomerania during the Weimar Republic," *German History* 9 (1991), 1–22.

———*The Confessing Church, Conservative Elites, and the Nazi State* (Lewiston, NY, 1986).

———*The Sanctity of Rural Life: Nobility, Protestantism, and Nazism in Weimar Prussia* (Oxford, 1995).

Barkai, Avraham, *Nazi Economics: Ideology, Theory, and Policy* (New Haven, 1990).

Barnett, Victoria, *For the Soul of the People: Protestant Protest against Hitler* (New York, 1992).

Bärsch, Claus-Ekkehard, *Erlösung und Vernichtung – Joseph Goebbels: Zur Psyche und Ideologie eines jungen Nationalsozialisten* (Munich, 1987).

Bauman, Zygmunt, *Modernity and the Holocaust* (Ithaca, 1989).

Benz, Wolfgang, *Herrschaft und Gesellschaft im nationalsozialistischen Staat* (Frankfurt a.M., 1990).

Berding, Helmut, *Moderner Antisemitismus in Deutschland* (Frankfurt a.M., 1988).

Bergen, Doris, "The Nazi Concept of 'Volksdeutsche' and the Exacerbation of Anti-semitism in Eastern Europe, 1939–45," *Journal of Contemporary History* 29 (1994), 569–82.

————*Twisted Cross: The German Christian Movement in the Third Reich* (Chapel Hill, 1996).

Besier, Gerhard, "The Stance of the German Protestant Churches during the Agony of Weimar, 1930–1933," *Kyrkhistorisk Årsskrift* 1 (1983), 151–63.

Bessel, Richard (ed.), *Life in the Third Reich* (Oxford, 1987).

————*Political Violence and the Rise of Nazism: The Stormtroopers in Eastern Germany 1925–1934* (New Haven, 1984).

Bienert, Walther, *Martin Luther und die Juden* (Frankfurt a.M., 1985).

Black, Peter, *Ernst Kaltenbrunner: Ideological Soldier of the Third Reich* (Princeton, 1984).

Blackbourn, David, *Marpingen: Apparitions of the Virgin Mary in a Nineteenth-Century German Village* (Oxford, 1993).

Blackburn, Gilmer, "The Portrayal of Christianity in the History Textbooks of Nazi Germany," *Church History* 49 (1980), 433–45.

Blaschke, Olaf and Frank-Michael Kuhlemann (eds.), *Religion im Kaiserreich: Milieus, Mentalitäten, Krisen* (Gütersloh, 1996).

Blaschke, Olaf, "Der Altkatholizismus 1879 bis 1945: Nationalismus, Anti-semitismus, Nationalsozialismus," *Historische Zeitschrift* 261 (1995), 51–99.

————*Katholizismus und Antisemitismus im Deutschen Kaiserreich* (Göttingen, 1997).

Bollmus, Reinhard, *Das Amt Rosenberg und seine Gegner: Studien zum Machtkampf im nationalsozialistischen Herrschaftssystem* (Stuttgart, 1970).

Borg, Daniel, *The Old-Prussian Church and the Weimar Republic: A Study in Political Adjustment, 1917–1927* (Hanover, NH, 1984).

Bracher, Karl Dietrich, *The German Dictatorship: The Origins, Structure and Effects of National Socialism* (New York, 1970).

Brakelmann, Günter, "Nationalprotestantismus und Nationalsozialismus," in Christian Jansen et al. (eds.), *Von der Aufgabe der Freiheit: Politische Verantwortung und bürgerliche Gesellschaft im 19. und 20. Jahrhundert* (Berlin, 1995), 337–50.

————Martin Greschat and Werner Jochmann, *Protestantismus und Politik: Werk und Wirkung Adolf Stoeckers* (Hamburg, 1982).

Bramwell, Anna, *Blood and Soil: Richard Walther Darré and Hitler's 'Green Party'* (London, 1985).

Braun, Christina von and Ludger Heid (eds.), *Der Ewige Judenhass: Christlicher Anti-judaismus, deutschnationale Judenfeindlichkeit, rassistischer Antisemitismus* (Stuttgart, 1990).

Bridenthal, Renate et al. (eds.), *When Biology Became Destiny: Women in Weimar and Nazi Germany* (New York, 1984).

Broszat, Martin, *German National Socialism 1919–1945* (Santa Cruz, 1966).

————*The Hitler State: The Foundation and Development of the Internal Structure of the Third Reich* (London, 1981).

Bruce, Steve (ed.), *Religion and Modernization: Sociologists and Historians Debate the Secularization Thesis* (Oxford, 1992).

Buchheim, Hans, *Glaubenskrise im Dritten Reich: Drei Kapitel nationalsozialistischer Religionspolitik* (Stuttgart, 1953).

Burleigh, Michael (ed.), *Confronting the Nazi Past: New Debates on Modern German History* (New York, 1996).

Burleigh, Michael and Wolfgang Wippermann, *The Racial State: Germany, 1933–1945* (Cambridge, 1991).

Burleigh, Michael, "Between Enthusiasm, Compliance and Protest: The Churches, Eugenics and the Nazi 'Euthanasia' Program," *Contemporary European History* 3 (1994), 253–63.

———*Death and Deliverance: 'Euthanasia' in Germany, 1900 to 1945* (Cambridge, 1994).

———*Ethics and Extermination: Reflections on Nazi Genocide* (Cambridge, 1997).

Burrin, Philippe, "Political Religion: The Relevance of a Concept," *History and Memory* 9 (1997), 321–49.

Cancik, Hubert (ed.), *Religions- und Geistesgeschichte der Weimarer Republik* (Düsseldorf, 1982).

Carr, William, *Hitler: A Study in Personality and Politics* (London, 1978).

Casanova, José, *Public Religions in the Modern World* (Chicago, 1994).

Cecil, Robert, *The Myth of the Master Race: Alfred Rosenberg and Nazi Ideology* (London, 1972).

Chickering, Roger, *We Men Who Feel Most German: A Cultural Study of the Pan-German League, 1886–1914* (London, 1984).

Childers, Thomas and Jane Caplan (eds.), *Reevaluating the Third Reich* (New York, 1993).

Christ, Herbert, "Der Politische Protestantismus in der Weimarer Republik: Eine Studie über die politische Meinungsbildung dürch die Evangelischen Kirchen im Spiegel der Literatur und der Presse," Ph.D. dissertation, Bonn, 1967.

Conway, John, *The Nazi Persecution of the Churches* (London, 1968).

———"Coming to Terms with the Past: Interpreting the German Church Struggles 1933–1990," *German History* 16 (1998), 377–396.

Dahm, Karl-Wilhelm, "German Protestantism and Politics, 1918–1939," *Journal of Contemporary History* 3 (1968), 29–49.

Deschner, Günther, *Reinhard Heydrich: A Biography* (New York, 1981).

Denzler, Georg and Volker Fabricius, *Christen und Nationalsozialisten: Darstellung und Dokumente* (Frankfurt a.M., 1993).

Dietrich, Donald, "Catholic Eugenics in Germany, 1920–1945," *Journal of Church and State* 34 (1992), 575–600.

Dobkowski, Michael and Isidor Wallimann (eds.), *Radical Perspectives on the Rise of Fascism in Germany, 1919–1945* (New York, 1989).

Eley, Geoff, *Reshaping the German Right: Radical Nationalism and Political Change after Bismarck* (New Haven, 1980).

———"What is Cultural History?," *New German Critique* 65 (1995), 19–36.

Elze, Martin, "Antisemitismus in der Evangelischen Kirche," in Karlheinz Müller and Klaus Wittstand (eds.), *Geschichte und Kultur des Judentums* (Würzburg, 1988).

Endres, Elisabeth, *Die gelbe Farbe: Die Entwicklung der Judenfeindschaft aus dem Christentum* (Munich, 1989).

Engelmann, Hans, *Kirche am Abgrund: Adolf Stöcker und seine antijüdische Bewegung* (Berlin, 1984).

Ericksen, Robert and Susannah Heschel, "The German Churches Face Hitler," *Tel Aviver Jahrbuch für deutsche Geschichte* 23 (1994), 433–59.

Ericksen, Robert, "A Radical Minority: Resistance in the German Protestant Church," in Francis Nicosia and Lawrence Stokes (eds.), *Germans against Nazism: Nonconformity, Opposition and Resistance in the Third Reich* (Oxford, 1990), 115–35.

———*Theologians under Hitler: Gerhard Kittel, Paul Althaus and Emmanuel Hirsch* (New Haven, 1985).

Falter, Jürgen, *Hitlers Wähler* (Munich, 1991).

Feige, Franz, *The Varieties of Protestantism in Nazi Germany* (Lewiston, NY, 1990).

Feiten, Willi, *Der Nationalsozialistische Lehrerbund: Entwicklung und Organisation* (Weinheim, 1981).

Fest, Joachim, *The Face of the Third Reich: Portraits of the Nazi Leadership* (London, 1970).

Field, Geoffrey, *Evangelist of Race: The Germanic Vision of Houston Stewart Chamberlain* (New York, 1981).

Fischer, Conan, *Stormtroopers: A Social, Economic and Ideological Analysis 1929–35* (London, 1983).

———*The Rise of the Nazis* (New York, 1995).

Ford, Caroline, "Religion and Popular Culture in Modern Europe," *Journal of Modern History* 65 (1993), 152–75.

Frankel, Jonathan (ed.), *The Fate of the European Jews, 1939–1945: Continuity or Contingency?* (Oxford, 1997).

Frei, Norbert, "Wie modern war der Nationalsozialismus?," *Geschichte und Gesellschaft* 19 (1993), 367–87.

———*Der Führerstaat: Nationalsozialistische Heerschaft 1933 bis 1945* (Munich, 1987).

Friedländer, Saul (ed.), *Probing the Limits of Representation: Nazism and the 'Final Solution'* (Cambridge, MA, 1992).

Friedländer, Saul, *Nazi Germany and the Jews: The Years of Persecution, 1933–1939* (New York, 1997).

Friedman, Jerome, "Jewish Conversion, The Spanish Pure Blood Laws, and Reformation: A Revisionist View of Racial and Religious Antisemitism," *Sixteenth Century Journal* 18 (1987), 3–29.

Furet, François (ed.), *Unanswered Questions: Nazi Germany and the Genocide of the Jews* (New York, 1989).

Gailus, Manfred (ed.), *Kirchengemeinden im Nationalsozialismus: Sieben Beispiele aus Berlin* (Berlin, 1990).

Gailus, Manfred, "Die andere Seite des 'Kirchenkampfes': Nazifizierte Kirchengemeinden und 'braune' Pfarrer in Berlin 1933–1945," *Berlin in Geschichte und Gegenwart: Jahrbuch des Landesarchivs Berlin* 14 (1995), 149–70.

———*Protestantismus und Nationalsozialismus: Studien zur nationalsozialistischen Durchdringung des protestantischen Sozialmilieus in Berlin* (Cologne, 2001).

Gay, Peter, *Weimar Culture: The Outsider as Insider* (London, 1968).

Gellately, Robert, *The Gestapo and German Society: Enforcing Racial Policy 1933–1945* (Oxford, 1990).

Gerlach, Wolfgang, *Als die Zeugen schwiegen: Bekennende Kirche und die Juden* (Berlin, 1987).

Germann, Holger, *Die politische Religion des Nationalsozialisten Dietrich Klagges: Ein Beitrag zur Phänomenologie der NS-Ideologie* (Frankfurt a.M., 1995).

Giesecke, Hermann, *Hitlers Pädagogen: Theorie und Praxis nationalsozialistischer Erziehung* (Weinheim, 1993).

Gilman, Sander and Steven Katz (eds.), *Antisemitism in Times of Crisis* (New York, 1991).

Goodrick-Clarke, Nicholas, *The Occult Roots of Nazism: Secret Aryan Cults and their Influence on Nazi Ideology* (London, 1992).

Gordon, Sarah, *Hitler, Germans, and the 'Jewish Question'* (Princeton, 1984).

Gotto, Klaus and Konrad Repgen (eds.), *Kirche, Katholiken und Nationalsozialismus* (Mainz, 1980).

Graml, Hermann, *Antisemitism in the Third Reich* (Oxford, 1988).

Greive, Hermann, *Geschichte des modernen Antisemitismus in Deutschland* (Darmstadt, 1983).

——*Theologie und Ideologie: Katholizismus und Judentum in Deutschland und Österreich 1918–1935* (Heidelberg, 1969).

Griffin, Roger, *The Nature of Fascism* (London, 1991).

Grossmann, Atina, "Feminist Debates about Women and National Socialism," *Gender and History* 3 (1991), 350–8.

Gutteridge, Richard, *The German Evangelical Church and the Jews, 1879–1958* (London, 1976).

Haas, Peter, "The Morality of Auschwitz: Moral Language and the Nazi Ethic," *Holocaust and Genocide Studies* 3 (1988), 383–93.

Hambrecht, Rainer, *Der Aufstieg der NSDAP in Mittel- und Oberfranken 1925–1933* (Nuremberg, 1976).

Hansen, Eckhard, *Wohlfahrtspolitik im NS-Staat: Motivationen, Konflikte und Machtstrukturen im 'Sozialismus der Tat' des Dritten Reiches* (Augsburg, 1991).

Harris, James et al., "Symposium: Christian Religion and Antisemitism in Modern German History," *Central European History* 27 (1994).

Harrison, E.D.R., "The Nazi Dissolution of the Monasteries: A Case Study," *English Historical Review* 109 (1994), 323–355.

Hayes, Peter, *Industry and Ideology: IG Farben in the Nazi Era* (Cambridge, 1987).

Heer, Friedrich, *Der Glaube des Adolf Hitler: Anatomie einer politischen Religiosität* (Munich, 1969).

Heilbronner, Oded, "The Role of Nazi Antisemitism in the Nazi Party's Activity and Propaganda: A Regional and Historiographical Study," *Leo Baeck Institute Yearbook* 35 (1990): 397–439.

——"Where did Nazi Antisemitism Disappear to? Antisemitic Propaganda and Ideology of the Nazi Party, 1929–1933," *Yad Vashem Studies* 21 (1991), 263–86.

Heineman, John, *Hitler's First Foreign Minister: Constantin Freiherr von Neurath, Diplomat and Statesman* (Berkeley, 1979).

Herf, Jeffrey, *Reactionary Modernism: Technology, Culture and Politics in Weimar and the Third Reich* (Cambridge, 1984).

Hermand, Jost, *Old Dreams of a New Reich: Volkish Utopias and National Socialism* (Bloomington, 1992).

Herrmann, Ulrich (ed.), *'Die Formung des Volksgenossen': Der 'Erziehungsstaat' des Dritten Reiches* (Weinheim, 1985).

Heschel, Susannah, *Abraham Geiger and the Jewish Jesus* (Chicago, 1998).

————"Nazifying Christian Theology: Walter Grundmann and the Institute for the Study and Eradication of Jewish Influence on German Church Life," *Church History* 63 (1994), 587–605.

Heschel, Susannah and Robert Ericksen (eds.), *Betrayal: German Churches and the Holocaust*, (Philadelphia, 1999).

Hirschfeld, Gerhard and Lothar Kettenacker (eds.), *Der 'Führerstaat': Mythos und Realität* (Stuttgart, 1981).

Höhne, Heinz, *Der Orden unter dem Totenkopf: Die Geschichte der SS* (Gütersloh, 1967).

Hölscher, Lucian, "Die Religion des Bürgers: Bürgerliche Frömmigkeit und Protestantische Kirche im 19. Jahrhundert," *Historische Zeitschrift* 250 (1990), 595–630.

Hong, Young-Sun, *Welfare, Modernity, and the Weimar State, 1919–1933* (Princeton, 1998).

Horn, Wolfgang, *Der Marsch zur Machtergreifung: Die NSDAP bis 1933* (Düsseldorf, 1972).

————*Führerideologie und Parteiorganisation in der NSDAP (1919–1933)* (Düsseldorf, 1972).

Housden, Martyn, *Resistance and Conformity in the Third Reich* (London, 1997).

Hübinger, Gangolf, *Kulturprotestantismus und Politik: Zum Verhältnis von Liberalismus und Protestantismus im wilhelminischen Deutschland* (Tübingen, 1994).

Hutchison, William and Hartmut Lehmann (eds.), *Many Are Chosen: Divine Election and Western Nationalism* (Minneapolis, 1994).

Hüttenberger, Peter, *Die Gauleiter: Studie zum Wandel des Machtgefüges in der NSDAP* (Stuttgart, 1969).

Iber, Harald, *Christlicher Glaube oder Rassischer Mythus: Die Auseinandersetzung der Bekennenden Kirche mit Alfred Rosenbergs 'Der Mythus des 20. Jahrhunderts'* (Frankfurt a.M., 1987).

Jäckel, Eberhard, *Hitler's World View: A Blueprint for Power* (Cambridge, MA, 1972).

Jochmann, Werner, *Gesellschaftskrise und Judenfeindschaft in Deutschland 1870–1945* (Hamburg, 1988).

Johnson, Marshall, "Power Politics and New Testament Scholarship in the National Socialist Period," *Journal of Ecumenical Studies* 23 (1986), 1–24.

Jones, Larry Eugene and James Retallack (eds.), *Between Reform, Reaction and Resistance: Studies in the History of German Conservatism from 1789 to 1945* (Providence, RI, 1993).

Kaiser, Jochen-Christoph, *Frauen in der Kirche: Evangelische Frauenverbände im Spannungsfeld von Kirche und Gesellschaft 1890–1945* (Düsseldorf, 1985).

————*Sozialer Protestantismus im 20. Jahrhundert: Beitrage zur Geschichte der Inneren Mission 1914–1945* (Munich, 1989).

Kater, Michael, *The Nazi Party: A Social Profile of Members and Leaders, 1919–1945* (Cambridge, MA, 1983).

Katz, Jacob, *From Prejudice to Destruction: Antisemitism, 1700–1933* (Cambridge, MA, 1980).

————*The Darker Side of Genius: Richard Wagner's Antisemitism* (Hanover, NH, 1986).

Kershaw, Ian, "Cumulative Radicalisation and the Uniqueness of National Socialism," in Christian Jansen et al. (eds.), *Von der Aufgabe der Freiheit: Politische Verantwortung und bürgerliche Gesellschaft im 19. und 20. Jahrhundert* (Berlin, 1995), 323–36.

————"Ideologue and Propagandist: Hitler in Light of His Speeches, Writings and Orders, 1925–1928," *Yad Vashem Studies* 23 (1993), 321–334.

————*Hitler* (London, 1991).

————*Hitler, 1889–1936: Hubris* (London, 1998).

————*Popular Opinion and Political Dissent in the Third Reich: Bavaria 1933–1945* (Oxford, 1983).

————*The 'Hitler Myth': Image and Reality in the Third Reich* (Oxford, 1987).

————*The Nazi Dictatorship: Problems and Perspectives of Interpretation*, 2nd ed. (London, 1989).

King, Christine, *The Nazi State and the New Religions: Five Case Studies in Nonconformity* (Lewiston, NY, 1982).

Kissenkoetter, Udo, *Gregor Strasser und die NSDAP* (Stuttgart, 1978).

Klee, Ernst, *Die SA Jesu Christi: Die Kirchen im Banne Hitlers* (Frankfurt a.M., 1989).

————*'Euthanasie' im NS-Staat: Die 'Vernichtung lebensunwerten Lebens'* (Frankfurt a.M., 1983).

Klein, Charlotte, *Anti-Judaism in Christian Theology* (Philadelphia, 1978).

Klönne, Arno, *Jugend im Dritten Reich: Die Hitler-Jugend und ihre Gegner* (Düsseldorf, 1982).

Koch, H. W. (ed.), *Aspects of the Third Reich* (New York, 1985).

Koonz, Claudia, *Mothers in the Fatherland: Women, the Family, and Nazi Politics* (New York, 1987).

Krebs, Albert, *Tendenzen und Gestalten der NSDAP: Erinnerungen an die Frühzeit der Partei* (Stuttgart, 1959).

Kremers, Heinz (ed.), *Die Juden und Martin Luther – Martin Luther und die Juden: Geschichte, Wirkungsgeschichte, Herausforderung* (Neukirchen, 1987).

Kremers-Sper, Thomas, "Antijüdische und antisemitische Momente in protestantischer Kapitalismuskritik," *Zeitschrift für Religions- und Geistesgeschichte* 44 (1992), 221–240.

Kren, George and Rodler Morris, "Race and Spirituality: Arthur Dinter's Theosophical Antisemitism," *Holocaust and Genocide Studies* 6 (1991), 233–252.

Kube, Alfred, *Pour le merite und Hakenkreuz: Hermann Göring im Dritten Reich* (Munich, 1987).

Kühnel, Franz, *Hans Schemm, Gauleiter und Kultusminister 1891–1935* (Nuremberg, 1985).

Kulka, Otto dov and Paul Mendes-Flohr (eds.), *Judaism and Christianity under the Impact of National Socialism* (Jerusalem, 1987).

Kupisch, Karl, "The Luther Renaissance," *Journal of Contemporary History* 2 (1967), 39–49.

Lächele, Rainer, *Ein Volk, ein Reich, ein Glaube: Die Deutschen Christen in Württemberg 1925–1960* (Stuttgart, 1994).

Lambert, Peter, "German Historians and Nazi Ideology: The Parameters of the Volksgemeinschaft and the Problem of Historical Legitimation, 1930–1945," *European History Quarterly* 25 (1995), 555–82.

Lamberti, Marjorie, *State, Society, and the Elementary School in Imperial Germany* (New York, 1989).

Lane, Barbara Miller and Leila Rupp (eds.), *Nazi Ideology Before 1933: A Documentation* (Austin, 1978).

Lane, Barbara Miller, "Nazi Ideology: Some Unfinished Business," *Central European History* 7 (1974), 3–30.

Lang, Jochen v., *Der Sekretär – Martin Bormann: Der Mann, der Hitler beherrschte* (Stuttgart, 1977).
Langmuir, Gavin, *History, Religion, and Antisemitism* (Berkeley, 1990).
——*Toward a Definition of Antisemitism* (Berkeley, 1990).
Larsen, Stein Ugelvik et al. (eds.), *Who were the Fascists: Social Roots of European Fascism* (Bergen, 1980).
Lebovics, Herman, *Social Conservatism and the Middle Classes in Germany, 1914–1933* (Princeton, 1969).
Lehmann, Hartmut, "Friedrich von Bodelschwingh und das Sedanfest: Ein Beitrag zum nationalen Denken der politisch activen Richtung des deutschen Pietismus im 19. Jahrhundert," *Historische Zeitschrift* 202 (1966), 542–73.
——"The Germans as a Chosen People: Old Testament Themes in German Nationalism," *German Studies Review* 14 (1991), 261–73.
Lehmann, Hartmut, and Guenther Roth (eds.), *Weber's Protestant Ethic: Origins, Evidence, Contexts* (Cambridge, 1993).
Lewy, Guenter, *The Catholic Church and Nazi Germany* (New York, 1964).
Ley, Michael and Julius Schoeps (eds.), *Der Nationalsozialismus als politische Religion* (Bodenheim, 1997).
Lidtke, Vernon, "Social Class and Secularisation in Imperial Germany: The Working Classes," *Leo Baeck Institute Yearbook* 25 (1980), 21–40.
Littell, Franklin and Hubert Locke (eds.), *The German Church Struggle and the Holocaust* (Detroit, 1974).
Littell, Franklin, "Inventing the Holocaust: a Christian's Retrospect," *Holocaust and Genocide Studies* 9 (1995), 173–91.
Lohalm, Uwe, *Völkischer Radikalismus: Die Geschichte des deutschvölkischen Schutz- und Trutz-Bundes, 1919–1923* (Hamburg, 1970).
Loth, Wilhelm (ed.), *Deutscher Katholizismus im Umbruch zur Moderne* (Stuttgart, 1991).
Lukacs, John, *The Hitler of History* (New York, 1997).
Martin, David, *A General Theory of Secularization* (Oxford, 1978).
Matheson, Peter (ed.), *The Third Reich and the Christian Churches* (Grand Rapids, 1981).
McKale, Donald, *The Nazi Party Courts: Hitler's Management of Conflict in his Movement, 1921–1945* (Lawrence, 1975).
Mehnert, Gottfried, *Evangelische Kirche und Politik, 1917–1919* (Düsseldorf, 1959).
Meier, Kurt, *Der Evangelische Kirchenkampf: Gesamtdarstellung in 3 Bänden*, 3 vols. (Göttingen, 1976–84).
——*Die Deutsche Christen: Das Bild einer Bewegung im Kirchenkampf des Dritten Reiches* (Göttingen, 1964).
——*Kreuz und Hakenkreuz: Die evangelische Kirche im Dritten Reich* (Munich, 1992).
Mensing, Björn, *Pfarrer und Nationalsozialismus: Geschichte einer Verstrickung am Beispiel der Evangelisch-Lutherischen Kirchen in Bayern* (Göttingen, 1998).
Michael, Robert, "Theological Myth, German Antisemitism and the Holocaust: The Case of Martin Niemoeller," *Holocaust and Genocide Studies* 2 (1987), 105–22.
——"Wagner, Christian Anti-Jewishness and the Jews: A Re-Examination," *Patterns of Prejudice* 26 (1992).
Michalka, Wolfgang (ed.), *Die nationalsozialistische Machtergreifung 1933* (Paderborn, 1984).

Mommsen, Hans et al. (eds.), *Industrielles System und politische Entwicklung in der Weimarer Republik* (Düsseldorf, 1974).

Mommsen, Hans, *From Weimar to Auschwitz* (Princeton, 1991).

Mosse, George, *Germans and Jews: The Right, the Left, and the Search for a 'Third Force' in Pre-Nazi Germany* (New York, 1970).

———*Nazi Culture: Intellectual, Cultural and Social Life in the Third Reich* (New York, 1966).

———*The Crisis of German Ideology: Intellectual Origins of the Third Reich* (London, 1964).

———*The Nationalization of the Masses* (New York, 1975).

———*Toward the Final Solution: A History of European Racism* (New York, 1978).

Mühlberger, Detlef, *Hitler's Followers: Studies in the Sociology of the Nazi Movement* (London, 1991).

Müller, Christine-Ruth and Hans-Ludwig Degener, *Warum sie sterben mußten: Leidensweg und Vernichtung von Behinderten aus den Neuendettelsauer Pflegenstalten im 'Dritten Reich'* (Neustadt a.d. Aisch, 1991).

Mybes, Fritz, *Agnes von Grone und das Frauenwerk der Deutschen Evangelischen Kirche* (Düsseldorf, 1981).

———*Geschichte der evangelischen Frauenhilfe in Quellen unter besonderer Berücksichtigung der Evangelischen Frauenhilfe im Rheinland* (Gladbeck, 1975).

Neliba, Günter, *Wilhelm Frick: Der Legalist des Unrechtsstaates* (Paderborn, 1992).

Niemöller, Wilhelm, *Die bekennende Kirche sagt Hitler die Wahrheit* (Bielefeld, 1954).

———*Der Pfarrernotbund: Geschichte einer kämpfenden Bruderschaft* (Hamburg, 1973).

Nipperdey, Thomas, *Deutsche Geschichte 1800–1866: Bürgerwelt und starker Staat* (Munich, 1983).

———*Religion im Umbruch: Deutschland 1870–1918* (Munich, 1988).

Noakes, Jeremy and Geoffrey Pridham, *Nazism 1919–1945: A Documentary Reader*, 3 vols. (Exeter, 1983–8).

Noakes, Jeremy, *The Nazi Party in Lower Saxony 1921–1933* (Oxford, 1971).

Norden, Günther van, *Kirche in der Krise: die Stellung der evangelischen Kirch ezum nationalsozialistischen Stat im Jahre 1933* (Düsseldorf, 1963).

———*Der deutsche Protestantismus im Jahr der nationalsozialistischen Machtergreifung* (Gütersloh, 1979).

Nowak, Kurt and Gérard Raulet (eds.), *Protestantismus und Antisemitismus in der Weimarer Republik* (Frankfurt a.M., 1994).

Nowak, Kurt, *'Euthanasie' und Sterilisierung im 'Dritten Reich': Die Konfrontation der evangelischen und katholischen Kirche mit dem 'Gesetz zur Verhütung erbkranken Nachwuchses' und der 'Euthanasie'-Aktion* (Göttingen, 1980).

———*Evangelische Kirche und Weimarer Republik: Zum politischen Weg des deutschen Protestantismus zwischen 1918 und 1932* (Göttingen, 1981).

Olender, Maurice, *The Languages of Paradise: Race, Religion and Philology in the Nineteenth Century*, trans. Arthur Goldhammer (Cambridge, MA, 1992).

Olenhusen, Irmtraud Götz von, *Jugendreich, Gottesreich, Deutsches Reich: Junge Generation, Religion und Politik 1928–1933* (Cologne, 1987).

Orlow, Dietrich, *The History of the Nazi Party: 1919–1933* (Pittsburgh, 1969).

Otto, Nans-Uwe and Heinz Sünker (eds.), *Politische Formierung und soziale Erziehung im Nationalsozialismus* (Frankfurt a.M., 1991).

Payne, Stanley, *A History of Fascism, 1914–1945* (Madison, 1995).

Peterson, Edward, *The Limits of Hitler's Power* (Princeton, 1969).

Peukert, Detlev, *Der Weimarer Republik: Krisenjahre der Klassischen Moderne* (Frankfurt a.M., 1987).

——*Inside Nazi Germany: Conformity, Opposition, and Racism in Everyday Life* (New Haven, 1987).

Phayer, Michael, *Protestant and Catholic Women in Nazi Germany* (Detroit, 1990).

Plewnia, Margarete, *Auf dem Weg zu Hitler: Der 'völkische' Publizist Dietrich Eckart* (Bremen, 1970).

Pois, Robert, *National Socialism and the Religion of Nature* (London, 1985).

Poliakov, Léon and Joseph Wulf (eds.), *Das Dritte Reich und seine Denker* (Berlin, 1983).

Preradovich, Nikolaus and Joseph Stingle (eds.), *'Gott segne den Führer!': Die Kirchen im Dritten Reich* (Leoni am Starnbergersee, 1986).

Pressel, Wilhelm, *Die Kriegspredigt 1914–1918 in der evangelischen Kirche Deutschlands* (Göttingen, 1967).

Priepke, Manfred, *Die Evangelische Jugend im Dritten Reich 1933–1936* (Hanover, 1960).

Prinz, Michael and Rainer Zitelmann (eds.), *Nationalsozialismus und Modernisierung* (Darmstadt, 1991).

Pulzer, Peter, *The Rise of Political Antisemitism in Germany and Austria* (Cambridge, MA, 1988).

Ramet, Pedro (ed.), *Religion and Nationalism in Soviet and East European Politics* (Durham, NC, 1989).

Rémond, René (ed.), "Special Issue: Anticlericalism," *European Studies Review* 13 (1983).

Reuth, Ralf, *Goebbels* (New York, 1993).

Röhm, Eberhard and Jörg Thierfelder, *Evangelische Kirche zwischen Kreuz und Hakenkreuz* (Stuttgart, 1981).

Roseman, Mark, "National Socialism and Modernization," in Richard Bessel (ed.), *Fascist Italy and Nazi Germany: Comparisons and Contrasts* (Cambridge, 1996), 197–229.

Rössler, Hans, "Die 'Euthanasie'-Diskussion in Neuendettelsau 1937–1939," *Zeitschrift für bayerischen Kirchengeschichte* 55 (1986), 199–208.

Rubenstein, Richard, "Religion and the Uniqueness of the Holocaust," in Alan Rosenbaum (ed.), *Is the Holocaust Unique? Perspectives on Comparative Genocide* (Boulder, 1996), 11–18.

——*After Auschwitz: History, Theology, and Contemporary Judaism*, 2nd ed. (Baltimore, 1992).

Rürup, Reinhard, *Emanzipation und Antisemitismus: Studien zur 'Judenfrage' der bürgerlichen Gesellschaft* (Göttingen, 1975).

Schellong, Dieter, *Bürgertum und christliche Religion: Anpassungsprobleme der Theologie seit Schleiermacher* (Munich, 1975).

Schieder, Wolfgang (ed.), *Religion und Gesellschaft im 19. Jahrhundert* (Stuttgart, 1993).

——(ed.), *Volksreligiosität in der modernen Sozialgeschichte* (Göttingen, 1986).

Schmuhl, Hans-Walter, *Rassenhygiene, Nationalsozialismus, Euthanasie: Von der Verhütung zur Vernichtung 'lebensunwerten Lebens,' 1890–1945* (Göttingen, 1987).

Scholder, Klaus, "Die evangelische Kirche in der Sicht der nationalsozialistischen Führung bis zum Kriegsausbruch," *Vierteljahrshefte für Zeitgeschichte* 16 (1968), 15–35.

———"Die Kapitulation der evangelischen Kirche vor dem nationalsozialistischen Staat," *Zeitschrift für Kirchengeschichte* 81 (1970), 183–206.

———*A Requiem for Hitler and Other New Perspectives on the German Church Struggle* (London, 1989).

———*The Churches and the Third Reich*, 2 vols. (London, 1987–8).

Schwartz, Michael, "Konfessionelle Milieus und Weimarer Eugenik," *Historische Zeitschrift* 261 (1995), 403–48.

Siegele-Wenschkewitz, Leonore (ed.), *Christlicher Antijudaismus und Antisemitismus: Theologische und kirchliche Programme Deutscher Christen* (Frankfurt a.M., 1994).

Siegele-Wenschkewitz, Leonore, *Nationalsozialismus und Kirchen: Religionspolitik von Partei und Staat bis 1935* (Düsseldorf, 1974).

Sluga, Hans, *Heidegger's Crisis: Philosophy and Politics in Nazi Germany* (Cambridge, MA, 1993).

Smelser, Ronald and Rainer Zitelmann (eds.), *Die Braune Elite: 22 biographische Skizzen* (Darmstadt, 1989).

———Rainer Zitelmann and Enrico Syring (eds.), *Die Braune Elite II: 21 weitere biographische Skizzen* (Darmstadt, 1993).

Smelser, Ronald, *Robert Ley: Hitler's Labor Front Leader* (Oxford, 1988).

Smid, Marikje, *Deutscher Protestantismus und Judentum 1932/33* (Munich, 1990).

Smith, Bradley, *Heinrich Himmler: A Nazi in the Making, 1900–1926* (Stanford, 1971).

Smith, Helmut Walser, *German Nationalism and Religious Conflict: Culture, Ideology, Politics, 1870–1914* (Princeton, 1994).

Sondheimer, Kurt, *Antidemokratisches Denken in der Weimarer Republik* (Munich, 1968).

Sonne, Hans-Joachim, *Die politische Theologie der Deutschen Christen* (Göttingen, 1975).

Speier, Hans, *German White-Collar Workers and the Rise of Hitler* (New Haven, 1986).

Sperber, Jonathan, *Popular Catholicism in Nineteenth Century Germany* (Princeton, 1984).

Stachura, Peter (ed.), *The Nazi Machtergreifung* (London, 1983).

———(ed.), *The Shaping of the Nazi State* (London, 1978).

Stachura, Peter, *Gregor Strasser and the Rise of Nazism* (London, 1983).

———*Nazi Youth in the Weimar Republic* (Santa Barbara, 1975).

Staffa, Christian (ed.), *Vom protestantischen Antijudaismus und seinen Lügen* (Berlin, 1993).

Stegemann, Wolfgang (ed.), *Kirche und Nationalsozialismus* (Stuttgart, 1990).

Steinweis, Alan, "Weimar Culture and the Rise of National Socialism: The *Kampfbund für deutsche Kultur*," *Central European History* 24 (1991), 402–23.

———*Art, Ideology and Economics in Nazi Germany: The Reich Chambers of Music, Theater and the Visual Arts* (Chapel Hill, 1993).

Stephan, Werner, *Joseph Goebbels: Dämon einer Diktatur* (Stuttgart, 1949).

Stephenson, Jill, *Women in Nazi Society* (London, 1975).

Stern, Fritz, *The Politics of Cultural Despair: A Study in the Rise of the Germanic Ideology* (Berkeley, 1961).

Stoltzfus, Nathan, *Resistance of the Heart: Intermarriage and the Rosenstrasse Protest in Nazi Germany* (New York, 1996).

Strohm, Theodor and Jörg Thierfelder (eds.), *Diakonie im 'Dritten Reich': Neuere Ergebnisse zeitgeschichtlicher Forschung* (Heidelberg, 1990).

Tal, Uriel, "Lutheran Theology and the Third Reich," in Paul Opsahl and Marc Tannenbaum (eds.), *Speaking of God Today* (Philadelphia, 1974), 87–96.

———"On Modern Lutheranism and the Jews," *Leo Baeck Institute Yearbook* 30 (1985), 203–13.

———*Christians and Jews in Germany: Religion, Politics and Ideology in the Second Reich 1870–1914* (Ithaca, 1975).

Thalmann, Rita, *Protestantisme et nationalisme en Allemagne de 1900 à 1945* (Paris, 1976).

Tiefel, Hans, "The German Lutheran Church and the Rise of National Socialism," *Church History* 41 (1972), 326–36.

Tilgner, Wolfgang, *Volksnomostheologie und Schöpfungsglaube: Ein Beitrag zur Geschichte des Kirchenkampfes* (Göttingen, 1966).

Tödt, Heinz Eduard, "Die Novemberverbrechen 1938 und der deutsche Protestantismus: Ideologische und theologische Voraussetzungen für die Hinnahme des Pogroms," *Kirchliche Zeitgeschichte* 2 (1989), 14–37.

Tracey, D.R., "The Development of the National Socialist Party in Thuringia, 1924–1930," *Central European History* 8 (1975), 23–50.

Turner, Bryan S., *Religion and Social Theory* (London, 1991).

Turner, Henry Ashby (ed.), *Hitler: Memoirs of a Confidant* (New Haven, 1985).

———(ed.), *Nazism and the Third Reich* (New York, 1972).

———(ed.), *Reappraisals of Fascism* (New York, 1975).

———*German Big Business and the Rise of Hitler* (Oxford, 1985).

Tyrell, Albrecht, *Vom 'Trommler' zum 'Führer': Der Wandel von Hitlers Selbstverständnis zwischen 1919 und 1924 und die Entwicklung der NSDAP* (Munich, 1975).

Volkov, Shulamit, *Jüdisches Leben und Antisemitismus im 19. und 20. Jahrhundert* (Munich, 1990).

Vondung, Klaus, *Magie und Manipulation: Ideologischer Kult und politische Religion des Nationalsozialismus* (Göttingen, 1971).

Vorländer, Herwart, "NS-Volkswohlfahrt und Winterhilfswerk des deutschen Volkes," *Vierteljahrshefte für Zeitgeschichte* 34 (1986), 341–80.

———*Die NSV: Darstellung und Dokumentation einer nationalsozialistischen Organisation* (Koblenz, 1988).

Ward, William R., *Theology, Sociology and Politics: The German Protestant Social Conscience 1890–1933* (Berne, 1979).

Weindling, Paul, *Health, Race and German Politics between National Unification and Nazism, 1870–1945* (Cambridge, 1989).

Welch, David, "Manufacturing a Consensus: Nazi Propaganda and the Building of a 'National Community,'" *Contemporary European History* 2 (1993), 1–15.

Wippermann, Wolfgang, *Faschismustheorien: Zum Stand der gegenwärtigen Diskussion* (Darmstadt, 1980).

Witt, Thomas de, "The Economics and Politics of Welfare in the Third Reich," *Central European History* 11 (1978), 256–78.

———"The Struggle against Hunger and Cold: Winter Relief in Nazi Germany 1933–1939," *Canadian Journal of History* 12 (1978), 361–81.

Wright, J.R.C., 'Above Parties': The Political Attitudes of the German Protestant Church Leadership 1918–1933 (Oxford, 1974).

Zabel, James, Nazism and the Pastors: A Study of the Ideas of Three 'Deutsche Christen' Groups (Missoula, MT, 1976).

Zahn, Gordon, German Catholics and Hitler's Wars (New York, 1962).

Zerner, Ruth, "German Protestant Responses to Nazi Persecution of the Jews," in Randolf Braham (ed.), Perspectives on the Holocaust (Boston, 1983).

Zipfel, Wilhelm, Die Kirchenkampf in Deutschland 1933–1945: Religionsverfolgung und Selbstbehauptung der Kirchen in der nationalsozialistischen Zeit (Berlin, 1965).

INDEX

INDEX

Bentheim, Fürst von, 187–8
Bergen, Doris, 6
Berlin, Diocese of, 71
Berlin-Brandenburg, 77,
    see also Brandenburg
Betcke, Werner, 197
Bhagavad-Gita, 234
Bible, biblical, 6, 11, 21, 27, 36, 41, 46,
    86–7, 89, 95–6, 115, 126, 136, 141,
    149–50, 210, 215, 254, 256, 259
  criticism, 32
  gospel, 145
  Gospel of John, 98
  Gospel of Mark, 98
  John 2:15, 32, 37
  John 8:44, 18
  John 10:12, 159
  Luke 17:21, 30, 79, 98
  Sermon on the Mount, 21, 234
  see also New Testament; Old Testament;
    Ten Commandments
Bismarck, Otto von, 82, 107, 126
Blomberg, Werner von, 183
Blöthner, Hans, 242
Bodelschwingh, Friedrich von, 159–60, 161,
    167, 181, 194, 200, 202
Boeckh, Rudolf, 200–1
Bohm, Walter, 157–8
Bolanden, Conrad von, 107
Bollmus, Reinhard, 127
bolshevism, bolshevik, 100, 122, 124–5, 182,
    213, 220, 254–6, 260, see also
    antimarxism; communism; marxism
Borg, Daniel, 43
Bormann, Martin, 23–4, 176, 202, 215, 218,
    220, 222–4, 226, 228–31, 236–7, 239,
    243–51, 259–60
Bornkamm, Heinrich, 69
Bouhler, Philipp, 236–41, see also Party
    Commission for the Protection of
    National Socialist Literature (PPK)
Bracher, Karl, 91
Brakelmann, Günther, 8
Brandenburg, 83, 103, 151, 187, see also
    Berlin-Brandenburg
Brandt, Rudolf, 131
Braun, Gerhard, 201
Braunschweig, 163, 179
Brethen, Council of 181, 184, 186, see also
    Confessing Church; Dahlemites
Broszat, Martin, 166
Brückner, Helmut, 73–4
Buddhism, 234

Brüning, Heinrich, 100
Brunstäd, Friedrich, 47
Bürckel, Joseph, 174–5
burials, 132, 223 see also funerals
Burleigh, Michael, 7, 194, 199, 202
Buß- und Bettag, 124
Buch, Walter, 22, 24–5, 32, 44, 46, 50, 55,
    58, 60, 74–5, 84, 111, 119, 154, 208,
    219, 225, 230, 235
Buttmann, Rudolf, 60, 78–80, 161, 162, 165,
    168, 212

Calvinists, Calvinism, 128–9, 156, 159, 235
Canterbury, Archbishop of, 174
capitalism, 42–3, 45–7, 88, 254, see also
    banks; mammonism
Caplan, Jane, 10
Caritas Association, 197, 198, 199, 200
Carson, Edward, 90
Casti connubii, 193
Catholic, Catholicism, passim, see also
    Ultramontanism
Catholic Youth of Germany, 212, 213,
    see also youth
Catholicism, political, 45, 56–7, 59, 82, 89,
    133, 252, see also Center Party
Center Party, 55–6, 65, 78, 81–2, 116–17, 120,
    128, 134, see also Catholicism, political
Chamberlain, Houston Stewart, 19, 31,
    39–40, 74, 96–7, 100–1, 108, see also
    Foundations of the Nineteenth Century
Charlemagne, 103, 131
Christ, 11, 13, 18–22, 24, 26, 27, 28, 30,
    31–2, 36–7, 39, 42, 44, 46–7, 49, 54, 55,
    65, 74, 77, 81–2, 86–7, 89, 95–7, 99,
    101, 103, 108–9, 112, 118, 124–8,
    131–2, 133, 141–2, 143, 145, 149–50,
    154, 172, 185, 186, 213, 237–8, 242,
    243, 254–5, 257–60, 262, 263, 265
  divinity of, 22, 27, 50, 96
  as a Jew, 33, 89, 107
"Christ Socialists," 44, 46, 125
Christian Boy Scouts of Germany, 212,
    see also youth
Christian-German movement, 75, see also
    German Christians (DC)
Christian Identity movement, 8
Christianity, passim, see also "active
    Christianity"; "positive Christianity";
    "practical Christianity"
Christian Parents' League (CEB), 210–12,
    see also National Socialist Parents'
    League (NSEB)

286

Christian Social Party (German), 42, 61–2
Christian-Spiritual Religious Association, 58,
  see also Dinter, Artur
Christian Trade Unions, 43
Christian Association of Young Men, 148,
  212, 215, see also youth
Christliche Welt, 38, 39, 73
Christmas, 55
Church Committees, 180, 183
Church Struggle (*Kirchenkampf*), 160–61,
  163, 166–7, 171, 175, 177–8, 179,
  184, 207
civil service, 120
Clerical Party (Austrian), 61
Coch, Friedrich, 212
Cold War, 266
communism, 41–42, 46, 48, 69, 76, 92, 115,
  117, 216, see also antimarxism;
  bolshevism; marxism
Concordat
  with Catholic Church, 64–5, 80, 139, 158,
    197, 211
  with Protestant Church, 71
Confessing Church (BK), 2, 4, 5, 11, 69, 101,
  118, 121, 128, 148, 149, 158, 162, 164,
  171, 174, 175–7, 178–86, 188, 200,
  207, 209, 215, 232, 235
  as SA men 148
  as members of the Nazi movement 163–4,
    223, 227–8
  see also Brethren, Council of; Dahlemites;
    Gospel and Church; Pastors' Emergency
    League; Young Reformers
confessions, confessional, 51, 85, 144
  divide, differences, 14, 45–6, 50, 51–66, 85
  see also "above confessions";
    anticonfessionalism; sectarianism
Consultants for Church Affairs, 72
Conti, Leonardo, 241
contraception, 48, 191, 193
Conway, John, 3, 4, 5 133, 155, 166
"coordination" (*Gleichschaltung*), 165, 188,
  189, 197, 207–10, 212, 215–16
Counterreformation, 45, 57, 90
Crusades, 266
Cultural Peace, Department of, 149, 182

Dahlemites, 183, 184–5, 186, see also
  Brethren, Council of; Confessing Church
Dalai Lama, 88
Darré, Richard Walther, 101–4, 110, 129,
  157, 220
Darwin, Darwinism, 35

"Death of God," 6, 12, 111
death penalty, 48
Delegate for Ideological Training, as
  potential state office, 240–42
Detten, Hermann von, 182
Deutsche Gotterkenntnis ("German
  conception of God"), 87–8
Dibelius, Otto, 69, 184–5, 186–7
Diehl, Guida, 204
Dinter, Artur, 19–20, 24, 27, 30–1, 32,
  58–63, 72, 87, 88, 92, 122–3, 153, 158,
  see also Christian-Spiritual Religious
  Association
Doehring, Bruno, 16, 64, 69–70

East Prussia, East Prussian, 76, 159, 180
  Synod, 223
Eckart, Dietrich, 17–19, 20, 23–4, 27,
  29–30, 31, 32, 36, 50, 53, 55, 58, 84, 88,
  92, 98, 107, 111
economics, economic theory, 22, 42, 46–8,
  262, see also "public need comes before
  private greed"; socialism
education, 71, 76–82, 122–3, 144, 211,
  246–7, see also National Socialist
  Teachers' League (NSLB); schools
Elert, Werner, 34, 135, 138
Eley, Geoff, 12
emancipation, Jewish, 33, 38–9
England, 155, 176
Enlightenment, 47, 80
Epp, Franz Ritter von, 67, 123, 173,
  175, 244
Ericksen, Robert, 8
Ernst Wurche Academic Guild, 227
eugenics, eugenicism, 12, 36, 190, 191,
  192–3, 203–4, 209
euthanasia, 194, 196, 201–2, 249, see also
  "T-4" Action
Evangelical-Lutheran Churches, Council of,
  181, see also Church Struggle

Fahrenhorst, Wilhelm, 119, 139
Fascism, Italian, 28, 64, see also Mussolini,
  Benito
Fatherland Party, 16
Feder, Gottfried, 41
Fest, Joachim, 245
Fighting League for German Culture, 92, 137
Fighting Ring of German Faith, 223,
  see also paganism
Finck, Bertha, 197, 205
"Final Solution," 235, 258, 261